"The distresses of the Army"

The Ephraim Blaine Letters

1780-1783

Joseph Lee Boyle

HERITAGE BOOKS
2021

HERITAGE BOOKS
AN IMPRINT OF HERITAGE BOOKS, INC.

Books, CDs, and more—Worldwide

For our listing of thousands of titles see our website
at
www.HeritageBooks.com

Published 2021 by
HERITAGE BOOKS, INC.
Publishing Division
5810 Ruatan Street
Berwyn Heights, Md. 20740

Copyright © 2021 Joseph Lee Boyle

All rights reserved. No part of this book may be reproduced or transmitted in any form or by any means, electronic or mechanical, including photocopying, recording or by any information storage and retrieval system without written permission from the author, except for the inclusion of brief quotations in a review.

International Standard Book Number
Paperbound: 978-1-55613-713-6

CONTENTS

Introduction v

Editorial Procedure xii

The Documents 1

Document Chronology 385

Index 398

INTRODUCTION

To paraphrase Nathanael Greene, "Whoever heard of a Commissary?" Among the many forgotten heroes of the American Revolution are the commissaries, the hundreds of men who worked to supply the fighting men with arms, clothing and food. In that, and every conflict, the fortunes of war are vastly affected by unspectacular activities such as the purchase and delivery of flour and meat.

The most persevering man among those feeding the Continental Army, was Ephraim Blaine of Carlisle, Pennsylvania. Though he complained repeatedly, and threatened to resign in twice in 1778 alone, he remained in an official post until November 1781, and then remained active in supplying the army under the new contract system, serving for seven consecutive years.

The intent of this work is to present the letters of Ephraim Blaine from 1780 through 1783. The majority of these come from the Ephraim Blaine Papers at the Library of Congress. These documents can be called the Commissary of Purchases letters. While Blaine wrote most of the letters, some were also written by George Morton, who served as Blaine's chief clerk.

Blaine (1741-1808) came to Pennsylvania from Ulster with his father, James Blaine, and family in 1745. During the French and Indian War he became commander of Fort Ligonier. Resigning from the army in 1763, he made his home in Carlisle, establishing himself as a large merchant, landowner, Indian trader, and one of the wealthiest men in interior Pennsylvania.

At the outset of the Revolution he assisted in raising a regiment of Associators and was serving as a purchasing agent in

Pennsylvania. In August 1777 when Congress elected him Deputy Commissary General of Purchases for the Middle Department. On December 2, 1779, he was promoted to Commissary General, a position from which he resigned on July 24, 1782.

In June 1775, the Continental Congress faced the problem of supplying the newly created Continental Army. The army around Boston was a spontaneous affair of the New England colonies, and the troops were supplied by their home towns. This method was immediately successful, but all were aware a more permanent method would be needed to pursue a successful war.

On June 16 1775, Congress established a Commissary General of Stores and Provisions, but did not establish an organizational structure. Joseph Trumbull of Connecticut was picked to head the new department.

Unfortunately a series of problems led to Trumbull's resignation in 1777. These were caused in part by intersectional jealousies, Trumbull's desire for cash commissions for his purchases, and inconsistent direction of the department by Congress. The single biggest problem was Congressional concern for frugality. Many thought that the existing system was too expensive, and should be replaced with a purchase by contract system.

The situation came to a head in early 1777. Trumbull had left a man named Carpenter Wharton to supply Washington's army in New Jersey while he returned to Hartford, Connecticut. Wharton was inadequate to the job, and the army had suffered during the Trenton-Princeton Campaign. Investigation led to a report by the Board of War in February 1777, which suggested separating the purchasing and issuing functions into two departments. Washington agreed with this concept, as he thought the job was too big for one man.

Trumbull was completely against the continuance of a fixed salary for himself, and suggested, as he had several times before, that he receive a commission on the money that passed through his hands. Though he was willing to see the department split into separate purchasing and issuing departments, he was disappointed by the lack of consultation he had expected from Congress in the planned reorganization. Meanwhile his absence from the army, while detained by Congress, had allowed a shortage of provisions to occur in the army. When he did rejoin the army, Trumbull found his staff in disarray and wrote on June 15, 1777, that "An Angel from Heaven could not go on long in my Situation."

On June 10, Congress approved detailed new regulations. These divided the Commissary into separate departments of Purchases and Issues, but established such detailed procedures and record keeping, that administration of the system was inevitably ineffectual. Fixed pay and rations for the staffs were continued, which was not well accepted in a time of rising inflation.

On June 18, Trumbull was elected as Commissary General of Purchases, with Charles Stewart of New Jersey established as Commissary General of Issues. The new organization led to a large number of resignations by various members of the staffs of both departments. Frustrated by not being paid a commission, and the fact that Congress would not even let him appoint his own deputies, Trumbull submitted his resignation to be effective on August 20.

On August 5, 1777, Congress picked William Buchanan, a Baltimore merchant, to succeed Trumbull. Buchanan lacked experience and assumed his duties during a crisis with a small and incomplete staff. He was being ordered to feed the major American army during four of the most active months of the war, with many vacant staff positions, and new men in some of the key jobs.

In the year 2021, it is common to pick up a telephone or turn on a computer and order innumerable objects from across the world, which can be shipped to you overnight. The choice of food products in supermarkets is ever expanding, and restaurants of all types and prices prepare ethnic foods never heard of in eighteenth century America. Communication was by horseback; if you needed to get meat from Connecticut, you sent a letter by an express rider, asking your assistant to buy barrels of pork or beef, or cattle and have them sent to you. Of course most rivers of any size had no bridges, so crossing was by ferry. A wagon with a load of supplies would do well to make fifteen miles a day on good roads. On roads of mud from rain or snow melt, progress was reduced considerably, and there are many references in contemporary documents to roads being totally as well as rivers, being impassable, particularly during the winter months. There were so many interdependent aspects in the transport system alone, that failure in any one, often resulted in food not arriving on time.

Consider that even the containers for transporting good were hand-made and expensive. Food that was not on the hoof was transported in barrels of various sizes. Obtaining and keeping barrels for transport and storage was a continual problem. Hoops were usually made of wood, not iron, and they were relatively fragile. They were difficult to store properly when empty, and if stored near an army encampment, were soon used for firewood. Another item now taken for granted is salt. As refrigeration and canning did not exist, salt was absolutely vital as a preservative for food. At the outbreak of the war, salt was being imported, but the British fleet interdicted supplies, which led to chronic shortages and even salt riots.

The commissaries also struggled with congressional inefficiency, poor wages, lack of cooperation from state and local authorities, disdain from Continental Army officers, and desperate financial problems. One historian commented that the chronic food shortages were "a great phenomenon of the Revolution—an almost starving army in a country of abundant food resources." Despite suffering much criticism and frustration, the commissaries were an absolutely vital link in winning the war. Their patriotism and espirit de corps, as well as concerns for honor and reputation, were every bit as strong as the men in "the fighting line."

Meanwhile the Commissary Department had to compete with civilian purchasers, speculators, and other branches of the American military. For example, each side had to provide food for its prisoners held by the other side. This required Elias Boudinot, the American Commissary General of Prisoners to purchase food and send it under a flag of truce to American prisoners. This was certainly necessary, but food that was eaten by American prisoners, was not available to feed Americans still under arms.

Only a small percentage of Americans in the twenty-first century are engaged in agriculture. But in the eighteenth century these percentages were reversed. William Hooper wrote in 1778 that "a Soldier made is a farmer lost." All the farmers on the firing line, and there were thousands, reduced the production of food, but did not diminish the number of hungry mouths.

In March 1778, the ineffective Buchanan resigned as Commissary General of Purchases. On April 9 Congress appointed Jeremiah Wadsworth in his place. On April 14, 1778, Congress adopted a new plan which instituted most of the recommendations that had been made by Trumbull during the summer of 1777. The Commissary General of Purchases had full control over his staff, and commissions on purchases were allowed to attract the most competent men. Ephraim Blaine, who had proved his effectiveness, continued in the Middle Department.

While the Commissary Department functioned relatively smoothly for the rest of 1778, problems began to multiply and by 1779 many complaints were being registered. These led to Wadsworth's resignation, and the appointment of Ephraim Blaine as Commissary General of Purchases on December 2, 1779, a position he held nearly the end of the war. Minor changes in 1780 led to another reorganization by Congress in November 1780, and a supply by contract system was eventually instituted. However the troops suffered intermittent food shortages for all the factors mentioned above and others, until the end of the war.

As Dr. Victor Johnson summed up "In a word, confusion reigned in an ever increasing tempo. The system was subject to many changes; and the commissaries general came and went with alarming regularity, Joseph Trumbull being followed by William Buchanan, Jeremiah Wadsworth, and Ephraim Blaine in the order mentioned."

Blaine's frustrations with the job can be judged by some of the letters published here. In September 1780, he wrote to the President on Congress: "I have been with them since the Year seventy six and never experienced the same difficulties in procuring Supplies of Provisions I have done this last six Weeks—" He also pointed out that feeding the French army had created problems: "I must beg leave to mention to you that our want of Meat is greatly owing to the Supply of our Allies...permit me to remind Congress that the cause of this misfortune is their admiting the French Agent to purchase

Supplies upon terms that were not in their power to grant their own Agents or those of the respective States—"

In October 1780, he wrote to Charles Stewart: "where the winter supplies and next summer are to come from god Knows for I dont." On May 1, 1781 he informed the Board of War that: "my disapointments have been so repeated and distresses of the Army so great that I have determined to quit the service." Fortunately he did not, a played a key role in supplying the troops at the Siege of Yorktown. March 1782 found him writing to Robert Forsythe, his deputy for the Southern Department that: "I am heartily tired of Public Service—Even after he left the department he was still vexed by his service as his accounts were not fully settled at the end of the Confederation and the final settlement was probably not completed until the 1790s.

The operation of the commissariat is well covered by E. Wayne Carp, *To Starve the Army at Pleasure: Continental Army Administration and American Political Culture, 1775-1781*, Chapel Hill: University of North Carolina Press, 1984, Victor Leroy Johnson, "The Administration of the American Commissariat During the Revolutionary War" Ph. D. diss., University of Pennsylvania, 1941, and Erna Risch, *Supplying Washington's Army*, Washington: GPO, 1981.

See also Joseph Lee Boyle, *"My Last Shift Betwixt Us & Death" The Ephraim Blaine Letterbook, 1777-1778* (Bowie, MD: Heritage Books, 2001, Anna A. Hays, "Colonel Ephraim Blaine: Commissary General of the Revolutionary Army," Read before the Association March 8, 1935 (Carlisle: The Hamilton Library Association, 1935) in vol. 6, Hamilton Library Association, Historical Papers, Willis Kocher, "Ephraim Blaine," *Cumberland County History* 3, 1 (Winter 1986), 3-17.

EDITORIAL PROCEDUURE

For the most part these letters were original entered in the letterbook in chronological order. In a few cases they were not in order and have been rearranged in this work to appear by date. Undated letters are assumed to have been written between the dates of letters preceding and following.

Letters are introduced by the names of the addresser and addressee. The dateline falls just below the heading though the original document may have it at the bottom. The complimentary close in brought up flush with the last paragraph. A descriptive note at the foot of each entry shows the location of the document presented, and identifies the recipient or recipients, where possible, the first time the individual appears.

These documents present a literal transcription with spelling, punctuation and grammar as they are found in the originals. Abbreviations and contractions are also preserved as they are found. As a letterbook was intended to serve as a reference for the author, abbreviations, misspellings, and errors are far more common than in the "fair copy" letters which have been drawn from other sources.

Capital letters follow the text of the original, although it is often a guess whether is a capital or not. Brackets indicate questionable or illegible words or letters. *Sic* is used sparingly as it would quickly detract from the text, given the numerous variants of spelling and oddities of expression. Crossed out material has been omitted. Margin notes are shown as postscripts, except where keyed to the body of the document.

The index includes the names of all mentioned persons. Mention of foodstuffs such as beef, pork and flour occur so frequently they have not been indexed. Less common foodstuffs such as tongue and bacon have been indexed.

Ephraim Blaine to Samuel Huntington

Philadelphia January 5th 1780—

Sir

I beg leave through your Excellency to acquaint Congress that I have receiv'd their late resolves respecting the new System of the Commissariate—As to my own Salary I make no doubt but Congress mean to make it equal to the great undertaking and trouble I shall have and humbly presume that ought to be in Specie or an equivalent—however this I shall submit to Congress and leave to their further consideration— All travelling Charges, Office Expences, Clerks &c must be paid—There are many matters which will require additional Resolves which are absolutely necessary, and to which I hope Congress will agree—This will put it in my power to appoint Men who will accept and be capable to executing—

The deputies ought to have one half pr Cent at least upon all disbursements, and the assistants who execute the purchases will not undertake for less than two pr Cent—some little less might do, provided there could be a great reduction of Posts— for where there is a small Post and an Issuing Commissary, the deputy Commissary of Purchases has to employ some Person to attend and procure Supplies for that place.

One Assistant must be allow'd me, who must constantly attend at Head Quarters—his business must be to answer such questions respecting the Supplies and Magazines as his Excellency thinks proper, and in my absence give the earliest Intelligence of his Excellency's Orders, the rout of the Army, and correspond with my Deputies, giving them such directions respecting Provisions, that constant and regular supplies may be secured for the Army—and settle such Accounts as are transacted in the vicinity of Camp—As this business will require an action person, and a Man of secrecy and Letters, hope Congress will allow a Salary as will enable me to obtain such a person.—

The Commissary General ought to have an Agent in each State who would superintend the State Purchasers and push them to execute their duty, without which I doubt the Supplies cannot be regularly obtain'd.—Shall the Commissary General with the sanction of the Board of War, have the regulating the pay of Coopers, Packers, Superintendents of Cattle, Drovers, Butchers &c?—

My entering upon the business at this season of the Year, when all the Magazines are nearly empty, Your Treasury nearly exhausted, all to this the most unreasonable and extravagant demands of people for every necessary of life— The disappointments of Coll. Wadsworth has met with in not being able to furnish his deputies with Cash, has depriv'd them of laying in the quantity of Provisions they otherwise might have done—and he informs me that I must not depend on Mr. Champion for further supply of Cattle, without he is furnish'd with Money for that purpose—those Circumstances give me much Concern, and will subject me to great difficulty to keep the Army supplied through the Winter.—Six Months must pass before we can have any advantage from Grass fed Beef— Suppose Salt Provisions equal to half the consumption for that time—but the difficulty of transportation to the Army before the Summer will be so great, that they ought to be fed upon fresh Meat.

Congress will please to take immediate Measures, and wrote to the Governor and Council of Connecticut, to give every possible assistance to procure all the fat Cattle in that State—And a sufficient Sum of Money for that purpose, ought immediately to be procured.—

Sir, You will please to inform Congress that I am ready when they enable me to enter upon the business of my Department, and will use my best endeavours to answer their expectations in procuring Supplies for the Army upon the most reasonable terms in my power—Also inform them that I hope

to keep the Army properly supplied with Bread 'till the first of May next which is now engag'd—
I have the honour to be with the greatest respect
Your Excellency's Most Obedient & most humble Servant
Eph Blain DC.G

His Excellency Samuel Huntington Esqr. President of Congress

Papers of the Continental Congress, Roll 182, i 165, p 311-12, National Archives. Huntington was a Signer of the Declaration of Independence, and President of the Continental Congress from September 28, 1779 to February 28, 1781.

Blaine to Moore Furman

Philada. 6th. Jany 1780—

Dear Sir

Your favour by Colo. Cox came safe to hand for which I Return you thanks and am Greatly Obliged to you for your attention in forwarding the supplies for our Army and fixing the Mill to grind Indian Corn which will greatly Supply our present want of flour—[three words illegible] be uneasy respecting more Corn which C. Dunham purchases. I will require as part of your Business and rest assured that you shall have my Commissions on the same I shall order them to desist their purchase the moment our Army has a temporary supply which I hope will be a very few days—I have ever experienced your rediness to serve the Public and render me Many Services—it wou'd give me great Satisfaction to have it in my power to return the Compliment, and I assure you—you have only to Command—my present undertaking is a very great one—what my Success may be in the execution time will discover, but the Present prospects are gloomy and do not promise fair—however I have a good Constitution and hope a good Conscience and nothing shall be wanting on my part to

execute, wishing you the Complimts. of the season, and all Possible happiness. I am with much Esteem and Reguard,
 Dear Sir
 Your Most Obedient and Most Hble Servt
 Eph Blaine
M. Furman Esqr.
a notation under the date shows "recd. 11th"

> Record Group: Department of Defense; Subgroup: Revolutionary War, Mss. 4740, Division of Archives and Records Management, New Jersey State Archives. Furman, of Trenton, New Jersey, was serving as a Deputy Quartermaster General.

Blaine to Jonathan Trumbull

Philadelphia, 9th. January 1780

Sir

Congress have alter'd the System of the Commissariate, & honor'd me with the new Appointment of Commissary General of Purchases. They have granted me a special Warrant for two hundred thousand Dollars to assist in the Purchase of fat Cattle in your State—Your Excellency will receive a Letter from Congress respecting the great want of Beef for the Support of our Army, & the necessity of immediate Measures being taken to afford them a regular Supply—you will therefore dispose of the Money to such Persons as your Excellency may judge equal to the Business. Should Mr. Champion undertake would wish him ye. preference but leave your Excellency to adopt such Measures as may answer the present Exigencies—

I mean to set out from this place about the 15th. for Hartford to wait upon your Excellency & Council & beg your Recommendation in the choice of a Deputy Commissary of Purchases for the State of Connecticut—

I have the honor to be with due respect—

                    Your Excellency's Most Obedt.
                        & Most Hble Servt.
                            Eph. Blaine D.C.G
His Excell. Govr. Trumbull

> Misc. Bd. 1780 January 9, Massachusetts Historical Society. Trumbull was the Governor of Connecticut at the start of the war, and was the only colonial governor to remain a governor after independence was declared.

Blaine to Samuel Huntington

                        Philadelphia January 12th 1780.—
Sir
Please to inform the Honorable Continental Congress that I accept of the appointment of Commissary Genl. of Purchases—and shall leave to their future consideration the Salary my services may entitle me to—

As it is my desire to perform this business with Oeconomy and reputation—previous to my entering on the execution thereof, I must be empowered by Congress to carry it through—and no other method remains, but to give such Commissions or Salaries, as will be an inducement for Men of business to accept—

I mean to set out for the Eastern States the beginning of next week, provided I have Returns from my assistants in the Middle Department before that time—and assure Congress that my best endeavours shall be used to engage Men who are active and approv'd of by the Executive authorities of such States as are necessary to have Deputies employ'd in—and should these not be willing to take less than two & one half pr Cent, which is not half their present Salaries at twenty for one, I beg the approbation of Congress for so doing—and expences to be allow'd them when called out of their district upon public business—When your Money appreciates, and the Public

Magazines afford a supply for your Army, I shall be happy in assisting Congress to reduce the Commission, and adopt a system of Oeconomy, by procuring the supplies on Contract.— or otherwise as Congress may approve.

The Resolve for allowing my Expences, Office, Clerks &c. has been by some means mislaid, as I have not receiv'd it from the Secretarys Office.—

The two hundred thousand Dollars granted me by Warrant last Satturday, have sent Governor Trumbull and wrote him to apply it to the immediate purchase of Cattle, and requested him to order them forward to our Army will all possible dispatch—

The present demand for Beef Cattle & Flour will inform Congress how necessary it is for them to furnish me with money to prosecute the purchases—

I am with all due respect Your Excellencys
Most Obedt. & most hum Servt.
Eph. Blaine D.C.P.
His Excellency Saml. Huntington Esqr
President of Congress—

>Papers of the Continental Congress, Roll 182, i165, 315-16. Note on the reverse shows "Read 13th."

Blaine to George Washington

Philada. 16th Jany. 1780

Please your Excelly.
Sir
Last Wednesday I accepted the Appointment of Commissary Genl. of Purchases and previous thereto had every assurance from Congress of their utmost exertions in furnishing Money and Recommending such Measures to the Executive Authorities of the United States as will not fail in enabling me to procure Ample supplies for the army—I am

Promised Instructions and money the 21st Instant at which time shall set out for Head Quarters on my way to the Eastward—my flour is coming on fast from Maryland and the Delaware State, and Your Excellency may be assur'd that I shall use every Possible exertion to lay in a Small Magazine to remedy against the breaking up of the frost—particular returns of the Supplies in the middle department shall be furnished your Excellency when I come up, the Governor and Council of Maryland deserve great Credit for their Spirited exertions to enable the Commissary's to procure supply upon Receipt of your letter and believe it will not be in the Power of Engrocers Speculators to hide or procure a Single barrel of flour, this will add Considerably to our Magazines—I am trying to engage a Gentlemen to take Mr. Flints Station at Head Quarters, and hope to Relieve him in a very few days—am with due Reguard,

                Your Excellencies
                Most Obdt. and Most Hble Servant.
                Eph. Blaine, C. G. P.

Genl. Washington

> George Washington Papers, Library of Congress. Addressed to Washington at Morristown, "favd. by Col Wadsworth"

Blaine to Isaac Carty

Sir

The Army's distress for bread is very great and on you and Mr. Ewing I must depend for their support, have therefore in the most Pressing terms to request you to use every possible means to procure flour also equal Dispatch in forwarding the same—should you not be able to procure sufficient Teams from the Quarter Master in your district, make application to Colo. Hollingsworth at the head of Elk who has many at his command, pray loose [sic] no time in this necessary business else the army will undoubtedly disband for want of bread which will be the most maloncholy Circumstance which has happened since the commencement of the present War, let me here [*sic*] from you by every opportunity also inform me what your present Success and prospects are respecting flour and the quantity you can forward weekly to this City—

    Am with much regard Sir,
      Your most Hble. Servt.
       Eph. Blaine C. G. of P.

To Major Carty

> *Delaware Archives: Revolutionary War* (Wilmington: Public Archives Commission of Delaware, 1919), 3:1354. Undated, This is published immediately before Blaine's letter to Carty of January 25, 1780. Carty was Commissary of Purchases for the State of Delaware.

Blaine to Isaac Carty

         Philadelphia, January 25th 1780

Sir

 Sundry parcels of Flour has come up from your district in very bad order, and neither Invoic'd, nailed or any thing done to the Casks have therefore to request you to give directions to the Millers to have their Flour properly Invoiced, nailed and lining Hoops upon the end of each Cask, the weight of the Flour mark'd with red lead or blacking upon the head of the Barrels, and branded with the Initials of your name—

 For Gods Sake forward all the Flour you can, and suffer none of the Waggons you load to take less than eight or ten barrles each—Upon your exertions depends the Supplies of our Army, and shall depend on your utmost endeavors to answer my expectations—Inclos'd you have an Order upon the Treasurer of your State for One hundred & seventy five thousand Dollars—This money must be laid out for your future purchases, as it is paid me on account of the new System of the Commissariate—Your other Accounts must be prepared for a final Settlement, and when adjusted Congress assures me they will furnish Money to discharge the ballances due to each of my Assistance—[sic]

Write my by every Opportunity and inform me of your success and am with great regard

Sir Your most Obedt. humbl. Servt.
Major Isaac Carty

> *Delaware Archives: Revolutionary War* (Wilmington: Public Archives Commission of Delaware, 1919), 3:1354.

Blaine to George Morton

Philada. 26th. Jany. 1780

Sir,

Gentlemen and people who have business at my Office will expect punctual attendance and speedy answers to what business they are upon, and the Office will gain Reputation if those rules are Observ'd—have therefore to request your steady attendance and when business call [sic] you away have Mr. Lyon in the Office, be very particular in answering all letters,—dismissing all persons who come with Accts. to settle, and careful in the Examination of such Accts, as you Receive till I return, be making every Preparation for a Settlement of Colo. Wadsworths & Mr. Buchanans Accts. and let no time be lost in the Office from this business—I shall write you from Camp, and inform you who the Person will be who I fix there as [ ] Commissary Genl. and shou'd there be a Appearance of want of any Kind of Provision shall write you, also Mention the demands of Supplies you will make from my Assistance, [sic] presume flour will be the Princaple—prepare a sett of books for my Acct. and have them made Middle siz'd. the Pork at Mr [Hug]leys have pack'd and forward it to Trenton by the very first Waggons give directions to Nihl. Patterson to send his pork to Pitts Town, apply to the Quarter Master and if he can furnish you with a Stove have One put in the Office, if he has none buy One,

Remain Sir Your Most Hble Servt.
Eph: Blaine C.G.P
Mr. Geo: Morton

> Papers of James G. Blaine and Family, Acc. 16,822, Container 3, Library of Congress. Morton was cashier and bookkeeper in the Blaine's Philadelphia office and contributed much to this correspondence.

Blaine to George Morgan

Prince Town 29 Jany 1780

Sir
I have done all in my Power to obtain Mony from the Treasury for my Department, but have been disappointed, the Treasury being of the Monies emitted & the Taxes coming in so very slow, have obliged Congress to delay the payment of large Sums wanting for the Commissary & Quarter Masters Departments, I have not been able to obtain a Shilling—if you find the Garrison at Fort Pitt in want of an immediate Supply of Provisions, you will apply to the Treasury board for a Sum sufficient to make the necessary Purchases in your District for the above purpose & I make no doubt they will furnish you with it, am now upon my way to new England, when I return will give you all the assistance in my power necessary for the present Demand of my Assistants in the Vicinity of Camp, you must therefore wait til Congress has it in their Power to obtain Mony by Taxes & Dispose of Bills of Exchange, without the immediate want of the Garrison at Fort Pitt call your attention in that,
& am with much Regard & Esteem Dear Sir
Your most Obedt. & most Humble Servt.
Col.Geo: Morgan

> Peter Force Collection, Mss. 17,137, Series 8D, Ephraim Blaine Papers, Library of Congress. Morgan had served as Deputy Commissary General of Purchases for the Western Department,

based at Fort Pitt, since 1777. He had left his post in early 1779 after conflicts with General Lachlan McIntosh, but was still conducting the business.

Blaine to Moore Furman

Trenton 29th. Jany. 1780—

Dear Sir

I call'd at your House but was so unhappy as to not see you, I suppose long Eer this Colo. Pettit has wrote you to Send all the Teams you had to spare to Philada. to forward Provisions to this place, there is loading there at this time sufficient for One Hundred and fifty Waggons and Stores daily coming on—have therefore to Request you to order to Philada. all the Waggons and sleds you can possibly Spare from Carrying on the daily Supplies to the Army at Morris—I shou'd wish to have all the Stores from Philada. to this place before the River breaks up, to effect which a Great number of Teams must come from You, am in Great haste Dear Sir,
    Your Most Obdt. Hble Servt.
    Eph: Blaine C.G.P

Colo Furman
A noted under the date reads "recd 30th the Business done"

> Record Group: Department of Defense; Subgroup: Revolutionary War, Mss. 4741, Division of Archives and Records Management, New Jersey State Archives.

Blaine to Jacob Cuyler

Morristown Feby. 1st. 1780

Sir

The System of the Commissariate being altered & Congress having accepted of Col Wadsworths Resignation, they have appointed me Commissary Genl. of Purchases for the United States, from your acquaintance in the Business & Character, wou'd wish your Continuation, & hope you will find the System tho a very poor one indeed, such as will afford you a subsistance to serve your Country, inclosed you have the Resolves of Congress on that subject, I am now on my way to Boston & intend returning your way, & be assured I shall make the Business of my Department as agreeable as possible, I have obtained an Order upon the Treasurer of your State for One hundred Eight three thousand Dollars which I have sent you by Mr [writer's blank] which you'll please to appropriate to the new Department; Congress have given me every assurence of Mony, & tho they have been this three Months past much distress'd by their Finances, yet they assure me the future prospects are very Considerable, & that they expect Mony sufficient to pay the Sums due Col. Wadsworth & amply supply his wants.

 Mr. Livingston one of your Delagates of Congress, has engaged a Considerable quantity of Wheat which he has upon his Farms (& has requested an appointment for one of his Neighbours for the Manor of Livingston) & Mrs. Mary Livingstons land in Albany County, I have given him an Appointment to Collect all the Wheat in those Estates, but left him subject to your further Orders & Directions, & have advanced Mr. Livingston an order in part payment of which have charged you with—the wants of the Army are great & require every possible Exertion & influance the Commissary are possessed of & beg you to use your utmost endeavours to procure as largely of Flour Wheat & Beef, & depend on my Exertions with Congress to procure Mony to discharge all your Debts & Contracts, am with much Esteem & Regard Sir
 Your most Obedt. Humble Servt.
Mr. Cuyler.

   Peter Force Collection, Mss. 17,137, Series 8D, Ephraim Blaine Papers, Library of Congress. Cuyler was Deputy Commissary General of Purchases for the Northern Department in New York. He had first been appointed in June 1777.

Blaine to Robert Hoops

Morristown Feby. 1st. 1780

Sir

The Garrison at West point is in great want of Bread therefore Request you upon Rect. of this to make application to Col Hooper for a Sufficient number of Waggons to forward with all possible Dispatch two hundred Barrels of Flour, shou'd you not have that Quantity ready you must apply to Arndt & Stroud to make up the Deficiency from their Magazine, the Distresses I have Experienced for want of a Regular supply of Mony for my Assistants gives me a great deal of uneasiness, & I feel for you & the rest of them being well acquainted with the Trouble you will have in being Dunned by the Farmers from all Quarters, but be assured that upon my Return from Hartford (where I am now going) that you shall be fully paid for your Purchases, & I have full assurance from Congress of Cash at that period, pray my good Sir procure all the Wheat & Flour you can & give me all possible Assistance to feed the Army when I return shall make your House on my way to Philadelphia & hope to have it in my Power at that time to alter the System of Purchases in your State & make the Business with your continuance, am with much esteem & Regard Dear Sir

Your most Obedient & most Humble Servant

Major Hoops

> Peter Force Collection, Mss. 17,137, Series 8D, Ephraim Blaine Papers, Library of Congress. Robert Hoops of Hunterdon County, New Jersey was a Major in the New Jersey Militia. At this time he was serving as a Deputy Quartermaster for the Continental Army and had been appointed a contractor for Sussex County to purchase supplies.

George Morton to William Evans

Philada. 4 Feby. 1780

Dear Sir

I received your favr. of the 3rd. Instant & note the Contents with regard to the Purchase of Flour; your own prudence must be your Government but it appears to me that the present rise of that Article is owing to the Mills being stopped by the Frost, if you can purchase Wheat reasonable you may get in Manufactured as soon as the Frost breaks up, perhaps the latter wou'd be the best plan, but as you are on the spot you must be the best Judge, you dont acknowledge the Receipt of Col. Blains letter of the 26th. Ulto. inclosing an Order for fifty thousand Dollars sent by Mr. Mc.Caraher, please mention it in your next, I am with much regard & Esteem Sir

  Your most Obedient Servant
    Geo Morton for E. Blaine Cy of Purchases
Col William Evans

> Evans and Haslet were Commissaries of Purchases for Chester County, Pennsylvania. Peter Force Collection, Mss. 17,137, Series 8D, Ephraim Blaine Papers, Library of Congress.

Blaine to George Clinton

Morris Town Feby 5th. 1780

Sir

Congress having appointed me Commissary General of Purchases for the Armies of the United States of America, & am now on my way to Boston to regulate the Business of my Department, I mean to make Albany on my Return, & do myself the Honor of waiting on your Excellency & Council, & have your approbation respecting the choice of a Deputy for your State from the Character I have had of Mr. Cuyler wou'd wish his Continuation, provided the new System of the

Commissariate is agreeable to him Inclosed you have a Letter from Mr. Livingston, am with all due Respect your Excellencys
   most Obedient & most Humble Servant
His Excellency Govr. Clinton

> Clinton was the Governor of New York. Peter Force Collection, Mss. 17,137, Series 8D, Ephraim Blaine Papers, Library of Congress.

Blaine to Morton

        Morris Town 5 Feby 1780—

Sir
 Pay Mr. John Thomas or his Order Twenty three thousand three hundred and sixty Eight Dollars which charge to Account of Majr. Hoops as that sum was paid to his Assistant James Little Miller at Hackets Town who is to account with Maj Hoops for the same
     Your humble servt
Mr. Geo. Morton Philada.
 G Morton for E Blaine CGofP

> Peter Force Collection, Mss. 17,137, Series 8D, Ephraim Blaine Papers, Library of Congress.

Morton to John Mitchell

        Philada. 5 Feby. 1780

Sir
Please furnish a Brigade of Waggons sufficient to Transport, eighteen thousand Weight of Pork in bulk, twenty Busls. Salt, twenty empty Barrells & one Beam & Scales, with five hundred of Weights from Smithfield to Philada to sett out if possible to morrow Morning, I am Sir
    Your most Obedient Servt

Geo Morton for E. Blaine
CGofP

Col. Jno. Michel DQMG—

>Mitchell was a Deputy Quartermaster General stationed in Philadelpha. Earlier in the war, he had served as a colonel of the Philadelphia militia, commissary of the Pennsylvania artillery, and mustermaster of the Pennsylvania navy. Peter Force Collection, Mss. 17,137, Series 8D, Ephraim Blaine Papers, Library of Congress.

Morton to Michael Kitts

Sir Philada. 5 Feby. 1780

You will proceed with the Brigade of Waggons (after taking in a pair of Scales & Weights) to Smithfield & carefully Weigh & Load a quantity of Pork now in Mrs. Naglies Sellar which was purchased by her late Husband Mr John Naglie for the use of the Army, also a quantity of Salt supposed to be about twelve Bushels, & twenty Pork barrels—

The Salt which is on the Pork must be shook off with care & measured together with that before mentioned & put into the empty pork Barrels, give Mrs Naglie a Rect. for the whole & keep close to the Waggons til their Loads are delivered to Col. Cowperthwaite in this City & get his Rect.

If the Waggons are not close you must put a sufficient number of empty Hhds. in them to make a Load when fill'd, be very exact in the Weight & Measure of the Pork & Salt & desire Mrs. Naglie or some person for her to be present. take a Cooper with you & if necessary a person to assist in Weighing & keep the Waggoners from pilfering on the Road, as your Father was with me at Smithfield he will be able to give you further directions,

I am Yours &c.
G Morton for EBlaine CGofPs

Mr Michl Kitts

Peter Force Collection, Mss. 17,137, Series 8D, Ephraim Blaine Papers, Library of Congress

Morton to Mrs. John Naglie

Philada. 6 Feby. 1780

Madam

Mr. Kitts who will deliver you this has Orders to Weigh & take charge of the Pork in your Cellar, also the Salt for which he will give you a Rect. you may depend that no advantage will be taken of your present Circumstances, on the contrary I am confident Col. Blaine will render you any Service in his power consistant with his duty to the Public & as soon as I am convinced that there is a Balance due you (which did not appear by the Accot. I took at your House) I shall be happy in paying it that you may be enable to settle what is yet due on Accot of Mr Naglie's Contracts

I am Madam
    Your very Humble Servant
        G Morton for E Blaine

Mrs. Naglie

Peter Force Collection, Mss. 17,137, Series 8D, Ephraim Blaine Papers, Library of Co

Blaine to the Board of War

Morris Town Feby. 6th. 1780

Gentlemen,

I have fixed the Business of my Department in such a Train, that I hope will afford such a timely & temporary Supply for our Army as will keep them afloat til I return from the Eastward, which Journey I mean to begin to Morrow, the Magazine at this place has equal to ten days Bread & twenty four of Meat for the Army, but it is highly necessary to have twice that Quantity before the breaking up of the Ice, as there will be no Possibility of Transportation by Land before that Period, & without great Exertions in forwarding the Stores from your City the Army will undoubtedly experience the Distresses for want of Bread they have lately done—

Request your application to the Quarter Master for the necessary means to forward every particular of Provision at the Head of Elk, Christiana & Philadelphia to this place with all possible dispatch, to remedy the aforesaid Evil—no Relief can be expected from Jersey, as they have been so agrieved in Collecting the Surplus of all Provisions in the State in our late Scarcity—I shall not delay longer than is necessary to execute the Business I am going on, the Success I meet with shall inform you by Post from Boston, & be assured every possible exertion in my Power shall be adopted to feed the Army, have the Honor to be with much Esteem & Regard—Gentlemen
　　　　　　Your most Obedient & most Humble Servant

> The Board of War was set up by the Continental Congress to oversee the war effort. At this time it included two members of Congress and three permanent members. In late 1779 the Commissaries of Issue and Purchases, and the Quartermaster General were place under its control. Peter Force Collection, Mss. 17,137, Series 8D, Ephraim Blaine Papers, Library of Congress.

Blaine to Jacob Cuyler

　　　　　　　　　　　　　　Morris Town Feby 6th. 1780
Dear Sir

　　I shall set out from this place to Morrow for Boston, perhaps delay three days at Hartford & four at Boston, & then return to this place, if you cou'd possibly make it convenient to meet me at West-point, wou'd beg you to favour me with a Line the first safe Opportunity to Boston, you making reasonable allowances for my Return can fix the time for our Meeting shou'd it answer your conveniency, am with much Esteem Sir

Your most Obedient Humble Servant
Mr. Cuyler   E. Blaine

Peter Force Collection, Mss. 17,137, Series 8D, Ephraim Blaine Papers, Library of Congress.

Blaine to Nehemiah Dunham

Morris Town Feby 6th 1780

Dear Sir
You will continue to make all the Purchases of Wheat & Flour in your Power, & wish you Credit for that purpose, & pray give me all possible assistance to feed the Army. I am now on my way to New-England, & upon my Return depend on being amply supply'd with Cash to discharge all your Public Debts & Contracts, as Congress have given me every Assurance of a full Supply at that Period, Col: Stuart will inform you of your wants, [sic] am with Regard & Esteem Dr Sir
Your most Obedt. Humle Servant
Mr. Nehemiah Dunham   E. Blaine

NB. You will oblige me by having my Mare brot. from Mr. Fackness's at Flemingtown, & upon my return shall discharge the Mony he paid Mr. King for keeping her & what Expences he may have had since he has had the Mare in keeping—

Nehemiah and Azariah Dunham had served Blaine as purchasers of food in New Jersey since 1777. Peter Force Collection, Mss. 17,137, Series 8D, Ephraim Blaine Papers, Library of Congress.

Blaine to Azariah Dunham

Morris Town Feby. 6th. 1780

Dear Sir

By a late Law in your State, I find that there are Contractors appointed to procure Supplies necessary for our Army in each County, & that the Legislative & Executive Authority have appointed you to superintend the whole, I request you to adopt the most proper means, to procure as largely of Wheat, Flour, and Beef Cattle, salt Beef & Pork as you possibly can; & give the necessary orders to your Contractors to Purchase such of those Articles as their respective Districts afford, our public Magazines are emty & the daily Consumption of Provisions will require your utmost exertions in feeding the Army—your former attention to public Business, & the exertions you have used to assist me in feeding the Army deserves the public's esteem & thanks for the same, & your attatchment to the Public cause, & Industry gives me great hopes of timely & regular Supplies from your State, & am fully convinced that every thing in your power will be done to comply with the Requisition of Congress, the Demands of your State & my Demands from time to time, the public Magazines must be your Deposits for Provisions, & the following will I presume be adapted by the Board of War, Trenton, Pittstown, Elizabethtown & Morristown—

I am now on my way to New England, & beg your very particular attention to the supplying the Army until I return, you will give the earliest Intelligence to my Southern Assistants & Mr. Morton who has my Instructions to comply with your Requisitions & use every Exertions to forward Supplies, you will also inform his Excellency Genl. Washington of the State of our Magazines twice a week & your expectations of Supplies—the Beef which is now Slaughtered, you will keep people employ'd daily in cuting & packing in Barrels & such Casks as you can procure for that purpose, & use no more Salt than will be necessary to keep it, til the middle of April, am informed that the Sutlers about Camp have a number of Hhds., & if those Gentry will take a reasonable Price purchase them all, & continue Killing all the

Cattle you can find Casks to pack in, you will order the person who has the care of this Business to have the Weights of Beef marked on each Cask & Hhd. & have the same Invoiced & delivered to the keeper of the Magazine. I shall write you from Hartford & give you every information respecting Beef Cattle, am with much Esteem & Regard, Dear Sir
  Your Most Obedient & most Humble Servant
    E. Blaine
Azariah Dunham Esqr.

  Peter Force Collection, Mss. 17,137, Series 8D, Ephraim Blaine
  Papers, Library of Congress.

Blaine to Conrod Theodore Wederstrand

Sir   Morristown 7th. Feby. 1780
  I have thought it prudent to keep the Cattle you have now on hand & have them provided for with Forrage in best manner you can, til the Beef already Slaughtered & that in the Possession of the Brigade Commissarys is made use of—those Commissarys who are out of Cattle & apply to you, give them orders upon Mr. Litle for Beef & direct him to give Rects. for Weight & Quantity delivered, Mr. Dunham will assist you in culing out such Cattle as will not answer to Slaughter & receive the same from you, I have directed him to procure keeping for same, you will use every Eaconomy in the disposal of the Cattle, & suffer none to be slaughtered that will risk condemnation, and with much Regard Sir
    Your most Obedient Humble Servt

Mr. Witherstrandt

Peter Force Collection, Mss. 17,137, Series 8D, Ephraim Blaine Papers, Library of Congress. Wederstrandt was an Assistant Deputy Commissary of Purchases for Queen-Anne's, Talbot, and below in Maryland.

Morton to Matthias Slough

Philada. 10th. February 1780

Sir

I have just now Recd. your favr. of the 3rd. Inst. that of the 27 Ulto. also came to hand since Col. Blaines departure—I find you misunderstood his Letter of the 25th. Ulto. with regard to the prices of Produce, which he dont mean to confine you in, your Commissions only are affected by the Resolve of Congress, which you have enclosed, at the same time I make no doubt but you will study to procure the Supplies your District affords on the most reasonable terms in your Power.—as to the Beef Cattle I am happy to acquaint you, there is now a very Plentiful supply at Camp, you will therefore keep yours til further Orders in their present situation, forward all the Flour you possibly can before the Roads break up, as it will be impracticable for some time after, & the Army shou'd at least have a Months provisions on hand—I am daily in expectation of Letters from Col. Blaine at Camp & shall give the earliest notice of anything respecting you, I am
Your most Obedient Servant—
Geo: Morton

Matthias Slough Esqr.

Slough was an Assistant Commissary of Purchases at Lancaster, Pennsylvania. Peter Force Collection, Mss. 17,137, Series 8D, Ephraim Blaine Papers, Library of Congress.

Morton to Conrod Theodore Wederstrandt

Philada. 12 Feby 1780

Sir

Your favour of the 7th. Inst. by Mr McCallaster came safe to hand & note the Contents, am glad you are in a fair way to Receive the amount of the Orders sent you on the Treasury of your State, since Col. Blaines letter to you of the 12 Ulto. there has been an alteration in the System of the Department, & he has accepted of the appointment of Commissary Genl. of Purchases, he sett out for Boston by way of Head Quarters the 26th. Ulto. in order to establish purchases in the Eastern states—

  I have paid your Order in favr. of Mr. for twelve thousand Dollars which is all that can be done for you til Col. Blaines return which will be about the middle of March. in the mean time be preparing your Accots. for a final <u>Settlement</u> up to the 15th. of January, & be assured Col. Blaine will use his utmost endeavours to procure a Sum equal to the Balance—you will receive herewith the Letters from your Assistants, I am in behalf of Ephm Blaine Esqr. Comy. Genl. of Purchases

     Your most Obedient Servant
       Geo Morton
C. C. Wederstrandt

Peter Force Collection, Mss. 17,137, Series 8D, Ephraim Blaine Papers, Library of Congress.

Blaine to Jonathan Trumbull

        Hartford Feby. 14th 1780
Sir,

  I arrived here yesterday from the Army which is now tolerably supplied with Provisions for a few Days, but from the many obstructions for their future Support, I am apprehensive they will soon be reduced to short Allowance unless this State take the matter of Supplies under their immediate Consideration & I flatter my self I shall meet with their Approbation & assistance as a Public Officer—& from my knowledge of those Gentlemens Countenance, & their past exertions who have gone before in Office I hope for Success

Notwithstanding the power I have of appointing Deputies in each State, I know it will be more agreeable to Congress that each State shou'd appoint their own Commissaries & will be satisfactory to me—as I must Visit the other New-England States & very little time to Spare, shall esteem it a particular favour of your Excellency & Council to take up the Business of my Department & lay it before your Legislature & fix the mode of Purchasing & a Deputy, that I may give him the necessary Direction to keep up the Supplies for our Army before I leave Town, am with all due Respect your Excellencys most Obedient & most Humble Servant
E. Blaine

Governor Trumbull

Peter Force Collection, Mss. 17,137, Series 8D, Ephraim Blaine Papers, Library of Congress.

Blaine to Jonathan Trumbull

Hartford 14 Feby. 1780

Sir

Finding the Assembly have declined appointing a Purchasing Commissary, & well knowing it was the desire of Congress that each State shou'd take up their Recommendation & appoint their own Agents, and as it is my desire to appoint a person of Reputation & Character, & one who will be agreeable to the State, wish your Recommendation of the Man & I shall appoint him I am with much Respect your Excellencys
Most Obedient & most Humble Servt.
Ephm Blaine

Governor Trumbull

Peter Force Collection, Mss. 17,137, Series 8D, Ephraim Blaine Papers, Library of Congress.

Morton to John Chaloner and James White

Philada 22nd. Feby 1780

Gentlemen

Yours of the 15th. Instant to Col. Blaine is just come to hand inclosing a resolution of Congress of the 11th. Ulto. & note the Contents—from the time the Convention Troops crossed the North River they were entirely supply'd thro. the Issuing Departmt til their Arrival at the Barracks in Albemarle County Virginia an exact return of which, properly Certify'd by the British Commissaries, I delivered to the Board of War being then in the Issuing Department & Commissary with the Troops of Convention on their March, I am Gentleman

Your most Obedient Servant for E. Blaine CG

Geo: Morton

Messrs. Chaloner & White

> Chaloner and White were Philadelphia merchants whom Blaine had appointed in 1777 as Assistant Commissaries of Purchases. They had left their government posts and gone into business together. Peter Force Collection, Mss. 17,137, Series 8D, Ephraim Blaine Papers, Library of Congress.

Morton to William Evans

Philada. 24 Feby. 1780

Sir

Your favor of the 18th. Inst. came to hand, & agreeable to your Request have enclosed you a Genl. Accot. Currt. from the 1st Jany. 1778 to December 1779 inclusive by which it appears there is a Balce. due you of £6.489..7..2 exclusive of your purchases in the Month of January last, enclosed you have a Coppy of the remarks made on your Returns, & request that you will procure such Vouchers & Rectify such Errors as are therein pointed out, after which there will be no obsticle in

your way for a final Settlement as soon as Col. Blaine returns from the Eastward, I am Sir
Your most Humble Servant
Geo: Morton

NB. procure such Vouchers as are wanting for Deliveries Col. Wm. Evans

> Peter Force Collection, Mss. 17,137, Series 8D, Ephraim Blaine Papers, Library of Congress.

Blaine to Samuel Huntington

Boston 25th Feby 1780

Sir,

I ariv'd here yesterday and never had such Difficulty travelling in all my life—when I came to Hartford the Governor and assembly were siting I made application to them requesting their nomination or appointment of a Deputy Commissary, assureing them it was the desire of Congress and much more agreable to me than one of my own choise—but doubting it wou'd be giving them great trouble and the prospects of procuring money to discharge such contracts as the deputy made for cattle has induced them to decline and leave the appointment to me—I waited upon the Treasurer delivered him letters and bill from the Treasury board, and presented him my two drafts the One for a Million of dollars when the bills are sold—the other for one and a half Million tax money—he gave me for answer, that there was no Money in the treasury—that he was now indebted five hundred thousand dollars an order Due Mr. Champion some time, and a Considerable sum to Mr. Colt and the Quarter Master, and that he did not know when it woud be in his power to answer my draft, that the first taxes was nearly all collected and the Money paid out for the use of the state and sundry other purposes—in this situation I am left a Stranger—without money and of Course few friends—the new system for the Commisariate reprobated and no person in Any Kind of business or capable willing to Accept—Mr. Champion who has acted as purchaser of live stock is approv'd of and deemed trusty and Exceedingly well acquainted with the business of his department—his assistants are numerouse as the [sic] have to go from House to House to purchase the farmers Cattle the [sic] have had two Pr Cent on all disburstment and reasonable charges when called out of their respective districts on public Business the [sic] have till last November been Pretty well supplied with money their purchases since that period have been chiefly on trust and the disappointments they have given the Princaple feeders of cattle has greatly injured their credit—(and what is still worse) has Prevented numbers from being able to fill their stalls with poor Cattle to Fatt, he also assured me the whole allowance offered by Congress is not sufficient to engage his most triffling assistants to continue. I have got him to forward the princaple part of all the cattle he has purchased to Head quarters which with whats in hand will be a sufficient supply till the first of April—

The treasurer of Rhoad Island and this state have answered my orders wish they had been Larger as I believe the [sic] were enabled to have answered them—part of those sums with what I can obtain at Hartford shall reserve for the purchase of beef Cattle—and will adopt some plann to engage proper persons to purchase and forward Supplies to our Army—shoud no Other Method do, necessity will Oblige me to continue them on the old terms rather than suffer the supplies to fail, which will undoubtedly be the case, as no person I can trust with the business will Accept on any other terms—and I shall depend on Congress for the confirmation of such Contracts and engagements and their adopting ways and means to procure money to enable me to Discharge the same— for without little can be done in this Country—I should be exceedingly happy in executing measures to procure the Necessary supplies for our army and adopting every plan of

economy possible—but from the Present prospects of money and the Avaricious disposition of people generally—and the inducements offered by Congress for the service of those who must Necessarily be employ'd in that business, I have great reason to doubt my success, and shou'd I fail shall be unhappy indeed—as the same time assure Congress that my greatest exertions and best endeavours shall not be wanting—am with the Greatest respect—your Excellencys—
Most Obdt. & Most Hble Servt.
Eph. Blaine C. G. P.
Saml. Huntington Esqr.

Papers of the Continental Congress, Roll 182, i165, p345-48, National Archives.

Blaine to George Washington

Boston 25th Feby 1780—

Please your Excellency
    Sir,
    I have not meet [sic] with the success I had Reason to expect in Connectticutt the Governor and Assembly have not taken up the Recommendation of Congress in Nominating or appointing a deputy Commissary to execute the purchases of their state—doubting it wou'd be Giving them Extraordinary trouble and the disapointment their agent might meet with in not receiving money to discharge his purchases and Contracts—the treasurer has also Paid out the Continental money for state and Other purposes which has deprived me of the payment of a Million and a half of dollars which I had an order on the Treasurer for this is a very considerable disapointment of which I have informd Congress also my doubts of supplies shoud the [sic] fail in furnishing me with money—
I find this country capable of affording large Supplies of beef cattle (but prices exceedingly high) and if Congress adopt a

proper plan and demand such supplies as each State can afford, and furnish me with money to Keep a Temporary supply in the magazines till their new system is properly set on foot—your Excellency need have little doubts respecting provisions—and be assured of my greatest exertions and every possible Attention to perform every part within the compass of my power—I delivered your letters to Major Talmage which he promised to Acknowledge by first Oppertunity—I have the honor to be with all due respect—
    Your Excellency's Most Obedt. and
    Most Hble Servt.
    Eph. Blaine C. G. P.
Genl Washington
In a different hand:
copy of the above except the final p[aragraph] transmitted Congress the 17th. March 1780

  George Washington Papers, Library of Congress.

Morton to Benjamin Rogers

          Philada. 25th. 1780.
Sir
  Your Letter of the 20th. Instant covering one from his Excellency Thomas Sim Lee Esqr. came to hand, Col. Blaine is gone to the Eastward & will not return before the middle of next Month, when you may expect his Answer, I enclose you a Coppy of the Resolves of Congress respecting the new System of the Commissaries Department for your perusal & remain Sir
    Your most Obedient Servant
      for Ephraim Blaine CG of P. Geo: Morton
Mr. Benjn. Rogers
Gunpowder falls Baltimore Co.

  Rogers was a Justice of the Peace in Baltimore County. Peter Force Collection, Mss. 17,137, Series 8D, Ephraim Blaine Papers, Library of Congress.

Morton to John Chaloner and James White

Philada. 25 Feby. 1780

Gentn.

You will receive herewith sundry Letters of the 10th. 12th. 23rd. & 27th. December 29th. Ulto: & 7th. Instant from Mr. Conrad Theodore Wederstrandt Assist Commissary of Purchases on the Eastern Shore of Maryland wherin [sic] he writes in the most pressing terms for Cash—that of the 27th. December, particularly mentions a quantity of Flour which Col. Ezekiel Forman spared for the use of the Army at a time when they were in the greatest want and as that Gentleman has called upon Col. Blaine for Money, I make no doubt but you will see the necessity of making application to the Honorable Board of Treasury for a Sum (if nothing more can be done) equal to Col. Foremans demands which shall be paid him on Acct. of Mr. Wederstrandt—

You have also a Letter from Major Isaac Carty dated the 19th. this moment come to hand to which as well as those from Mr. Wederstrandt must refer you for particulars—

I am Gentn. Your Most Obt Servt.

Geo: Morton In behalf Col. E. Blaine CG of P

Messrs Chaloner & White—

Peter Force Collection, Mss. 17,137, Series 8D, Ephraim Blaine Papers, Library of Congress.

Morton to Jacob Arndt and Jacob Stroud

Philada. 26th. Feby. 1780

Gentlemen

Your favr. of the 19th. Instant came to hand this day & am sorry you met with so much difficulty in the execution of your Duty. I must request that you wou'd continue to Act, at least til Col. Blaines return (which will be about the middle of next Month) & til you have laid out the Amot. of the Order sent you on Accot. of the new System. in the mean time your Accots. in the old Department shall be examined as soon as you please to bring them for Settlement.

If you can't dispose of the L O Certificates for the full Value you may return them, & your Accot. shall have the Credit for such part of them as are unapproiated—
I am Gentlemen, in behalf of Col Blaine CG of P.
                    Your very Humble Servt.
                            Geo. Morton
Messrs. Arndt & Stroud

> Their company was serving as purchasers for the Commissary Department at Easton, Pennsylvania. Peter Force Collection, Mss. 17,137, Series 8D, Ephraim Blaine Papers, Library of Congress.

Morton to Peter Aston

                              Philada. 9 March 1780
Sir
The present is to request that you woud as soon as possible send to this Office a Return, of what Wheat & Flour there is on hand in your District, what you have lately forwarded to Camp & what prospect you have of future Supplies, this requisition is in consequence of an Order from the Honorable Committee of Congress, to furnish them with an Accot. of the Quantity of the above Articles in the hands of Col. Blaines Assists. in the middle Departmt:, must therefore request your attention thereto, as well as to forwarding an immediate Supply of Flour to Camp if Practicable

    I received a Letter from Col. Blaine at Boston, wherein he desires that you shou'd have the Cattle which you have Kept thro' the Winter, good Beef ready to deliver his Order next Month
              Remain Sir Your most Obedt. Servant
                            Geo Morton

Peter Aston Esqe: Reading

> Aston was an Assitant Commissary of Purchases at Reading, PA. Peter Force Collection, Mss. 17,137, Series 8D, Ephraim Blaine Papers, Library of Congress.

Morton, Circular, to Robert Buchanan, Patrick Ewing, and Jacob Giles Jr.

Philada. 9th. March 1780

Sir

I am sorry to inform you the Army are like to suffer their former Distress for want of Bread, if not timely relieved by the Zealous exertions of Col. Blaines Assistants, in your State, & to you in particular we must look, as your situation makes you capable of rendering more immediate Supplies—

I have orders from the Honorable the Committee of Congress, to obtain a Return of all the Wheat, Flour &c in the Possession of the Purchasing Commissaries in the Middle Department, to effect which I must request you immediately to furnish me with an Acco^t. of the Quantity now in your District & what prospect you have of future Purchases—together with what you have lately forwarded—

I received a Letter this day dated at Boston the 24 Ulto. from Col. Blaine, he desires that you wou'd forward all the Flour you possibly can without delay. I am Sir

Your most Humble Servant
Geo: Morton

Robert Buchanan
Patrick Ewing
Jacob Giles

> Buchanan was Assistant Commisary of Purchases for Baltimore; Ewing was Assistant Commissary of Purchases for Cecil County, Maryland. Giles held the same post for Harford County, Maryland. Peter Force Collection, Mss. 17,137, Series 8D, Ephraim Blaine Papers, Library of Congress.

Morton to Isaac Carty

Philada. 9th. March 1780

Sir,
I received your favors by Messrs. Crosby & Bell, & wou'd have wrote you by the former but at that time no answer had been given to your application to the board of Treasury. Mr. Bell waited on them in person, & to him I must refer you for their Answer—

The distress which the Army are again like to experience for want of Bread, has induced a Committee of Congress to call upon me for a Return of all the Wheat, Flour &c in the possession of Col. Blaines Assistants in the middle Department, to effect which I must request you immediately to furnish me with an Accot. of the Quantity now in your District & what prospect you have of future purchases—

I mentioned your situation to Col. McKean who is a member of the Committee aforesaid, & that I was apprehensive the Supplies wou'd be held back for want of Mony, he assured me you shou'd be furnished with the needful

I must entreat you to exert your self at this critical Period in forwarding all the Flour you possibly can, & besides the Credit you will get from Congress & Col Blaine on this Occasion, you will have the Secret satisfaction of rendering an important Service to your Country, I am Sir wh. respect
   Your most Obedient Servant
    Geo: Morton
let me hear from you immediately in this Subject
Major Isaac Carty

> Peter Force Collection, Mss. 17,137, Series 8D, Ephraim Blaine Papers, Library of Congress.

Morton to John Chaloner and James White

Philada 9 March 1780

Gentlemen

 Inclosed you have a Letter from Mr. Robert Hoops A. Cy. of Purchases for Sussex County new Jersey by which you will see that he has drawn, an Order on Col. Blaine in favr. of the bearer Mr. Increase Carpenter for Eighty one thousand three hundred & Sixty one pounds for Cattle purchased from him in the Months of November & December last, he wishes to represent the matter to the Honorable the Board of Treasury & I beg leave to refer him to you for that purpose, I am Gentleman

    Your most Obedient Servant
      Geo: Morton

Chaloner & White Esqrs:

Peter Force Collection, Mss. 17,137, Series 8D, Ephraim Blaine Papers, Library of Congress.

Morton to the Committee of Congress

Estimate of Flour expected to be delivered into the Magazine at Philadelphia in the Course of 3 Weeks, March 9th. 1780

	Barrels
From Conrod C. T. Wederstrandt,	
Eastern Shore Maryland	1.000
Robert Buchanan Baltimore	.500
Patrick Ewing Head of Elk	.500
Isaac Carty Delaware State	.500
	2.500

Gentlemen

 The above is an estimate of Flour which may reasonably be expected to be delivered into the Magazine at Philada. in the course of three weeks or a Month, at the same time, I beg leave to observe, that I believe a much larger is contracted for, which I reason to fear [sic] will be detained for want of Mony, shall Write to Coll. Blaines Assistants in Maryland & the Delaware

States for a particular Return of what they have on hand, which when obtained shall be transmitted you immediately, I have the Honor to be Gentlemen
            Your most obedient & most humble Servant
                  Geo Morton
The Honorable the Committe of Congress.

    Peter Force Collection, Mss. 17,137, Series 8D, Ephraim Blaine Papers, Library of Congress.

Morton to Azariah Dunham

                              Philada 9 March 1780
Sir
    Col. Stewart delivered me a Letter the 4 Inst. from Col. Blaine dated at Morristown the 5th. Ulto. by which I find you were to Act for him (in the absence of Col. Stewart) til his return from the Eastward, I was much surprized yesterday on being call'd before the Honorable the Committee of Congress to answer for the want of Bread in the Army, of which I never had the least information from you or any other person at Camp, I must request that you will in future give me the earliest information from time to time of the state of your Supplies, that I may use my endeavours to prevent a future Scarcity, I am Sir in behalf of Col. Blaine CG
            Your most Obedient Servant
                    Geo. Morton
A Dunham Esqr. Morristown

    Peter Force Collection, Mss. 17,137, Series 8D, Ephraim Blaine Papers, Library of Congress.

Morton to William Evans

                              Philada. 9 March 1780
Sir

Your favour of the 7 Instant I received & observe the Contents—Flour at present is much wanting, must therefore request that you wou'd forward every Barrel you have on hand to this place, & purchase as much more as lye in your Power at the price mentioned in your Letter, as to fresh Provisions you must do as you think best, but by all means secure Flour for which purpose you must lay out what Mony you have in the County Treasury & you may depend upon having an Order sent you from Mr. Rittenhouse as soon as Col. Blaine returns
    I am Sir Yours &ca
      Geo. Morton
W. Evans
P.S. you will herewith Receive your Accot. Currt. which has waited some time for an Opportunity

Peter Force Collection, Mss. 17,137, Series 8D, Ephraim Blaine Papers, Library of Congress.

Morton to Mathias Slough

          Philada. 9 March 1780
Sir
 Since the Receipt of yours of the 26 Ulto. I received a Letter from Col. Blaine dated at Boston the 24th. of February, wherein he desires that you will keep the Beef Cattle (agreeable to his former Orders), til his Return which will not be til the begining of next Month.
 I have this day received Orders from a Committee of Congress to obtain an exact Return of what Flour is in the hands of the Purchasing Commissaries in the middle Department, in complyance with which must request you will send immediately an Accot. of what is in your District, & what you have forwarded lately to Camp if any. you will lose no time in forwarding what you have on hand, as the Army is likely to experience a want of Bread—I can give you no Assistance with Money at present, & remain

             Your most Obedient Servant
                             Geo. Morton
Matts. Slough Esqr. Lancaster

   Peter Force Collection, Mss. 17,137, Series 8D, Ephraim Blaine
   Papers, Library of Congress.

Morton to Conrad Theodore Wetherstrandt

                         Philada. 9th. March 1780
Sir
     Prior to the Rect. of your favor of the 21st. Ulto. I laid your sundry Letters of the 10. 12. 23 & 27 December 29 Jany & 7 Feby. before the Board of Treasury, & particularly represented the Transaction between you & Col. Ezekl. Foreman, who had call'd upon Col. Blaine for Cash on Accot. of the Flour delivered you, but the Board have not yet done any-thing in your Favor.
     I have received Orders from the Honorable the Committee of Congress to obtain a Return of what Flour & Wheat is in the hands of the Purchasing Commissaries in the middle Departmt. in complyance therewith I must request you to furnish by the return of the Post an accot. of the Quantity of Wheat & Flour you have in your District & also how much you have forwarded to the Landings on the Delaware, this information is absolutely necessary for the Wellfare of the Army, & will be a means of procuring you a Sum of Mony to enable you to discharge your Debts—
     As I have given Congress an Assurance of a very considerable Quantity of Flour from your District in the course of 3 Weeks from the present time I must entreat you to use your utmost exertion in forwarding every Barril you possibly can.
     I am Sir Your most Obedient Servt.
                             Geo. Morton
C. C. T Wetherstrandt Esqr.

Peter Force Collection, Mss. 17,137, Series 8D, Ephraim Blaine Papers, Library of Congress.

Morton to Conrod Theodore Wederstrandt

Philada: 13 March 1780

Sir

Since my Letter to you of the 9th. Instant I recd yours of the 4th & am sorry to hear that you have met with so much difficulty from the interference of the Commissioners, you have inclosed a Coppy of an Invoice of Sixty Barrels of Flour sent up from Johnny-cake landing, which I suppose to be part of your Purchases it has been inspected & Weighed at the Magazine here & falls short of the Original Invoice 6 Ct..0..22 request you to make enquiry into the matter, & have the Delinquents whither Waggoners or Flatmen punished as the Law directs I am Sir
 Your Obedient Servant
 Geo Morton

C. C. T. Wederstrandt

Peter Force Collection, Mss. 17,137, Series 8D, Ephraim Blaine Papers, Library of Congress.

Morton to John Chaloner and James White

Philada 14 March 1780

Gentlemen

You have inclosed a Letter from Messrs. Morris & Hugg Assist. Coms. of Purchase for the Western District, New Jersey, & also a List of Debts due for Pork &c. contracted for by them I need not inform you that its not in my Power to give them any assistance with Mony, & for want of that necessary Article a considerable Quantity of Salt provisions which lies in Bulk is likely to Spoil

I am Gentlemen Your most Obedient Servant
Geo: Morton
Messrs: Chaloner & White

> Peter Force Collection, Mss. 17,137, Series 8D, Ephraim Blaine Papers, Library of Congress.

Morton to James McCallaster

Philada. 14 March 1780

Sir
Your favr of the 7th. Inst. pr Mr. Noble inclosing two Returns I Recd. & am sorry its not in my Power to pay that Gentn. any Money on your Acct, I expect Col. Blaine from the Eastward the first on next Month I am Sir
Your Humble Servant
Geo: Morton
James Mc.Callaster Esqr.

> This was probably James McAlister, who was an Issuing Commissary in Berkley County, Virginia. Peter Force Collection, Mss. 17,137, Series 8D, Ephraim Blaine Papers, Library of Congress.

Morton to the Board of Treasury

Philada. 17 March 1780

Gentlemen
I take the Liberty of inclosing you a Letter from Mr. Patrick Ewing AComy. of Purchases at the Head of Elk dated the 3rd Instant to Col. Blaine, the contents of wh. I communicated to Mr McKean Congress. he has given Mr Ewing expectation of a Sum of Mony equal to the purchase of Eight or Ten thousand Bushels of Wheat, which he can procure in a short time in his District. for the above purpose he requires a Warrant on the Treasury of the State of Maryland for five

hundred thousand Dollars as appears by his Letter to me of the present date which you have also Inclosed, as Mr. Ewing has been waiting in Town several days, I beg to be favoured with your Answer as soon as convenient, I have the Honor to be in Behalf of E. B. CG of P.
      Your most Obedient Servant
        Geo. Morton
The Honble Board of Treasury

> The Board of Treasury was a standing committe of five members of the Continental Congress. Peter Force Collection, Mss. 17,137, Series 8D, Ephraim Blaine Papers, Library of Congress.

Morton to Benjamin Stoddert

        Philada. 17 March 1780
Sir
  The Return requested by the Honorable Board of Warr of the Quantity of Provisions in the Possession of the purchasing Commissaries in the Middle Department, it is not in my Power to furnish at present, shall Write a circular Letter to Col. Blaines Assistants for an Accot. of what remains on hand in their respective Districts, a General Return of which shall be transmitted you as soon as possible, I am Sir
    Your most Obedient Servant
Benjn. Stoddart Esqr. Secretary

> Stoddert was Secretary to the Board of War and later the first Secretary of the Navy. Peter Force Collection, Mss. 17,137, Series 8D, Ephraim Blaine Papers, Library of Congress.

Morton, Circular to Assistant Purchasing Commissaries in the Middle Department

        Philada: 17 March 1780
Sir

Sir
 The board of War have call'd upon Col: Blaine for a Return of the provisions in the possession of his Assistants in the middle Department, to effect which I must request an immediate Return of what remains on hand in your District
  I am Your most Humble Servant
   Geo: Morton
Circular

> Peter Force Collection, Mss. 17,137, Series 8D, Ephraim Blaine Papers, Library of Congress.

Blaine to George Clinton

Sir, Fish Kill 19th March 1780.
 The delays I meet with at Boston and Connecticut depriv'd me the Oppertunity of waiting upon your Excellency and the Assembly while Conveen'd at Albany. I went within a few miles of your House but being inform'd there was no Certainty of your being home for some days (the roads being exceeding bad) concluded it was best to proceed on my Journey to Head Quarters; shoud been happy in seeing your Excellency, and having your approbation in the continuance of Mr. Cuyler in Office, or a Recommendation of some other Person; a line from your Excellency upon that Subject by first post shall acknowledge a particular favour. The magazines being nearly exhausted, it will require my greatest Exertions and that of every person in the Department, to procure a sufficient supply of bread and beef to feed our army till after harvest; indeed, if we accomplish it I shall be exceedingly happy and hope we shall never experience such a Scarcity and want of Provisions in future,
  Remain with all due Respect, your Excellency's, Most Obdt. and most Hbl. Servant
   Eph. Blaine, C. G. of Purchases.
Gov'r Clinton.

Public Papers of George Clinton, First Governor of New York, (Albany: James B. Lyon), 5:544.

Morton to John Chaloner and James White

Philada: 20 March 1780

Gentlemen

I received the Inclos'd from Major Carty this Instant in answer to my Letter to him of the 9th. Instant, if you think it will answer a good purpose, I beg you to lay it before the Honorable Board of Treasury, the Provisions contracted for in his District chiefly remain in the hands of the former Owners, & without Mony they will not admit of its being forwarded for the use of the Army, I am

Gentlemen Your most Obedient Servant
Geo: Morton

Messrs: Chaloner & White

Peter Force Collection, Mss. 17,137, Series 8D, Ephraim Blaine Papers, Library of Congress.

Morton to Benjamin Stoddert

Philada. 21 March 1780

Sir

Robert Irwin of Hanover settled his Accots. in Col. Blaines Office last August since which he has not acted in any Capacity in the purchasing Department

I am Sir Your most Obedient Servt.
Geo Morton

Benjamin Stoddart Esqr. Secretary

Peter Force Collection, Mss. 17,137, Series 8D, Ephraim Blaine Papers, Library of Congress.

Morton to Ephraim Blaine

Philada. 23 March 1780

Dear Sir
Your favr. by Col. Stewart dated the 5 Ulto. did not come to hand til the 4th: Inst: & shortly after I received your Letter from Boston, & am sorry you met with so much Difficulty in Traveling, but I have reason to think the badness of the Roads was the least of your Trouble, prior to the Rect. of your Letter from Morristown, I had accepted & paid orders from different Quarters to nearly the Amot. of what you left in my Hands, but your draft in favr. of Mr. Thomas for Cash advanced Major Hoops being presented, I paid him & put others off who I thought were not so well entitled to Cash, that in favr: of Mr. Erskine came to hand some time after but it was not in my Power to pay it til this day to Mr. Flahavan he having agreed to take it in Certificates, Mr: Dunham has never thought proper to give me any information respecting the Supplies at Camp, & the first I heard of a Scarcity was from a Committee of Congress about two weeks ago, since which I wrote pressingly to your Assistants, in Maryland & the Delaware States, as I did before to such as cou'd render Supplies by Land, but not having Mony to pay off their old Contracts, I fear will make them hold back the Supplies, indeed Carty says Publickly that if he is not furnished with Mony, he will keep the Supplies in his hands as Security, & tho' Wederstrandt is not so open, I believe his intentions are the same

Repeated applications have been made by Chaloner & White in favor of N Dunham & Major Carty without effect, & in consequence of advice from Mr. McKean one of the Honorable Committee of Congress, I took the Liberty to make an application to the board of Treasury on the new System in favour of Mr. Ewing for a Sum of Mony (five hundred thousand Dollars) equal to the Purchase of Eight or Ten thousand Busls. of Wheat, but after keeping him in expectation for five or six days the application shared the same fate as those from the old Department, Flour is offering for Sale every Day & Chaloner & White have no Mony to purchase—

I Recd: a long Letter yesterday from Major Forsyth to you, he & all his Assistants in the Southern Department absolutely refuse to act under the new System, the Convention Troops are likely to Starve & no Mony to purchase Provisions for their Support, to conclude every thing wears a gloomy aspect. I wish to God you were once more in Philada., I am Sir with due Respect
Your most Obedt: Servant
Geo: Morton
PS. Mrs. Blaine & Family are well, I purchased Oats for your Horses & charged Bobby to see them fed two or three times a day
Col. Blaine

> Peter Force Collection, Mss. 17,137, Series 8D, Ephraim Blaine Papers, Library of Congress.

Morton to Conrod Theodore Wederstrandt

Philada. 25 March 1780

Sir

Your favour by Mr. McCallaster of the 20th. Currt. I received, I sent you a Circular Letter of the 17th. post, requesting a Return of the Provisions of all Species on hand in your District to which I beg your attention, if you cant be exact you must come as near the quantity as possible, & mention the places where it is deposited

I accepted you Order in favr. of Mr. McCallaster, not having Cash at present to pay him, but hope it will answer his purpose; have your Wheat Manufactor'd & forward the Flour with all possible dispatch, or the Army will undoubtedly suffer
I am Sir

                    Your Most Obedient Servant
                            Geo: Morton
C. C. T. Wederstrandt

>Peter Force Collection, Mss. 17,137, Series 8D, Ephraim Blaine Papers, Library of Congress.

Morton to Henry Miller

                                    Philada. 25 March 1780
Sir
    I delivered your Letter of the 20th. to General Schuyler, which he laid before Congress, & this Minute he has given me for answer, that they understood you had Contracted for the Flour on public Accot. before you sent in your proposals I am
Sir
            Your most Obedient Servant
                    Geo: Morton
Col. Henry Miller

>Miller was an Assistant Commissary of Purchases at York, Pennsylvania. Peter Force Collection, Mss. 17,137, Series 8D, Ephraim Blaine Papers, Library of Congress.

Blaine to George Clinton

                                Fish Kill 19th March 1780.
Sir,
The delays I meet with at Boston and Connecticut depriv'd me the Oppertunity of waiting upon your Excellency and the Assembly while Conveen'd at Albany. I went within a few miles of your House but being inform'd there was no Certainty of your being home for some days (the roads being exceeding bad) concluded it was best to proceed on my Journey to Head Quarters; shoud been happy in seeing your Excellency, and having your approbation in the continuance of Mr. Cuyler in

Office, or a Recommendation of some other Person; a line from your Excellency upon that Subject by first post shall acknowledge a particular favour. The magazines being nearly exhausted, it will require my greatest Exertions and that of every person in the Department, to procure a sufficient supply of bread and beef to feed our army till after harvest; indeed, if we accomplish it I shall be exceedingly happy and hope we shall never experience such a Scarcity and want of Provisions in future, Remain with all due
Respect, your Excellency's,
Most Obdt. and most Hbl. Servant
Eph. Blaine,
C. G. of Purchases

Gov'r Clinton

Public Papers of George Clinton, First Governor of New York, (Albany: James B. Lyon), 5:544.

Blaine to Samuel Huntington

Sir

Philadelphia 29th March 1780

My duty to the Public requires that I shoud report to the Honorable the Congress the State of the supplies as well at Head Quarters, as in the Eastern States The Provisions collected in Jersey in pursuance to the late Requisition of his Excellency General Washington & the other Supplies collected are nearly expended, not a single Bullock now in Camp & only Salt Provisions equal to twelve Days remained in the Magazine there. The Magazine at West point affords but a Temporary supply and twenty five or thirty fatt Cattle pr Week will be wanting; otherwise the Garrison will certainly be distressed in a Short time.—General Poors Brigade, Colonels Moyland Sheldon & Greens Regiments & the prisoners at Rutland have not been regularly supplied with Bread.—Little Flour can be procured in that Country but Indian & Rye Meal, this with Rice which is in the Magazine must support those Troops.—

The Governor & Assembly of Connecticut declining the Appointment or recommendation of a Deputy Commissary to superintend the purchases of that State, & rather than let those Troops suffer for want of Bread and have the Supplies of Beef retarded, I took upon me the power (which I hope Congress will approve of) to reappoint Coll. Champion with a Commission of two pr Cent on his Expenditures, he to pay all his Assistants thereout.—On the same terms by the approbation of the Council of Massachusets Bay, I appointed Charles Miller Esquire, & for the State of Rhode Island Asa Waterman—to all those Gentlemen I have engaged the like Commission of two pr Cent—

The Magazines of Salt Provisions in the Eastern States very inconsiderable—the whole in the Middle Department with about four hundred head of Fat Cattle which I have had fed thro' the Winter will about feed the Army with Meat up to the 10th. of May, & if the Contracts my People have made for Flour are comply'd with (which I have reason to think disappointment of Money has induced some people to hold back) there will be sufficient of Flour and Indian Meal to serve the Army up to the Middle of June.—It therefore requires the speedy & serious attention of Congress to enable me to keep up the Supplies for the Army—

The Laws in this State and New Jersey will prevent an former Deputy or Assistant from making any Contracts in future, and the pressing demands for Money to fulfill those already made are numerous & in many cases realy distressing—

The Vicinity of this State, Delaware & Eastern Shore Maryland to the Grand Army will require instant Exertions from the new Commissioners, to furnish the quoto's required by Congress, <u>on the speedy Collection & delivery</u> of which, I think the very existence of our Army depends, & the forwarding it to Camp is a matter of great importance

I have to add that Congress may depend on the Exertion of my abilities to execute the trust resposed in me, but let me entreat your Honorable Body that I may be supported in going thro' it with your Countenance & as much Money as the Treasury can from time to time furnish to procure Supplies. I have no greater Ambition than to deserve your Approbation by feeding your Troops, & convincing Congress & his Excellency General Washington that they may rely on the Activity & integrity of their faithfull Servants—

Mr. Cuyler of New York State will continue for the present—Major Forsyth who has the direction of the Southern Department, informs me his Assistants have all resigned, & that the Provision made by Congress is not sufficient to Support any Man who attends to the Business, & adds that he will render the public every Service in his power till a new appointment takes place—

Your Agent at Boston has above twelve hundred Hogsheads of Sugar & some Rum yet on hand, the Rum I have ordered to Camp when the Roads will admit—As the price of Sugar was low at Boston, postponed selling any, and gave directions to Captain Bradford to Ship in different Bottoms for this City four hundred Hhds, knowing it would bring the public a much greater price, this I hope will meet the Sanction of Congress.—I have many things to communicate which wou'd be too tedious by Letter, therefore when convenient request a Conference with a Committee on the Business of my Department

  I have the Honor to be with much respect
    Your Excellencys Most
      Obedient and Most Hble Servant
        Eph. Blaine, C. G. P.
His Excellency Samuel Huntington Esquire

Note: received March 30.

Papers of the Continental Congress, M247, Roll 182, i 165, p 349-51, National Archives.

Blaine to the Board of War

Philada. April 3rd. 1780

Honor'd Gentlemen

Inclosed you have Coppy of Letters to Congress & the Treasury-board respecting the Supplies of the Army, also an estimate of Sums of Mony necessary to procure Flour Wheat & Beef Cattle contracted for & not delivered this Sum is absolutely necessary to procure a temporary Supply for the Army, until the State Commissioners are in motion, therefore Request your immediate attention to this Business & the wants of the Northern & Southern departments as represented by Mr. Cuyler & Major Forsyth, I am with due Respect
    Honor'd Gen. Your most Obedient
     & most Humble Servant
      E. Blaine

Honble. Board of War

Peter Force Collection, Mss. 17,137, Series 8D, Ephraim Blaine Papers, Library of Congress.

Blaine to Nathanael Greene

Philada. April 3rd. 1780

Sir

Underneath you have my Opinion of a proper Rout for Troops to march to the Southern States from Morristown Head Quarters Vizt. Curryels Ferry, Lancaster, Yorktown, Fredericktown, Nowlands Ferry Potowmack, Lewisburgh, twelve miles South, at these places there are small Magazines of Provisions which will be sufficient to supply the Troops

passing through, & I believe it is the nearest & best Rout for the Troops towards South Carolina & the most fertile parts of the Country to furnish Provisions and Forrage, I am not acquainted with the fixed places for Magazines in Virginia & North Carolina, but am of Opinion it will be impossible to feed a Number of Troops without they pass through the Country contiguous to those Magazines & States, am with much Esteem & Regard Dear Sir
    Your most Obedient
     & most Humble Servant
      E. Blaine CG of P.
Genl. Greene QMG

 Peter Force Collection, Mss. 17,137, Series 8D,   Ephraim Blaine Papers, Library of Congress.

Blaine, Circular to John Chaloner, & James White, Nicholas Patterson, William Evans, Arndt & Stroud, Peter Aston, Matthias Slough, Cornelius Cox, Henry Miller, James Smith, and William Maclay

(Circular)
           Philada, April 5th. 1780
Sir
Congress having call'd on the several States to furnish their Quoto of Supplies for our Army & to adopt their own ways & means to procure the same in consequence of which the Executive Council have appointed Commissioners in each County—you are immediately on Rect. of this to decline making any future Purchases, & prepare your Accots. with all possible dispatch for a final Settlement. forward all your Beef Cattle without delay to Morristown Head Quarters & such Quantities of Flour as you have on hand deliver over to the Issuing Commissary, all the residue of Stores & Offalls from grinding Wheat to the Forrage Master, & have your Accots.

regularly closed accompany'd with compleat Vouchers for delivery the Commissioner for your County [*sic*]

I shall furnish you with Mony as soon as in my power to obtain it from Congress, pray pay immediate attention in forwarding all your Beef Cattle & Flour, as the Army are in a Distress'd situation for want of Supplies, let me have a Return of the Amot. of Supplies remaining in your District with all possible Speed & be particular respecting Quantity, Quality, & price, that I may be enabled to lay an estimate before the Board & obtain Mony to pay each of you by first Opportunity & believe me to be with much regard

    Your most Obedient &
     most Humble Servant
      E. Blaine CG of Purs.

Chaloner & White	Nicholas Patterson
William Evans	Arndt & Stroud
Peter Aston	Matthias Slough
Cornelius Cox	Henry Miller
James Smith	Wm Maclay

  Peter Force Collection, Mss. 17,137, Series 8D, Ephraim Blaine Papers, Library of Congress. Patterson was a Commissary of Purchases in Bucks County, Pennsylvania. Smith was a Commissary of Purchases at Carlisle, Pennsylvania. Maclay was a Commisary at Sunbury, Pennsylvania

Blaine to Thomas Sim Lee

         Philadelphia April 5, 1780

Congress having call'd on the respective States to procure their Quoto of Supplies for the support of our Army and as I have ever experienced the most ready Disposition in your Predecessor, Self and Council to render every possible Assistance for the support of the Army, and indeed their present Existence is in a great measure owing to the Exertions of your State and Jersey. As I shall continue at the head of the

Commissaries Department and wish Active Men to be appointed to execute the Purchases in the sundry States I take the Liberty of pointing out an easy Method to procure the Supplies demanded from your State. The Head of Elk, Baltimore, George Town and Frederick Town are pointed out as proper Places for Magazines and will be continued, also Fort Frederick while prisoners are kept there.

The Commissioners of Elk & Baltimore ought to have a joint Appointment, then there will be no Contrast in their purchases, and they will have it in their power to command all the Supplies on the Eastern Shore & that part of the Western Shore contigeous to the Bay. George Town and that part of your State adjoining the Potomack another District, Frederick County to Supply Frederick Town Magazine and Washington County the Prisoners at Fort Fredk

Mr Ewing has done my Business at the Head of Elk, Mr Buchanan at Baltimore, Mr Richardson George Town, Mr Murdoch Frederick Town and Col. Rawlings at Fort Frederick, they are well acquainted with the Business and I have ever found those Gentlemen attentive to execute my Orders with Care and Fidelity, and if they are disposed to continue and Your Excellency & Council think proper to Appoint them I am confident you will find them, faithful & capable of furnishing the Supplies and fully answering your Expectations and the Public. Mr Calhoon, Mr Rodgers and Mr Spear of Baltimore have made Application to superintend the Purchases of that district, they are all attentive good Men, your Excellency & Council will Appoint which of them you think proper, provided Mr Buchanan declines serving. I shall be happy in giving you any Information respecting Supplies.

    & have the Honor to be with much real
        Regard & Respect, Your Excellencys
            most Obedient & most Humble Servant
                E. Blaine CG of Ps.
His Excellency Thos. Simm Lee Esqr.

Peter Force Collection, Mss. 17,137, Series 8D, Ephraim Blaine Papers, Library of Congress.

Blaine, Estimate of Money Due to the Commissary Staff

Estimate of Money due to the several Deputy & Assistant Commissaries of Purchases employed under the direction of Ephraim Blaine C. G. of Purchases.—

Names	District	Amount
Noah Emory	New Hampshire	40.000
Charles Miller	Massachusetts	137.500
Oliver Phelps	Ditto	44.124..9.4
Asa Waterman	Rhode Island	
Henry Champion	Connecticut	75.000
James Watson	ditto	74.025
Jacob Cuyler	New York	500.000
Udney Hay	ditto	150.000
Anthy. Broderick	New Jersey	16.7000
Azariah Dunham	ditto	450.000
Nehemiah Dunham	ditto	75.000
Robert Hoops	ditto	120.000
Morris Hugg	ditto	90.000
Robert L Hooper	Pennsylvania	129.000
Chaloner & White	ditto	50.000
George Morton	ditto	300.000
Evans & Haslet	ditto	25.000
Matts. Slough	ditto	30.000
Cornelius Cox	ditto	32.000
James Smith	ditto	375.000
William Stuart	ditto	2.500
William Maclay	ditto	37.500
Isaac Carty	Delaware	114.384..8..2
Whitehead Jones	ditto	14.604..7..2
Patrick Ewing	Maryland	
Richard Dellam	ditto	

George Murdoch	ditto	350.000
C. T. Wederstrandt	ditto	
Thomas Richardson	ditto	
Robert Forsyth	Southern Deparmt.	937.500

£ .270.838..14..8

N.B. Exclusive of the above considerable quantities of Provisions have been taken by Detachments of the Army the Amount of which cannot be Ascertained.
Philada: 6 April 1780

Eph. Blaine C.G.P

Papers of the Continental Congress, Roll 182, i165, p 412, National Archives.

Blaine to the Board of Treasury

Philada. 10 April 1780

Gentlemen

It is not in my Power to delay the people that has been waiting for Mony in Town longer than this day, the Delay Mr. Champion has met with will be of fatal Consequences, the supplies of Meat are nearly expended & not a single Bullock can come from the Eastward til this Gentlemans return & we are daily loseing Quantities of Wheat & Flour which has been contracted for & delivered into Mills this three Months past, I beg that your Honble Board wou'd inform me what I am to expect & enable me to give the necessary information to those Men who are so impatiently waiting, I am Gentlemen

Your most Obedient Humble Servt.
E. Blaine CG of P.

Honble Board of Treasury

Peter Force Collection, Mss. 17,137, Series 8D, Ephraim Blaine Papers, Library of Congress.

Blaine to George Washington

Philadelphia 10th. April 1780.

Please your Excellency,

It has not been in my Power to obtain a single Shilling of Mony from the Treasury board; my people are so much Indebted, that their Credit is quite exhausted with the Country, my first Object was to procure Mony, to enable Mr. Champion to keep up a supply of Beef-Cattle, his Son has been several Days here on that Business, this day I have obtained Orders on the Eastern States for a considerable Sum, which if Honored will enable him to purchase Beef sufficient to feed the Troops stationed in the Eastern States & Jersey up to the 1st of July—they have promised me an additional Sum, to secure some Contracts for Flour, which, with what I have in hand, will be equal to serve the Troops up to the 1st. of August next, at which time if the new System takes place, and the Commissioners act with Spirit supplies will be coming into the Public Magazines—I shall return to Morris, the moment I obtain the Sums promised me by the Treasury-board, and dispose of the same, and give necessary directions to keep forwarding the Supplies—your Excellency may be assured of my greatest exertions to keep up regular Supplies for the Support of your Army—

The Treasury being exhausted, my Agents greatly Involved, the delay of our Public finances, and the General change in the System of the Quartermaster & Commissary-General Departments, has made my Office, one of the most disagreeable, Man ever experienced—indeed nothing wou'd induce me to continue under present appearances, but the Duty I owe my Country, & Regard to your Excellency, which ever shall be motives to command my best Services, & surmount every other Difficulty—

I have the Honor to be with
due Respect Your Excellency's

most Obedient & most Humble Servant
Eph: Blaine C.G.P

N.B

I recd. your Excellencies letter late last night, after writing the above, and have to inform you that a Quantity of salt Provisions is on its way, and at Trenton, and between two and three Hundred head of Cattle will be at Camp the middle of next week, I have not Obtain'd a Return the Quantity of salt Provisions in the hands of my people but believe three thou. Barrels the princaple part of which is ordered for Head Quarters, I have flour Plenty on the way to Trenton, and hope the salt Provisions will be sufficient to secure the troops till we can be supplied with Grass beef, Remain &ca &ca.

Eph. Blaine C.G.P

His Excellency Genl Washington
Main body of letter not in Blaine's hand, N.B. on is.

George Washington Papers, Library of Congress.

Blaine to Moore Furman

Philada. 11th Apl. 1780

Dear Sir

I recd. a Letter from Head Quarters last night, giving the most alarming Acct. the want of salt Provisions and very little flour—for god sake my Dear Sir, use your best Endeavour to forward supplies else the army must disband for want of what little Provisions we have in the Magazines, am with real reguard Dear Sir,

Your Most Obdt. Servt.
Eph Blaine C.G.P

addressed: Public Service Colo. Moore Furman D.Q.M.G Trenton   favd by Genl Irvine

Record Group: Department of Defense; Subgroup: Revolutionary War, Mss. 4742, Division of Archives and Records Management, New Jersey State Archives.

Blaine to Moore Furman

Philada. 12th Apl. 1780

Dear Sir

The army is in great want of Provisions and without your assistance in procuring Teams will undoubtedly disband. Mr. Nehemiah Dunham has a Quantity of beef and Pork at Penny Town and Aimell, there is about One Hundred and fifty barrels at Corryells ferry if not lately remov'd, beg you to forward these Provisions to a[   ] as meat is much wanting—I have n[   ] Experienced such distresses as lately, [   ] want of money will undoubtedly be fatale to the army—the disapointments my people have given the farmers and the large sums they are indebt'd has Quite exhausted their Credit and I do not Know the Commissary that can have Credit to purchase a single bullock, [writer's blank] thousand daily after me for money has made my House and Office disagreable and the moment I have some little matters Settled shall take my departures for some Private place where my Crediters cannot find me, Am with much regard Dr. Sir Yours &c &c

Eph: Blaine CGP

Addressed: Public Service
Colo. Moore Furman D.Q.M.G Trenton

Record Group: Department of Defense; Subgroup: Revolutionary War, Mss. 4743, Division of Archives and Records Management, New Jersey State Archives. Missing words due to a tear in the manuscript.

Blaine to Thomas Sim Lee

Philada April 15, 1780

Sir

There is a Quantity of Rum belonging to the Public (& which is much wanting) in your City, it has been represented to the Commercial Committee that the person with whom it is in charge makes a very unreasonable demand for Storeage, & therefore beg your Excellency & Council, to order the Rum on board one of your State Vessells or any other that will deliver it to the Commissary at the Head of Elk, as I intend for Annapolis in a few weeks, will settle the Freight & pay the Gentlemn who has the Demand for Storage the valuation of any two Gentlemen.
    Your Excellencys most Obedient
     & most Humble Servant
      Eph Blaine C. G. P.
His Excellency Thomas Sim Lee Esqr.

> Bernard Christian Steiner, ed. *Archives of Maryland, Journal and Correspondence of The State Council of Maryland 1779—1780*, (Baltimore: Maryland Historical Society, 1924), 43:472.

To Robert Buchanan

         Philada. 20th. April 1780
Dear Sir
  The Maryland Troops will be at this place to day on their way to the Southward, I believe it is intended they shall go by water, there is no Salt Provisions at the Head of Elk therefore on Rect. of this request you & Mr. Donaldson to forward without a moments delay fifty Barrels of Beef to that place, I agree to your paying what Mony remains in your hands to Mr. Wederstrandt, shall be glad how soon you & Samuel render your Accts. for a final Settlement,
    am with Esteem & regard Dear Sir
      Your Most Obedient Humble Servant
       E. Blaine CG of Ps.
Robert Buchanan Esqr. Baltimore

Blaine to Johann De Kalb

Philada. 21 April 1780

Sir

Shou'd the Troops under your Command go from this by Water, Christiana Bridge & Head of Elk, the places you will be furnished with Provisions—when at Elk & you find it will be dangerous going by Water, the Troops can be supply'd with Provisions at Baltimore GeorgeTown or Alexandria, Fredericksburg & the Stages from that Southerly, you'll oblige me when you fix your Rout of March for Information, that I may write Major Forsyth to make the necessary Provisions for your Men, I have the Honor to be with much Respect
    Your most Obedt. Servant
        E. Blaine CG of P.
Genl. DeCalb.

Major General De Kalb, commanding the two Maryland brigades, was heading to South Carolina to attempt to relieve the enemy's siege of Charleston. Peter Force Collection, Mss. 17,137, Series 8D, Ephraim Blaine Papers, Library of Congress.

Blaine to Robert Forsyth

Philada. 30th. April 1780

Dear Sir

The Maryland & Delaware Troops are now on their March from this to the Southward & are to go by Water from the Head of Elk to Richmond, Major Lees Corps the upper Roads by Leesburg, my Dear Sir do for Godsake use your every Exertion to have them properly provided for, I have some Weeks ago made application to the Treasury board & Board of War for Mony or a Warrant for your use Mony is not at present in their Power to give but have assurances of an Order on your State for a considerable Sum this Week & shall send it by the Post, we are much in want of Salt Provisions if in

your power to spare us any send it without delay those Vessels which carry down the Troops will be an excellent Oppory & beg you to embrace it Remain Dear Sir
Your very Humble Servt.
E Blaine CG of P

Major Forsythe

> Blaine appointed Forsyth of Fredericksburg, Virginia, Deputy Commissary General of Purchases for the Southern Department on December 2, 1780, though he had been acting in the department for long before that. Peter Force Collection, Mss. 17,137, Series 8D, Ephraim Blaine Papers, Library of Congress.

Blaine, House Rental Agreement

This is to Certify that I have taken a three Story House of Jacob Hiltzheimer the Corner of Market & Seventh street for which I am to pay him at the rate of One hundred pounds Specie Pr Annum to be left at any time by giving one Months previous Notice the rent Commencing the 1st. May Inst 1780.

Eph Blaine

Witness George Nelson

N. B. Col. Blaine dld up the key of the House Septmr. 5th. 1781

Peter Force Collection, Mss. 17,137, Series 8D, Ephraim Blaine Papers, Library of Congress.

Blaine to Robert Forsyth

Philada. 6 May 1780

Dear Sir

I have obtained an order upon the Treasurer of your State for one Million five hundred thousand Dollars which I have endorced payable to you, this Sum I hope will be in the Power of the Treasurer to discharge, wch. will in some measure enable you to pay part of your Debts & Contracts, the

Continental Treasury have had no Mony since last January & the Treasury board have been often distressed to discharge trifling Orders, the Credit of all Public Officers in the middle & Eastern Departmt, is quite exhausted & scarcely will any person Credit them for one hundred of Flour, God grant us a Speedy relief else the Army must disband for want of subsistance, send me what assistance you can in Salt Provisions & beg to hear from you by every Opportunity—I remain with much Esteem & Regard Dr Sir
  Your most Obedient Servant
    E Blaine
Major Forsyth

> This was in the letterbook between letters of May 27, 1780. As Blaine was writing on May 24 to beg for money for Forsyth, the correct date may be May 26. Peter Force Collection, Mss. 17,137, Series 8D, Ephraim Blaine Papers, Library of Congress.

Blaine to Nehemiah Dunham

         Morris Town 8 May 1780
Sir
  I have been informed sundry persons from whom you purchased Wheat last January have lately threatned taking the same away owing to the disappointment they have met with in not being paid their Mony, an attempt of that kind wou'd be of dangerous consequences & not only subject you to censure but be a means of starving the Army, upon Rect. of this request you to have the Wheat removed to some Millers care, who will immediately have it Ground, Mr. Berry Q Master at the White-Horse will furnish you with the necessary Teams for that purpose, & shou'd any of the Wheat be removed inform me by Express that I may make application to his Excellency Genl. Washington for an Officer & Guard to Seize both the person & property & have them brought to Head Quarters forward all

your Salt provisions without a moments delay—let me hear from you be every Oppy. & believe me Sir
Your most Obedt. Humble Servt.
E. Blaine
Nehemiah Dunham

> Peter Force Collection, Mss. 17,137, Series 8D, Ephraim Blaine Papers, Library of Congress.

Morton to William Stewart

Philada. 9 May 1780

Sir
Agreeable to your Request I inclose you an order upon Mr. D Riddock for Beef & Flour, & five Barrils Whiskey for the use of the Post at Wyoming, Liquor is a very scarce Article at Camp & the above Quantity is as much as can be spared you at present, Mr. Risburg writes you by this Opportunity
I am Sir Your Most Obedient Servt.
Geo Morton
Mr. Wm. Stewart

> Stewart was a Commissary of Purchases at Wyoming, Pennsylvania. Peter Force Collection, Mss. 17,137, Series 8D, Ephraim Blaine Papers, Library of Congress.

Blaine to Robert Hoops

Morris Town 9 May 1780

Dear Sir
We are in the greatest want of Meat provisions, it not [sic] in your power to procure a Quantity of Shadfish a few Waggon load fresh wou'd answer a good purpose, & if in your power to procure a Quantity for Gods sake have it done & forward them without delay, I make no doubt you will give us every Assistance, in your power to feed the Army, I shall be

delay'd here several Days, & intend making your House on my Return to Philada, favour me with a Line by first Opportunity & believe me with much Regard Dear Sir
        Your most Obedt. Servant
            E. Blaine
Major Hoops

> Peter Force Collection, Mss. 17,137, Series 8D, Ephraim Blaine Papers, Library of Congress.

Blaine to Robert Lettis Hooper Jr.

                          Morris Town 9th May 1780

Dear Sir

    The Army has not one days Subsistance of Meat, for God sake my Dr: Sir use your utmost exertions to procure Teams to furnish all the provisions at your Post else we shall Starve, I gave orders some time ago to forward a Quantity of Salt Provisions (which lay at Reading) to your Town. this I have has [sic] been comply'd with, and I make not the least doubt of your best endeavours to forwd. the same, favour me with a Line & believe me with much regard. Dr Sir
        Your most Humble Servant E. Blaine
Col. Hooper

> Hooper was a Deputy Quartermaster General at Easton, Pennsylvania. Peter Force Collection, Mss. 17,137, Series 8D, Ephraim Blaine Papers, Library of Congress.

Charles Stewart and Blaine to George Washington

                          Morris Town 9th. May 1780

Sir

    Since the return presented Your Excellency by Chas. Stewart, on the fourth Instant, Seven hundred Barrs. of Flour and India Meal, has been received at this Magazine, and only Eleven Barrels of Beef and pork and thirty head of Cattle from Lancaster.

It is truely distressing to Us, to inform Your Excelly. that the supply of Meat will be totaly exhausted on friday next at farthest, The Flour now here will suffice, if made into Bread as has lately been the practice, for fifteen or sixteen days, and by advice from Trenton, We are certain that fifteen hundred Barrells of Flour, is at that Post and on the Road from thence to Camp; One hundred Barrells of which Chas Stewart has ordered to Kings Ferry for the Use of the Garrison at that point, and One other hundred [sic] Barrells, to be delivered The Commissary General of prisoners for the Use of The Prisoners, at New York & Long Island

Whether any Shad, will speedily be brought into Camp in pursuance of C. Stewarts application to Mr. Dunhams Assistants We do not yet know.

We beg leave to Suggest that We think the State of Pennsylvania could furnish a supply of Meat, in a Short space, Bucks, Chester & Lancaster Countys, more particularly and part of Berks, feed a great many Cattle and the Owners of the Meadows, near Philada. have pretty large Stocks; The mode of getting them speedily, and that without present money, We presume can be only by a Military command, from Your Excellency. New Jersey has freely, and greatly distressed herself, to supply the wants of the Army last Winter, New York has the Garrison at West point to support, Pennsylvania We think must therefore be the Object: And as that State has furnished very little supplys for six months past We beg leave to add that a present support ought now to drawn [sic] from that Contry, or Your Army be distressed, and perhaps disband.

We are with the greatest respect
                Your Excellencys most Obedient Servants,
                        Chas Stewart Commissary General of Issues
                        Eph. Blaine C.G. of Purchases

P.S. The Commissary of Purchases has ordered

from Philada. & Salem	220 Bbls pork
from Coryells ferry	50 Bbls pork & Shad
from Reading & Easton	200 Bls Beef
from Dover	100 Bls pork

He has also Wrote Col. Champion repeatedly to purchase and forward Fatt Cattle as fast as possible, as the Supply of the Army after the 15 May would depend on his exertions & Success.

> George Washington Papers, Library of Congress. Stewart of Hunterdon County, New Jersey, served as Commissary General of Issues from June 18, 1777 to July 24, 1782.

Charles Stewart and Blaine to Committee of Congress at Headquarters

Morristown, 9th May, 1780.

Gentlemen,

The distresses of the Army are such as require the attention of all concerned for their support: We have delivered our sentiments to his Excellency of this date, inclosed is a copy for your perusal Your present local situation with the Army prompts us to trouble you.

We are with proper respect,
Your most obedient servants.
Charles Stewart C. G. Ius
Ephraim Blaine, C. G. purchases
The honorable the committee.   copy.

> Papers of the Continental Congress, M247, r22, i11, p333, National Archives.

Blaine to Henry Champion

MorrisTown 10th May 1780

Dear Sir

I have not had a Letter from you this four Weeks which gives me great uneasiness, all the provisions in the Vicinity of Camp is consumed & we can have little relief but from you, for Gods sake my good Sir use every possible exertion to keep us supply'd else the Army must Starve, we can have no Supply in the middle State [sic] til grass Beef is fit for use, I hope you have obtain'd all the Mony upon those Orders sent you & that you have had it in your power to procure a large number of Cattle, such a Number of the Militia being call'd out in Actual service in the Southern States will deprive us from receiving any supply of Salt pork, resting assured of your best endeavours to procure us Supplies & that you will adopt every means of forwarding the same,

  I am Dear Sir
    Your most Obedient Humble Servant
  E. Blaine CG of Ps.

Col. Champion

> Champion had been a major purchaser of livestock in Connecticut since 1777. Peter Force Collection, Mss. 17,137, Series 8D, Ephraim Blaine Papers, Library of Congress.

Blaine to Isaac Carty

Morristown 12th May 1780

Sir

We are in the greatest want of salt provisions and without great Exertion the Army will undoubtedly suffer, upon rect of this request you to forward to Trenton every bll you possibly can, and if in your Power beg you to purchase all the pork you can, and give me Information and I shall contrive ways and means to Pay the same

  am in Hast Sir

Your Obedt. Hble Servt.
Major Carty

> *Delaware Archives: Revolutionary War* (Wilmington: Public Archives Commission of Delaware, 1919), 3:1355

Blaine to Robert Hoops

MorrisTown 12 May 1780

Dear Sir

Your two favours I received pr the Express, & make no doubt every Assistance in your power will be afforded us to feed the Army, & be assured your aid never was more wanting than at the present Moment, I am well acquainted with the Difficulties & Distresses you labour under for want of Mony, & rest assured of my best endeavours to relieve you from so disagreeable a Situation when in my power, that part of my Letter which you quote was meant to sundry persons who publickly declared holding back Supplies for want of Mony when I receive my dismission from this place, shall do myself the Honor of waiting on you upon my return to Philadelphia am with much regard Dear Sir

Your most Obedt. Servant
E. Blaine CG of Ps.

Major Hoops

> Peter Force Collection, Mss. 17,137, Series 8D, Ephraim Blaine Papers, Library of Congress.

Blaine to Conrod TheodoreWederstrandt

MorrisTown 12 May 1780.

Sir

Being call'd in by Congress to settle not only my former but present Accots., have to request you to use every possible Exertion to prepare & bring in yours for a final Settlement, I

have assurances from Congress of immediate payment of all Monies due in my Department & I authorize you to inform every person with whom you have had public Dealings that my best endeavours shall not be wanting to obtain the Sums due my Deputies upon settlemt. of their Accots, the more expeditious you are in this Business the better chance you will have of payment as Congress propose selling Bills of Exchange to a very considerable Amount, the Accots. of Mr. Harrison & Mr. Horsey wch. I have had the perusal of, cannot agree to your settling wh them in the manner they have charged, nor will I agree to any other allowance but five pr Ct., for Receiving in paying for cuting up & Salting pork, Receiving in delivering & paying for Wheat & Flour, except Store Rent which is a just & Reasonable charge, five pr Ct. is a much higher Commission than any Agents have upon the Continent & is a very generous allowance for all the Trouble & Expence those Gentlemen have had & to which I mean to confine you.—I dread the dissolution of the Army for want of Meat for Gods sake forward with all possible dispatch all your Salt provisions & if in your power to purchase try to procure two of three hundred Barrels of Pork, beg you not to fail in the Execution of this Business immediately on your Return, & favour me with a Line of information by first safe Opportunity, believe me with regard Sir
     Your most Obedient Humble Servant
      E. Blaine CG of Ps.
C. C. T. Wederstrandt

  Peter Force Collection, Mss. 17,137, Series 8D, Ephraim Blaine Papers, Library of Congress.

Blaine to John Davis

          Morris Town 14th May 1780
Dear Sir,

We are in the Greatest distress for want of Provisions. my brother has been Wrote to two [sic] forward all he has in the Magazine at Carlisle, do my dear Sir, use your usual industry to forward all the Provisions at that Post, Jersey is so Exhausted we Can have no relief either in bread or beef—hope to set out next Wednesday or Thursday for Philada. and shall only stay two Days there till I set out for Carlisle make my love to Mrs. Davis and all friends and
    believe me with much Reguard Dr. Sir
     Your Obdt. Hble Servt.
      Eph Blaine C.G.P.
Colo. Davis

  Davis was a Deputy Quartermaster General at Carlisle, Pennsylvania. Peter Force Collection, Mss. 17,137, Series 8D, Item 32, John Davis Papers, Roll 81, Volume 5, Library of Congress.

Blaine to George Washington

Morristown 18 May 1780

Please your Excellency
  One Hundred & forty barrels of the Salt provisions mentioned in my last Return has been delivered at the Magazine the residue I look for daily which is all I have any expectation of, <u>and when that is used</u>, the Supplies of Meat will depend on Col. Champion I gave him very pointed Instructions in February last and has wrote him Frequently since, to arrange Matters in such a manner as wou'd afford us an Ample supply of Meat from the 10th of this Month till the middle of July and furnished him with the principal part of what money I obtain'd from Congress for that purpose. I have had no late information from him of his success or what Number of Cattle he can forward this and the next month. (but hope they will be considerable) every means in my power shall be adopted to keep up the supplies of meat but doubt its Impossible, [sic] shou'd Col. Champion fail of my expectations, I shall try to

procure some Beef Cattle below Philadelphia, which shall be forwarded with all possible dispatch, Remain with due Respect Your Excellencies
Most Obdt. and Most Hble Servant
Eph: Blaine C.G.P.
N B. Col. Stewart & Mr. Dunham will give you the necessary information respecting supplyies in my absence.
Genl. Washington

George Washington Papers, Library of Congress.

Blaine to Isaac Carty

Philada. 20th May 1780
Sir

The army is in the most dreadful Situation for want of Meat, and without an Immediate supply must disband, have therefore in most Pressing terms to request you to forward every barrel of salt Provisions which you have purchased or Contracted for, and Assure the persons to whom you are indebted that I shall enable you to pay them the first Money I receive and will make proper allowances to those who have suffered; but insist on your Immediate procuring and forward all brought or contracted for. If you cou'd make any purchases of Salt beef or pork try to secure all you Possibly can and inform me by first Opportunity the Quantity and Price, I will see paid any Shallop Men or Waggoneers you may Employ to forward the supplies to our army, write me by first Opportunity and believe me Sir
Your most Hub Servt.
N. B. pray enquire in any Cattle can be purchased in your State
Major Carty

Delaware Archives: Revolutionary War (Wilmington: Public Archives Commission of Delaware, 1919), 3:1355.

Blaine to Joseph Reed

Sir,   Philada, 20th May, 1780
    I left Head Quarters late on the evening of eighteenth, and find it will be impossible to feed the Army, without the Aid of the Legislative authority impowering their Commissioners to purchase or to take Cattle where they can find them fit for use.
    The want of Money last fall deprived the Agents from securing any large quantities of Salt Provisions, and the severity of the winter has deprived many of the Connecticut Farmers from feeding Cattle, on whom our principal dependance was for Beef; those circumstances, and our Salt Provisions being exhausted, has reduced the Army to half allowance of Meat; indeed on this day there is not a single pound in Camp.
    This State is capable of furnishing a considerable number of Stock Cattle, which will make good Beef if proper means are adopted to colect them. I would beg leave to point out to your Excellency the proper places:—the County of Chester and the Meadows on Delaware, Lancaster, Bucks & York Counties; indeed, a few may be provided in each County. The States of Jersey and New York has been so drained we can expect very little Assistance from them; therefore, without your speedy Aid in giving a Supply of Meat, the Army must undoubtedly disband for want of that necessary Article. Would beg your Excellency to give immediate Orders to the County Contractors to enter upon the Execution of their respective Purchases with all possible dispatch, as a very few Days will reduce me to want every necessary for the Army, and oblige me to call on the Contractors for the Supplies required from this State.
                I am, very respectfully
                    Your Excellencies most obedient

                & most Hble. Servant,
                     Eph Blaine C.G.P.
Directed, Public Service.
His Excellency Joseph Reed, Esquire. Present.

    Reed was then serving as President of the Supreme Executive Council of Pennsylvania, analogous to being governor. The letterbook copy reads "impossible to feed the army with meet," and show Berks, not Bucks County. Samuel Hazard, ed., *Pennsylvania Archives*, 1st. series, vol. 8 (Philadelphia: Joseph Severns & Co., 1853), 260.

Morton to Isaac Carty

                            Philada. 20th: May 1780
Sir
    Your favour of the 12th. Instant by Mr Bell came to hand: since which Col. Blaine has returned from Head Quarters, where he left the Troops in the greatest distress immaginable for want of salt Provisions and at this time there is not an Ounce of Meat fresh or salt at Camp or in this City—Col. Blaine begs that you would exert yourself at this critical period in forwarding on Salt Provisions, if you can furnish the Army with three Days supply of that necessary Article, it will be a very essential piece of service, you may be assured of a proportion of the first money that come in to this Office, which hope will be in a very few Days—
    You will procure the necessary Waggons & Shallops for transporting your Wheat to Mr. Tatnalls Mill at Brandywine in Order to have it manufactur'd—as there is some Arm'd Vessels gone down the Bay, there will be no danger of it falling into the hands of the Enemy—
                I am Sir Your Most Obt Servt
                      Geo. Morton
Inclosed you have a Letter from Col. Blaine, he goes to Camp again on Monday.—

Major Isaac Carty   Assist Commissary of Purchases

Delaware Archives: *Revolutionary War* (Wilmington: Public Archives Commission of Delaware, 1919), 3:1357-58

Blaine to George Washington

Philada. 21st May 1780

Sir,

The Executive and Legislative authority of this state are dissatisfied with my Representation to your Excellency, and insist that the State cannot produce any beef of consequence. I have assured them it can and pointed out the places where—upon which they have permited me to purchase from those Persons in the best manner I can, and given me Orders upon the County Treasurers for money to pay the same—I shall be able to send off a drove of about fifty Cattle next tuesday Morning from the Meadows, and hope in a few days to make up One or two more—I have fallen upon a plan last night which will produce three Hundred and odd barrels of salt Provisions, this I shall be able to forward by Wednesday next—One Hundred Barrels of Pork was forwarded yesterday for Trenton, and I expect One Hundred more from Maspillion Landing in a day or two—

The assembly have Repealed the Law for which all State Officers were to Receive their saliries in wheat, and have made another to receive their pay in the new Money, and to take it in pay for taxes, the Merchants have had a meeting and have agreed to take it as gold and Silver, this Act of the assembly and the Agreement of the Merchants will certainly give it a Currency, and enable the State Contractors to procure Considerable Quantities of Provisions—your Excellency may be assured of my utmost Exertions to feed the Army and Studying every means to procure supplies—

           I have the honor to be very Respectfully
                 Your Excellencies

                    Most Obdt. and Most Hble Servt.
                        Eph: Blaine C.G.P
Genl. Washington

    George Washington Papers, Library of Congress.

Blaine to the Treasury Board

                                Philada. 24th May 1780
Gentn.
 The Letters which are now before you from Major Forsyth points out his distresses for want of Money, the daily demand which will be made upon him for the Supply of our own and the Convention Troops will be very great and require a large sum of Money, he is now indebted to the State of Virginia about eight hundred thousand Pounds that Currency, you will please to report a Warrant in my favour upon that State for as large a Sum as you think can be paid—Messrs. Ewing and Wederstrandt of the Eastern Shore of Maryland are indebted at least One Million and a half Dollars for Provisions purchased under my Direction as D. Comy and Suits are commenced against them for the nonperformance of Contracts with Sundry persons, and what is still an additional misfortune several of them hold back the Articles purchased 'till they are paid the Balance due, perhaps eight hundred thousand Dollars will be necessary for the above purpose, this Sum would beg you to grant a Warrant for in Order to enable me to get the Provisions out of their hands—The Merchants in this City upon my request have lent me such quantities of their Store Provisions as they could conveniently Spare from their immediate use, which I have punctually promised to pay as soon as the Public Magazines will admit—I have also purchased upon two weeks Credit Live Stock and Salt Provisions equal to two hundred & fifty thousand pounds, this Sum would wish to pay agreeable to my Contract and beg you

to enable me to discharge the Same, there are many other Persons who are embarrassed exceedingly but shall not trouble you with their representations, you will greatly Oblige me by reporting those matters to day as I am obliged to leave town tomorrow

    Have the Honor to be very Respectfully
    Gentn. Your Most Hble Servant
      Eph Blaine
Honorable Treasury Board

> Peter Force Collection, Mss. 17,137, Series 8D, Ephraim Blaine Papers, Library of Congress.

Morton to Peter Aston

          Philada. 25 May 1780

Sir On receipt of this you will collect all the Cattle you have on hand and send them by the nearest route to Messrs. Little & Jones's place at Dragon Neck New Castle County, making a Return to Col. Blaines Office of the number of each kind, their Age and quality. as these Cattle, you say are the only obstacle in your way for a final Settlement, you will after delivery repair to Philadelphia with your Accts. fully prepared for that Purpose—Am Sir
    Your very Hble Servt
      Geo: Morton
Mr. Aston—

> Peter Force Collection, Mss. 17,137, Series 8D, Ephraim Blaine Papers, Library of Congress.

Blaine to the Board of War

         Philada 25 May 1780

Gentn.

You'll please to remember that in my Letters and Returns to your Honorable Board in Febry: and March last. that the Flour purchased & contracted for by my Deputies and State Agents of Maryland would not be more with Economy, than would feed the Army up to July or beginning of August next—The want of Money has been the occasion of my Deputies losing considerable quantities of the Flour purchased which will deprive me of feeding the Army longer than the first of July. we have had little or no Assistance from the States since the requisition of Congress and in that Resolve Congress have made their Estimate far short of the quantity requisite for the yearly support of the Army and its dependencies—and have proposed giving Credit to each State respectively for the quantity of each Article furnish'd since the first day of last December—this will nearly excuse the States of New York & Jersey, Delaware and Maryland will be considerably in advance to the Public. This Flour nearly all consumed and none coming into the Public Magazines—should an additional demand be made for the supply of our Allies how is it to be complied with? The Agents of this State have not yet began their purchase—my Deputies being largely indebted to the County cannot purchase on Credit tho' considerable quantities have been in their power, which is daily consuming and ingroced—the Delaware State I am informed have taken off the embargo, and sundry Persons are now loading Vessels with that necessary Article—The Situation of that State is such as can command or aggregate all the Surplus of Flour in a very few Days from the best Wheat Country in America, the Eastern Shore of Maryland and Pennsylvania—and the delay of the State Agents in entering upon this Business will give the person purchasing Flour an Opportunity of ingrocing the whole—I would also beg leave to request you to ask Congress what is done with the Indian Corn they requested the States of Virginia and Maryland to purchase last fall upon my representation to them of the Scarcity of Bread—this Corn would wish you to order deliver'd to me as a reserve against future needs, and shall have it carefully stored in the Neighbourhood of Trenton where it will be convenient to our Army—

I am sorry your Application in my favour of yesterday to the Board of Treasury has not been complied with, the monies wanted for Major Forsyth is for the Pork purchased thro' the last Winter under the direction of Col. Wadsworth Comy General and which he cannot furnish without money to pay the same a Supply of One thousand Barrels of Pork is a matter of such consequence as not to be delay'd a moment—I made a further Application to the Treasury Board for one Million five hundred thousand Dollars, for Purchases made under my direction as Deputy Commissary, to enable me to pay the Sums due Mr. Wederstrandt & Ewing of the Eastern Shore of Maryland, eight hundred thousd. of which is essentially necessary to enable them to obtain a quantity of Flour and Pork which is detain'd by the persons who took in the same 'till they are paid the Balances due—I have a Warrant in my favour upon the State of Maryland which is yet unpaid, but cannot think of paying it toward the purchases made under the direction of Colonel Wadsworth without the Treasury Board give me Credit for the same—

My doubts of the Army suffering for want of the necessary Supplies of Provisions is well grounded and I am apprehensive (& indeed certain) measures will be delay'd 'till it is too late—be assured my representations proceed from no other motive than a desire to feed the Army and keep them from disbanding—

I have the Honor to be Gentn very respectfully—
    Your most obt Hble Servt
        E. Blain

Board War

Peter Force Collection, Mss. 17,137, Series 8D, Ephraim Blaine Papers, Library of Congress.

Blaine to the Honorable Committee of Congress

Philada. 25th. May 1780

Gentlemen

I have been exceedingly busy since Col Matthews left Town trying to procure & forward Stores in the best manner I could without Money—I have borrow'd from the Merchts. two hundred barrels of Beef & Pork & purchased from others one hundred Barrels—One hundred barrels of Pork forwarded the 23rd. and this day One hundred & ninety Barrels of Pork with Sixty Head of Cattle which I have taken from the Grazers below this City—I shall set out tomorrow for Lancaster & Tulpahocking and hope to make up a Drove of One hundred head perhaps more, the moment I see those Cattle secured shall lose no time 'till return to Head Quarters which will be about the sixth of June—be assured of my utmost Exertions in procuring and forwarding Supplies and being at Head Quarters with all possible dispatch—I hope to have some little more Assistance from Delaware & Maryland say five hundred Barrels, of this shall give you the earliest notice—

I have the Honor to be
very Respectfully Gentn.
Your Most Obt. & Hle Servt.
Eph: Blaine, C. G. P.

The letterbook copy shows it was addressed to the committee at Morristown. The original shows the committe received it on May 30. Papers of the Continental Congress, Roll 182, i, 165, p. 319, National Archives.

Blaine to Charles Stewart

Philada. 26th May 1780

Dear Sir

I am Just seting out for Lancaster and hope in two or three days to send you a drove of Cattle from that place, before this reaches you my drove of sesseiyers [*sic*] By Michl. Kitts must have arriv'd. since I came here have forward'd five Hundred and odd barrels of salt Provisio[ns] two Hundred of which I borrowed from the Merchants, One Hundred purchased, and two Hundred and sixty came from below. I shall have One thousand barrels of Pork from Major Forsyth without the Governor and Council of Virginia detain it. and perhaps four Hund. Barrels more in adition to my Return made his Excellency Genl. Washington, and two or three Hundred barrels of fish, I have Receivd a letter from my old friend Colo. Champion, which Breaths nothing but Misfortunes, want of money, and Scarcity of cattle—the disapointments people have met with in not being paid their money, has depriv'd them of filling their Stalls with poor Cattle to Fatt. however the whole of his Representation is to explain the Reasons why he will fall short of the number of Cattle I required him to furnish—be assured of my best endeavours and utmost Exertions to Keep up supplies, and if I had money cou'd Accomplish it—this State though Council and assembly are siting, and well acquainted with the wants of our army, will give me little Assistance, (and I have great doubts of the performance of their Contractors) I shall stay four days in the Neigh bourhood of Lancaster, using force, when fair Words will not answer in geting what fatt Cattle is in that Neighbourhood from my Kinsmen, Mrs. Blaine is to meet me there, and from whence I shall Return to Camp—had I money or power, the Meadows below Town wou'd in twelve or fifteen days produce a few Hundred good Cattle, and I shall try dam'd hard to get them, but Present prospects are gloomy—my dear Sir I hope you will persevere in your former plann of contriving ways and Means to add to our Reduced Magazines—and depend on my doing the same, the following intiligence I will give you as a Secret and in Confidence—our Accts. from Charles Town indicate Hard times, the Enemy had got through the advance Works and had got Possession of the drounded ditch our Battaries within eighty yards of each Other, and the smallest cannon upon those Works are twenty four Pounders, a Continual Skirmishing, and Constant rattle nothing but Sulfer fire and smoak since the fifteen till the 20th. except, on the 21st. we had a sessation of Army for six hours, when it is said Genl. Lincoln proposed giving up the Town upon having a priviledge of Marching of his Army and a protection to the purses and Properties of the people in town, this Clinton Refused and Refer'd him to his proclamation, upon which our Genl. sent him a Verbal Messenger & told him he was well Acquainted with his intentions, & was determined to defend the Town till the Last extremity—god protect him poor Gentleman my doubts are great, this Keep to your selfe,—your friends in Town are well, write me by every Oppertunity and

believe me with much Esteem and Reguard,
Dear Sir Your Most Obdt Hble Servt.
Eph Blaine CGP.

Colo. Stewart
Public Service   Colonel Charles Stewart
                 Commissary General of Issues
Pr Express—   Head Quarters

Charles Stewart Papers, 1752-1818, Collection 262, New York State Historical Association.

Blaine to George Washington

Philada. 27th. May 1780—

Please Your Excellency
Sir

I have used every Endeavour since I left Camp to procure and forward Provisions, and have met with some success—the Merchants of this City have lent me two hundred Barrels of Beef and Pork, I have purchased one hundred barrels, and taken Sixty Head of Cattle from the Graziers below this City, hope to make up two hundd. more in this and

Lancaster County—two hundred Barrels of Pork came from below yesterday, & with what Major Forsyth can spare from Virginia, expect to make up One thousand Barrels, exclusive of my Return to your Excellency at Camp—be assured of my utmost Exertions in adoptg: Ways and Means to obtain Supplies, tho' I am loaded with debt and have not had a Shilling this two months—inclosed you have an Extract of a Letter receiv'd from Major Forsyth yesterday—
   I am with all due Respect Your Excellency's
    Most Obedt & Most Hble Servant
     Eph. Blaine C.Gn.
His Excellency General Washington

  George Washington Papers, Library of Congress.

Blaine, Circular to Conrad Theodore Wederstrandt, Patrick Ewing, Robert Buchanan, and Thomas Richardson

(Circular)

            Philada. 27 May 1780
Dear Sir
  The Scarcity of Mony in the Fall & Winter have been the means of my Deputies all disappointing me in the Quantity of Salt Provisions I had reason to expect from them, this with the Severity of the Winter depriving many Farmers from feeding Cattle, has reduced us to the greatest Difficulty's for want of Meat, I obtained a Warrant from Congress upon Mr. Harwood your State Treasurer——Dollars of wch. have enduced [*sic*] payable to your Order, beg you to pay as little of this Mony to discharge your old Debts as possible & adopt every means in your power to procure all the Salt provisions & Shad fish your District can afford, I am confident notwithstanding the many Difficulties & embarrasssments you have met with as a Public Officer, that your Attachmt. for the General cause of America

will surmount all other considerations & that you will use your utmost Exertions in this time of Distress to render me every Assistance in your Power, you will bring in your Accots. as soon as possible for a final Settlemt. favour me with a Line by every Oppy. & believe me with Esteem & Regard Dr Sir
     Your most Obedt. Humble Servt. E Blaine
Mr. Wederstrandt
Ewing
Buchanan
Richardson
for the Sums Endorces see the Acct. Book

> Richardson was an Assistant Commissary based at Georgetown, Maryland. Peter Force Collection, Mss. 17,137, Series 8D, Ephraim Blaine Papers, Library of Congress.

Blaine to Thomas Sim Lee

             Philada: 27 May 1780
Sir
 A few days will consume all the Salt Provisions in our Magazines, little in this part of the Country & no Mony to buy it with, the severity of last Winter & backwardness of this Spring will deprive of any fresh Beef til the latter end of July or begining of August, shou'd we have Assistance from our Allies as is certainly expected, every possible Exertion to supply them & feed our own Troops will be necessary have therefore to beg the Aid of your Excellency & Council to adopt ways & means to secure all the Salt provisions in your State I obtained an Order from Congress early in April for One Million Eight hundred twenty two thousand five hundred & thirty three Dollars & 30/90, payable as endorced to my Deputies, this Mony is to enable them to pay part of their old Debts & secure all the Salt provisions they possibly can, shou'd their purchasing be contrary to the Laws of your State, wou'd wish your Excellency to give permission, or order your

Contractors to secure all the Salt provisions within their respective Districts the Requisitions of Flour call'd for by Congress for the Support of the Army from the States will not be adequate to the Consumption, therefore they shou'd make an additional Demand, we hourly expect to hear of the French Fleet being on our Coasts; every good Man here wishes their first Object may be Charlestown if they are not there very soon doubt the Consequences, shou'd they come to New York I have not the least doubt but two Weeks after their Arrival within the Hook, Genl. Washington will be compleatly in possession of the City of New York & its dependancies, & that I shall be able to agragate such a Quantity of salt provisions as well give our Army three Months Supplies & procure a Sufficient Magazine of Salt to serve the Continent two Years, we had two different Accots. of the Arrival of the Fleet off sandy Hook but is yet premature—

  I beg leave to inform your Excellency & Council that you have the warm acknowledgmts. of the Commander in Chief for your Exertions in procuring Supplies, & it is greatly owing to you that I was able the feed the Army with Bread thro the Winter, & be assured I am happy in all Companies of having an Opportunity of declaring how much the United States are indebted to you for the Supplies rendered I have the Honor to be very respectfully, Your Excellencys
    Most Obedient & very Humble Servant
    E. Blaine

Governor Lee

  Peter Force Collection, Mss. 17,137, Series 8D, Ephraim Blaine Papers, Library of Congress.

Blaine to Azariah Dunham

        Philada. 27th. May 27 1780

Dear Sir

No immediate prospects of Money nor will there be any 'till the New Money comes out and Congress dispose of their Bills of Exchange which is now much talked of—I have been using every possible endeavour to procure and forward Supplies, but have not met with the Success I had reason to expect—I borrow'd from the Merchants of this City two hundred Barrels & I bought from sundry persons one hundred—two hundred came from below, which have been forwarded with a Drove of Cattle taken from the meadows—I am just now setting out for Lancaster where I expect to raise a considerable Drove and immediately upon my return from thence shall proceed to Camp—

My good Sir use every means in your power to add to our reduced Magazines—present my best Compliments to Mrs. Dunham and your good family & believe me with much Esteem & regard Dear Sir

Your most Obt. Hble Servt.
Eph Blaine CG of P—

Azariah Dunham Esqr.

Peter Force Collection, Mss. 17,137, Series 8D, Ephraim Blaine Papers, Library of Congress.

Blaine to Christian Wirtz

Lancaster County, June 5th, 1780.

Sir,

The Garrisons at Sunburry and Wyoming being nearly exhausted of what Flour they had, and as the supply of those places are an Object of Immediate Concern, have therefore in the most pressing Terms to request your utmost exertion in procuring three hundred Barrels Flour, and deliver the same into the Magazine at Etherton, in order that it may be forwarded to the above mentioned posts, while the River admits of Navigation—beg your attention to this Business in

preference to any other, as the Wants of the Troops at those places will admit of no delay, and their supplies depends on your County and Cumberland.
Am with Esteem, Sir, yr most obdt H. Servt,
Ephraim Blaine, C. G. Ps.
Christ. Wirtz, Contractr for Lanc. County.

> Wirtz was a purchasing contractor at Lancaster, Pennsylvania. Samuel Hazard, ed., *Pennsylvania Archives*, 1st. ser. (Philadelphia: Joseph Severns, 1858), 8:304.

Blaine to Circular

Circular

Philada: 8 June 1780

Sir

You will deliver the Beef Cattle & Sheep you have collected for the use of the Army to Capt. William McCauley who has my Orders to Receive the same & Give you a Rect. for the Number Age & estimated Weight of such Cattle & Sheep as you may deliver, I have given him Instructions how to have them provided for & forwarded to Head Quarters Morris Town, am with much Regard Sir
Your most Obedt. Humble Servt.
E B, CG of Ps.

> The recipients were not identified. Peter Force Collection, Mss. 17,137, Series 8D, Ephraim Blaine Papers, Library of Congress.

Blaine to William McCauley

Philadelphia 8 June 1780

Sir

Your favr. by Mr. Hunt came safe to hand & am happy to find you have a prospect of rendering me a supply of Beef I have wrote the other Commissioners of your County to deliver

over all the Cattle & Sheep they Purchase to you, & requested them to be particular in geting a Rect. from you, & give you the same Caution about the Rects. you give, as those Cattle will all be Recd. from you by estimation, have them collected to the best pastures you can procure near Curryells Ferry & keep them till my further Orders, it will be necessary to have a carefull person to Attend them til they are drove for Head Quarters, you will have them all Branded with a Continental Brand Iron in case any shou'd Stray that you may find them—Mony I have none to send you, when in my power shall furnish you with a Sum to defray the Expence of driving them to Camp & pay Pasturage I remain Sir
    Your Obedt Humble Servant
      E. Blain CG of Ps.
Cap McCauly

  McCauly/McCauley has not been identified. Peter Force Collection, Mss. 17,137, Series 8D, Ephraim BlainePapers, Library of Congress.

Blaine to the Board of War

            Philada. 13 June 1780—
Gentn.
  The time is nearly elapsed when the Flour procured by my Deputies and Assistants will be consumed and I see very little appearance of any coming into the Magazines except from Maryland State—the Spirit of Monopoly which prevails, and numbers of People whose daily Proffession it is to traffick in this Article gives me reason to doubt that all the Surplus of Flour in Jersey, Pennsylvania Delaware & Maryland States will be very Shortly consumed or, what is equal, out of our reach, Those Reasons with the Stagnation of my Agents Purchasing, induces me to represent to your Honorable Board my doubts respectg the Supplies of our Army—I have two Weeks Supply at the Magazine at Morris Town and perhaps two more between the Magazines at Trenton Christeen Bridge

and the Head of Elk, little or none coming in—when this is consumed our whole dependence must be on the State Agents, and they ought to secure a supply of last Years Crop sufficient to serve us up the Christmas, as before that Period we should put but little dependence on the new—The State Agents should adopt immediate Measures to Secure all the Surplus, which if neglected be assured your Army must Starve for want of Bread this I thought it my duty to represent to you—I have also to mention that my Special promise lays with a number of Grazers for Cattle taken when our Army was in distress for want of Beef—likewise for a quantity of Salt Provisions collected in this City besides a number of other demands which your Honorable Board are well acquainted with—in my last Letter to you I requested a Warrant on Mr. Hillegas for two hundred & fifty thousand Pounds in order to enable me to pay those debts and Contracts—I find there has been no report made nor Money granted—I have now to request your Honorable Board to apply for a Warrant equal to the above Sum or for what Money may be procured from the Sale of the Sugars; this beg you to lay before Congress as I am distressed by the repeated Applications of the People who are very pressing for their Money—

 I have the Honor to be with every Sentiment of respect—
  Gentn. Your most Obedt
   and very Hble Servt—
    Ep Blaine C.G.P.

Honorable Board War

 Peter Force Collection, Mss. 17,137, Series 8D, Ephraim Blaine Papers, Library of Congress.

Blaine to the Board of War

          Philada. 13 June 1780

Gentlemen

Major General Gates— upon representation of Col. Broadhead commandant of the Garrison at Pittsburgh of the want of Provisions gave Orders to Mr. McCalister my Agent to procure a Supply to relieve the wants of that Post, & being destitute of Mony & means to enable his to obtain the same, has influence with Mr. Noble who waited on you & borrow'd of him thirty thousand Dollars, as this Gentleman had no connection with Public Business & lent Mr McCalaster that Sum merely to serve the public wou'd wish your Honorable Board to adopt some mode to enable me to pay him

Underneath you have my Answer to your Queries of this Morning from the best Information I have been able to Collect Vizt.

1st. the Garrison at West point have only a temporary Daily supply of Provisions

2d & 3d. there is one Months supply of Flour in the Magazine at Morristown, Trenton Christiana Bridge & Elk, three days supply of Meat in Jersey & with the Exertion of this State & what little Assistance my Deputies can give may carry us to the first of July

4th. the State [sic] Pennsylvania Delaware & Maryland must be principally depended on for Flour, all the middle States can furnish assistance in Beef, after the first of July a very considerable Supply from the State of Connecticut

5th. The Flour for supplying Westpoint must be sent from our Magazine in Jersey & the Salt provisions must be procured in the State of Connecticut, have been informed a prize Brig was brought into the Harbour at New London the other day with twelve or fifteen hundred Barrels of salt Provisions was this public Property it might be brought by Water within forty or fifty miles of Westpoint,

I remain Gent.
Your most Obt. Humble Servant
E. Blaine CG of Ps.

Honble Board of Warr

Peter Force Collection, Mss. 17,137, Series 8D, Ephraim Blaine Papers, Library of Congress.

Blaine to Robert Forsyth

Philada. 13 June 1780—

Sir

I have delay'd your Express ever since he came up expecting to have obtain'd Orders upon the State of Virginia in your favour, which I had a prospect of 'till this morning, but have failed, there is only one remedy left which I am adopting at Present, and hope yet to succeed which will put it in your power to pay off the Sums of Money which you have borrow'd from the State and enable you to prosecute your purchases a little farther. this Sum will be granted to discharge your purchases under Col. Wadsworth—Why in the name of God have you delay'd forwarding the Salt Provisions? the Governor and Council have no power over those Provisions nor ought you to have hesitated a moment after receivg. my Letter and that from the Board of War, except such as might be necessary for the Troops station'd in and passing thro your District—you have Grass Beef from North Carolina six Weeks sooner than us, therefore request you to send us every Gammon, pound of Bacon and Barrel of Pork you can possibly spare as our Army is in the greatest distress for want of Provisions and now taking the Field.—The Enemy have been out for several Days and appear prepared to open the Campaign, I believe we shall have a very Active Summer if our Southern Army are made Prisoners of War as reported this two days—Why in the name of God did they remain in a place where they were liable to be surrounded without an amply Supply of Provisions, Ammunition, Men &c—the most damn'd Misfortune that has happen'd since the commencement of the War—the Treasury Board have Resolved that no Money shall be granted any Officer without regular Estimates of his Disbursments and Purchases this you will comply with—the New System for the

Government of the Quarter Master & Commy Genl. is not yet agreed upon therefore cannot inform you but hope to have it in my power by next post—Write me by every Opportunity and give us every possible Assistance, believe me with much Esteem & regard—
    Dear Sir Your most Obt Hble Servt—
      Eph Blaine CGP
Major Forsyth—

> Peter Force Collection, Mss. 17,137, Series 8D, Ephraim Blaine Papers, Library of Congress.

Morton to Robert Hoops

          Philada. 17 June 1780
Sir
  Your favour of the 15th. Inst. pr Mr. Hanshaw came to hand this Morning w. your Accots. but not in proper form as the purchases & Expences are blended together & the whole made out in one Return instead of being Monthly—you must also distinguish your Purchases since the 15 Jany from those made under Col. Blaine a DCG, any Accots that are yet outstanding you will bring into your Monthly Returns agreeable to your Contracts, tho' you may not be able to procure Vouchers to support the charges at present
  Mr Howells case is very hard all that can be done for him is to accept his Order payable when in Cash if he can procure Credit in Town on them Terms
  Col. Blaine sett out for Camp on tuesday & will perhaps see you before his Return, I remain
      Your most Obedt. Servant
        Geo Morton
Major Hoops

> Peter Force Collection, Mss. 17,137, Series 8D, Ephraim Blaine Papers, Library of Congress.

Morton to James McCallaster

Philada. 17 June 1780—

Sir

Your favour by Mr. Noble came duly to hand, and also your Monthly Returns and after repeated Applications and Representations in his favour (which have not yet come to an Issue) I was obliged to borrow thirty thousand Dollars from Messrs. Chaloner & White which I paid him yesterday on your Acct—Col. Blaine left this a Tuesday [sic] for Head Quarters, where he expects to be detain'd a week or ten Days—on his Return, suppose he will write you fully on the Subject of your Letter—remain—

Sir Your very Hble Servt. Geo: Morton

Mr. Mc.Calester

> Peter Force Collection, Mss. 17,137, Series 8D, Ephraim Blaine Papers, Library of Congress.

Blaine to the Committee of Congress

Morris Town 26th, June 1780

Gentlemen

The Campaign being Oppened and Several matters relative to my Office at Philadelphia necessary to be settled, before I proceed to North river—the treasury calling upon all public Officers for an Immediate settlement of their Accts. which is impossible to be attended to by the princaple Staff Officers of they [sic] Army till the close of the Campaign, Money wanting to procure stores for his Excellency's family during the Summer: Necessaries for your use, and sundry Other Articles to buy which cannot be done without,—this business will Require my attention a few days in Philadelphia, and be assured of my returning as speedily as possible, I have the honor to remain, very Respectfully, Gentlemen

Your Most Obdt.

Humble Servant
Eph. Blaine C.G.P

Honble. Committee of Congress

> Papers of the Continental Congress, Roll 182, i 165, p 321, National Archives.

Morton to William Evans

Philada. 28th June 1780

Sir

You will forward what Cattle you have purchased immediately to this City, where they will be provided with good pasture and be ready to go to Camp on the shortest notice Should they be wanting there—

I am Sir Yours &
Geo. Morton

Col Evans—

> Peter Force Collection, Mss. 17,137, Series 8D, Ephraim Blaine Papers, Library of Congress.

Blaine to the Board of War

Philada. 29 June 1780.

Gentlemen

The method of supplying the Army of the United States being in some measure altered, & each of my Deputies destitute of Mony, & deprived of every Means of Purchasing, I have reason to doubt some of the Established Posts & Garrisons will suffer for want of Provisions, there is Fort Pitt & Wyoming claimed by different States and not property attended to by any, the resources of the Country adjoining is by no means adequate to the Consumption of Provisions—are their Supplies to depend on the Activity of the Contractors & purchasers of the Counties Aajacent?—

The Article of Flour gives me great concern and I fear much our distresses for want of it the Crops now in the ground are exceeding light and will afford the Farmer a small pittance for his Labour and we ought to put no dependance upon New Flour before next January—what is now in the Country will be daily carrd. off and consumed by various means, and without immediate Exertions of the respective States or their Officers to secure every particle each State can Spare, you will find my fears well grounded and at a time when it will not be in your power to remedy the Evil—

I have not heard what has been done with the Indian Corn which Congress gave directions to the States of Maryland and Virginia to purchase last Winter for the use of grinding for Bread; no part of this Corn came to my Care—I beg your Honorable Board would direct all this Corn to be deliver'd to me or my Assistant at Trenton—I shall take proper care to have it Stored in Mills in that Neighbourhood and have it as a reserve against want when our Troops are preparing to go into Winter Quarters, without which or a Magazine of Flour at Trenton, they will undoubtedly experience the same distresses they had last Winter

Inclosed you have an Estimate of Debts which I have contracted and for which I beg an Order upon the Treasury Board to enable me to Discharge the Same—All my Supplies of Provisions are nearly exhausted and the daily existence and Support of the Army will depend on the Exertions of the State Agents—

    I have the Honor to be very respectfully
     Gentn. Your Most Obt Hble Servant—
      Eph Blaine CG P

Honorable Board War

<small>Peter Force Collection, Mss. 17,137, Series 8D, Ephraim Blaine Papers, Library of Congress.</small>

Blaine to Samuel Lyon

Philada. 2 July 1780

Sir

The movement of the Enemy & our Army taking the Field obliged me to go to Camp the day after my return from Carlisle which has been the means of my not writing you before this your proportion of the State Mony. & Instructions you have long since Recd. from the President & Council & hope it will be in your power to purchase such Articles as you are desired to procure & have it deposited agreeable to my Directions

The supplies of all the Troops stationed at Wyoming Sunbury & the frontiers of [writer's blank] & Bedford Counties must depend on you & Mr. Wertz of Lancaster, I have ordered him to forward to Susquehanna for that purpose 300 Barrels of Flour the residue must come from you & all the Beef Cattle, send no Cattle this way except you can spare them from the Consumption of the Troops at Carlisle & upon those Stations the necessary persons must be employ'd to take charge of the Cattle & at Carlisle, one or two Butchers, my Brother will inform you what may be Necessary, you must agree with those persons upon the most reasonable Terms you can, do not confine your self to the Quantity of Provisions ordered to be purchased by Council, but purchase every Article of Provisions & Liquor necessary for the ample Supply of those who are intitled to draw paying particular attention to keep the Magazine at Carlisle well supply'd with Provisions the pay of Drovers & Butchers & all aditional Articles which you may purchase over your Instructions must be a Continental Charge, which as well as your own Service I shall take care to procure you Mony to Discharge, the pay allowed to the Commissioners is left to the Governor or Council & I make no doubt they will make it Right, you must Keep Duplicate Invoices of all your purchases, one to be delivered the

Continental Agent, & the other to be your Voucher with his Rect. for the Delivery my Brother has the form of keeping the Accots. & can give you proper Directions on that Head Mrs. Blaine & Children are well & Joins me with Love to you & Sister & believe mw with much Respect
        Yours Affectionately
           E Blaine CG of P.
Saml. Lyon Esqr.

> Lyon was Assistant Commissary of Purchases for Cumberland County, Pennsylvania. He later became a clerk in the Office of Finance. Peter Force Collection, Mss. 17,137, Series 8D, Ephraim Blaine Papers, Library of Congress.

Blaine to Peter Aston

                              Philada. 3 July 1780

Sir
    In 1778 no Butchers had more than 40 Dollars pr Month & that was continued til August 1779, since the Master Butchers at posts have been allow'd 60 Dollars where they had an Allowance of drawing one Ration let not any dispute arise which may delay your settlemt., the Butchers & those people who have demands for Services may have their pay settled in future as you bring down their Accots. to be adjusted at time of settlemt. my hurry in Business now when the Campaign is opening will prevent the settling my Accots.— Mr. Morton will pay every possible Attention to that Business, I remain Sir
        Your most Obedt. Servant
          E. B. CG of Ps.
Mr. Peter Aston

> Peter Force Collection, Mss. 17,137, Series 8D, Ephraim Blaine Papers, Library of Congress.

Blaine to Robert Forsyth

3 July 1780—

Dear Sir

Your favour of the fifth Ulto. came to hand and am exceedingly sorry for the distresses of the Southern States, and doubt it will be some time before we retrieve our Losses in that Country—we are making every preperation to flog the Enemy in this quarter, and our hopes were great had our Ally arrived when first expected, but we have no certain Accts. of their being on our Coast Yet and every days delay will be much to our disadvantage—

The change of the Commissaries and want of Money has made our Business both precarious & difficult & very few persons can transact any Business under those Embarrassments—I make no doubt you have had your Share of them, and their is great trouble in agregating Supplies for the Troops now in your District—I have used every method in my power to obtain Money from the Treasury Board or Orders to cover your Draft upon the Treasury of Virginia but in this I have fail'd—Make out an Acct against Col. Wadsworth of all your Purchases prior to the first of March, since that period your purchases must come under my Notice—you will also make out an Estimate of all your disbursements and Purchases, since the first of March, giving Credit for the Sums receiv'd and send those Estimates with all the Accts. you can possibly collect by first Safe Opportunity and be assured of my best Endeavours with the Treasury Board to obtain payment—they are determin'd not to grant Money without them—

The New Arrangement of our Department is not properly Settled tho' there has been a Committee at Camp some weeks and have not yet finished the Quarter Masters Business, the moment they have settled mine shall inform you—They have assured me that genteel Salaries in Specie or an equivalent will be allow'd the Officers. if your State have complied with the

requisitions of Congress in furnishing Provisions and as you will have to receive those Supplies, would wish you to have particular Care taken of the Beef Cattle—small ones will answer as well for Summer use as grown Cattle, and as I doubt we shall be scarce here next fall, would wish you to send me to this City under the direction of carefull drovers, from six hundred to One thousand good large grown Cattle—that number will enable me to lay in a large Magazine of Salt Provisions—they ought to be here by the first or middle of September, pray attend to this Business and the forwarding your Estimates and Accompts—The loss of your Pork has been a very trying Scene to me, indeed so great was the Shock and disappointment I have scarce got over it—pray send me all the Bacon and Hams you possibly can Spare—
  Am with much real Esteem & regard
   Dear Sir Your most Obt Hble Servt
    E Blaine CG of Ps.
Major Forsyth—

> Peter Force Collection, Mss. 17,137, Series 8D, Ephraim Blaine Papers, Library of Congress.

Blaine To Nicholas Lutz

Sir   Philada. 3 July 1780

 You will supply the Commissary of Issues at Reading with what Provisions may be necessary for that Post & engage a Butcher to Kill what Cattle may be wanting, give him so much pr head for Slaughtering & Weighing out to the Commissary, be particular in taking duplicate Rects. for all provisions so delivered, those Expences which come not under your Direction as State Agent must be Continental charges & wch. I will take care to discharge as such, I Remain
   Sir Your most Humble Servt.
    E Blaine CG of Ps.
Mr. Lutz

Lutz was a militia colonel and served as a commissioner to purchase supplies in Berks County, Pennsylvania. Peter Force Collection, Mss. 17,137, Series 8D, Ephraim Blaine Papers, Library of Congress.

Blaine to Charles Stewart

Philada. 3rd. July 1780

Dear Sir,

  This State has made little or no preparation towards laying up a magazine, I have not been able to here [sic] of a single barrel of flour and but a small Quantity of rum, the Commissioners make Poor progress, indeed the principle misfortune is the people have not confidence in the money and will sell little property for it, the cattle they are colecting are generally poor and small and will fall short of the Quantity demanded from this State—the business the Merchants are upon will afford us a temporary supply, though not come up to their Expectations—when thats done we shall be where they began, and worse, those Circumstances make me dread the close of the campaign indeed we shall feel hunger before that period, or get our supplies from Monsiure who has Permission from Congress to purchase supplies with the new State money (in each State) if that will not answer to facilitate their Purchases (to [ever har]d) how will poor State and continental agents manage with Light Paper and Often without that. Congress are or Ought to be dd.—and every days transactions convince he that fall far short of our expectations, I wou'd not remain a moment in the Service was it not the Esteem I bear our worthy Commander in chief and my distress'd country—your friends are all well and Long to see you, the rum & Other Provisions in Store which are triffling shall be all forwarded, I shall proceed with the utmost dispatch in a few days to head Quarters and Request you not to leave it untill I come; I will not have it in my power to Obtain money to purchase

Necessaries for his Excellency and family, do have your system fixed with the Committee of Congress else all your people will leave you to look for Others, they are Quite Dissatisfied, my respects to all friends, and believe me with much Esteem, and
    Regard, Dear Sir,
      Your Most Obdt. Hble Servt.
       Eph. Blaine C.G.P.
Coll. Stewart:

Public Service. Charles Stewart Esquire
      Commissary Genl. of Issues
      Head Quarter[*sic*] New Jersey

  Charles Stewart Papers, 1752-1818, Collection 262, New York State Historical Association.

Blaine to Joseph Baker

          Philada. 4 July 1780

Sir
  I am inform'd by the Council of your State that they have appointed you to purchase the Article of Meat—have therefore to request you to use your utmost endeavours to procure all the good Meat Cattle you possibly can and have them properly provided with good pasture—forward One hundred Head Weekly, and as I expect in the course of four Weeks our demand will be treble what it now is, request you to be prepared to furnish me with thrice the quantity now demanded—I am preparing for Camp where I shall be glad to hear from you by every Opportunity—
    remain Sir Your most Obt. Hble Servant
      Eph Blaine C.G.P.
Joseph Baker Esqr.
Westborough—

Baker, of Westborough, Massachusetts, had been appointed by the state legislature to purchase cattle in Middlesex and Worcester Counties and forwarding them to the army. Peter Force Collection, Mss. 17,137, Series 8D, Ephraim Blaine Papers, Library of Congress.

Blaine to Charles Miller

Philada. 4 July 1780

Sir

Your two favours of the 16th. May & 7th. June came safe to hand, & should have answer'd them long before this but being absent prevented me—Am well satisfied with the Appointments your State have made—the New Arrangement of the Commissariate is not yet settled therefore cannot inform you, but presume I shall be allowed a Deputy Commissary General for each State or at least one for two States, should that be the case shall be happy in happy in having it in my power to give you the Appointment—

The Committee of Congress have made the demand on your State of their quoto of Suppies—should that prove insufficient a further purchase must be made on Continental Account—the quantity of Beef Rum and Salt required from you is very considerable—the moment I receive Instructions to lay up Magazines of Salt Provisions shall give you instructions how to dispose of the Salt—

Upon rect. of this wish you to forward One hundred Hhds of Rum to West Point, and oblige the Carters who receive it from you to deliver it, at the landings upon the North River, and request you to employ a carefull person to proceed with Carters [sic] and take charge of it, and see that it is deliver'd at the aforesaid place, without Waste or Adulteration—fifty Teams will carry that quantity, but should you find it difficult to engage so many at one time, send forty or fifty Hogsheads together I will not agree to have it unloaded on the way as it is Subject to peculation and great loss—

You must continue to procure such Supplies on Continental Acct. as your State is not call'd on for, to serve the Troops which are Station'd there, and I shall use my Endeavours to procure Money to enable you to pay the Same

I am preparing for Camp where I shall be glad to hear from you by every Opporty and remain with regard

     Your Most Obt Hble Servant
      Eph. Blaine CG of Ps.
Charles Miller Esqr.

> Miller, of Boston, had been appointed Deputy Commissary of Purchases, for Massachusetts. Peter Force Collection, Mss. 17,137, Series 8D, Ephraim Blaine Papers, Library of Congress.

Blaine, Advertisement for a Runaway

Five Hundred Dollars Reward.

RUN AWAY on the fifth instant, a Negro man named SAM, twenty two years of age, five feet ten inches high, a stout well made fellow, speaks good English, and plays on the violin, has been bred to farming business. Whoever delivers him to the subscriber shall be entitled to the above reward.

July 6.   EPHRAIM BLAINE,

> *The Pennsylvania Packet or the General Advertiser*, July 11, 1780; July 15, 1780; July 18, 1780.

Blaine to Joseph Hugg, John Patton, John Ladd Howell, and the Executors of George Eichelberger

      Philada. 9th. July 1780
Sir

The frequent applications I have made for the Settlement of your Accounts & the little attention paid to my many Requests makes me doubt some kind of neglect or Fraud has attended your Transactions while in Public employ—the injury done your own Reputation by thus delaying ought to influence you to use every possible Exertion to put a final settemt. to those Accots. by which means you will relieve the Distresses of thousands who cannot receive the sums Due until my Accots. are prepared for a final Settlement with the Treasury board

    I now for the last time inform you that unless you render your Accots. to my Office immediately for Settlement that I will undoubtedly commence Actions in behalf of the United States against you which will be very disagreeable to Sir
                Your Humble Servant
                E Blaine CG of Ps
Jo: Hugg   Col. Jno. Patton
John Lad Howell
The Exrs. of Geo: Echelbarger

> All of the men had been Assistant Purchasing Commissaries before 1780. Hugg at Gloucester County, New Jersey; Patton for "the Northern Parts of the Western Shore of Maryland"; Howell for the Middletown, Delaware area; and Eichelberger out of York, Pennsylvania. Peter Force Collection, Mss. 17,137, Series 8D, Ephraim Blaine Papers, Library of Congress.

Blaine to John Little

                                    Philada. 1 July 1780
Sir
    Such confusion has arisen from the receiving & delivering public Cattle & the frauds which people may commit in changing Cattle which are not Branded, the care which ought to be taken in seeing the Cattle kept in good pasture, will require the Care & Attention of some person who can be rely'd on for that purpose, you will therefore please to undertake this Business & keep regular Accots: of all the Cattle which you may now Receive also all Recievals & Deliveries, Mr. Geo: Kitts will receive the Cattle necessary for the Issuing

Store & attend to that Business, his Son Michael with the Necessary hands must be employ'd as Drovers, the first Business will be to cull out all the Cattle fit for Slaughtering & send them to Camp except what may be wanting for the use of this post, the next Duty is to have all the Cattle Branded & see them properly provided with pasture, & to have such as may Occasionally be fit for Beef forwarded to Camp; the small Cattle & Cows will answer for Slaughtering at this post, when you meet with large Oxen or Cattle which may answer for Winter Beef, have such saved for our winter Magazine, for your Service in the execution of this Business you will be properly rewarded by
    Sir Your Most Obedient Humble Servt.
    E. B CGP
Capt. John Little

 Little was a resident of Philadelphia. Peter Force Collection, Mss. 17,137, Series 8D, Ephraim Blaine Papers, Library of Congress.

Blainne to the Commercial Committee of Congress

Ephraim Blaine Esqr.
   Commissary Genl. of Purchases
1780   To Chaloner & White   Dr.
May 5 To 2 Hhds Sugar dd. M. O'Hara
    23..1..4@£305   7102.2..10
 6 To Cash lent him   1.875
 25 To ditto pd. Geo: Kitts   750
 31 To ditto pd. Fradis for Beef   5.512..10
 " To ditto pd. Livy Hollingsworth   4.050
June 1 To 2 Hhds Sugar dd: P: January   20.0.22
    @ £250   5.049..2.1
 13 To Cash paid S. Hugg   633..15
  To ditto pd. George Kitts   750
 16 To 2 Hhds Surgar dd. Jones & Singer

25..3..2 @ £200	5.153..13..6
20 To 1 ditto delivd. John Darah	
12..2..11 @ £200	
	2.519..12..9
23 To 1 Bbl. 2..0..4 @ £210	427..10
To 1 do. deld. S. Smith	
2..0..17 200	430..7..6
	£34.253..13..2

Gentn.

The above quantities of Sugar has been deliver'd and Sums of Money paid the Persons therein mention'd, they having large Sums due them from the Public for purchases made under my Directions and are not only under heavy Losses owing to the depreciation of the Currency, but exceedingly distressed for Money to Answer their private purposes, and which I thought it my duty in justice to relieve therefore request you Honorable Board to Apply to Congress for a Warrant in my favour for this Sum, in order to settle th Accts—

        have the Honor to be
          with the greatest Respect,—
            Gentn. Your most Obedt. Hble Servant
            Eph. Blaine C.G.P,

Philada. 13 July 1780
Honorable Commercial Committee—

> Papers of the Continental Congress, r182, i165, p353-55, National Archives.

Blaine to Samuel Lyon and Christopher Wirtz

(Circular)

            Philada. 13 July 1780

Sir

    Any supplies the Bearer Mr. Willm. Stewart may want for the Garrison at Sunbury or Wyoming you will please to

furnish him with & his Rect. shall be acknowledged as a sufficient Voucher for the same, the want of Provisions at those places will require great exertion in you to keep them supply'd, with the Troops stationed in your District, beg you to pay proper attention to this as well as to my former Instructions, I remain with much Regard Sir
    Your most Obedt. Humble Servant
      E. Blaine CG of P.
Mr. Saml. Lyon
Chrisr. Wirtz Esqr.

  Peter Force Collection, Mss. 17,137, Series 8D, Ephraim Blaine Papers, Library of Congress.

Blaine, Advertisement for a Runaway Slave

Five Hundred Dollars Reward.
RUN AWAY on the fifth instant, a Negroe man named SAM, twenty two years of age, five feet ten inches high, a stout well made fellow, speaks good English, and plays on the violin, has been bred to farming business. Whoever delivers him to the subscriber shall be entitled to the above reward.
July 6.
    EPHRAIM BLAINE.

The Pennsylvania Packet or the General Advertiser, July 15, 1780.

Morton to the Board of War

Estimate of Money wanting to Purchase Provisions for the Mercury Packet July 17. 1780

11 Barrels of Beef & Pork @ £550	6.050	" "
1 Ct. Rice	150	" "
6 Bushs. Peas or Beans @ 26.5/	157	10
	£ 6357	10

Gentn.

    The above Articles are not to be had at the Magazine and the Commissioners of the Navy have given Orders that them & some other Stores should be deliver'd to Capt. Brown, of which the Inclosed is a Copy—As Col. Blaine is at Camp I take the Liberty of requesting that a Warrt. may be Issued in his favour for the above Sum, and the Provisions shall be immediately procured & deliver'd agreeable to the requisition of the Navy Board, otherwise the Vessel will meet with unnecessary delay

        I have the Honor to be, Gentn. &c
           Geo. Morton for Col. E. Blaine
Honorable Board of War

      Peter Force Collection, Mss. 17,137, Series 8D, Ephraim Blaine Papers, Library of Congress.

Blaine to George Washington

                      Camp Prakeness July 19th. 1780—
Please your Excellency

    The prospects of future supplies for your Army and the manner in which they are to be procured is a matter of the utmost Consequence, and gives me great Uneasiness, which I think my duty to represent to your Excellency in Order if possible to remidy the same before it may be too late—

    Sundry of the States have Complyed with the requisitions of Congress and appointed their Agents and Contractors to Execute their Purchases. Others of the States have not come into the measure but have Appointed Agents & made them subjects to my Orders, those who have Complyed with the requisitions of Congress have neither made their Contractors subject to my directions or Military Law—A great Majority of those Persons are People who have not the least Idea of the daily Consumption of the Army, and the bad Consequences should those supplies fail; I have it not in my power to bring them to Account should they prove Delinquents in Answering my demands, which I have many reasons to doubt will be the Case.

My Deputies have principally been oblidged to desist from Purchasing some Months past. The Continental Magazines nearly Exhausted of every specie of Provisions, such of my People as have a Privilidge to purchase are often without Money, when they have it are Oblidged to Use Aarguments with the People to Purchase such articles at they have to sSpare—Congress have given a Permission to the French Consul to purchase Provisions where it may suit him for the French Fleet and Armament, And if the New States Money will not Answer the Purpose of Procuring his supplies, He is to make such other Payments as may answer (which of Course will be hard Money) this will Effectually prevent my Assistants from obtaining a single Article untill the Gentleman's Purchases are Compleat, what Inducement Congress had for granting a Privilidge to the Consul of their ally's which their Own Agents were deprived off is to me a matter of Astonishment and Concern, when at the same time the States were Called upon by that Body for a Sufficient supply of Provisions for the whole, the Consequence of which will be your Army will starve if Force and Active Exertions are not used to procure their Supplies in this Situation is my Department, without Money, without means of obtaining the supplies, your Excellency looking to me for the support of the Troops, and liable to your Displeasure if I should fail—I must therefore beg Leave to inform you that I Cannot on any Account whatever be Answerable to your Excellency for the wants of the Army, at the same time be assured of my Utmost Exertions and Constant Attention to procure the supplies as far as in my power, or untill some mode is pointed Out by Congress which may have the desired Effect.

The Season now fast Advancing in which I ought to be making preparation for Laying up Magazine's of Salt

Provisions near where your Excellency may suppose the Winter Cantoonments of the Army will be, without which the Troops can never be regularly supplied, as it will be necessary to prepare large Quantities of Salt, and have Cooper's Employed to prepare stuff for Barrells, would request your approbation in naming those places—The southern District will scarsely be able to feed the Troops now on that station, the supplies of flour come very slowly in the Middle States, Indeed little can be Expected before the Winter, Except from the State of Maryland (without Force is Used) The Bankers will not be able to fulfill their Engagements for some Considerable time, Pennsylvania will furnish a Considerable Quantity of Rum and Salt, And I hope with what little Beef we can pick up the Eastern Department will afford a tolerable supply of live Cattle, There is now upon the Communication from the Head of Elk, Trenton & the upper Road to New Windsor, Five thousand barrels of Flour (Exclusive of what the Merchants have) which is the residue of Our Continental Supplies.

                I Remain with all due Respect,
                    Your Excellencies Most Obedient
                      and Most Humble Servt:
                        Eph. Blaine C.G.P.

Genl. Washington

    George Washington Papers, Library of Congress.

Morton to Jacob Giles Jr.

                            Philada— 19 July 1780

Sir

    Inclosed you have a Copy of your Acct. Current as it now stands, Balance in favour of Col. Blaine £4.469..6..8—if you have any other charges to bring in they shall be placed to your Credit, and the sooner the Acct. is finally closed the

better, the Vouchers you sent up are put in their proper places and such of them as were not charged are enter'd—
I am Sir Your most Obt Servt
Geo: Morton

Jacob Giles Esqr.

Peter Force Collection, Mss. 17,137, Series 8D, Ephraim Blaine Papers, Library of Congress.

Morton to Conrad T. Wederstrandt, Patrick Ewing, Isaac Carty, and Thomas Richardson, Circular, Undated.

Sir—
A requisition is made by the Navy Board for a quantity of Provisions &c for the Frigate Confederacy & other Continental Vessels in the Harbour—Amongst other Articles Peas & Beans are much wanting and cannot be had here, you will therefore forward any you may have on hand to this City as soon as possible—Beef and Pork are also much wanting, if you can forwd. some it will be very Acceptable—
I am Sir, for Col. E. Blaine
Your Hble Servt Geo: Morton

T. Wederstrandt   Patk. Ewing
Isaac Carty   Thos. Richardson—

Peter Force Collection, Mss. 17,137, Series 8D, Ephraim Blaine Papers, Library of Congress.

Morton to Thomas Harwood

Philada. 22 July 1780

Sir
Your favor of the 13 Inst. giving an Accot. of your being in Cash to discharge the Balance of the Warrant in your hands, I received & wou'd have sent for the Mony before this time but for want of an Express, Col. Blaine drew in you [*sic*] the 13th.

in favor of Col Moses Rawlings for 61.298 54/90 Dollars. which must be deducted from the Sum mentioned in your Letter, the Balance will be 70.446 11/90 which you'll please pay to the Bearer Mr. Christian K[u]khoof & his Rect. will be a sufficient discharge for the payment of the Warrant, I hope the Express will arrive in time as the Mony is much wanting I remain

    Your most Obedt. Servant
    Geo Morton for E. Blaine CG of Ps.
Mr. Harwood

> Harwood was Treasurer of the Eastern Shore of Maryland. Peter Force Collection, Mss. 17,137, Series 8D, Ephraim Blaine Papers, Library of Congress.

Morton to Nicholas Lutz

        Philada. 24 July 1780
Sir

  Your favour of the 23d. Inst. came to hand in Answer thereto, am to inform You that Colo. Blaine is now at Camp, shall Write him on the subject of your Letter, and what ever Orders he gives as to the Supplying you with Money shall be immediately comply'd with—
    I am sir Your most Obedient Sert.
    Geo: Morton
Nicholas Lutz Esqr.

> Peter Force Collection, Mss. 17,137, Series 8D, Ephraim Blaine Papers, Library of Congress.

Blaine, Receipt

Recd. Camp Prackness 26th. July 1780 of Mr. John Pape by the hand of Andrew Muirhead Waggoner five Casks of Hams said to Contain one hundred and five, weighing One thousand and forty One pounds

Eph Blaine C. G. of P.

Record Group: Department of Defense; Subgroup: Revolutionary War; Roll 13, Mss. 4738, Division of Archives and Records Management, New Jersey State Archives.

Blaine to William Greene

Head Quarters, Near Kings Ferry 30th. July 1780—
Sir
The Committee of Congress at Head Quarters calling upon the States for supplies for Our Army during the Campaign, and as I have had no Advice from my Agent of his being Continued in Office by your Legislative or Executive Authority, Nor do I fully Understand in what manner your State supplies are to be Appropriated, whether the French Agents Apply to you for part of their Provisions, or have Commissioners of their Own purchasing (if the latter), request your Excellency & Council to Adopt some method of forwarding the Supplies required of your State to Genl. Washington's Head Quarters, all Expence of Transportation out of your State becomes a Continental Charge, and when in my Power to Obtain the returns of Expenditures from your Agent, shall Obtain money or orders from Congress to repay you whatever Sum may Attend the forwarding the Supplies of my Department—The Army is hourly Increasing and the daily Consumption of Provisions will require every possible Aid the States can give us, Please to Inform who is Appointed your State Agent, and in what manner the French Troops are supplied with Provisions—I have the Honour to be very respectfully,

Your Excellencies, Most Obedt. hble Servt:—
Eph Blaine C. G. of Purchs.

Governor Greene—

Docketed "Ephm Blains letter of July 30th. received August 6th 1780" Greene was the Governor of Rhode Island. William Greene Papers, Mss 468, Rhode Island Historical Society.

Morton to the Board of War

Philada. 31 July 1780—

Gentn.

On Stateing Mr. Jas McCalisters Accts. there Appears to be a Balance of Thirty Odd Thousand Pounds due him from the Public for purchases made in Berkley County Virginia since January last, he is in great distress for Money and without your Aid Colo. Blaine is not Able to relieve him.—

If your Honorable Board should think proper to report a Warrant to the Board of Treasury in favour of Colo. Blaine for a certain Sum it shall be paid Mr. Mc.Calister in part of the Bala. Which is due him—Inclosed you have a Rough Sketch of his Acct. Current which can't be finally Settled Owing to some other Charges yet to be brought in

I have the Honor to be &ca.

George Morton for Ephm, Blaine CG of P

Honble Board War

Peter Force Collection, Mss. 17,137, Series 8D, Ephraim Blaine Papers, Library of Congress.

Morton to John Chaloner and James White

Gentln.

Philadelphia 1st Augt. 1780—

In my Letter of the 25th February last I mention'd the Circumstances of Mr. Foremans claim for Flour deliver'd Mr. Conrad Theodore Wederstrandt in Septr. 1779, and requested you to make Application equal to Mr. Formans demands—I find by a Letter from Mr. Wederstandt dated the 13th. Ultimo that he has never been able to Pay Mr. Forman any part of the Sum due him on that Acct., which he Ascertains to Amount to £29.051..7..6 calculating the Flour at the Current price at the time of delivery and including the Charge of Transportation to the Head of Elk, which Col. Forman had done at his own Expence—request you to make Application for that Sum in any way that may be most likely to Obtain it—from the nature of the Transaction, Mr. Forman is certainly intitled to an equal quantity of Flour, as it was spared for the Army on Loan and would Amount at this Time to a Sum considerably more than that before mention'd—

I am Gentn. Your most obt: sert—

Geo. Morton for E. Blaine Esqr. CG of Ps.

Messrs. Chaloner & White
Agents for Col. Wadsworth, late D.C.G.P.

Papers of the Continental Congress, Roll 95, i78, v9, p 371, National Archives.

Blaine to the Board of War

Peeks Kiln 2d. Augt 1780

Gentlemen

This Night the Army will consist of thirteen Brigades at this place the daily Consumption of Provisions is very great. Beef Cattle comes in very slow, Our Magazine of flour very inconsiderable and without the greatest Exertion in each State in furnishing the Supplies required the Army cannot be fed For God Sake press Pennsylvania and those States Southerly to give every possible assistance. I am afraid the demand of Beef for supplying the french Troops will reduce our weekly supplies—I expect Letters from the Superintendants of Purchases of Massachusets Bay and Col. Champion this Evening or to morrow from which I shall be able to judge what Returns of Cattle he can furnish weekly upon which will give you the earliest Information

I have the Honor to be with much respect
Your most obedt. Hble Servt
Eph Blaine C. G of P.

Honble Board of War
A true Copy

Maryland State Archives, MdHR 4566-58.

Blaine to Thomas Sim Lee

August 3, 1780 Kings Ferry

Sir

The Committee of Congress at Head Quarters having Called upon the States to furnish Supplies of Provisions for Our Army (during the Campaign) which is Increasing fast, and makes the daily Consumption of Provisions very Considerable, and will require every possible Exertion of the States to keep them supplied. Your State is requested to furnish for the Commissary Department, Two Thousand five hundred barrels of flour and one hundred forty three Thousand and Thirty five pounds of Beef Monthly, and thirty Thousand weight of Bacon for the Campaign. There is fourteen Brigades Assembled in this Neighbourhood, and recruits hourly Coming in, which with the followers of the Army, now Consume One hundred Barrels of flour and Sixty five head of Cattle daily. The Requisition made by the Committee of Congress upon the respective States for Provisions, are Calculated to supply Our Army, which is very Shortly Expected in the field, and without a speedy Complyance they Cannot long subsist, have in the most pressing Terms to request your Excellency & Council, to urge your State Commissioners, to use every possible Exertion, to facilitate their respective Purchases and beg your Excellency not to Confine them to the Quantity requested from the State, (whatever they Exceed) I shall take particular Care to make it a Continental Charge, and Engage to see your State paid first

Costs & Charges. The flour you will Order delivered to the Commissary at the Head of Elk or Christiana Bridge, The Cattle to Capt John Little of Philadelphia, whom I have Appointed to Superintend that Business and to forward them regularly by Droves to Head Quarters. I shall be happy in Adapting any measure which will make the delivery of Supplies Easy to your State, and not be prejudicial to the United States. The sudden move of Our Army from Jersey to this place gave me hopes of being in New York in a very few days, but Sir Henry Clintons speedy return from his Intended Expedition against the French at Rhode Island, with all his forces, has Occasioned his Excellency Genl Washington to postpone that Attempt for the present. We are now recrossing North River and going to take Post at Dobb's ferry, Eighteen Miles below this, where I presume we shall remain, untill we have Accounts of the Arrival of the second Division of the French fleet.

Eph. Blaine C. G. of Purch^s

Bernard Christian Steiner, ed. *Archives of Maryland, Journal and Correspondence of the Council of Maryland November 13, 1780 - November 13, 1781*, (Baltimore: Maryland Historical Society, 1927), 45: 39-40.

Blaine to Joseph Reed

Toppan, August 3, 1780.

Honoured Sir,

The Consumption of Provisions have Increased this Eight days past, and without the States use four-fold Exertions, the Army cannot long Subsist; there is now but Ten days' flour within the Neighborhood of Camp, King's ferry and Morris Town, Six days supply of Beef, and little or no Rum; and what distresses me beyond measure, I have this moment been Informed that the Magazine at Trenton is quite Exhausted, and all the flour & Rum there would not Load One Brigade of Waggons.

 Supplying the French Army at Rhode Island, has held back part of the Supplies of Beef I had reason to Expect from the Eastern States; this gives me reason to doubt I shall fall far short of a Sufficiency of that Article, without great Assistance from the Southward—much Dependance is put on your State for flour; therefore pray, your Excellency and Council to give us Immediate relief and every possible Assistance, else the Army must undoubtedly disband for want of Subsistance. Marquis La Fayette is just returned from Rhode Island, and brings little news, Except the French Army are in great spirits, and with the Militia was well prepared to have received Sir Henry Clinton & his Army, had he proceeded as was Expected. I Believe the Army will remain here several days. I have the Honor to be very respectfully,

      Your Excellencies Most obedt Hble. Servt,
        Eph. Blaine, C. G. P

Directed, Public Service.
His Excellency, Joseph Reed, Esqr, President of the State of Pennsylvania, Philadelphia.

> Samuel Hazard, ed., *Pennsylvania Archives*, 1st. series, vol. 8 (Philadelphia: Joseph Severns & Co., 1853), 479-80.

Blaine to Joseph Reed

        Kings Ferry August 3d. 1780—

Sir

 The Committee of Congress at Head Quarters having Called upon the States to furnish Supplies for Our Army (during the Campaign) which is Increasing fast, and makes the daily Consumption of Provisions very considerable, and will Require every possible Exertion of the States to keep them Supplied—

 Your State is Requested to furnish five hundred barrels of flour, Two hundred & Twenty five hogshead of Rum & 166,835 pounds of Beef pr Month—there is fourteen Brigades Assembled in this Neighbourhood, and Recruits hourly comeing in, which with the followers of the Army, now Consume, One hundred barrels of flour and Sixty five head of Cattle daily—The Requisitions made by the Committee of Congress upon the Respective States for Provisions, are calculated to supply Our Army which is very shortly Expected in the field, And without a speedy Complyance they cannot long subsist,—have in the most pressing Terms to beg your Excellency and Council to press the State Contractors, to use every possible means to facilitate their Respective Purchases, forward the flour & Rum, agreeable to the Orders of the Committee—The Beef Cattle will be Received by Capt: Little at Philadelphia, whom I have appointed to superintend that Business, and forward them by Droves to Head Quarters—I shall be happy in Adopting any measure which will make the delivery of Supplies Easy for your State—

Our sudden March from Prackness in Jersey to this place made me Conclude that a very few days would bring us into New York, but Sir Henry Clinton's speedy Return from his Intended Expedition to Rhode Island, has prevented his Excellency General Washington from proceeding further—We are now Recrosing North River and ging to take post near Dobbs ferry, which is Eighteen Miles below this place, and I presume we shall Remain there until the Arrival of the Second Division of the French Fleet—

I have the Honor to be with Great Esteem
  Your Excellencies Most Obedt. hble Servt.—
   Eph Blaine C.G. of Purchs.
His Excellency Joseph Reed Esqr:—

 Samuel Hazard, ed., *Pennsylvania Archives,* 1st. series, vol. 8 (Philadelphia: Joseph Severns & Co., 1853), 480-81.

Blaine to Caesar Rodney

     Kings Ferry August 3d. 1780—

Sir

The Committee of Congress at Head Quarters having Called upon the States to furnish Supplies for Our Army (during the Campaign) which is Increasing fast, and makes the daily Consumption of Provisions very Considerable, and will Require every possible Exertion of the States to keep them supplied—Your State is requested to furnish five hundred barrels of flour, Seventy One Thousand Six hundred & Seventy five pounds of Beef pr Month and five Thousand pounds of Bacon for the summer, There is fourteen Brigades assembled in this Neighbourhood, and Recruits hourly Comeing in, which with the followers of the Army, now Consume One hundred barrels of flour and sixty five Beef Cattle daily—The Requisitions made by the Committee of Congress upon the respective States for Provisions were calculated to supply Our Army which is very shortly expected in the field, and without a speedy Complyance they cannot long subsist—have in the most pressing Terms to beg your Excellency and Council to Urge your State Commissioners to use every possible means to facilitate their Respective Purchases, and Request your Excellency not to Confine them to the Quantity required, whatever their Purchases may Exceed your Quota. I shall take Care to have it settled in my Continental Accounts and See you paid Costs & Charges—

Your flour & Bacon must be delivered the Keeper of the Magazine at Philadelphia or Trenton, and your Beef Cattle to Capt. John Little of Philada: whom I have Appointed to superintend that Business, and forward them by Droves to Head Quarters—

I have the Honor to be very Respectfully
   Your Excellencies Most Obedt. & very hble Servant
      Eph Blaine C.G. of Purchs.

Addressed: Public Service
Caesar Rodney Esqr.
Governor of the State of Delaware Dover—

Rodney Family Papers, Roll 1, Container 2, Library of Congress.

Morton to James McCallaster

Philada. 3 August 1780—

Sir

You will furnish the Issuing Commissary at Martinsburgh with such quantities of Provisions & Liquor as will be necessary for the Consumption of that Post, so long as it shall be continued by the Board of War or Commissary General of Issues out of the Stores purchased on Account of the State of Virginia and his receipt will be a Sufficient Voucher for the delivery of such Supplies—
I am Sir, for Ep Blaine Esqr C.G.P.
Your most Obt servt.
Geo: Morton
James McCalester Esqr.
Commissary Berkley County, Virginia.
Present—

Peter Force Collection, Mss. 17,137, Series 8D, Ephraim Blaine Papers, Library of Congress.

Morton to William Maclay

4 August 1780—

Sir

Your favour of the 23 Ultimo pr Capt Clingham came safe to hand & am sorry for your Distress on public Acct.—but it is such as the greatest part of those who have been employ'd in the Staff now experience—have inclosed your Letter to Col. Blaine at Camp & be assured he will take every step in his power to relieve you—In the mean time when ever you think proper to attend with your Accts. for Settlement, you shall meet with all possible dispatch from—

Your Obt Servt
Geo: Morton

Mr. Maclay   Sunbury—

Peter Force Collection, Mss. 17,137, Series 8D, Ephraim Blaine Papers, Library of Congress.

Blaine to the Committee of Congress at Headquarters

Clarks Town 7th. August 1780—

Gentlemen,

The Army is now Large and hourly Increasing, which makes the daily Consumption of Provisions very great, it takes now One hundred barrels of flour & fifty head of Cattle of such as Often come on—I have much Concern about it, and doubt the supplies will not come in equal to the Demand, especially if the Army Increases which I Expect—The Magazine at Trenton is quite Exhausted. Not a Barrell of flour there when the last Waggons went for Loading, not more flour in the Neighbourhood of Camp than will supply the Troops for Eight days, Exclusive of what is in Sussex County, and about the same supply of Beef Cattle, The supplies of Beef are by no means Equal to my wishes, have not have a Bullock this four Weeks from the State of Connecticut; to keep up a plentifull supply for the present Army we Ought to Receive upward of One hundred barrels of flour and at least Sixty head of Cattle daily, these Circumstances I thought it my duty to mention to you and Beg your Honors to Use every means to pressure the States to Comply with your Requisitions, and furnish their Respective Quotas punctually—

I have the Honor to be very Respectfully—Gentlemen
Your most Obedt: hble Servt:—
Eph. Blaine C.G.P

The Honourable Committe of Congress Head Quarters

Papers of the Continental Congress, Roll 182, i 165, p 323-24, National Archives.

Ephraim Blaine to George Clinton

Tappan August 9th 1780

Sir,

The Committee of Congress at Head Quarters having Called on the States to furnish Supplies for our army during the Campaign which is Increasing fast & makes the daily Consumption of Provisions very Considerable, and will require every possible Exertion of the States to keep them supplied.

Your State is requested to furnish one hundred & forty barr's of flour and seventy one thousand six hundred & Seventy five pounds of Beef p Month; there is fourteen Brigades assembled in this neighbourhood and Recruits hourly coming in, which with the followers of the army, now Consume one hundred barrels of Flour, & Sixty five Beef Cattle daily. The requisitions made by the Committee of Congress upon the respective states for Provisions were Calculated to supply our army, which is very shortly Expected in the field, and without a speedy Complyance they cannot long subsist.

The supplies Demanded from your state is ordered to be deposited at Albany, I suppose with an Intention of supplying the Troops stationed on your Frontiers. I have been Informed that will not be sufficient, as an additional number of Troops are Called into the field. Have, therefore, in the most pressing terms to request your Excellency, to give Col. Hay, or the State Commissioners, orders to Extend their Purchases, to procure all the flour & Beef your state can possibly furnish, whatever Sum that may Exceed your Continental Supplies, I shall take proper Care to have it settled and either Pay your state the money, or obtain an order upon you from Congress for that purpose. I am much Concerned for the supplies of our army, and doubt the want of Punctuality in the state agents forwarding their respective Quotas, we shall be reduced to great Distress &

difficulty. We have much hopes from the assistance of your state, and your Excellency may depend, was it three fold, we shall stand in need of it.

> I have the Honor to be with every Sentiment of Regard
> your Excellencies most Obed't & most h'ble Serv't
> Eph. Blaine C. G. Purch's.

Gov'r Clinton

> *Public Papers of George Clinton, First Governor of New* York, (Albany: James B. Lyon, 1914), 6:92-93.

Blaine to George Morton

> Tappan 18th. August 1780,

Sir,
Pay John Talbot or his order Six Hundred and forty Dollars for two months service.
> Your Hble Servt.
> Eph. Blaine C.G.P.

Mr. Geo: Morton   Philada.
reverse: Col. Blaines Order in favour of
> John Talbot 18th. August 1780

> Peter Force Collection, MS 13,778, Series 8D, Roll 74, Frame 601, Library of Congress.

Morton to Robert Hoops

> Augt. 10. 1780—

Sir
Your favour of the 6 Inst pr Mr. Hynshaw came safe to hand with your Accts. of Purchs. &c:—I send you herewith a Copy of the remarks made in the course of the Examination & also the whole of your Returns & Vouchers for deliveries which were not made out in proper form—Mr. Hanshaw knows what will be necessary to compleat them—The two

Sums mention'd in your Letter are Orders drawn by Col. Blaine at Morris Town in Favour of Messrs. J. Thomas & Jno: Erskine, being so much advanced to James Little Miller at Hacketts Town on your Acct.—you will Settle with him for the Expenditure of the Money and oblige him to produce proper Vouchers to Support his Acct. after which you can Include it (with any other charges you may have to make) in a Return for June—have paid Mr. Hynshaw Nine hundred Dollars on your Acct. & furnished him with a State of your Acct Currt—
  I am sir for Ep Blaine Esqr. CGP.
    Your Most Obt servt
     Geo: Morton
Major R. Hoops—
Belvedere—

  Peter Force Collection, Mss. 17,137, Series 8D, Ephraim Blaine Papers, Library of Congress.

Blaine to George Clinton

          Tapan 14th August 1780.
Sir,
  The army is now become numerous and Consumes large Quantities of Provisions daily, Our Continental Supplies are quite Exhausted, and our Total dependance is on state supplies, agreeable to the Requisition of Congress and their Committee at Head Quarters, We are now without a magazine of any specie of Provisions, feed from hand to mouth (on the Receivals of this day, depends the Issues of tomorrow); in this Critical Situation is an army, which Consumes Twenty five thousand rations daily. A great number of those Troops, for want of Provisions in Camp, Under those Circumstances, a failure of two days supply, might be attended with the most fatal Consequences, which might not be in the power of his Excellency the Commander in Chief to prevent. Have, therefore, in the most pressing Terms to request your

Excellency & Council to use every possible measure which may facilitate the Purchases required of your state, and order Punctuality, in delivering & forwarding the same. I have great reason to doubt the want of spirit & Exertion in many of the agents who are Impowered to Purchase, which I hope will be a sufficient Apology for my being so Pointed on that head, Shall take it a particular favor to have a line from you, informing what your prospects are respecting supplies.
    I have the Honor to be very respectfully,
      Your Excellencies Most Obedient
       and most Humble Serv't
        Eph. Blaine C. G. P.
Governor Clinton

Public Papers of George Clinton, First Governor of New York, (Albany: James B. Lyon, 1914), 6 100-101.

Blaine to William Greene

            Tappan, 14th August, 1780.
Sir,—

  The army is now become numerous, and consumes large quantities of provisions daily. Our Continental supplies are quite exhausted, and our total dependance is on state supplies, agreeably to the requisition of Congress, and their committee at headquarters We are now without a magazine of any species of provisions; feed from hand to mouth (on the receivals of this day depend the issues of to-morrow). In this critical condition is an army which consumes twenty-five thousand rations daily. A great number of those Troops have lives which have not been enured to the hardships of the field, or want of provisions in camp, Under these Circumstances, a failure of two days' supply, might be attended with the most fatal consequences, which might not be in the power of His Excellency the commander-in-chief to prevent—have therefore in the most pressing terms to request Your Excellency and Council to use every possible measure which may facilitate the purchases required of your state, and order punctuality, in delivering and forwarding the same.

I have great reason to doubt the want of spirit and exertion in many of the agents who are empowered to purchase, which I hope will be a sufficient apology for my being so pointed on that head.

Shall take it a particular favor to have a line from you, informing what your prospects are respecting supplies.

Your Excellency's most obedient
and most humble serv't,
Ephraim Blaine, C. G. P.

To Governor Greene

John Russell Bartlet, *Records of the State of Rhode Island and Providence Plantations in New England* (Providence: Alfred Anthony, 1864), 9: 303.

Blaine to William Livingston

Tappan, 14th. August 1780—

Sir

The Army is now become Numerous & Consumes large Quantities of Provisions daily. Our Continental Supplies are quite Exhausted, and Our Total dependance is on state supplies, Agreeable to the requisition of Congress, and their Committee at Head Quarters—We are now without a Magazine of any Species of Provisions; feed from hand to Mouth, (On the receivals of this day, depends the Issues of tomorrow) in this Critical situation is an Army which Consumes Twenty five thousand rations daily—A great Number of those Troops New Levies, have which have not been enured to the hardships of the field, or want of Provisions Camp, [*sic*] Under those Circumstances a failure of two days supply might be Attended with the most fatal Consequences, which might not be in the power of his Excellency the Commander in Chief to prevent—have therefore in the most pressing Terms to request your Excellency & Council, to Use every possible measure which may facilitate the Purchases required of your State, and order <u>Punctuality</u> in delivering and forwarding the same—

  I have great reason to doubt the want of spirit & Exertion in many of the Agents who are Impowered to Purch[ase,] which I hope will be a sufficient Apology for my being so pointed on that head—

  Shall take it a particular favor to have a Line from you, informing what your Prospects are respecting [sup]plies.

     I have the Honor to be very Respectfully
       Your Excellencies Most Obedient & Most
       Humble Servt.—
       Ephraim Blaine, C. G. P.

Livingston was Governor of New Jersey. William Livingston Papers, Roll 12, New York Public Library.

Blaine to Thomas Sim Lee

August 14, 1780 Tappan

Sir

  The Army is now become numerous and Consumes large Quantities of Provisions daily. Our Continental Supplies are quite Exhausted and our Total dependance is on State supplies, agreeable to the requisition of Congress and their Committee at Head Quarters. We are now without a Magazine of any Specie of Provisions, feed from hand to mouth (on the receivals of this day, depends the Issues of to morrow) In this Critical situation is an Army which Consumes Twenty five thousand rations daily. A great member of those Troops, new Levies which have not be [*sic*] enured to the hardships of the field, or want of Provisions in Camp. Under these Circumstances a failure of two days supply might be Attended with the most fatal Consequences, which might not be in the power of his Excellency the Commander in Chief to prevent. Have therefore in the most pressing Terms to request your Excellency & Council to use every possible measure which may facilitate the Purchases required of your State, And Order punctuality, in delivering & forwarding the same.

I have great reason to doubt the want of Spirit and Exertion in many of the Agents who are Impowered to Purchase, which I hope will be a sufficient Apology for my being so pointed on that head.

Shall take it a particular favor to have a Line from you informing what your prospects are respecting supplies.

       Eph. Blaine C. G. of Purch^s
Governor Lee

>Bernard Christian Steiner, ed. *Archives of Maryland, Journal and Correspondence of the Council of Maryland November 13, 1780 - November 13, 1781*, (Baltimore: Maryland Historical Society, 1927), 45:47-48.

Blaine to the Committee of Congress

          Tappan 15th. August, 1780—

Gentlemen,

The Army daily Increasing and a Declention of Supplies, makes me dread the most fatal Consequences—Our Continental Magazines are quite Exhausted in every part of the United States & No other method of procuring Provisions, but through the respective States.

The requisition of Congress upon the States was Calculated to Supply the American Army and its dependancies, That made by your Honorable Committee was to answer the Demands of the Campaign, agreeable to a Calculation for that purpose, many of the States have done little, others are moving slowly, and those who are using their utmost Exertions, will fall short of the Supplies required—

I have this day received Advice that there is little flour at Elk, Christiana, and the Communication to Trenton, of Course the supply of that Article must fail, the States who are called upon for Cattle are also Tardy, The Army now feed from hand to mouth (On the receivals of this day, depend the Issues of tomorrow). In this Critical situation is an Army which consumes Twenty five Thousand Rations daily, two thirds of which are new Levies not acquainted with the hardships of the field or want of Provisions in Camp. under those Circumstances, two days failure of Supplies might be attended with disagreeable Events, which might not be in the power of his Excellency the Commander in Chief to remedy—have therefore to Request you to use every possible measure with Congress, and the Executive Authorities of the respective States, to pay due Attention to your demands, A neglect of which will be a Dissolution of the Army—

In the former System of the Commissariate, all Persons Employed in the Department were by a resolve of Congress Exempted from Militia duty and fine, the Persons Employed in Philadelphia are all Classed and fined, without they Render Personal Service; my Cashire, who has the principal direction of my Office when Absent, the Receival of all Letters and Settlement of Accounts, but One Clerk to assist in transacting the whole of my Business, Several other Persons Employed as Receivers and Drovers of cattle, those Persons have scarcely a daily Subsistance, and without they are Exempted from those fines, which they are not able to Pay, I must be under the Necessity of shutting up my Office, and all Business Cease—

One of my Clerks is fined Four thousand Dollars, the other Eleven hundred Pounds, have not been informed what the other Persons have to Pay—I Request your Answer to this matter, as they have Wrote me if the Public do not Exemp them from Payment of their fines, Necessity will oblige them to quit my Office—

You may rest Assured of my Utmost Endeavours to keep up Supplies, but present prospects are not favourable, and believe my Endeavour will prove Ineffectual without the States use four fold Exertions—
  I have the Honor to be with every Sentiment
    of Respect Your Most Obedient Humble Servt.
      Eph. Blaine C.G.P.
The Honorable Committee of Congress—

Addressed: Public Service
    The Honorable Committee of Congress
    Head Quarters

Papers of the Continental Congress, M247, Roll 182, i165, p327-28.

Blaine to George Washington

      Tapan Manleys Mills 15th. Augst. 1780—
Please your Excellency
  I have been several Weeks much distressed about the resources of Provisions and the manner of procuring & forwarding them, under those Circumstances I have with great Concern seen your Army Increasing, and no decisive measure taken by many of the States to support them, I have but very little hope of a Temporary and seasonable supply to Answer your Excellency's Expectation, The Continental Magazines are quite Exhausted and afford no relief—the failure of supplys coming from Trenton I doubt will deprive [sic] a distribution sufficient to keep the Army from Mutiny and Discontent, The Army is now fed from hand to Mouth, to Add to the misfortune, Four Thousand five hundred Militia are on their way to Camp, depending on the Public Magazines—Could your Excellency Insure that Service of those Men when wanted, would wish them delayed, untill we are in a better way to have them feed—[sic] I have this day received Advice of

little flour being on the Communication from the Head of Elk to Trenton—

Since the requisition of Congress, The Active Men who have with me in Business this four Years, and on whom I could have put the greatest dependance for relief in the hour of Distress, and was well acquainted with the Nature of supplies, are principally left Out in the state Arrangements, New persons appointed who are strangers to the Business, few of which have spirit or perseverance to procure the supplies their respective Districts can furnish, though they have Law to support them in siezing any thing wanted for the Army, Nor have they an Idea of the disagreeable and fatal Consequences One days failure of supplies have with the Soldiery—thus am I left to struggle with Difficulties unsurmountable, and without four fold Exertions in the States must Undoubtedly End in a dissolution of the Army—Your Excellency may rest Assured of my Constant and Utmost Exertions, happy indeed if my Efforts prove successfull, and distressed beyond measure should they fail—

I have the Honor to be very respectfully
Your Excellency's Most Obedient
and Most Humble Servt.
Eph. Blaine C. G. P.

George Washington Papers, Library of Congress.

Morton to Ludowick Weltner

Philada. August 17th:—80

Sir

Your Letter of [writer's blank] Inst. to Col. Blaine wherin you request a Supply of Provisions for your Regiment, came to hand—Col Blaine has given Instructions; long since to Mr. Samuel Lyon Commissioner of Purchs. for Cumberland & Mr. Wertz of Lancaster, not only for the Supply of your Regt.

with Provisions &c. but the other posts on the Frontiers—you will therefore make known your wants to those Gentlemen, who I make no doubt will give you every Assistance in their power—
  I am Sir for E. Blaine Esqr:
    Yours &c &c
      Geo: Morton
Lt. Col. Weltner Northumbd:

> Weltner was Lieutenant Colonel of the German Regiment then stationed in Northumberland County. Pennsylvania. Peter Force Collection, Mss. 17,137, Series 8D, Ephraim Blaine Papers, Library of Congress.

Morton to John Weitzel

          Philada: 17 August 1780
Sir
  In answer to your Letter of the 9th: Instant to Col. Blaine, I am to inform you that Mr: Samuel Lyon Commissioner of Purchases for Cumberland & Mr. Wertz for Lancaster, have Instructions from Col. Blaine to Supply the posts on the Frontiers with such provisions & Liquor as they may want from time to time—you will therefore make Application to them for that purpose & I make no doubt of their Exertions to afford you a regular Supply—
  I am Sir for E. Blaine Esqr. CGP
    Your most Obt servt.
      Geo: Morton
John Weitzel
A.C. of Issues Sunburry—

> Weitzel was the Assistant Commissary of Issues at Sunbury, Pennsylvania. Peter Force Collection, Mss. 17,137, Series 8D, Ephraim Blaine Papers, Library of Congress.

Morton to Nicholas Lutz

17 August 1780

Sir

You will receive herewith an Order upon Jacob Shoemaker Esquire Treasurer of your County for twenty thousand Dollars which you are to lay out in Beef for the Supply of the Post at Reading
   I am Sir—Your most Obt Servt.
     Geo: Morton For Ep Blaine Esquire C.G.P.

Nichs. Lutz Esqr.
Reading—

> Peter Force Collection, Mss. 17,137, Series 8D, Ephraim Blaine Papers, Library of Congress.

Morton to Samuel Lyon and Christian Wertz

Sir

Col. Blaine has recd. Sundry Letters from the Frontiers respecting the scarcity of Provisions, particularly from Col. Weltner Commt. of the German Regt. at Northumberland & Mr. John Weitzel Issuing Commissary at Sunburry. As I have referred them in part to you for a Supply, I beg leave to remind you of Col. Blaines Instructions on that head & request your Attention thereto—
   I am Sir Your Hble Servt
    Geo: Morton

Saml. Lyon

> This is addressed to "Chrr. Wertz" This is probably Christian Wirtz. Peter Force Collection, Mss. 17,137, Series 8D, Ephraim Blaine Papers, Library of Congress.

Morton to John Weitzel

Philada: 17 August 1780

Sir

In answer to your letter of the 9th: Instant to Col. Blaine, I am to inform you that Mr: Samuel Lyon Commissioner of Purchases for Cumberland & Mr. Wertz for Lancaster, have Instructions from Col. Blaine to Supply the posts on the Frontiers with such Provisions & Liquor as they may want from time to time—you will therefore make Application to them for that purpose & I make no doubt of their Exertions to afford you a regular Supply—

I am Sir for E. Blaine Esqr CGP
Your most Obt servt.
Geo: Morton

John Weitzel A.C. of Issues Sunburry—

> Peter Force Collection, Mss. 17,137, Series 8D, Ephraim Blaine Papers, Library of Congress.

Morton to Nicholas Lutz

Philada: 23rd. August 1780

Sir

The present serves to Acknowledge the rect. of yours of the 21st: Instant—Am sorry the Treasurer is not able to answer the Order sent you, as that is the only possible method of Supplying you, the Treasury here being quite exhausted—

It will be of no use to send you another Order 'till that you have is paid, must therefore request you to use your Credit for the Supply of the Post untill Money can be procured—

I am Sir For E. Blaine Esqr. CGP.
Your most Obt Servt
Geo: Morton

Nicholas Lutz Esqr
Commr. Birks County

> Peter Force Collection, Mss. 17,137, Series 8D, Ephraim Blaine Papers, Library of Congress.

Blaine to Richard Kidder Meade

Sir,

The report of the Commissaries is two true, there has been little meat for this day—about sixty barrels of salt Provisions expected from Kings Ferry, I have been looking this two days for a drove of cattle from Mr. Dunham, two from Massachusetts, the present prospects for meat is not favourable, as few of the State agents are punctual, have not have a Bullock from the State of Jersey since the first of Ap^l except seven exclusive of the drove sent up by Major Lees Officers from Monmouth, few of which were fitt for use, I shall waite on his Excellency two Morrow,
   and Remain Sir,
     Your Most Obedt. Hble Servt.
      Eph. Blaine C.G.P

Monday Evening 10 OClock 21st Augt. 1780,

> Meade was an Aide-de-Camp to George Washington.
> George Washington Papers, Library of Congress.

Blaine to Robert Hanson Harrison

       Camp Orange Town 22nd Augt. 1780,
Sir,
 All the cattle receiv'd at Head Quarters from Colonel Champion since the first of april is eight hundred and thirty seven head, perhaps near six hundred more has been delivered at West Point and its dependancies for the use of the troops

stationed there, I presume the State of Conecticutt ought not to have credit for more than two thirds of said number, as Colo. Champion had a priviledge of Purchasing in the State of Massachusetts bay,

> I remain with much Esteem and reguard
> Sir your Most Obedt. Servt.
> Eph. Blaine C.G.P

Colº. Harrison

> Lieutenant Colonel Harrison served as Military Secretary to George Washington. George Washington Papers, Library of Congress.

Morton to Archibald Dick

Philada: 23rd. August 1780

Sir

The bearer Mr. John Steen informs me he has four Continental Cattle which were kept on his Plantation thro' the Winter, one of them is an Old Cow with a Calf which is not likely to make beef—I think you had better have her & the Calf Sold at public Vendue and pay Mr. Steen his charge for pasturage if reasonable—the other three send up to this City, and any Expence for driving I will pay to your Order together what may [sic] be wanting after Selling the Cow, to pay the pasturing—

> I am Sir Yours &c.
> Geo: Morton

Major Dick—

> Dick, of Delaware County, Pennsylvania, had served in the Quartermaster Department under Nathanael Greene. Peter Force Collection, Mss. 17,137, Series 8D, Ephraim Blaine Papers, Library of Congress.

Morton to James McCallaster

Philadelphia 1st. Setemper 1780. [*sic*]

Sir,

Your letter of the [6]th. Ultimo did not come to my hands till this moment and agreeable to your request have drawn an Order for this payment of the Warrant, which you have inclosed. am sorry for your indispostion & remain
Sir Your verry Humble Sert
Geo: Morton

James McCalester

Peter Force Collection, Mss. 17,137, Series 8D, Ephraim Blaine Papers, Library of Congress.

Morton to Alexander Blaine

Philadelphia 5 Septr. 1780

Sir

Your favour by Mr. Swim came to hand which I have sent to Col. Blaine pr Express—I thought it unnecessary for Mrs. Swim to proceed any farther as I know it's not in Col. Blaines power to give you the least Assistance with Money—I also sent Mr. Lyons & Mr. Raineys Letters to Camp—suppose Col. Blaine will write them by first Opportunity
Yours &c.
Geo: Morton

Mr. A. Blaine—

The brother of Ephraim Blaine, Alexander was Commissary of Purchases at Carlisle, Pennsylvania. Peter Force Collection, Mss. 17,137, Series 8D, Ephraim Blaine Papers, Library of Congress.

Morton to James Smith

Philada. 5 September 1780

If you have any Cattle on hand Col. Blaine requests that you would forward them to Camp without a moments delay as the Army are like to be in want of Beef—he also requests that you would prepare your Accts. for a final Settlemt. and bring them to his Office for that purpose, without which it will be in vain for him to attempt to procure Money for you— Yours &c

Geo: Morton

Major Smith—

> Peter Force Collection, Mss. 17,137, Series 8D, Ephraim Blaine Papers, Library of Congress.

Blaine to George Washington

Philada. 12th. Septemr. 1780

Please your Excellency

I have laid the wants of your Army before Congress and pointed out the uncertainty of State Supplies and assured them without the most peremptory demand upon the States for a speedy and full compliance with their requisition & the most vigorous Exertions of the States in executing the Army cannot be fed, and from the repeated want of Supplies I had not the least hope of being able to lay up one Barrel of Salt Provisions—they have appointed a Committee of six Members to confer with me upon ways and means to remove the present wants and guard against future—the Members are Genl: Sullivan, Mr. Samuel Adams, Genl. Cornell, Genl: Scott, Colonel Bland and Mr: Jones, they shew a disposition of doing everything in their power to feed the Army—I have inform'd them, it was Your Excellencies Orders to me (exclusive of the prest. supplies of the Army) to make immediate preperations for laying up Magazines of twelve thousand Barrels of Salt Beef, and Sixteen thousand barrels of Flour—the places of deposit, Albany, Clavarack, Newborough, Pitts Town, Easton and Philadelphia, and to use every possible Exertion to have this Business executed before the severity of the next Winter sets in, in Order to prevent the distresses your Army experienced last Winter and Spring for want of Provisions—to shew them the necessity for adopting immediate measures to enable me to comply with your Order I have laid before them an Estimate of the Expence of transportg: the Salt to the places of deposit, making of Barrels & the number of Cattle necessary to comply with your Excellencies Requisition—

The Governor & Council of this State have assured me they will in three Months from this date, deliver weekly into the public Magazines, twelve hundred Barrels of Flour, this with what Assistance I shall get from the neighbouring States will afford you a regular Supply of Flour—

I started from this yesterday seventy head of Public Cattle eighty more will move to morrow and I have made Application to the Governor & Council, to assist me in procuring five hundred Head from the Meadows below this City—if I am successfull they will start in four days from this—

Mr. Dunham Agent for Jersey has assured me the Contractor of Monmouth County has purchased one hundred Cattle, exclusive of those which Genl. Furman took from the Inhabitants—Sixty head purchased by the Commissioner in Salem County and Sixty in Cumberland County which were all order'd to Camp—

Your Excellency may rest assured of my utmost endeavours to keep up a regular Supply—but the present mode of purchasing without Money, and no Immediate hopes of any gives me great uneasiness—

I have the Honor to be with the greatest respect
Your Excellencies Most Obedient

& Most Hble Servt—
Eph. Blaine C.G.P.

His Excelly Genl. Washington
Addressed to Washington at Head Quarters, "favour'd by Col. Pickering"

George Washington Papers, Library of Congress.

Blaine to Samuel Huntington

Philada. 15th: September 1780

Sir

The distresses of our army has been the Occasion of my coming to Town at this time—I have been with them since the Year seventy six and never experienced the same difficulties in procuring Supplies of Provisions I have done this last six Weeks—None of the States have near complied with the requisition of the Honorable Congress—those failures causes a scarcity of Provisions which gives his Excellency General Washington ye: greatest uneasiness, by having hourly complaints from the Inhabitants in the Neighbourhood of his Army, who are plundered of every Necessary of life by a Starving Soldiery which is not in the power of human nature to prevent—The present support of our Army in a great Measure is owing to the Supply of Meat I have had from Massachusetts Bay—

I must beg leave to mention to you that our want of Meat is greatly owing to the Supply of our Allies (and that wicked disposition <u>Self</u>, which at this hour of distress prevails too much in America) permit me to remind Congress that the cause of this misfortune is their admiting the French Agent to purchase Supplies upon terms that were not in their power to grant their own Agents or those of the respective States—Colo. Champion who was my Deputy to execute the Purchases of

Beef in the four Eastern States until last May or June has been since Appointed by the Executive & Legislative authorities of the State of Connecticut their Agent to procure the Supplies of Beef and Flour required from that State—he has also contracted with the French Consul to Supply the French fleet & Army at Rhode Island with Beef—he informs me he is not confined by his Contract to the State of Connecticut, but may purchase in any other of the Neighbouring States, and has actually employ'd People who have purchased a considerable number of Cattle with hard Money in the State of Massachusetts, which I have since seized, and I have it from good Authority, when our Army was destitute of a single Bullock for several Days in Camp, the Contractors for the Army of France had six or eight hundred Cattle upon Rhode Island besides a considerable number of Sheep—were the State Agents upon a footing with those of France, and had the means wherewith to secure Supplies, I should be under no uneasiness, as there is plenty for present purposes for the Support of both Armies—but I carry the Idea further; there is a prospect of those Troops being here the whole Winter, as least until Christmass—they may have a view of layg: up a very large Magazine of Salt Provisions, and I make no doubt have Salt & Casks for that Purpose—what confirms me in this Oppinion, the Agent in this City has Contracted with Major Smith at Carlisle for five hundred Head of Cattle to be deliver'd in the month of October—

The Season is now at hand in which every preparation ought to be made for laying up Magazines of Salt Provisions—the Salt ought to be on the Spot, and Barrels ready for that purpose—His Excellency Genl. Washington has pointed out the proper places of Deposit; a memorandum of which I have laid before your Committee, for their immediate Consideration; and if this Business meets with the least delay the Army cannot be fed thro' the Winter—It is necessary to deposit about eight thousand Barrels at Philadelphia, Easton & Pitts-Town—how are the cattle to be procured? there is no Beef demanded from this State, or the State of Delaware, and very little can be furnished by Jersey—the Quantity demanded from Maryland is order'd to be reserved for the Southern Army, & the requisitions of Congress request Meat from Virginia and North Carolina sufficient for an Army of Seventeen thousand Men—The daily Consumption of beef in this State and Maryland, exclusive of the Militia exceed Six thousand Rations—Those places all destitute of meat and People calling upon me to Supply them, without money without means—

My present doubts of feeding the Army is very great and I have much concern about it—I have ever taken pleasure in being in my Countrys Service & thought it my duty to render every Aid in my power—my close attention to that duty I hope has met your Approbation, and that of the Commander in Chief, but from the present Appearance of furnishing Provisions and the many disappointments I have met with in keeping up a regular Supply, I shall not only lose Reputation but be liable to the Insults of two thirds of the Army, and without Immediate Measures are taken, which may secure a timely and plentifull Supply I cannot think of Continuing longer in the Service—

I have Agents to Appoint to Supperintend the Business of my department in the respective States—Persons to employ in making Barrels and preparing places for Salting Provisions, the Receivers of Cattle, Drovers & Butchers who are employ'd with the Army have never receiv'd one Dollar since last March, and as no regular System is adopted for my Government or any rate laid down to direct me how or in what manner to settle with those Persons who may occasionally be employ'd in the Department, request that Congress may point out the mode & how I am to obtain Money to discharge the same—

The State of Pennsylvania have given me Assurances of twelve hundred Barrels of Flour being deliver'd Weekly into the Public Magazines for three Months—The Army have been Destitute of rum three weeks pray how is it to be procured—great quantities is now in this City for Sale upon reasonable terms—I wish part of it could be procured—

> I have the Honor to be with Great Esteem
> Your Excellencies Most Obdt. Hble Servt:
> Eph. Blaine C.G.P.

His Excellency Samuel Huntington Esqr President of Congress
Notation shows it was received on September 16.

> Papers of the Continental Congress, Roll 182, i 165, pages 357-60, National Archives.

Blaine to Caesar Rodney

Philadelphia, 17th Septr 1780,

Sir,

Inclosed you have a Letter from Congress Respecting the wants of our Army—which beg your immediate attention, I have come from head Quarters upon that business and cannot think of returning untill I see it put into execution—the grand army Including the Garrison at West Point and the followers of the Army who are entitled to draw provisions exceed twenty four thousand, and were seven days without one Ounce of meat except what was taken from the Inhabitants in the neighbourhood, those wants of provision with hourly complaints from the people who are plundered of every Necessary of life by a Starving soldiery, gives his Excellency Genl. Washington the utmost Distress—

your Excellency will adopt the most Immediate Measure to procure the Cattle requested from your State I shall appoint a Man to receive them at Wilmington or Chester by Estimation who will give Proper Receipts for the neat-weight of beef—the wants of the army will sufficiently appologize for my

reminding your Excellency that the utmost Exertion ought to be used in procuring those Cattle—
I have the honor to be with the Greatest Respect
Your Excellency's Most Obdt.
and Most Hble Servt.
Eph Blaine

Govr. Rodney Dover

> Peter Force Collection, Mss. 17,137, Series 8D, Ephraim Blaine Papers, Library of Congress.

Blaine to Mr. Jones

Philada. 18th. Septr. 1780

Sir   Your favour with Major Lee's Horse came safe to hand and Observe the Contents, I am sorry to here [sic] the Cattle you have in charge are in bad order as the Army is in the greatest distress for want of beef, indeed have been five days without a single Ounce, I have sent Joseph Carson down to Bring up all which can possibly be used and to settle with you the number which are there, any poor Milch Cows and Calves which are there with those I have directed him to fix with you the avarage weight also to Value all the Calves, if there shou'd be any Cows forward with Calves have directed Mr. Carson to Exchange them for beef—
I am Your Obedt. Hble Servt.
Eph Blaine

Mr. Jones

> Peter Force Collection, Mss. 17,137, Series 8D, Ephraim Blaine Papers, Library of Congress.

Blaine to Zebulon Butler

Philada. 18th. Septr. 1780

Sir,

Your favour of the fourth Inst. came safe to hand, and delay'd your Express Several day [sic] expecting to Obtain mony or some Other means to procure supplies of Provisions, agreable to the present system the States are to furnish the supplies for our army, they have been so exceeding dilatory that the army has been Several days at different times destitute of one Ounce of Meat of any Kind,—and are now in the most disagreable situation for want of that Article, I have it not in my power for the present to give you any assistance, but that of Flour, but advise you to appoint Mr. Stewart or some Other person to procure supplys in the following Manner and give Certificates for the Same, Vizt—to purchase in the old way for hard Money, fixing the price, for which give a Certificate bearing an Interest of five pr Cent untill paid, which Certificate is redeemable in the Current money at the exchange fixed in the City of Philadelphia in the time of Payment, in this way you must try to procure a supply of meat, when in my power to give you any assistance you have only to Command, wou'd wish you to secure all the Wheat you can in your Country as it will undoubtedly save a great Expence of transportation, wish to here [sic] from you by every Oppertunity,
    and am Sir, Your Most Obedt Servt.
    Eph Blaine C.G.P
Colo Butler Wyoming

> Butler was Colonel of the Third Connecticut Regiment, then in the Wyoming Valley, Pennsylvania. Peter Force Collection, Mss. 17,137, Series 8D, Ephraim Blaine Papers, Library of Congress.

Blaine to David Deshler

    Philada. 20th Septr. 1780
Sir
 His Excellency Genl. Washington has ordered me to make preparation for Laying in a Magazine of salt Provisions and flour at Easton, you will use your utmost endeavour to

procure two thousand good seasoned barrels for the above purpose exclusive of what may be necessary for the supply of the post untill next August, be very particular in having your barrels made of good seasoned Stuff and double the Quantity of hoops commonly put on tight Barrels, let nothing delay this Business and we must be prepared for salting down beef the first part of Novr. next, if you can exceed the above mentiond Number of barrels please to inform me how many. The coopers who are employed at the Public factory, must be furnished with fitness rations while engaged in that business and as there is no Issuing Commissary at Allen Town the Comy. at Easton ought to furnish them with Provisions Monthly and take their Rects. for Such Quantities of Flour beef and Whiskey delivered them for their Rations—When in my power to obtain Money shall furnish you with such Sums as will pay the expence of barrels and pray inform me by any first Oppertunity the number of barrels you may think of procuring, I am Sir
    Your Most Obedt. Hble Servt.
    Eph Blaine CGP
Colo. Deshler

> Deshler was a purchasing agent in Northampton County, Pennsylvania. Peter Force Collection, Mss. 17,137, Series 8D, Ephraim Blaine Papers, Library of Congress.

Blaine to Nehemiah Dunham

         Philada: 20th. Septemr. 1780

Sir
  His Excellency General Washington has order'd me to make preperations for laying in a Magazine of Salt Provisions and Flour at Pitts Town—You will do your utmost endeavours to engage between this and the first of December next, two thousand five hundred Barrels, which must be made of good Season'd Stuff, and twice the quantity of Hoops commonly put on Barrels—Would wish you to have a Couple of Vaults or

Granaries made in order to pack the Beef first in Bulk, from whence you take it up and pack it into Barrels, this will enable you to continuing Slaughtering & packing away provided you fall short of Cask—the Salt I will Order from this City and give you directions to have it put into good tight Casks which will answer to put Beef in after they are Emptied of the Salt—

I am inform'd there are Public Stables one or two of which you must have the use of while Slaughtering, and have the necessary Alterations made which may Answer your purpose—I am not yet able to inform you where the Cattle are to come from, which will answer for the above purpose, but presume principally from the Eastern States—however must inform you that I shall expect you prepared to begin to Salt down Beef by the first of November next—great care and Eoconomy must be used both in Cutting and Salting such Meat as may be intrusted to your Charge and you must be particular to put two hundred and twenty pounds in each Barrel, branding it with your name and marking the end of the Cask with the No. Pounds of Beef which it Contains—The Tongues must be Salted down with such parts of the Heads & hearts as will be usefull—I shall be able to furnish you with a Sum of Money to enable you to advance the Coopers when they Contract with you—

Congress have not yet pointed out the daily pay you will be entitled to receive for executing this Business, but have every reason to believe it will be worth your Acceptance—When you inform yourself of the Number of Coopers you may engage & the quantity of Barrels they Contract for, please give me information by first Opportunity—

I am Sir Your most Obedt Hble Servt—
E. Blaine C.G.P

Mr. N. Dunham

Peter Force Collection, Mss. 17,137, Series 8D, Ephraim Blaine Papers, Library of Congress.

Blaine to Samuel Adams and the Committee for the Commissary Department

Philada. 20th Septr. 1780.

Gentlemen

One of my drovers who left Camp last tuesday informs me the Army was then without meat, that the Brigade Comy. was waiting a whole day at the bullock Guard for his Cattle, and that he was Inform'd forraging parties were sending out to colect supplies. I wish to god some measure may be taken which will afford Immediate Assistance, the Consequence of those failures of Provisions is not only total destruction to the Inhabitants near Camp but causes great disertion in the army, five or six hundred Cattle may be Purchased between this City and New Castle, provided money cou'd be procured to pay the Graziers one half the sum to Enable them to Stock their lotts with poor Cattle, then will wait three Months for the residue, pray urge this State to give an Immediate supply of part of the meat required from them and wou'd wish you to apply to Maryland for four or five hundred head, which the [*sic*] can procure without delay, I am very respectfully Sir
Your Most Obedt. Hble Servt.
Eph Blaine C.G.P

The Hble Saml. Adams & the Comtte. for Comy. Departmt.

> Adams was a Delegate to Congress from Massachusetts. Peter Force Collection, Mss. 17,137, Series 8D, Ephraim Blaine Papers, Library of Congress.

Blaine to Joseph Reed

Philada. 21st. Sepr 1780

Sir

His Excellency Genl. Washington has directed me to Lay up Seven thousand Barrels of salt Provisions in this City

Easton and Pitts Town And One thousand barrels at Carlisle—exclusive of the above small Parcels Ought to be salted up where posts are Established to secure the troops Against want next winter and Spring, to Answer the above purpose, ten thousand bushells of salt is necessary and will be Immediately wanted—have therefore to request your Excellency and Council to adopt some plan of Procuring that Quantity and give Directions to your agents to deliver the same to my Order—I should wish to have an Oppertunity of speaking with the Council and giving them my Opinion respecting Small Magazines of salt Provisions,

  Am very respectfully Your Excellencies,
  Most Obedt. & Most Hbl Sert.

 Peter Force Collection, Mss. 17,137, Series 8D, Ephraim Blaine Papers, Library of Congress.

Blaine to the Board of War

          Philada: 22nd. Septr. 1780
Gentn.

 I am directed by His Excellency General Washington to making immediate Preperations for laying up Magazines of fourteen thousand Barrels of Salt Provisions upon North River, at Philada., Easton & Pitts Town. Inclosed you have an Estimate of the Exps. of Cask—I find it impossible to make any Contract with the Coopers without one half the Money being advanced upon engaging with them—If not immediately furnish'd with a Sum sufficient for that purpose I cannot obtain Casks, have therefore in the most pressing terms to request you to adopt some means to enable me to proceed in executing a Business of such great Importance—

   I have the Honor to be very respectfully
    Yours &c. &c—
    Eph Blaine CGP
Honl. Board War

14.000 Cask @ 7/3 to 7/6 Specie pr Bbl

    Dollars
    Suppose the Former, Exchange at 73—   851 666 2/3
           Eph Blaine C.GP

Peter Force Collection, Mss. 17,137, Series 8D, Ephraim Blaine Papers, Library of Congress.

To Daniel Brodhead

Philada. 22nd. Septr. 1780.

Dear Sir,
    The deranged situation of the department over which I preside, and the total want of money has prevented me from taking any notice of the Westren department (Indeed the means I was deprived of when Congress called upon the united States for a full supply of Provisions for the support of the Continental Army—my apprehensions of your Garrison suffering for was on Subsistance being a Country disputed, and much exhausted and reduced by the depradations of the Savages, was very great, and I represented my doubts to Congress and the board of war—the [sic] are exceedingly distress'd for want of money and not the least Prospects of any for many months, indeed the [sic] are destitute of a single dollar in their Treasury and cannot for the present pay their Clerks and persons employ'd in their Respective Offices in this City money sufficient for their daily support, under like Circumstances are all public departmt. and in the midst of Plenty our Army Starving two days in the week—I am happy in finding You have adopted a Measure to Keep the Garrison supplied, and be assured there is none Other can take place for some time, if you have any Immediate expectation of money to answer that purpose you may be assured you will meet with

disappointment—therefore have to request you to give Mr. Duncan every Possible assistance and let him Continue to give such Certificates as you have directed, I presume that Country up the Manongahala will afford a Sufficient Quantity of beef and pork and I wish Immediate measures may be taken to procure it, I am at a loss to Know how you are for salt if not sufficient to answer the purpose of salting down what meat can be purchased there, Request to be inform'd by very first Oppertunity and I shall send a Quantity up to Carlisle or Canoyajy provided Pack Horses can be ready to transport it from that place, to Pitts burgh I wish to here [sic] from you by first safe Oppertunity

    and am with much Esteem and regard
      Dear Sir Your Most Obdt. Hble Servt.
      Eph Blaine C.G.P
Colo. Broadhead Fort Pitt

> Brodhead was Colonel of the Eighth Pennsylvania Regiment, and then in command of the Western Department. Peter Force Collection, Mss. 17,137, Series 8D, Ephraim Blaine Papers, Library of Congress.

Blaine to David Duncan

Sir,   Philada. 22nd. Septr. 1780

 Your sundry favours came safe to my Office and shou'd have been answered before this but my absence with the Army prevented, I am happy in finding Colo. Broadhead has adopted the method you inform he has done, to feed the Garrison and Keep the troops from disbanding—

 the treasury has been destitute of money since last Apl. and Congress have not a Single dollar in the Continental treasury to pay any person, nor is there any appearance of any for some Considerable time indeed I have no Expectation of any before next January

You will continue to adopt every prudent measure taking the advice of Colo. Brodhead to feed the Garrison, and use your utmost endeavour to prepare a Magazine of salt Provisions for next Winter and Spring without which the [*sic*] cant be supported—I have had no Return of the Stores there and am entirely at a loss to know how you are situated for salt—of this wish to be inform'd by very first Oppertunity and Quantity can be sent you to Carlisle or Canoyajy in order to be transported by Pack Horses—your Country up the Manangahela River will I make no doubt afford a Sufficient supply of beef and pork, and you must contrive Immediate measures to obtain it, at the same time give the people full Assurance of a punctual and faithful paymt. of all the certificates you give for the above purpose for which I pledge my honor—

Congress have not settled the pay of Persons employ'd in my department but have given me assurance it will be generous and in Specie or the exchange, therefore beg you not to be under any apprehension on that head, the winter supply of your Garrison gives me great concern and the Season being so far advanc'd will require your Utmost exertion, wish to hear from you by Every Opportunity

and remain Sir Your
Most Obedt Hble Servt.
Eph Blaine C.G.P

(Mr David Duncan Fort Pitt)

> Blaine had appointed Duncan as an Assistant Commissary of Purchases for the Western Department in 1777. Peter Force Collection, Mss. 17,137, Series 8D, Ephraim Blaine Papers, Library of Congress.

Blaine to Charles Stewart

Philada. 22nd. Septr. 1780.

Dear Sir,

I have had little in my power through Several meetings with a Committee of Congress, they seem much disposed to feed the Army and have passed sundry Resolves respecting supplies—but the want of money Obliges them to leave the Execution to the respective States—and I fear the same Inactivity Prevails with their Officers which we have Experienced heretofore, and we shall still be distress'd for want of a Regular support—Congress have wrote the most pressing letters to the Eastren States upon the subject of beef, and inform'd them of the Fatal consequences which must attend a failure of Supplies—they have made very pressing and Immediate demands, upon the bank for five hundred head of cattle this state 1251, Jersey 375, and Delaware 530,—the State of Delaware are now purchasing their Cattle, and I expect a drove from them the day after to Morrow—this State has been tedious, being Part of three days engaged upon that business, but the report of this evenning is favourable and I have had assurances of their full and Speedy complyance, your State I make no doubt will exert themselves as usual and fully comply with the triffling demand made from them—the Bank refused having any thing to do with the purchase of Cattle, owing to their reduced funds—though Congress proposed giving them credit for the amount of the Cattle Purchased, out of the Quantity of Flour Promised. I have prevail'd on Congress to make a Special demand of five hundred Cattle from the state of Maryland, which the [sic] have done and Requested me to proceed there to Morrow, this I shall do—and have not the least doubt of being successful, shall also endeavour to have Brought forward One or two thousand barrels of Flour, though Congress have some time ago passed a Resolve reserving the Provisions of the State of Maryland for future purposes and the southern Army, though the requisitions of meat from Virginia & North Carolina are sufficient for the supply of seventeen thousand men One year—the Bank go on slowly in the purchase of Flour—this State have given me assurances of twelve hundred barrels being being delivered into the Magazine at Easten and this place weekly for three Months, this I am afraid they will not perform—they have assured me their Quoto of rum is delivered and the [ ] of money prevents them from buying [P], though cheap and very plenty—

Present appearances now in this Place are exceeding disagreeable, Congress are much distress'd for want of money and cannot obtain a dollar from any of the States, I have given up making application for money to pay old debts and have only applied for money to enable two or three people I have engaged to procure me a few beef barrels, and pay my Expenciss to Mary land and back, but this the [sic] have not been able to Grant me, Immediately upon my Return shall proceed to Camp,

     I remain with much Reguard
      Dr. Sir Your Odbt. Hble Servt.
       Eph. Blaine C.G.P.

Public Service Charles Stewart Esquire
      Commissary Genl. of Issues
      Head Quarters

<small>Charles Stewart Papers, 1752-1818, Collection 262, New York State Historical Association.</small>

Report of Pay Due

An Estimate of Pay due the receivers of Cattle drovers Coopers and Butchers since my entering upon the Business of the department untill the first of Octr. 1780,

One Inspector of Cattle 1st. March	7/6
10 Receivers of Cattle at sundry places	5/
15 Butchers with the Army to the 1st July	3/9
32 ditto from 1st July to the 1st Octr	3/9
6 ditto at West Point at its dependancies	3/9

6 Coopers at Carlisle upon Artificers pay	5/
4 ditto Easton	5/
4 Butchers in Philadelphia	3/9
1 Ditto Trenton 1 Morris 1 Pitts Town	
One Brunswick 1 White House 5 Butchers @	3/9

Peter Force Collection, Ms 17,137, Ephraim Blaine Papers, Library of Congress.

Blaine to Samuel Adams

Philada: 1st: October 1780

Gentn.

The want of Rum in the Army is very great, they have not had One Days allowance this four Weeks & the Season is now at hand in which the Soldiery cannot be contented without it—there are large quantities in the City for Sale and in my Oppinion can be purchased upon exceedingly good terms provided Means can be adopted to make payment—I presume by purchasing two hundred Hogsheads three Months Credit might be obtain'd for one half the Amount, & that would give a considerable Supply to the Troops—

I thought it my duty to mention this matter to you and as the same time wish you to think of some Measure to secure part of said Rum in order to Supply the Army with an Article, the want of which produced so much discontent—

I have the Honor to be very respectfully—
  Gentn. Your most Obt Hble Servt.
   Eph Blaine CGP

The Honble. Saml. Adams Esqr. Chair Man Committee &c.

Peter Force Collection, Ms 17,137, Ephraim Blaine Papers, Library of Congress.

Blaine to Jacob Morgan

Philadelphia 3rd Octr. 1780

Sir

The army are likely to be distress'd for want of Flour and the first of this month had but two days supply in the Magazines, have to request you to inform me what your Prospects are respecting flour, and what has been delivered into the sundry Magazines Since the appointment of the State Agents this youl be particular in making me a return off, [sic] the wants of the Army will require the Utmost exertion of the State Officers to Keep them properly supplied—have therefore in the most pressing terms to intreat you to use every endeavour to procure and forward flour Else they will undoubtedly disband for want of a supply of that Article,

I am Sir
Your Most Obdt. Servt.
Eph Blaine

Jacob Morgan
Supt. of Purchases for the State of Pennsylvania

> Peter Force Collection, Ms 17,137, Ephraim Blaine Papers, Library of Congress.

Blaine to Charles Stewart

Philada. 3rd. Octr 1780—

Dear Sir,

Your favour by Miller came safe to hand, and it gives me much concearn to here [sic] of your reduced Magazines, I have done every thing in my power and Congress seem much alarmd at my representations and have passed sundry resolves which the [sic] think sufficient to command supplys, but it is left with the states to execute and we shall be where we were and Nothing effectual will be done—Flour beef and rum are in Great plenty but no public officer able to purchase <u>without</u>

money without any Other means—and it appears to me Congress have no Immediate measures in View to Obtain money of any Kind—how we shall carry through this winter distresses me indeed, I fear that the army Cannot be kept together—Pennsylvania will Certainly disapoint in the Quantity of Flour they have promised the Bank move[s] Slowly and cannot do much, the supplies of Maryland are in part reserved for the Southern Army therefore we can have little from that State, where the winter supplies and next summer are to come from god Knows for I dont. Six or Seven hundred Barrels of Flour will be forwarded from the bank and Other places in this City this Week, perhaps an equal Quantity the three following Weeks, but this will by no means be sufficient this month and begining of next ought to Store Our Magazines in Jersey with four or five thousand Barrels exclusive the Consumption of the Army in Order to ensure the army bread through the winter, we cannot expect Jersey will be able the ensuing Winter to do any thing, and the disapointments the inhabitants have meet with in not Receiving their money has cowed the minds of the best Whigs in the State, and should a Scarcity take place little can be expected from them,

After I have set out on my Journey to Annapolis I was taken with the fever which has prevaild much in this City and was confind Eight days to my bed, am now Quite recovered and hope in a few days to set out for Camp, I have done every thing I can with Congress except Obtaining their Scanction to purchase two hundred Hhds. of rum which I have been pushing them hard for—what my Success is two Morrow [sic] will determin—this State Delaware and Mary land are Purchasing some few Cattle, but those ought to be salted down if to spare at Pitts Town If I succeed in the purchase of Rum I shall take care to have it sent forward before I leave this Dam'd place—I cannot get money sufficient to bear my Expences to Camp, I shall be Obliged to [Sha]le the whole way a method of travelling I ever hated—Inclosed you have this days news Paper the affair of Wicked Arnold engroces the whole conversation of this City, he is undoubtedly the damdest Villain upon earth, his intention to have taken Genl. Washington to me is a Crime ten fold greater than giving away West Point, he must fall a Victum to us One day or Other—he have Certainly some Military Characters which will venter far is ever he may be in our reach—I have no news worth Communicating only this City is Poverty struck for want of money, and your pockets can hardly contain what is sufficient for your daily Support—

      I remain with much Real Reguard Dear Sir
        Your Most Odbt. Servt.
         Eph Blaine C.G.P

Colo. Stewart

Addressed: Public Service
    Colonel Charles Stewart Comy. Genl. of Issues
        Head Quarters
Mr Miller: Express

<small>Charles Stewart Papers, 1752-1818, Collection 262, New York State Historical Association.</small>

To Unidentified

Sir   Philada. 4th. Octr. 1780
  Since writing you the Other day I recd. your favour by Mr. Boeman and have been inform'd by the Govr. and Council that Mr. Pery is appointed agent for Westmoreland County, his Orders will only extend to the purchase of Flour and salt and I presume his Quoto is by no means Equal to the supply of the Garrison of Pitts burgh—

<small>Peter Force Collection, Ms 17,137, Ephraim Blaine Papers, Library of Congress.</small>

Blaine to the Committee of Congress

Sundry Queries for the Consideration of Honble. Committee of Congress to which the Commissary Genl. of Purchases begs an Immediate Answer—

Philadelphia 5th. Octr. 1780—

first The States being called upon by Congress to furnish Supplies for our Army—and as

no Regulation or System is laid down for my Government how am I to agree or fix the pay of Persons employ'd in my department—

2ndly. Where more Provisions are Necessary for supplyg. troops than the Requisition

made from any Respective State how is it to be procured & Paid for—

3rdly. The Garrisons of Pittsburgh Northumberland and Wyoming are three Frontier

Posts, of Consequence—and now destitute of Provisions no method is pointed out

for furnishing them with meat—if Immediate measures are not taken to lay up a winter supply those Places must be Evacuated—Pennsylvania agreeable to his Excellency Genl. Washington orders are to furnish flour—Expresses are now in

Town waiting for my directions on that Subject.

4th. How are all the posts in Pennsylvania and the Delaware State to be supplied with meat. in the Requisitions of Congress none is required from those States—(now is

the time to make Provision) if delayed—the people must be discharged who are in public Service

5thly. all Posts in the State [*sic*] of Massachusetts bay New Hampshire and Rhode Island are in the same situation for Flour how are they to be supplied and the Flour paid

for—

6thly. Large quantities of Spirits, Rum and Cattle taken in the vicinity of Camp by Order of his Excellency General

Washington, which he has given me Express Orders to Settle & pay—how am I to obtain Money—

I am Gentleman

Your most Obedt Hble Servt.

Eph Blaine C.G.P.

The Honorable Committee of Congress—

Peter Force Collection, Ms 17,137, Ephraim Blaine Papers, Library of Congress.

To Jacob Cuyler

Philadelphia 6th Octr 1780

Dear Sir

Your favour of the 14th. September came safe to hand, and I feel for your distress & that of Every faithful Officer in my department who have done their duty. The public finances appear so low that I have doubts of their being Able to discharge our demands for some Months, but nevertheless they have given me assurance that measure [sic] shall be adopted to pay all Ballances due upon settlement of Public Accounts. you will try to prepare your Accts. for a final Settlement and wish you to have them Immediately Settled with your Continental Auditors of Accts. for the Northern department and Obtain duplicate Abstracts of your Accts. Current Certified by those Gentlemen which forward me by first safe Oppertunity and rest assured of my Utmost Endeavour to Obtain you payments—Money or an Order upon your Loan Officer is not in my power to Obtain, nor will Congress do any thing untill Accts. are settled, nor can you attemp without Injury to your selfe to make the person's to whome you are Indebted any Allowance for the Depreciation of our money, the people to Whome you are indebted must have Patience at the same time assure them that every Means in power shall be made use of to Obtain Money, and I am fully persuaded Congress are disposed

to pay every person Justly when in their power,
>I am with Much regard Dear Sir
>>Your Most Obedt. Hble Sert.

Peter Force Collection, Ms 17,137, Ephraim Blaine Papers, Library of Congress.

Blaine to Charles Miller

>Philada. 6th. Octr. 1780.

Dear Sir

I hope ear this Reaches you that the Princaple part of the salt which I ordered to Springfield and Clavarack is forwarded, I beg you my dear Sir to loose not a moments time in Executing this business the salt is now wanted. I am using every means in my power to Obtain Money from Congress when I accomplish it shall save you a part and give you the Earliest Information—make every possible Preparation to secure a plentiful supply of Provisions for the troops Stationed in your District through the winter (you may Justly Answer how can you execute without Money) but I request your Repeated Application to your Governor & Council for their Assistance in this business without which I fear you will fail and the troops in Public Employ must disband for want of the necessary support, but when the Consider [sic] that Congress have no money, and that all Supplies furnished the united States will be made good to each Respective State and the Consequence that must attend a neglect of laying in supplies at this Season, I make not the least doubt the [sic] will afford you Every Necessary Assistance, the purchases and Expenditure of money which you have made under my direction settle with the Public Auditors of your State, and Obtain duplicate Abstracts of your Acct. Current Certified by those Gentlemen, which forward me by first safe Oppertunity. Congress has given me assurence of adopting measures to pay the Ballance of all

settled Accts, wish to hear from you by very first Safe Oppertunity, and am Dear Sir
>Your Most Obdt Hble Servt.
>>Eph Blaine C.G.P

Chs. Miller Esqr Boston

>Peter Force Collection, Ms 17,137, Ephraim Blaine Papers, Library of Congress.

To Unidentifed, Incomplete

>Philada. 7th. Octr. 1780—

Dear Sir,

>Your sundry letters came to my Office While I was at Camp, else the [sic] shou'd have been answered ear this—Congress have not fixed with me a new system nor Pointed out the pay of my Agents, but they have assured me it will be generouse and in Specie or the exchange and that they [sic] will arange my department the moment the [sic] have a little leisure from the business of the Army—the new mode of Procuring supplies through State Commissys. I have no hopes from, the consequence will I doubt be a disolution of the Army [sic] for want of necessary subsistance—but as that is the method pointed out we must Acquiese and give it every possible assistance.

>Inclosed you have a Return of Supplies which Congress have Required from the State of Virginia North and South Carolinas I expect little can be procured from south Carolina, but you must press North Carolina and Virginia for a full complyance with the requisitions of Congress and Oblige them to deliver as much of the meat Kind in pork and Bacon as you Possibly can Obtain—you may Receive Part of the Cattle from their Agents by Estimation Especially where there are a Number of troops to feed, I presume they have appointed County Contractors who are to procure such Quantities of Provisions as may be assessed in each Respective

County—when those provisions are delivered at the proper places of deposit, great care must be taken to see that the [*sic*] are well cured of Proper Quality, and the Compleat Quantity put in each bbl when you

> From the context, this was probably intended for Robert Forsyth. Peter Force Collection, Ms 17,137, Ephraim Blaine Papers, Library of Congress.

Blaine to Tench Tilghman

Philada. 7th. Octr. 1780

Dear Sir

I shou'd have wrote you Long ear this but the delay I have met with in the business of my dept. has deprived me of any agreable Subject respecting supplies—

I was ordered by Congress to the Delewarr and Maryland State upon the business of Flour and beef Cattle, but being taken sick coud not Proceed, Expresses was sent on with the Dispatches and I hope to have great relief from those States—an Immediate Demand is made upon Delewarr for their Quoto of flour which is three thousand Barrels, five thousand is Requested from the State of Maryland and ten from this State—when I came to this City the agent gave me assurance of twelve hundred Barrels being delivered weekly into the Magazine at this place and Easton and, that, that Quantity wou'd be weekly Delivered untill it exceeded ten thousand Barrels, for which he had Contacted with Mr. Vandering and the Miller in the Neighbourhood of this City and County. This Induced me to believe a Regular supply for the Army was secured, and if in my Power to cary the Requisition of Congress with the State of Maryland and Delewarr it wou'd secure us against want of bread in the winter, and provided active Measures are taken to procure, the greatest part of that Quantity is now Manufactured and laying in the Mills—the next article is rum and beef which I am doing all in my power about, twelve hundred head of cattle are now apurchasing and I shall use every possible dispatch to forward them as they come in. I have prevaild with the Committee of Congress with whome I have had several meetings to enable me to purchase two hundred Hhd. of rum in this City (which is very low) and if the [sic] can furnish me with bills of Exchange to pay One half the sum three months Credit can be Obtained for the residue, in which Purchase the public will save a Million and a half of Dollars and the army Obtain a supply of that Necessary Article—the Committee have agreed and will Immediately Report if Congress Pass it I shall make the purchase next tuesday and Wednesday and have it forwarded from this place with some flour, with which Mr. Morris will proceed to Camp, Congress appear much distress'd about the wants of the army and I am Convinced are disposed to do every thing in their Power to prevent it, and have wrote in the most pressing terms to the Respective States upon the Subject of Supplies, and was money in their Power they wou'd Advance it to enable me to make the necessary Provisions—but that they are deprived of and it lays with the states to execute and I fear their slow method of Procuring supplies with still lay us under difficulties—

be assured my utmost Endeavour shall be used to prevent distresses which I much fear, and before I leave the City shall try to adopt means to prevent it—inclosed you have a Return of the Quantity of Flour forwarded since the first of this Month eight hundred barrels will go from here next week—

Congress have suspended Genl. Gates Command to the southward and ordered and enquiry into his Conduct, and resolv'd that his Excellency Genl. Washington shall direct an Officer to take command of the southern Army Private letter from Gentlemen in the Military line are put in his favour, Mr. Morris will have charge of a pipe of wine for his Excellency which I hope will go safe—favour me with a line by first safe Oppertunity, and believe me

with much Esteem and Regard Dear Sir
Your Most Obdt. and Most Hble Servt.
Eph Blain C.G.P

Colo. Tilghman

> Tilghman was an Aid-de-Camp to Washington. Peter Force Collection, Ms 17,137, Ephraim Blaine Papers, Library of Congress.

Blaine to Charles Stewart

Philada. 8th. Octr. 1780.

Dear Sir,

I delay'd Miller six days expecting to have caried the purchase of two hundred Hhds. Rum with Congress but as yet have not Succeeded, the Committee have reported and if the [sic] can furnish me with bill of exchange to pay half the amount three Months Credit can be Obtain'd for the residue, the rum can be purchased from six & six pence to seven Shilling pr Gallon on an excellent Quality. this purchase will undoubtedly save the Public a Million and a half of dollars, and give the army a good supply—I hope to have it settled two morrow if that shou'd be the Case the Purchase shall be made Immediately and the Rum forwarded under the Care of Mr. Morris, Congress are disposed to do every thing in their power and have wrote the most pressing letters to the states upon the subject of supplies, the [sic] have made an Immediate demand upon the Delaware State for their Quoto of Flour, which is three thousand barrels, five thousd. they have demanded from the State and Maryland and ten from this State, when I came to this City the agent assured me twelve hundred barrels of Flour shou'd be delivered weekly in the Magazine in this City and at Easten, and that that, Quantity wou'd be weekly delivered untill it Exceeded ten thousand barrels which Quantity he had contracted for with Mr. Vandering and the Miller in the neighbourhood of this City and County, they are doing all the [sic] can but Hazelwood has not been able to furnish them with what

money he promised, this ten thousand Barrels with what the Bank might forward I thought wou'd secure us a plentiful supply of Bread until the first of January, or February, and if I cou'd cary the requisition of Congress with the State of Deleware and Mary land for the eight thousand barrels and have it forwarded to Trenton before the Navigation cou'd by impeaded by frost, we shou'd be secure against the wants of Bread through the winter, but how in the name of god are we to do for meat, twenty hundred head of cattle are now purchasing, those ought not to go to Camp but shou'd be salted here and at Pitts Town, Inclosed you have a Return of the flour forwarded since the first of this Month,—The Medical and Hospital department have just been aranged by Congress and finished Last night, Inclosed you have a list as far as my Memory serves from Seeing the Record, &c., give my love to those of our Acquaintance and let them Know I hope to see them very soon, Mr. Risburgh was taken with the fever Yesterday and is very Ill, no person in this City escapes it, your son and Mr. Nisbit is recoverd and geting well,—Genl. Gates by a Genl. Resolves of Congress Yesterday is Suspended from the Southern Command and his Excellency Genl. Washington is directed to order an Officer to take the Command of the southern Army. Private letter from Military Characters in the southern army are not in his favour, I recover slowly from my fever I have not rais'd a perpendicular this two weeks, Mr. Morris will set out next tuesday or Wednesday for Head Quarters, by whome I shall write you particularly
    and Remain with much Real Reguard
    I am Sir Your Most Obdt. Hble Sert.
      Eph. Blaine C.G.P

Charles Stewart Papers, 1752-1818, Collection 262, New York State Historical Association.

Blaine to Asa Waterman

          Philada. 10th. Octr. 1780.
Sir
  I have not heard from you a long time, your Silence made me conclude you have declined all public Service of which I was Inform'd the Other day by a Letter from Governor

Greene. I wish you to prepare and settle your Acct. with the Auditors of the United States in the Eastren deptmt. for the purchases you have made under my direction, and Obtain duplicate Abstracts of your Acct. Current Certified by those Gentlemen specifying the Quantity and cost of each Article purchased. One for the treasury Office and the Other for my Vouchers, those Accts. you will Please to forward to my Office by first safe Oppertunity—Congress have given me assurance of adopting Measures to pay the Ballances of all settled Accts. wish to hear from you by first Oppertunity
    and Remain Sir Your Most Obdt. Hble Servt.
        Eph Blaine CGP.
Mr. Asa Waterman

> Waterman was an Assistant Commissary of Purchases at Providence, RI, and later a Deputy Commissary of Purchases at Norwich, CT. Peter Force Collection, Ms 17,137, Ephraim Blaine Papers, Library of Congress.

Blaine to Nehemiah Dunham

                Philada. 13th. October 1780—
Sir
    Inclos'd you have a Warrant upon Joseph Bordin Esqr. Continental Loan Officer for your State for Eleven Thousand, Six hundred and Sixty Six Dollars in the New money Which is to pass One for Forty—One fourth is only Allot'd for your Use to Purchase Casks, the Other I will Call on you for When on my way to Camp
    I have been very Ill with a Fever else you shou'd have heard from me Long ere this for God Sake use Your Utmost Endeavours to procure Casks upon the best Terms you can & have the Other preparations made for Slaughtering & Salting any repairs which are Necessary make Application to Colo. Neilson Who is appoint'd Qr. Master for Your State favour me with a Line the first safe Oppertunity

       & I remain Sir Your most humle. Sert—
       E Blaine C. G. P.
N Dunham Esqr—

> Peter Force Collection, Ms 17,137, Ephraim Blaine Papers, Library of Congress.

Morton to David Deshler

                  Philada. 16 October 1780

Sir

    Your favor of the 13 inst. to Colo. Blaine came to hand he desires me to inform you that he has Nothing to do with Flour Casks as they are demanded from the State by Congress and come Immediately under your Notice as a Commissioner—You will make a Return by first Oppertunity of the Number of Beef Barrels Only, on hand in Your District and Also of the Stuff you may have proper for making such Casks—The Waggoner with deliver you Twenty One Bushells Salt which is all he can take as One of his Horses is Lame—
    I am Sir your most Obt. Sert.
        G Morton

Colo. Deshler
PS procure all the Beef Barrels you can—

> Peter Force Collection, Ms 17,137, Ephraim Blaine Papers, Library of Congress.

Blaine to Samuel Huntington

                  Philada. 17th. Octr 1780

Sir

    Permit me thro' your Excellency to remind Congress about the Supplies of our Army which gives me much real concern and uneasiness—they are now fed from day to day, and Scarcely a week has pass'd this three months that they have not been one or two days wanting either Bread or Beef,—

Your Magazines are now destitute of Flour, Bread, Beef, Pork, Fish, Salt, Rum and none upon the Continent to my Knowledge can furnish one Days Supply—The States of N. Hampshire and Massachusetts Bay are our princaple dependence for Beef—the French being station'd at Rhode Island has deprived the Agent of that State from giving any Assistance; indeed he is hard put to it, to feed the Continental Troops on that Station & the State Officers of Connecticut told his Excellency General Washington at Hartford that little could be expected from that State—I have no relief from the State of New York for the main Army—they have not been able to furnish their frontier Posts with Beef—I have had frequent applications for Supplies & they have actually had two or three hundred Head of Cattle from the Committee of Massachusetts Bay—Jersey can furnish but little Beef and not a large quantity of Flour—their quota of supplies must be furnished between this & the first of January. I believe there is not above one quarter of their supply of Meat due—Pennsylvania as yet have deliver'd very little flour, no Salt nor do I know of them buying any Cattle—Sickness prevented my going to the State of Delaware & Maryland, therefore can't inform you what is done in those places—The enclosed coppies of Letters will shew you the situation of the Southern Department. Major Forsyth my Deputy, I expect him every moment who will give your [sic] further information—

All the Garrisons and posts in the Middle Department are destitute of Provisions, and no Means in my power of relieving them—The season is now advanced and passing, in which quantities of Beef ought to be procured and laid in at those places, otherwise the troops must disband for want of Subsistance—

I am distressd to think how the Army is to be kept together thro' the Winter—it will be impossible without large quantities of Beef is laid in upon the North River contiguous to West Point, and at the Magazines in Jersey—there is a very poor prospect at present, as the daily Support of the Army leaves none for that purpose—The Supplies of Fresh Meat must undoubtedly fail in the Winter, and without large Magazines of Salt Meat are procured in due time the Army cannot be fed—those are matters which require immediate consideration & if delay'd may be attended with the most serious Consequences which cannot be remedied—

There are large demands against me since last Spring and early in the Summerpart for the Seizure of Rum by order of his Excellency General Washington at the time when our Army march'd from Morristown against the Enemy when in Jersey, which he gave me express Orders to Settle and pay for—All the Persons, Receivers of cattle and Butchers who are in my employ with the army, have received no pay since my entering upon the Business of the Department—those with the former Sums will Amt: to two hundred thousand Pounds, which I beg & request Congress to enable me to pay, without which it will be Impossible for me to stay in Camp—

Since the Month of July and last of September in the Vicinity of the Army, and Garrison of West Point, there has been seized from Sundry Persons above twelve thousand Gallons of Rum, and Orders and certificates given upon me for payment—the People are very importunate for their money and give me great trouble—What I can do with them under present Circumstances?—The want of Rum in the Army causes great uneasiness amongst the Soldiery more particularly, when there is the least scarcity of Provisions, and the consequence of not having a regular Supply, causes seizures and those generally at thirty or forty Pr Cent above the price it might be procured at—

The present mode of procuring Supplies from the States has left no method Pointed out for my Government; or direction in fixing the pay of my Deputies & such other persons as may be occasionally employ'd in the Department—I

wish Congress to point out a regular line for my future Conduct, and fix the pay of the Persons I have engaged—some of them have been employ'd a considerable time & are desirous of knowing what they are to have for their Services—
I have the Honor to be
with much Respect Your Excellencys
Most Obedient & Most Humble Servant
Eph. Blaine C.G.P.

His Excellency Samuel Huntington Esquire—

reverse: Read   Referred to Mr. Henry
                Mr. Mathews
                Mr. Clarke

Papers of the Continental Congress, r 182, I 165, p. 361-64, National Archives.

Blaine to Henry Hollingsworth

Philada. 20th. October 1780

Sir
The bearer William Willson Drover called upon me this day to deliver One hundred and eighty four Head of Cattle which he says came from you, without either paper or Invoice, as part of the Immediate Supply of Cattle recd: from your State for the present use of the Army—I must confess I was astonish'd upon Examination & am sure no person in their Common Senses could attempt to purchase such Cattle for present use without an Intintion of imposing either upon the State or the U. States I shall give no rec^t. nor will I be accountable for the Cattle as they do not answer for present use—indeed many of them cannot be kept alive thro' the winter—The Agent who has purchased them ought to be prosecuted and damages recover'd for attempting to buy such Cattle & ever discharged from Public trust—If you act

as Agent for the State I request that no Cattle may be forwarded but such as are Beef fit for immediate use and that you will give Orders for disposal of those Cattle—I have given directions to a person who has provided them with pasture until I hear from you—

                I am Sir Your Hble Servt.
                Eph Blaine CGP

Col. H. Hollingsworth

> Hollingsworth was a Deputy Quartermaster General at the Head of Elk, Maryland. Peter Force Collection, Blaine Letterbook, Roll 75, f1354-55, Library of Congress.

Blaine to Henry Champion

Philada. 24 October 1780

Sir

I have been some considerable time Absent from the Army, who have been Scantily Supply'd all Summer With Beef they are now Without One days Provision at Camp and their Whole dependance must be on the Eastern States Else they Cannot be fed, pray my dear Sir give me every Assistance in Your power and forward all the Cattle You possibly can next Month What can be Spar'd from the dayly Supplies of our Army, I mean to Salt down at West point & in Jersey the Season is near Approaching in which salt provisions ought to be laid up—You will extend Your Views towards a proper quantity of salt beef for Supplying the different posts in Your State untill next Summer, Allowing Two days in seven fresh—Exclusive of the Above about 500 Barrels to be laid up in the Western part of the State for the Use of our Army next Summer and all the Pork you can possibly Secure—In my Estimation to Congress, I suppose you can Obtain Four Thousand Barrels, should you fall short of that Quantity more beef must be Added—

I have Wrote your Son, to Obtain a return of all the Supplys of provisions furnish'd by you since last January, giveing Cr. for all the Cattle You Purchas'd in the State of Massachusetts—Or any other as well as those Procur'd under Colo. Wadsworth as my self—Congress have Call'd on me for this return and I wish to have it by first Opportunity—

Your Accounts of Purchases under my directions Wish you to Settle with the Auditors of the Eastern department, and Obtain duplicate Certificates of Your a/c. of Purchases and Expidentures of Money, Specifying the quantity, quality and Price of each Article, One of those Accots to be Lodg'd with the Treasury Board upon which I will Obtain you the Balance due—and the Other as a Voucher for my Office, those are matters I wish you to attend to, let me hear from you by every Opportunity—

I remain Sir &ca.
E Blaine C.G.P.

Colo. Champion—

Peter Force Collection, Blaine Letterbook, Roll 75, f1354-55, Library of Congress.

Blaine to Henry Champion Jr.

Philada. 24th. Octr. 1780.

Sir

I forwarded an order to my assistant at Camp desiring him to Inclose it to you by first safe Oppertunity, amounting to five thousand and thirty dollars two third of the new money, upon the Loan Officer of your State, this will enable you to defray part of the expenciss of forwarding Cattle and paying Drovers &c.—you must use every possible Means of economy in the disposal of this Money—Congress have called upon me to furnish them with Accurate Returns of all the supplies of Provisions furnish [sic] by each Respective State since the first of Last January,—you will Immediately upon Receipt of this make application to your father and the Other State Agent and Obtain an Acct. from them of all the Provisions furnished as above specifying the Quantity of each Article, Quality and price, and forward the Same to me by first Oppertunity. you will also Obtain from your father the Accts. of what Cattle he purchased in the State of Massachusetts bay & the Other Neighbouring States—

Our want of beef is great you must press your father to force his Purchases and forward all the Cattle you can, the season is near advanced in which Quantities of salt Provisions out [sic] to be laid up, but as my intentions are to salt the Princaple part of what beef can be spared from the daily supplies of the Army, at West Point, I have wrote your father to lay up salt beef equal to the Consumption of your State sufficient to secure untill next Summer allowing two days fresh in Seven to be issued—Exclusive of the above you must demand five hundred Barrels to be laid up in the Western parts of the State, and four thousand barrels of Pork shou'd the agent fall short in the Quantity of Pork—a little more beef must be added Consult your father upon the Subject of salt Provisions and Inform me what may be depended on, when I receive your State Returns I shall be able to Know the Quantity of beef due deducting as much Pork as may be purchased, upon which I shall make my estimate and Inform you of the weekly demand, that I must Depend on from you—I hope shortly to be able to give you a further Supply of money—Congress have not fixed the pay of my Deputies but I have Reason to believe it will be in Specie or the exchange, (and Generous) pray forward all the Cattle Possible next Month and write me by every Oppertunity, I remain with much Regard Sir

        Your Most Obdt Hble Servt.
        Eph Blaine
Majr. Henry Champion Junr.
DCG Colchester

Henry Champion Jr. was a Deputy Commissary of Purchases at Colchester, Connecticut. Peter Force Collection, Blaine Letterbook, Roll 75, Library of Congress.

Blaine to Nehemiah Dunham

Philada. 24th October 1780

Dear Sir

Congress have Called on me for an accurate return of all the Supplies furnish'd by Respective States since the 1st Jany last either by Colo. Wadsworth my Self or the State Commisrs. you will therefore favour me with a Return without delay—the Season is now at hand in Which preparation Ought to be made to lay up Supplies of Salt Provisions, you with therefore Extend Your Views to secure all the Beef & Pork you possibly can, I have reason to suppose the principle part of all the Beef you can furnish will be us'd Fresh, without Larger supplies Comes from the Eastern States, but in my Estimation to Congress I have fixed Jersey at Four Thousand Barrels of Pork this quantity I am sure you Can procure provided the County Contractors do their duty—You will procure all the Tight Barrels you can in the Neighbourhood of Morris and have such of the Old as is at the Magazine repair'd—If Cattle can be Obtain'd I mean a Large Magazine at Pitts Town—I hope to set out for Camp in a few days & shall take your Town in my way—I have been very Ill with a Fever & Flux since I saw you but am recover'd and find my self geting Very hearty, no Immediate prospects of Money, Congress assure me Payment when my Accounts are Settled in the New Money 40 for 1 or the Nominal Sum When their Treasury will Admit of Payment in Continental, favour me with a Line by first Opportunity, and believe me with much Esteem & regard—
 Yours & ca.
 E Blaine CGP

Colo. Dunham

Peter Force Collection, Mss. 17,137, Series 8D, Ephraim Blaine Papers, Library of Congress.

Blaine to Noah Emory

Philada. 24th October 1780

Sir

Congress have called upon me for a Return of all supplies of provisions furnish'd by the respective States since the first of January last, therefore have to request you to forward to me Without delay a return of all supplies sent on to the Army and Issued in the State since the above mention'd time

The Army are poorly supplied with Beef you will therefore use your utmost exertion to forward all you possible can before the 15th. of next December, let me have regular Returns Monthly in future and give me every information respecting Supplies—

I am &ca—
E Blaine C G P

Noah Emory Esqr.—

Emory was a purchasing Commisary in New Hampshire. Peter Force Collection, Ephraim Blaine Letterbook, Library of Congress.

Blaine to Charles Miller

Philada. 24th Octr. 1780

Sir,

Your favour of the 16th. Ulto. came to hand yesterday and that inclosing your Returns receiv'd this Morning at the post Office—I am much distress'd in finding your State have not laid in their Quota of salt long before this. you must press their Executive to enable you to forward six thousand bushells of salt to Clavarac without a single Moments delay, no Cause whatever must Prevent you from dispatching this business as the Magazine of salt Provisions for the Garrison of West Point and all the post [*sic*] upon North River and the Frontiers of New York State are entirely depending on you for salt, Obtain Casks for this Purpose by every Means you can I will be able to forward you an Order next week to pay for them shou'd the state supplies not enable you to forward that Quantity upon Rect. of this, you must compleat it out of the salt you Mention being in the Magazine. I will Indemnify you and procure an Order from Congress for the whole Quantity, you must extend your Ideas to laying in a sufficiency of salt Provisions to Answer the Consumption of your posts untill next Summer, and procuring all the pork Possible which must be Receiv'd for the Army let me hear from you by every Oppertunity, and let no business whatever delay you forwarding the salt, I am with much Esteem & Regard Sir

     Your Most Obdt. Hble Servt
     Eph Blaine CG.P.

Mr Miller Boston

Peter Force Collection, Mss. 17,137, Series 8D, Ephraim Blaine Papers, Library of Congress.

Blaine to Samuel Huntington

         Philadelphia 26th October 1780

Sir

The States of Massachusetts Bay & Pennsylvania have been exceeding dilatory in procuring their quoto of Salt, and I fear I shall meet with disappointment in the quantity immediately wanted—Six thousand Bushels have been ordered some considerable time ago to Clavarac North River, from Boston—the Agent there informs me in his last Letter that there is no Salt in the Public or State Magazine except what is mention'd in the following Extract—Vizt:

"There is about five thousand Bushels of Salt in the Magazine in this State, but remains a matter in dispute whether

it is the property of the Continent or Mr: Livingston—the matter stands thus—Mr: Livingston of Charles-town South Carolina loaded a Ship with Rice for the Continent, and order'd her to this Port, she was blown off to the West Indies, the Master sells the Rice, takes in a Cargo of Salt, on his Arrival here Mr: Livingstons friends claims it as his property; but finally consents it should be stored in the Magazine until the determination of Congress was known—now if you would have it forwarded you must apply to Congress for their Orders to take the Salt—you must send on Money to purchase Casks to put it in, and to pay the Transportation, otherwise it cannot be moved—
  Yours &c. &c.
  Charles Miller
  D. C. G of Ps

  The above is taken from Mr: Millers letter which I receiv'd by last Post, upon which I should wish a speedy determination of Congress in Order that the Salt may be forwarded—
  I beg leave to mention Sir, if Congress can adopt Measures to enable me to procure three thousand Head of Cattle, exclusive of their late Requisitions upon this and the neighbouring States, now is the time as Cattle are plenty—it will lay up a Supply at their different Post and Garrisons, and Establish a Magazine in Jersey, without which many if those places must be Evacuated— have the Honor to be with every Sentiment of Regard—
  Your Excellencies Most Obedt:
  & Most Humble Servant
  Eph. Blaine, C.G.P.

His Excellency Samuel Huntington Esquire

reverse: Read Referred to Mr. Duane Mr. Adams Mr. Fell

The clause for enabling the comy genl to purchase of cattle referred to the comme on ways and means

> Papers of the Continental Congress, r 182, I 165, p. 373-4, National Achives.

Blaine to the Treasury Board

Philada: 26th: October 1780

Gentlemen

The bearer Major Forsyth, Deputy Commissary General of Purchases for the Southern Department, is come from Virginia with his Accts. prepared for a Settlemt: As many Questions may be necessary to Ask him respecting the Expenditure of Public Money, which in his absence I can not possibly answer—I beg you to give directions to the Chamber of Accounts to examine his Returns of Purchases and disbursements of Money & settle the same

I have the Honor to be with much Esteem & regard—
Gentn. Your Most Obt. Servt.
E. Blaine CGP

The Honorable Treasury Board—

> Peter Force Collection, Mss. 17,137, Series 8D, Ephraim Blaine Papers, Library of Congress.

Blaine to the Board of War

Philada. 27th. Octor. 1780

Gentlemen

I have given orders agreeable to your directions to procure the Flour with all Possible dispatch and have employ'd a person to Pick up all he can in the City from Waggoners and

Others Part of the money will be Immediately Wanting to pay persons from the Country,
    I am very respectfully
        Gentlemen Your Most Obdt. Hble. Servt.
        Eph: Blaine CGP

The Honble. Board of War—

> Peter Force Collection, Mss. 17,137, Series 8D, Ephraim Blaine Papers, Library of Congress.

Blaine to Joseph Carleton

                Philada. 28th. Octr. 1780

Sir
    Inclos'd you have an Estimate the sum which I suppose may purchase five hundred bbls. flour, part of the Money will be Immediately Wanting, I remain Sir
    Your Most Obdt. Hble Servt.
      Eph Blaine CGP

Joseph Carleton Esqr.
Pay Master the Board of War

NB. Estimate of Cash wanting to procure 500 Barrels of Flour Vizt—
500 Bbls. @ 224 lb. is 1.000 [Ct] @ £85 £85.000-"-"
    Casks   @ 6   3.000
                                   £88.000 "-"

> Peter Force Collection, Mss. 17,137, Series 8D, Ephraim Blaine Papers, Library of Congress.

Blaine to Udny Hay

                Philada. 29 October 1780

As to cash none can be expected until the new Money is in Circulation—I have obtain'd a Warrant upon the Loan Officer of New Jersey for fourteen thousand Dollars of the New Money, in order to pay for Casks Six thousand Dollars of which Shall forward to you in a few Days, for that purpose.

I have hopes of receiving a Warrant to answer your demands with printed Certificates, of which shall give you the earliest information—

I have no power whatever in advising you to give any other than the price stipulated by Congress—and I could wish you to seize and make Examples of those People who purchase without Public Authority in your State—

You must adopt such measures with the Inhabitants of the Hampshire Grants as will enable you to procure what Provisions they may have to Spare—I shall use all the influence in my power to obtain Money to enable you to pay for the Cattle purchased in the Grants, and such other Contracts as you are obliged to make for Supplying the Posts on your frontiers—

I am well acquainted with the Characters of your Legislative and executive Bodies & am well convinced every thing in their power will be done to assist you in Supplying the Posts and feeding the Army, and I hope their Treasury will very Shortly be in a better Situation—

I have had in View the Magazine of Salt Provisions, which his Excellency General Washington mention'd being laid in upon the North River, some considerable time ago, and gave you Directions last August about Cask [sic] which I hope your Credit has been able to obtain

Would wish you to fix two principal places of Slaughter and have all your Casks collected their [sic] for packing—

I wrote Mr: Chas. Miller, my Agent at Boston, in the Month of August to procure tight Barrels Sufficient to pack Six thousand Bushels of Salt and forward it with all possible dispatch to Clavarac the Barrels would not only answer the

Transportation of the Salt, but serve you to pack Beef in—he has informed me a Considerable number is now on the way to Clavarac—I hope the whole will arrive in good time to answer your wants

By the bearer of this I have wrote to Committee at Springfield to push their Purchases of Cattle, and after forwarding two hundred and fifty weekly to Camp—the residue to be sent to such places as you should direct—you will therefore write them immediately upon that Subject—I have reason to hope they will be able to forward four thousd: Cattle in the Course of next month

Extend your Views to laying up as large a Magazine as you possibly can and write to Mr: Miller at Boston to forward more Salt—I have desired him to comply with your requisitions for the Article—You will also adopt Measures to procure all the Pork you can & if possible let none escape you—this will be an Article much wanted next Summer—

Agreeable to the late regulation of the Hospital Department, the purveyors are to order the Stewards to provide Vigetables and other small Articles for such Hospital, & the Commissary of Issues to Issue provisions to the Stewards upon the Physicians Orders—

The moment my Departmt: is properly arranged & I can procure a little Money and some Orders upon the State Treasurers, & Establish a Magazine at Pittstown, I will return to the Army, from whence I shall pay you at Visit at Fish-Kills—

  I remain with much Esteem & regard—Sir
    Your Most Obedt Hble Servant
      Eph Blaine CGP

Col. Udny Hay
D. C. G. Ps. Fish Kill

> Hay had been an Assistant Deputy Quartermaster General, and was serving as a Deputy Commissary General of Purchases at Fish Kill, New York.

Peter Force Collection, Mss. 17,137, Series 8D, Ephraim Blaine Papers, Library of Congress.

Blaine to Samuel Osgood and the Committee of Purchases at Springfield

Gentlemen   Philada. 29th Octr 1780

Your favour of the sixteenth came safe to hand yesterday I am well convinced the means afforded you to execute the arduous business to which you have been appointed was by no means adequet, and the Embarrassments you have meet [sic] with and want of Money has made it almost Impossible to execute—under those difficulties I have been astonished how you have succeeded so far in forwarding supplies—

the exertions of your State Merit the thanks of Congress and I have Assured them the support of the army with meat has been principally owing to your supplies—your steedy attention to Public business has my Approbation and permit me to return you my thankfull Acknowledgements for the faver, at a time when our distriss'd Country never wanted your Services more—His Excellency General Washington has given me a direction to Lay up Magazines of salt Provisions up North River, for which purpose I have Ordered Six thousand bushl, of salt being sent from Boston to Clavarac—some considerable time ago I gave directions to Colo. Hay to procure four thousand barrels for that Purpose, and wrote Mr. Miller of Boston to purchase tight Barrels to forward the salt to Clavarac which will make about fifteen hundred more, which will be the prinicaple part of what salt Provisions can be laid up on North River, as Colo. Hay has the Management of this business you will take his Directions where to forward the Cattle after deducting two hundred and fifty head which must be regularly forwarded to the army weekly—I hope in the course of next month you will be able to send forward three or four thousand head of Cattle for the use of the army and the above Purposes exclusive of laying in a sufficient supply for the Consumption

of the State at the proper Magazines. add to the above One hundred head of Stall'd Cattle to be deliver'd at head Quarters weekly and every week through the winter and spring, in fixing the Quotas for each Town wou'd wish you to have this in View and make you Calculations from the last Week in December untill the middle of June which is about the time Grass beef is fit for use. Congress have called upon me for a regular return of the provisions furnish [sic] by each respective State, and are laying their Estimates for the ensuing year which will be transmitted the Executive of each State by the first of Decr. next, those demands will be very Considerable, what the States are Difficient of the Requisitons of the 25th of last February they will have to make up in the present demd, of Congress—I am fully convinced every thing in your power will be done to comply with my requests, and am
    with much Real Esteem and Reguard,
      Gentlemen Your Most Obdt. Hble Servt.
      Eph Blaine C.G.P

Saml. Osgood Esqr, and the
Committee of Purchases at Springfield

> Osgood was later a member of Congress, and in 1789 President Washington appointed him as his first Postmaster General. Peter Force Collection, Mss. 17,137, Series 8D, Ephraim Blaine Papers, Library of Congress.

Blaine to Oliver Phelps

          Philada: 29 October 1780

Sir
  Your favour of the 17th: Instant came to hand yesterday and am fully satisfied you will use every possible Exertion in forwarding the Supplies—Col. Pickering the present Quarter Master General has wrote his Agent in your State to give every

possible Assistance & for which purpose has sent them Orders for Considerable Sums of Money—

His Excellency General Washington has given me Orders to lay up large Magazines of Salt Provisions upon the North River & I have given directions to Col. Hay Agent for the State of New York to procure all the Casks he possibly could for the above purpose—You must continue to forward to Head Quarters two hundred and fifty Head of Cattle weekly and the surplus must be sent to such places at Col. Hay shall direct—Exclusive of the above you must lay up a sufficient Supply for the Consumption of the Posts within your State to serve until the Middle of next June, allowing two days fresh Meat to be issued in Seven to the Troops who are entitled to draw Provisions—& in fixing the quoto's for each Town you must observe that I shall, at least, demand One hundred Head of Stalled Cattle to be deliver'd at Head Quarters weekly from the middle of December until the 15th. June next The requisition of Salt from your State is 12.126 Bushels, 6000 of which I have given directions to Mr. Miller to forward to Clavarack for the purpose of laying up Magazines of Salt Provisions, part of the residue will answer to Salt Provisions in the State for—Would request you to make a requisition of one or two thousand Barrels of Salt Pork from your State, provided so much can be procured, for which they shall have Credit for so much Beef this to be collected as near North River as possible and reserv'd for the use of our Army next Summer—You will lay up reasonable quantities of Beef at the Magazines pointed out by the Commander in Chief agreeable to the foregoing Instructions to serve the Stationed and passing Troops and what Barrels you have in the County of Berkshire within twenty Miles of NRiver would wish you to fill them with Beef, and as many more as you can procure, provided there is a good Road to Transport it to NRiver

Congress have called upon me to furnish them with accurate Returns of the Supplies furnished by each State since the first day of January last, you will therefore with all possible dispatch furnish me with a particular Return of the Supplies furnished by your State since the appointment of the Committee specifying the Number quantity, quality, and Amount of each Article—

Pray dont delay the Return—you will also send me an Acct. of your Expenditures of Money—let me hear from you by every Opportunity and
    believe me with much Regard
     Your most Obt. Hble Servant
      E. Blaine CGP
Oliver Phelps Esqr:
Granville—

> Phelps was Deputy Commissary of Purchaes at Granville, Massachusetts. Peter Force Collection, Mss. 17,137, Series 8D, Ephraim Blaine Papers, Library of Congress.

Blaine to Charles Miller

Philada. 30th. Octr. 1780

Sir

Your favour of the 11th. came safe to hand yesterday before it arriv'd I obtain'd an Order of Congress for the salt which you have Inclos'd. I am happy in finding the State has given you Authority to take the Salt and enabled you to forward it. pray sent of [*sic*] thousand Bushl. the residue of your Quota will answer Other purposes,

I hope to obtain a warrant for a Considerable sum upon your State treasurer in the course of this week and when Accomplished shall take the first safe Oppertunity in forwarding it to you,

the Low state of our public Finances has deprived Congress of drawing for any money indeed the Scarcity of that article is the Cause of all our Mis fortunes Provision was never Plenties in those States—I shall lay your letter before Congress

and use my utmost endeavour to procure money to answer your demands—I wish you to inform me what the tallow you mention wou'd bring at Public Sale, it is much wanted here the Army is not half supplied with soap and Candles—if the price at Boston will Replace an equal Quantity here, deducting Risque and Freight I shall make application for an Order to sell it—the exertions of your state have been very Considerable and the necessity of the army being supplied with rum & salt will I make no doubt Induce them to give you every Possible assistance in procuring those Articles and having them forwarded before the season Prevents, let me here [*sic*] from you by every Opportunity and
believe with much Reguard Sir
Your Most Obdt Hble Servt.
Eph Blain CGP

Chs Miller Esqr.

Peter Force Collection, Mss. 17,137, Series 8D, Ephraim Blaine Papers, Library of Congress.

Blaine to Henry Champion

Philada. 30th Octr. 1780

Dear Sir

I wrote you the Other day by Post and requested your sending me a return of all the Provisions furnish'd by your State since the first of Last January, I beg no time may be lost in forwarding it as Congress have called upon me for an Immediate Return of the supplies furnish'd by the respective States in order to make their Estimates for the ensuing Year—

You must forward all the Cattle possible before the fifteen of decemr. next, what can be spared from the daily Cumsumption of the Army I mean to have salted in the Neighbourhood of Camp, and call upon the State Agent to arange his purchases in such a way as to be such a way as to be enabled to deliver you One hundred and thirty head of stalled

Cattle every Week from the 15th. of Decr. untill the middle of June next at which time Grass fed beef becomes fitt for use. this with the requisions from Other States will Afford a temporary supply of Fresh meat, upon a very Contracted Calculation and exclusive of State Consumption—you will demand as Large a Quantity of Pork as you think the state can procure or has to Spare, and have it Collected as near North River as Possible, consult your father upon the supplies of meat and give me the earliest information you can has your Agents delivered no Rum we are much in want of it, the Quantity Required is very Considerable, be very particular in making your Monthly returns and send me your Accts and Expenditures of Public Money, in Order that I may obtain a Warrant for the pay ment of the sum, write me by every Opporty. and
                believe me with much regard Dr: Sir
                    Your Most Obedt. Hble Servt.
                    Eph Blaine C.G.P

Majr. Henry Champion
Colchester

> Peter Force Collection, Mss. 17,137, Series 8D, Ephraim Blaine Papers, Library of Congress.

Blaine to Samuel Huntington

                              Philada. 31st Octr: 1780,
Sir
    I Obtaind an Order of Congress upon Mr. Thos. Smith Loan Officer for money to enable me to begin the purchase of One thousand head of Cattle, and endeavoured last night to contract with the princaple Graziers for haf that number The resolutions of the 25th. February last confine the price of Beef deliver'd before the 1st. of December to five Dollars & a half The Neat hundred, [*sic*] a price for which I cannot obtain a

Single Bullock—The French Agents I have been informed have made Considerable Contracts for Cattle, five or Six hundred of which, I believe, was deliver'd yesterday and have given from fifty to fifty five Shillings pr neat hundred the Butchers who are buying for themselves & Merchants exceed that Price, therefore it will be in vain for me to attempt to Purchase without giving what others are—I beg that Congress would immediately consider this matter, as the delay of a Day or two may loose [sic] me the Offer of a Considerable number of good Cattle—

The Southern Department is now destitute of every kind of Provisions—Major Forsyth who Superintends that District is in town, he assures me without the utmost Exertion the Army cannot be fed thro' the Winter, and that the State Agents in Virginia have not been able to feed the passing and Convention Troops—

Major Forsyth and his Assistants have Superintended the Business of the Departmt. since the State Agents began to Act, and has given great Attention—Congress have not impowered me to fix his Salary and that of those imployed under him—he is disposed to Continue in the Service provided it is worth his attention—he is a Man of Business and a useful Officer therefore beg that Congress would enable me to give him Instructions to proceed upon the Business of the department without delay—Inclosed you have his Returns of the Supplies purchased by the Continental and State Agents in the States of Virga. and North Carolina since the first of January last, except what the State Commissary of North Carolina procured for the Militia, returns of which Major Forsyth could not obtain—

The Expresses from the Commanding Officers at Pittsburgh & Wyoming have been delayed four weeks in Town, those Garrisons are if great distress for Meat, how shall I make Winter Provision for them?—

I have the Honor to be very respectfully
Your Excellencys Most Obedt Hble Servant

—E Blaine

P. S.— General Greene has made Application to me for some necessaries for Family use and wishes if the Public can with Conveniency afford a little Wine, the Magazine affords none of the Articles he wants—is he to have them & how are they to be provided?—E B

> Peter Force Collection, Mss. 17,137, Series 8D, Ephraim Blaine Papers, Library of Congress.

Blaine, Circular to John Patton, C. T. Wederstrandt, James Smith, Joseph Hugg, Morris & Huff, John Ladd Howell, Patrick Ewing, Matts. Slough, John Chaloner & James White, Azariah Dunham, Peter Aston, William Maclay, William Stuart, Henry Miller, Robert Lettis Hooper Jr., and Isaac Carty

Philada. 1st Novr. 1780,

Sir

the delay you have made in the Settlement of your Accts. has not only subjected me to great difficulty and expence, but has been a loss of reputation with the Public, and a great Injury to Individuals who have had Just claims against me for monies due—I have long since assured you that I had the promise of Congress for the payment of what Ballance was due upon Adjusting my public Accounts, but this I have been prevented of (owing to your Neglect) have therefore in the most Pointed terms to request you to attend at my Office without a moments delay prepared for a final settlement of your Accounts, and I have also to Request that your Accounts and Receipts for purchases and Vouchers for delivery may be Regular and Correspond with cash Other Else you will meet with difficulty in settling—a neglect or further delay will reduce me to the disagreeable necessity of Bringing Actions against you in

behalf of the united States—no excuse whatever will be admitted for longer delay,
>I remain Sir
>>Your Most Obedt. Hble Servt.
>>>Eph Blaine C.G.P.

To whom the Circular Letters were Sent—
John Patton C. T. Wederstrandt Jas. Smith Joseph Hugg Morris & Huff John Lad Howell Patrick Ewing Esqr. Matts. Slough Chaloner & White, Azh: Dunham Peter Aston Wm: Maclay Wm. Stuart, Henry Miller R. L. Hooper Isaac Carty

> In the list of to whom the circular was sent, Smith, Maclay, Stuart, and Carty have "Settled" written next to their names. Peter Force Collection, Mss. 17,137, Series 8D, Ephraim Blaine Papers, Library of Congress.

Blaine to Abijah Phillips

>Philada. 2nd. Novr. 1780

Sir
>Your favour I recd. yesterday and have sent the bearer Mr George Kitts to Receive what public Cattle are in your Care, you will chuse a person who is a Judge of cattle in behalf of your State with Mr Kitts in behalf of the public to value the weight in beef of such cattle as you have ready to deliver; for which and the number of cattle he will give you a Rect.
>>I am Sir Your Most H Sert
>>>Eph Blaine C.G.P

Mr. Abijah Phillips

> Phillips was a merchant at Wilmington, Delaware and was issuing provisions there, and was transporting soldiers by water to Philadelphia. Last name also appears as Philips. Peter Force Collection, Mss. 17,137, Series 8D, Ephraim Blaine Papers, Library of Congress.

Blaine to Joseph Reed

Phila, 9th November, 1780.

Sir,

I have one thousand Head of Cattle to Slaughter for Barreling, and want a sufficient quantity of Salt immediately for that purpose; in adition to the above, three thousand Bushels will be absolutely necessary to Supply the Posts in this State and Jersey without a moment's delay.

Your Excellency will please to remember that Council was informed of the reduced State of our Magazines some time ago, & the necessity there was of laying in a Supply of Salt. I now take the liberty of informing you that I have no other remedy but by applying to you & Council for an immediate Supply of that necessary Article. The Season being so far advanced will admit of no delay as the Cattle are daily loosing Beef.

I have reason to believe the Pennsylvania Line with some others of the Army will be Cantooned upon the Communication between Coryell's Ferry & North River the ensuing Winter.—In Order to prevent such distresses as they experienced going into Quarters last Year for want of necessary Subsistence, a Magazine of Flour and some Beef ought to be laid in at Trenton & Easton before the severity of the Winter; have therefore to request your Excellency & Council to adopt such Measures as will throw in a supply of the Provisions required from this State to answer the above purpose, without which it will be impossible to secure a regular Supply for them.

I have the Honor to be very respectfully your
Excellency's most Obt. & very Hble. Servt.,
Eph. Blaine, C.G.P

His Excellency Joseph Read, Esquire, Present.

Samuel Hazard, ed., *Pennsylvania Archives*, 1st. series, vol. 8 (Philadelphia: Joseph Severns, 1853), 608.

Blaine to George Washington

Philada: 10th. Novr. 1780

Please Your Excellency

Sickness, disappointments in the Business of my Department and want of Money has been the Cause of my delaying so long in this City—I have considerable prospects respecting Supplies & am convinced Congress are disposed to have every thing done in their power—

I have been adopting every possible measure to lay up small Magazines of Flour and Beef to prevent the like distresses the Army experienced last Winter—I have in part accomplished it & have now on hand One thousand Head of Cattle, and hope some more will be procured, principal part of which I mean to Salt at Pitts-town, and if the State of New York are able to Supply the Garrison at West Point with Flour, I hope to throw in Six thousand Barrels at Trenton & Easton before the Frost Impedes the Navigation—

I gave Col. Hay Instructions last August to use his utmost Influence to procure a large number of Cask [*sic*] on North River & wrote my Agent at Boston to forward Six or eight thousd. Bushels of Salt to Clavarac, in Order to lay up a Magazine of Salt Provisions at that place & near West point, and have advice of a considerable quantity of Salt being on the Road some considerable time ago—

Congress have called upon New-Hampshire, Massachusets Bay & Connecticut to furnish One thousand Head of Cattle weekly from the first of October last, for ten Weeks—the Surplus from the daily Supply of the Army to be Salted—

The State of Massachusets Bay have Sessed [*sic*] their different Towns, twenty four hundred thousand Weight of Beef to be delivered in the Course of this Month I have wrote pressingly to the Committee & my Assistant at Springfield to forward a Supply of two hundred Hed [*sic*] Weekly for the Consumption of the Army, and the residue to send to the order Colonel Hay for the purpose of Salting, to whom I have wrote on that Subject—

The moment I can dispatch Major Forsyth (my Agent in the Southern Departmt.) after General Green, and obtain a small Sum of Money, I shall proceed to Camp and wait your Excellency's Orders, and give Attention to the Magazine upon the North River—

I presume Col. Hamilton will deliver you the requisitions of Congress upon the States for the ensuing Years Supplies, they have demanded an Ample Supply of Meat, and largely of other Articles, it looks well upon paper and I pray God it may be half executed—I have had a meeting with our Assembly and have great hope from their Exertions, they shew a disposition of providing all they possibly can for the Army—

I have the Honor to be with the greatest respect—
Your Excellencys Most Obedient
& most Hble Servant
Ephr. Blaine

His Excellency Genl. Washington

George Washington Papers, Library of Congress.

Blaine to Samuel Huntington

Philada 12 November 1780
Sir
It is not my desire to give Congress unnecessary trouble respecting supplies, or find fault with the mode adopted by the States ro procureng those required but when the Existance of the Army depends on the Execution, it is my duty to represent

to Congress those who are delinquent, that measures may be taken to prevent a failure of Supplies—

I have been informed this day by the Agent for Kent County, that the Legislature of the Delaware State have adjourned until some time in January, and have done nothing Effectual towards furnishing the supplies required from them last Year—The Agents complain that they cannot obtain the quantity of flour required, and that the People are evading the Law by Paying their Assessments in the ordinary kind of Grain & green Corn,—he also informs me that three Vessels are now loading off Willmington, the Characters of the owners such as do not entitle them to any Advantage from these States—I have also been informed that three or four Vessels are now preparing to fall down the River for the above purpose, and if some Measure is not speedily taken to prevent, it may be attended with disagreeable Consequences—

It appears to me astonishing why the Deleware State have not complyed, with the Requisitions of Congress in furnishing their quoto of Supplies, before they took off the embargo there is no State in the thirteen can furnish their quoto with the same Ease & Expence—I wish to God Congress would adopt some mode to seize the Flour now Shipd: & Shiping as the Quoto of that State—They have only deliver'd fifty Head of the Cattle required by a Resolution of Congress stated the 15th. of September last—

I have purchased four hundd. and fifty head of Cattle at about Eight pounds ten Shillings hard or the Exchange—those Cattle will near the price fixed by Congress, but the Vilainy of Persons who are daily engaged in depreciating the Paper Currency has engaged me in disputes with all the People I have been dealing with about the Exchange—which I shall be obliged to leave to Merchants—Two hundred Cattle are to be furnish'd for the Garrison at Fort Pitt, and One hundred for Wyoming. to Accomplish which & make the Purchase of One thousand Hedd, I request another Order may be drawn in my favour upon Mr. Smith, to enable me to compleat said purchase—

Inclosed you have a Letter from Major Forsyth to which I beg the Attention of Congress—

I have the Honor to be with the greatest
Respect your Excellencys Most Obedt: & Most Humble Servant
Eph. Blaine
Commissary General of Purchases

His Excellency Samuel Huntington Esquire
On reverse: "Recd 14.—
Referred to Mr. Duane Mr. Henry Mr. Ingersol"

Papers of the Continental Congress, r 182, i 165, p. 379-81, National Archives.

Blaine to Zebulon Butler

Philad: 12 November 1780

Sir

The want of Money & Congress not having it in their power to procure Cattle in any other way but from the States has been the Cause of Mr Foreman so long in this City—I have this day Order'd him fifty Cattle from the Supply we have at this Post, and have given him an Order for fifty more at Easton—those Cattle are all you can depend on thro' the Winter—I hope you have a Sufficiency of Salt to Cure the Meat—

The Cattle will turn out better than they look as they have been drove above two hundred Miles before they were delivd. to Mr. Foreman—I have given Mr. Foreman and Order upon the Commr. of Cumberland County for forty Bbls of Flour and two Hhds Whiskey—this you will endeavour to get up before the Frost impedes the Navigation in your River—What Flour you can procure in the Neighbourhood of the Garrison for the Support of your Troops will be a great saving to the Public allowing you to give the same price which Flour is worth in Cumberland and Lancaster County's and if you can Supply them without bringing any from below—I wish you to have it done—

I shall be happy in contributing any thing within the limit of my duty to make your Command at Post Agreeable & am with Esteem—Sir

Your most Obt. Hble Servant
E. Blain CGP

Col. Zebn. Butler
Commt. Wyoming—

Peter Force Collection, Mss. 17,137, Series 8D, Ephraim Blaine Papers, Library of Congress.

Blaine to Nehemiah Dunham

Philada. 18th Novr. 1780,

Sir

By Mr. George Kitts you will Receive two hundred head of Cattle some of which are not so good as I could wish, you will provid for them in the best mannor you can untill the are slaughtered Immediately upon the return of the Drovers the will proceed with another drove of Better Cattle than those you will now Receive, I shall endeavour to send you five hund. head from this place and perhaps some from head Quarters. I hope to be with you next thursday or Friday and beg you may not be from home or Pitts Town,

I remain Sir
Your Most Obdt Servt.
Eph Blaine C.G.P.

Mr. N. Dunham

Peter Force Collection, Mss. 17,137, Series 8D, Ephraim Blaine Papers, Library of Congress.

Blaine to Robert Elliot

Philadelphia Novr. 20th. 1780—

Sir
You will procure upon the best terms you can and without a moments delay One hundred head of good Beef Cattle and have them carefully delivered to the deputy Commissary Genl. of Issues at Fort pitt, for every hundred weight of Beef hide and Tallow so delivered I promise to pay you fifty shillings Species or current exchange in Continental money—the mode of delivery to be agreed upon by you and the Commissary, and I presume the best method will be to have proper Judges to Class the Cattle and agree on three to be slaughtered to terminate [sic] the weight of the Drove, I also agree to pay all reasonable expences which may attend said Cattle from Fort Cumberland to Pittsburgh

Given under my hand at Phia this
20th. day of November 1780
E: Blaine C:G:P

Mr. Robt. Elliot

> Elliot has not bee identified. Peter Force Collection, Mss. 17,137, Series 8D, Ephraim Blaine Papers, Library of Congress.

Blaine to Samuel Huntington

Philadelphia 20th. Novr. 1780—

Sir,
I have purchased seven hundred Head of the Cattle for which I had the Order of Congress, and contracted for One hundred and fifty more to be deliver'd at the Garrison of Fort Pitt, but am far short of Money to pay for them—A number of the People from whom I purchased are waiting in town for their Money—I request Congress to grant me a Warrant for a Sum, sufficient for the above purpose—the Cattle will Avarage

between eight and nine pounds hard Money or the Current Exchange—

I am ordered by His Excellency General Washington to proceed to North River, and hope to set out next Thursday, previous to which would wish the business of my departmt. so aranged as to inform the People, who I have employed what Acknowledgments they are to have for their Services—I have fixed no Salary or daily pay to any of them—

I am much concern'd about the Southern Department—my Agent Major Forsyth is here setling his Accounts; if he is retained in the Service, some Regulation will be necessary to fix the pay of the Deputies and such persons as they are under the necessity of Employing—

I have the Honor to be with the greatest Respect—
Your Excellencies Most Obedient Humble Servant
Eph. Blaine C. G. P.

Honorable Samuel Huntington Esquire
On the reverse: "Read the same Referred to Mr. Duane
Mr. Henry Mr. Ingersol"

Papers of the Continental Congress, r 182, i 165, p. 383- 4, National Archives.

Blaine to Caesar Rodney

Philadelphia Novr. 20th. 1780—

Sir

I take the liberty of addressing you upon the Subject of supplies for our Army and am sorry to inform you I have been Exceedingly disapointed in my expectations from your State—the quantity required is very small and no state in the union can furnish the requisitions of Congress with the same ease—very little of the last years supplies has been furnished and I have been informed your Legislature has broke up and adjourned untill the latter end of January next without doing

anything Effectual toward furnishing the supplies due and preparing for the present—and that they have taken off the Embargo and given free liberty for exporting Flour which will not only deprive yourselves but your Neighbouring States from being able to procure their Quotas—in the requisitions for the ensuing year a quantity of Salt provisions is required from your State, and without the States are punctual in complying in hurring [sic] the salt provisions in due Season the Army cannot be fed through the ensuing Summer I know it is your desire to see ample provision made for our Troops and I beg and intreat your Excellency to adopt every possible measure to comply with the triffling demand made on your State, your Salt Provisions ought to be procured in the season after Beef & Pork is plenty—I have the honor to be very respectfully—
    Your Excellencys
     Most Obedient Humble Servt.
      Eph: Blaine
G. Rodney—

> Peter Force Collection, Mss. 17,137, Series 8D, Ephraim Blaine Papers, Library of Congress.

Blaine to Frederick Augustus Conrad Muhlenberg

      Philadelphia Novr. 20th. 1780—
Sir,
  I take the liberty of adressing your Honble House upon a Subject which ought to take their immediate and most serious Consideration (that is the supplies of our Army) the disapointment I met with last Summer in Obtaining provisions, and the distresses the Army were often reduced to needs no painting as I believe every member in your Honble House is well informed of it, the season is almost past in which Magazines of Salt provisions ought to be procured without which it is impossible to feed the Army the quantity required from this State is but very trifling and if proper methods are

adopted in due time (while Grass Beef is to be purchased) can be procured with great ease—I would wish to point out to your Honble House the places of deposit which will make the business easy to the State, secure a supply of Provisions to those Troops who may intitled [sic] to draw from you, add considerably to our public magazines and secure your Army against want through the Winter—

The Article of Flour will be much wanted, and five or Six Thousand Barrels ought to be through [sic] into the Magazines at Easton and Trenton before the frost impedes the Navigation of the Delaware and the roads get bad, my reason for pressing this idea upon your Honble House, is, the Winter Cantoonments of Pennsylvania line with some others of the Army will be on the communication between Curryells ferry and North River, and if measures are not immediately taken to through [sic] in supplies at the above mentioned places before the severity of the Winter, the Army will undoubtedly be reduced to the same distress they were going into quarters last Year

I have experienced a great want of regularity in the States forwarding the supplies required by Congress—whether from a neglect of their publick Agents, the want of money or power to Execute I will not presume to say, but there is a great difficiency of supplies required which is the cause of the Army being often destitute of Provisions, I shall be happy if in the line of my duty I can render the state any Service, and your Honble House have only to Command.— I have the Honr to be with the greatest respect sir
        Your Most Obedient Humble Servt.
        Eph: Blaine

Fredk. Mullenburgh Esqr.
Speaker of the Honble House of Assembly—

Muhlenberg had just been elected Speaker of the Pennsylvania House of Representatives and was later the first Speaker of the U. S. House of Representatives. Peter Force Collection, Mss. 17,137, Series 8D, Ephraim Blaine Papers, Library of Congress.

Blaine to Thomas Sim Lee

Philadelphia 20th. Novr. 1780—.

Sir

I expected to have done myself the Honor of waiting upon your Excellency and Council at Annopolis but the wants of the Army in a great measure prevented, my Business was the Supplies of the Army and the requisitions of Congress from your State.

I take the liberty of Suggesting a few things to your Excellency and Council respecting securing the Supplies in due time which may be a real advantage to your State, as well the United States.

Our Army will never be properly fed until our Magazines afford a Barril of well cured Salt Provisions for every Man who is entitled to draw Rations to hold up the Idea of feeding them with fresh Beef is absurd and this Continent cannot furnish it. there remains no certain Method but by using every Exertion in the full Season, when Grass Beef and Pork are plenty, to procure as amply as our Exigencies may require.

A considerable quantity of Beef may be salted up in your State at the Magazines pointed out by His Excellency General Washington, and every advantage ought to be take by the State Commissioner in the Pork Season to secure as largely as possible of that usefull and necessary Article otherwise the Monopolizers & Engrossers will have it all bought up for other purposes than for the Army.

Larger Magazines ought to be collected at Elk or the Head of the Bay which will be convenient for either the northern or Southern Army as their Exigencies may require, this beg your Excellency and Council will pay attention to.

I wish to be informed who you have appointed Superintendant of your State Purchases in Order that I may be informed from him the Success your Agents have in executing their respective Purchases from month to month and give him such instructions respecting the Deposit of Provisions as I may receive from the Commander in Chief.

I have a quantity of Salt at the different Landings upon the Eastern shore which was deposited there for the Purpose of salting Pork last Fall, this Salt you may have the loan of until next Spring. Mr Wederstrandt of Wye River will render you an Account of it, to whom I have given directions to deliver it your Order and take receipts for the Quantity.

A number of Cattle forwarded by some of the Agents upon the Eastern shore are exceeding Ordinary, indeed Fifty of them in such a Condition that I think they will hardly survive the Winter. I have given directions to have them sold for the best Price they will bring.

The public is much indebted to your State for their Exertions last Year and I pray God the may pursue the same line of Conduct ensuing, without which it will be impossible to feed the Army.

I have the Honor to be Very respectfully Your
Excys. Most Obedient & Most Humble Servt.
Ephraim Blaine, C. G. of Purchases

Bernard Christian Steiner, ed. *Archives of Maryland, Journal and Correspondence of the Council of Maryland November 13, 1780 - November 13, 1781*, (Baltimore: Maryland Historical Society, 1927), 45:189-90.

Blaine to William Livingston

Philadelphia 22d. Novr. 1780—

Sir

I Expected to have done myself the Honor of waiting upon your Excellency and Council at Trenton, upon the Subject of supplies for the Army, and the requisitions from Congress upon your State for the ensuing years provisions. the Army will never be properly fed untill our public Magazines Afford a Barrel of well cured salt provision for every Man who is entitled to draw Rations, to hold up the Idea of feeding them regularly upon fresh Beef is absurd, and while there is so great a demand for Forage this Continent cannot furnish it—Now is the season for procuring beef and pork and I beg and request your Excy and Council immediately to adopt measures to take the advantage of it, a few Weeks delay'd will put it into the hands of Engrocers and Monopolizers—A great Number of which wou'd see the Army extirpated—provided they could answer their purposes and make a little money. I do not wish to find fault with the mode adopted by the respective States in procuring supplies but many are exceedingly difficient and none have come up to the requisition made by Congress—I have reason to believe many of the Contractors are exceedingly negligent in doing their duty and have experienced it last summer in your state indeed had little on none assistance from your Agents through the summer. many of the Commissioners who are appointed by the Legislature think themselves subject to no other order and pay little regard to the directions of the superintendant. if you can put confidence in your first Officers, a power by law ought to be given them to displace any Agent who is guilty of the least neglect of duty and appoint another in his place—this with a penalty might oblige many of them to do their duty which now neglect it—I have reason to believe a considerable part of the Army will be Cantooned between Curryells Ferry & North River and if provision is not made in due time they will Experience the same distress's going into Quarters they did last Winter—And the Inhabitants subject to plunder and Insult, which is not possible to prevent a Starving

Soldiary from commiting—And those are Misfortunes that cannot be avoided in any other way but by keeping up a regular supply of provisions—Let me intreat your Excy and Council to use means to procure meat while it is in your power, if neglected I dread the consequences will be the disolution of our Army—

By a late resolution of Congress the States are requested to make regular Monthly returns to the Board of War and my Office. I request your Excellency to give positive directions to your State superintendant to be very particular in making his returns to me—

I have the Honor to be with the greatest respect—
Your Excys Most Obedient Humble Servt.
Eph. Blaine CGP

Govr. Jerseys—

Peter Force Collection, Mss. 17,137, Series 8D, Ephraim Blaine Papers, Library of Congress.

Blaine to William Churchill Houston

Sir

it will take a Million of Dollars to pay my Contracts for beef to discharge the people who are in Town waiting two hundred and fifty thousand dollars will be Absolutely necessary exclusive those Granted Yesterday for which the [*sic*] have my Special Promises, you will greatly Oblige me by having a Warrant passed in my favour for the above Mentioned Sum—I am with Respect your Obdt. Hble Servt
Eph Blaine C.G.P

Thursday Morning 23rd: Novr. 1780
Honble Mr. Huston
Docketed: Letter from Ephm Blaine Esqr. to W. C. Houston Esqr. read 28d. Novr. 1780, referred to the Board of War.

Houston was a Delegate to Congress from New Jersey. Papers of the Continental Congress, Roll 182, i165. p385, National Archives.

Blaine to the Board of War

Philadelphia Novr. 24th. 1780—

Gentlemen

Having this Morning recd. sundry questions from you to which I beg leave to make the following answers, and intreat your immediate attention thereto, that means may be adopted to enable me to fulfill my engagements to those from whom I have purchased Cattle

Answer first—I do not consider myself vested with any Authority to purchase provisions without an Order of Congress, Board of War or the Commander in Chief.—

2ndly.—A resolution of Congress calling on the State of Pensylvania for One thousand Head of Cattle—the State declining the purchase and Congress furnishing me with an Order upon the Loan Office for Six hundred thousand Dollars, I thought myself justifiable in purchasing the Number first requested by Congress.—

3dly. I have had no Order to purchase any kind of provisions this three Months except the Cattle, and between four and Five hundred Bbls of Flour I am purchasing by Order of the Board of War—

4thly. The Amount of my purchases of Cattle is Six hundred and Eleven thousand Six hundred and Eight pounds 12/2. I have recd. Six hundred thousand Dollars, three of the persons from whom I have purchased, is to waite three months for One hundred and thirty thousand pounds which make the Ballance immediately wanted, Two hundred and fifty Six thousand Six hundred and Eight pounds some shillings—

The above answers and the inclosed Account will inform you the Number of Cattle I have purchased, and Amount in Continental money, also how they are disposed off, [sic] such sums as are due the persons who are in Town waiting I request

and intreat your Honble Board to enable me to discharge, I have given them assurances of ready pay and upon that principle have recd. their Cattle
I have the honor to be with the greatest Esteem
Gentlemen Your Most Obedient Humble Servt
E: Blaine

Honble Board of War—

> Peter Force Collection, Mss. 17,137, Series 8D, Ephraim Blaine Papers, Library of Congress.

Blaine to Frederick Augustus Conrad Muhlenberg

Philadelphia Novr. 28th. 1780—

Sir
I am ordered by his Excy. Genl. Washington to proceed to Clavarac up the North River to endeavour to lay up a small magazine of Salt provisions for the support of the Garrison at West point and its Dependancies through the Winter.—

I know the Commander in Chief has great hopes from the Exertions of this State in procuring the supplies required from them by Congress—and previous to my seting out wou'd wish to know what plan your Honble House is about to adopt that I may be enabled to give him information upon that subject a prospect of a temporary supply will give him great pleasure the quantity of Salt provisions required from this State will do little more than answer your own demands and if measures are not immediately taken you will find difficulty in procuring it and a very heavy additional expence Beef is now plenty cheap and can be easily purchased—To answer the demands in the state at the Established Magazines it will require the under mentioned quantity of Salt provisions to feed the Troops, up to the first of July next, allowing your Commissioners to furnish two days fresh meat in Seven—add to that the adition of your recruiting parties which I presume will be in difft. parts of the State—the Garrison at Fort Pitt has been distressed for meat all Summer and are now without a week's allowance for the whole Winter—

	Bbls. Beef	Do. fresh	
Pittsburgh	500	375	30,000
Carlisle	200		
	200	for the use of Northumberland County	
Lancaster	250		shou'd they have any disturbance
Reading			by the Indians next Spring—
Easton	100		
Phia.	1000		
Army—			

The Cantoonment of the Pennsylvania line with some others of the Army is at the Old Hutts near Morris-Town and in order to secure them a regular supply through the Winter a quantity of Provisions ought to be ordered into the Magazines at Easton and Trenton before the severity of the Winter this I beg may take the immediate Attention of your House without which they certainly cannot be regularly fed I have the Honor to be—

    Very respectfully Sir
     Your Most Obedt. Humble Servt.
      E. Blaine
Honble F. Mulinburgh—

> Peter Force Collection, Mss. 17,137, Series 8D, Ephraim Blaine Papers, Library of Congress.

Blaine to the Board of War

        Philadelphia Novr. 29th. 1780—

Gentlemen

Upon examining the System prepared by your Honble Board for the regulation of my department I wou'd beg leave to make the following remarks Vizt.—

The Commissary General to reside with the Main Army is impossible—was he a person newly appointed who had no connection with the Public heretofore, he can never settle his Accounts there—they are an Object of too much Consequence to keep with the Army, and I presume he cannot answer the purposes of his appointment without having an Office convenient to the Board of War and Treasury Board and there collect his Accounts of purchases and Returns for a final settlement and in his absence have a careful steady person to attend his Office and make application for such sums of money as may be necessary from time to time to discharge the Debts of his Department; the pay of this person ought to be more than the Clerks employed in public Offices.—

That the pay of the Commissary Genl. & his Deputy and allowance of provision and Forage shall be mentioned distinctly as also the pay and allowance of his Assistant and Clerks.—

Suppose the Resolve thus—

That the Commissary Genl. of purchases reside as much with the Main Army as the business of his Department will admit off [sic]—and that he keep his Office convenient to Congress and the Board of War there to Receive his Accounts & returns and settle the business of his Department.—

That he be allowed an Assistant to reside with the Main Army whose pay shall be Seventy five Dollars pr month, two Rations pr Day and Forage for one Horse—

The that Commissary Genl. of purchases Appoint a receiver of Cattle to remain with the main Army, whose business shall be to superintend the Butchers and deliver out the Cattle & Beef to the Brigade Commissarys, whose pay shall be [writer's blank] pr month One Ration of provisions pr day and forage for one Horse.—

That the Commissary Genl. of purchases make monthly reports to the Board of War and Commander in Chief the State of the Magazines, and every three Months make regular

Returns of all persons by him employ'd, Specifying for what time, at what place, and on what terms they are engaged—And of all provs. recd. from what state and the quantities delivered to the Issuing Commissarys' Specifying their Names and at what post—

The foregoing remarks you will please to consider if they appear to you reasonable and consistent with the public Inertest adopt them.—

I am Gentlemen &c—
E Blaine

Honble Board of War—

> Peter Force Collection, Mss. 17,137, Series 8D, Ephraim Blaine Papers, Library of Congress.

Blaine to Joseph Reed

Philada. 1st December, 1780.

Sir,

By a resolution of Congress passed last Tuesday all the Artificers in this State are ordered to Carlisle, and I am directed to prepare a Magazine of Salt Provisions for their Support. The quantity of Flour and Rye Spirits which you have directed the Commissioners of that County to Purchase will be sufficient for their Consumption, but Meat will be immediately wanting; have therefore to request your Excellency & Council not only to make Provision for that Post, but add two hundred Barrels as a Magazine for the use of Northumberland County in case the Indians should make any attempt upon the Frontier settlements.

Underneath you have an Estimate of the quantity of Provisions necessary for the State Consumption until the 1st of July next—this ought immediately to be procured while Beef is plenty; if delayed it will cost the State one third more.

Your Excellency will see the necessity of the measure, and I make no doubt will adopt Ways & means to answer the Demand.

I have the Honor to be very respectfully
Your Excellencies most Obedt servt,
Eph. Blaine C. G. P.

Govr. Reed

Estimate of Provisions necessary for the Consumption of the Posts in this State.

Posts.	Pounds fresh Beef for sixty Days.	Bbls salt Provisions for 152 Days.
Philadelphia,	60,000	760
Pittsburgh, &c.	27,000	342
Carlisle,	12,000	152
ditto for Cumberland		200
Lancaster,	15,000	190
Reading,		50
Easton,	6,000	76
	120,000	1,770

Commencing the 1st Instant and ending 30 June, 1781.
Philada. 1 December, 1780

N. B. The Consumption at the Post of Carlisle will be one half more than mentioned above, owing the the Artificers being Order'd there from Philada. since the Estimate was made.

His Excellency Joseph Reed, Enquire, Present. [sic]

The letterbook copy dated November 30, the letter refers only to a "Magazine of provisions" and "you have directed the Commissioners of that County to Purchase will be insufficient for their consumption" Samuel Hazard, ed., *Pennsylvania Archives*, 1st. series vol. 8 (Philadelphia: Joseph Severns, 1853), 630-31.

Blaine to Robert Forsyth

Philadelphia 2d. December 1780—

Sir

Herewith you will receive your appointment as Deputy Commissary of purchases for the Southern department the new system under which you Act points out your line of duty the exertitions [sic] of the States in procuring supplies you are well acquainted with, and the tedious manner in which they furnish—therefore your Orders cannot be to explicite [sic] and pressing and all your applications ought to be early, you will be very particular in making monthly Returns to the Commanding Officer of the Department and me, and do not attempt to purchase or order the purchase of any Article without a written order from the Officer Commanding—

You will extend your views to laying up as large Magazines of Beef & pork as you possibly can procure from the Southern States, and press the Legislative and executive authorities to be punctual in complying with the requisitions of Congress, the fresh Beef required you will demand in Monthly proportions as the Exigencies of the Army may require and write in the most positive terms to the States to procure their quota's required in due time without which the Army cannot be regularly supplied

I hope the Southern State [sic] will give you a power of suspending such of their Agents as are not punctual in furnishing the supplies required, indeed I cou'd wish you to have the appointment of new ones on whose Activity you could rely for supplying the Troops, Pork is an Article of the greatest consequence get all you can—

Pray let your delay be as short here as possible and proceed with all expedition to the Southern Army make your necessary arrangements and take the directions of Genl. Greene in establishing your Magazines. Make them as few as possible you can provided they are in places of safety—I request your particular attention to making Monthly Returns and giving me every Information respecting your Department, & remain—
with much Esteem Sir Your
Most Obedient Humble Servt.
E: Blaine

Major Forsyth—

NB Those whom you were obliged to employ at principal places of deposite of provisions and who had no advantage of Commissions pay them the sums allowed assistants but no Rations or forage, make them as few as possible—
Yours & ca. E: Blaine C:G:P

Sir

Agreeable to a resolution of Congress passed the 30th. Novr. last I do hereby appoint you Deputy Commissary General of Purchases for the Southern Department, you are to pay due attention to the Orders of the Commanding Officer of the Southern army, and be very particular in the duties of your Department agreeable to said resolution and the Instructions herewith given you—

Given under my had [*sic*] at Philadelphia this 4th. day Decr. 1780
E: Blaine C:P: P

Major Forsyth—

Blaine to the Treasury Board

Philadelphia 4th. Decr. 1780—
Gentlemen
    I shall be absent some time from this City, and previous to my return there may be sundry Applications for money due upon settlement of Accounts in my Office, I leave the Bearer Mr. George Morton to attend to that business, any application from him you will consider as from me, upon settlement of Major Forsyths Account you will please to grant him an Order for the Ballance and add two hundred and Fifty Thousand Dollars, twice that sum being due for purchases made by his Agents since his Departure from North Carolina.—
    I have the honor to be with the greatest respect
        Gentlemen Your Most Obedient Humble Servt.
           Eph. Blaine
                Commisary General of Purchases
Honble the Treasury Board

> Papers of the Continental Congress, M247, r95, i78, v9, p413, National Archives.

Blaine to the Board of War

Philadelphia 4th. Decr. 1780—
Gentlemen
    Your favor inclosing the resolutions of Congress Ordering the Artificers in the State of Pennsylvania to Carlisle I received, and observe the Contents—I can adopt no measure to furnish Provisions at that post but by application to the State, I have wrote the President in Council and Assembly pressingly upon that Subject and have laid before them an Estimate of the supplies necessary for that and the sundry other posts in this State, and beged of them to make such provision as wou'd answer those demands, it lays with them to Execute and I doubt their Commissioners will not facilitate the

necessary purchases in due time—I have the honor to be very respectfully—
> Gentlemen Your Most Obedt. Humble Servt.
> E. Blaine

Honble Board of War

> Peter Force Collection, Mss. 17,137, Series 8D, Ephraim Blaine Papers, Library of Congress.

Blaine to Thomas Sim Lee

Philadelphia December 8, 1780

Sir

The distresses of the Army for want of Bread and my great fears respecting their present & future supply will sufficiently Appologize for my troubling your Excellency & Council so often with the Business of my Department.

The depreciated State of our Currency, the Spirit of Monopoly which so generally prevails with mankind, & the temper of the Farmers to hold back from Sale such produce as they have to spare, is very alarming and makes me dread a Disolution of the Army for want of Bread, indeed I despair of being able to procure one third of the quantity demanded for the ensuing Years Supply on any terms without the aid of the Legislative Authorities, and the most vigorous measures adopted to secure every Bushel of Wheat & Barrel of Flour either in the Speculators or Millers Possession & procuring the residue which is to spare. The Millers & Speculators in your State have I presume bought up considerable Quantities, I wish it could be secured and means taken to stop their future purchases while the wants of the Army are so great   As the Season is now at hand in which the Navigation of Chesepeak & Delaware will be obstructed with Ice & cut off all Communication of Supplies by Water which is the only easy mode of transporting Provisions towards Camp.

I have some time ago given directions to my Assistants in your & Delaware State, to rise their utmost exertions to forward every ounce of Flour in their Possession before the 20th Instant & have to request your Excellency & Council to order the State Commissioners which were appointed last Spring & this Fall, to deliver over to my Assistants all Flour which remains in their Possession, who have directions to forward the same, Mr Dallam has been lately delivering Mr Smith (Agent for the French Consul) a considerable quantity of Flour which I expected, it is very hard that his Magazines should be fill'd with Flour when I can assure your Excellency our Army has been seven Days without Bread, and preparing to go into Winter Quarters with empty Magazines, the Idea distresses me exceedingly. Your Excellency & Council will please to take these matters into your most serious Consideration & adopt such measures as will enable my Assistants to obtain all the spare Flour in State else the Army will undoubtedly Suffer. I was happy when at Annapolis in finding your Honourable Assembly disposed to render every Aid to procure the quota of Flour & to detect all kind of Monopoly of Provisions, which will be of infinite service to the public

Eph. Blaine C.G.P.

> Bernard Christian Steiner, ed. *Archives of Maryland, Journal and Correspondence of the Council of Maryland, 1779-1780,* (Baltimore: Maryland Historical Society, 1924), 43: 381-382.

Morton to Donaldson Yeates

Philadelphia Decr. 8th. 1780—

Sir

Your favor to Col Blaine of the 5th. Instant came safe to hand with Forty three Head of Cattle for which you have a rect. inclosed, and also for One hundred and Eighty four Head recd. in October last, I laid a state of the Cattle before the Board of

War and they have Ordered Sale to be made of such as are unfit for present use

            I am Sir Obedt. Servt.
            Geo: Morton for Colo. E: Blaine C:G:P
Colo. Yates

> Yeates was a Deputy Quartermaster General at the Head of Elk, Maryland. Peter Force Collection, Mss. 17,137, Series 8D, Ephraim Blaine Papers, Library of Congress.

Morton to the Board of War

                                        Philadelphia Decr.
Gentlemen

Mr. Donaldson Yates sent up yesterday forty three head of Cattle in part of the requisition of Congress 21st. September last for 500 head Nt Catt—those Cattle Mr. Kitts reports are by no means fit to Slaughter nor will they answer to keep through the Winter (if forage could be procured for that purpose) being composed of Bulls Old Cows and two Year Old Stears all of them small—A Number of Cattle recd. on the same Acc before Colo. Blaine wou'd not give a rect. for but had them put in pasture and wrote to the Agent of the State of Maryland respecting them; Mr. Yates insists upon a rect. for the Cattle—I therefore request that your Honble Board wou'd be pleased to give me Orders for the disposal of them, in such manner as you may think proper—

            I have the Honor to be
                Your Most Obedient Servt.
                      Geo: Morton

Honble Board of War—

> This appears beetween letters of December 8 and December 9. Peter Force Collection, Mss. 17,137, Series 8D, Ephraim Blaine Papers, Library of Congress.

Morton to Jacob Morgan

Philadelphia 9th. December 1780

Sir

There is not more salt in the Magazine at this place than will serve to Salt the Beef now killing for three Days—must therefore request that you will adopt the most Speedy measures in you power to through [*sic*] into the Magazine a quantity of that necessary Article in part of the Quota of this State—the delay of but a very few days may be a considerable loss to the public—and we have no prospect of a supply from any other quarter—

I am for E: Blaine Esqr.
   Your Most Obedt. Servt.
    Geo: Morton

Colo. Jacob Morgan

> Peter Force Collection, Mss. 17,137, Series 8D, Ephraim Blaine Papers, Library of Congress.

Morton to Jacob Morgan

Philadelphia December 9th. 1780

Sir

One hundred and Fifty Bushells of Salt will be sufficient with what is now in Store to salt in bulk what Beef may be killed here in the course of Ten days—Three or four hundred Bushells ought to be immediately sent to Carlisle in Order to be forwarded from thence to Fort Pitt, before the Roads are impassible, for the purpose of laying in Magazine [*sic*] of Salt provisions for the consumption of the Troops stationed there 'till July next—I shall advise you when a further quantity will be wanting at this place and remain—

   Your Obedt. Servt. Geo: Morton

P. S rum is much wantg for the Butchers packers &ca.
Colo. Jacob Morgan—

> Peter Force Collection, Mss. 17,137, Series 8D, Ephraim Blaine Papers, Library of Congress.

Morton to Udny Hay

Philadelphia December 9th. 1780—

Sir

Major Hale will deliver you two Warrants for Three Hundred Twenty three thousand Nine hundred & Five Dollars each, one on Nathl. Appleton Esqr. C: L: Office Massachussits Bay, and the other on Abraham Yeates Esqr. C: L: Office State of New York—These Warrants were granted for the express purpose of paying Major Hale and Mr. T Donnel the sum due the former is Two hundred forty One thousand and Ten and Four hundre [sic] Six Thousand Eight hundred Dollars to the latter. this money must not by any means be appropriated to any other use you will therefore use your best endeavours to procure it for the Gentlemen for whom it is intended—Mr. Donnel is not in Town but suppose he will wait upon you as soon as he is informed of this Matter—

I am &ca for Colo. E: Blaine
Your Most Obdt. Servt.
Geo: Morton

Colo. U. Hay A S New York—

> Peter Force Collection, Mss. 17,137, Series 8D, Ephraim Blaine Papers, Library of Congress.

Morton to Joseph Reed

Philada., 11th December, 1780.

Sir

Your favour of the 9th. Instant to Col. Blaine I received late in the Afternoon, and have done every thing in my power to give your Excellency the best information on the subject of it, which you will find in the inclosed Estimate. Sussex County was part of Colonel Hooper's district, therefore part of the Sum affixed to his name may be due to Persons in the State of Jersey.

I have the Honor to be Your Excellency's
most Obedt & most Hble. servt,
Geo: Morton, for
E: Blaine, Esqr., C. G. of Ps.

Directed, Public Service,
His Excellency Joseph Reed, Esquire, Present.

> Samuel Hazard, ed., *Pennsylvania Archives*, 1st. series vol. 8 (Philadelphia: Joseph Severns, 1853), 646.

Morton to Blaine

Philadelphia 12th. December 1780

Dr. Sir

Your favor of the 7th. I recd. this Day and Observe the Contents, have given Mr. Kitts directions about the Beef and tongues for Mrs. Mathews; the Cattle shall be forwarded to Pitts-town agreeable to your Orders—Mr. Yeates sent up Forty three head of Cattle last week on Acct. of the State of Maryland and worse if possible than any we have received heretofore—Mr. Kitts refused to make an estimate on them, and I was under the necessity of representing them to the Board of War—their Orders was, that such as were not fit for present use shou'd be Sold. shall Advertise tomorrow and appoint a day of Sale as soon after as convenient—Mr. Hiltzheimer has refused to deliver any forage on your A/c, have therefore defered geting your Mare from Grovers 'till some other provision can be made for her—

Mr. Ramsay has recd. two hundred Bbls. of Flour from Smith and Matthews—Eighty six of which was forwarded to Trenton yesterday, the remainder will follow directly. Shall wait upon Colo. Hazelwood on the Subject of Flour; I made an Application to Colo. Morgan a few days since for salt for the Beef kiling here and also for four hundred Bushells to be sent to Carlisle for Pittsburgh &c. he has promised to comply immediately with the Demand—

Talbot, Kiersly, Eliot &ca. &ca. are still unpaid not a Shilling from any quarter since your departure—Yes this Morning [*sic*] Mr. Hilligas has recd. a Million and a half from the Eastward, but it is so inadequate to the demands against him that he says he will report it to the Treasury and take their Orders for the disposal—I shall sue for your proportion and send the Virginians to make a poor Mouth in support of it—Mr. Hollingsworth is very uneasy about his Money—no Bills yet put into the hands of Mr Smith—Jack shall be disposed off [*sic*] agreeable to your directions—

   remain Sir Your Most Obt. Servt.
    Geo: Morton

Colo. Blaine—

<small>Peter Force Collection, Mss. 17,137, Series 8D, Ephraim Blaine Papers, Library of Congress.</small>

Morton to the Treasury Board

    Philadelphia 13th. December 1780

Gentlemen

 I should be sorry to give you unnecessary trouble but the importunities of a Number of people from whom Colo. Blaine has purchased Cattle are so constant and pressing that the present application is unavoidable.—

 The inclosed letter from Colo. Brodhead will evince the necessity of enabling Mr. Elliot to comply with his Contract to deliver One hundred head of Cattle at Fort pitt—to accomplish this he only wishes to receive the Ballance due him for One hundred and twenty five head delivered here pr estimate laid before your Honble Board—Three persons from Virginia and Maryland who furnished Cattle have been waiting in town near a Month, the greatest part of the time on public Expence—Mr. Kiersly who representation [sic] you will receive herewith, has delivd. [writer's blank] Head of Cattle since his estimate was made Amounting to—[writer's blank] I make no doubt by you [sic] will consider his disagreeable situation—

    I was informed yesterday by Mr. Hilligas that he has recd. a sum of money from the Eastward, but it is so inadequate to the demands against him he intends to take your Orders for the disposal—if your Honble Board would be pleased to direct that Colo. Blaine shou'd be paid the Amount of his Warrant (Four hundred and Seventy thousand Dollars) and enable Mr. Smith to pay the whole or part of the Warrants on him—it wou'd in some measure stop the Clamour of his numerous Creditors—he has not yet received any part of the Warrant on the Managers of the lottery Office

                    I have the Honor to be Your Most
                          Obedient Humble Servt.
                            Geo: Morton for
                                  E: Blaine Esqr. C: G: P.

Honble Treasury Board

    Peter Force Collection, Mss. 17,137, Series 8D, Ephraim Blaine Papers, Library of Congress.

Morton to the Treasury Board

                          Philadelphia 14th. December 1780
Gentlemen

    The bearer Capt. Mc.Connel will deliver you a Warrant drawn on the supreme Executive Council of this State the 16th. November last for Two hundred and Sixty Eight thousand and Forty 30/90 Dollars for the purpose of paying for rum seized at

Camp and also a letter from his Excy. the president advising that the present State of the Treasury does not admit answering it if there were no other Objections—Capt. Mc.Connel and the other persons from whom the Liquor was taken will be thankfull to your Honble Board if you can advise some other mode of payment—
   I have the Honor to be for Colo. Blaine
    Your Most Obedt. Servt.
     Geo: Morton

Honble Treasury Board—

  Peter Force Collection, Mss. 17,137, Series 8D, Ephraim Blaine Papers, Library of Congress.

Morton to Ezekiel Forman

      Philadelphia December 22d. 1780—
Sir
 Your favor of the 18th. to Colo. Blaine came to hand and also a Letter from Colo. Butler, in answer thereto must inform you that by a late regulation of Congress for the Commissary General of purchases Department—he is not authorised to make any purchases whatever without a Special order from Congress, the Board of War or Commander in Chief—nor is he allowed to appoint any Assistant, except one Deputy with the Southern, and an Assistant with the Main Army, you are consequently to depend entirely upon the state Commissioners for Supplies and make application to such as are most convenient to you for what provisions you may stand in need of from time to time.—
 Colo. Blaine has already furnished the Council with an Estimate of provisions necessary for the Consumption of your Post and I hope they will take measures to supply you
  I am Sir Your Obedt. Servt.

Mr. Forman—

Peter Force Collection, Mss. 17,137, Series 8D, Ephraim Blaine Papers, Library of Congress.

Blaine to Unidentified, Probably Noah Emory

New Windsor, 25th Decr. 1780

Sir,

Your favour of the 16th, ultimoe Came safe to hand Enclosing a return of State supplies but very imperfect—you will be very particular in preparing your Accts. for a final settlement by the first of next month, the new Arangement of the Quarter Master and Commissary's departments orders the Receival and forwarding of all public Stores, to be perform'd by the Store Keepers appointed by the Quarter Master Genl.—

You Will Obtain monthly return of all supplies furnished by your state and be very particular in mentioning the Quantity Quality, estimation and price of each Article so Received and delivered, which form into One General Account, which must be Accompanied with Certificates of the estimation, and Receipts for delivery.—and where unavoidable losses has happened depositions on Oath must be produced as Vouchers, mentioning the cause why it was so—

make out a General Account of your Expenditures of money, regularly supported with Vouchers which are to be numbered & properly [   ]ed as you enter them, and at the Bottom of your Account Current enter your own pay at seventy five dollars pr month the new money which is the sum allowd by Congress from the time of you appointment untill the time you finish your Account which request may be about the fifteenth of January, and forward them to me by some careful person without a moments delay, in Order that I may present them to Congress for and obtain money or an Order for the Ballance due you (Request you not to neglect this business under any pretence whatever,) any supplies which may be on hand you will attend to see it forwarded with all Possible dispatch—what cattle you forward see that proper measures are adopted to provide them with the

Necessary forage, I wish to here [sic] from you by Return of the Express,

   and remain with much Reguard Dr. Sir.
    Your Most Obdt. Servt.
     Eph. Blaine C.G.ofP.

Mr. [Emory]

  Misc. Bd. 1780 December 25, Massachusetts Historical Society.

Morton to Blaine

         26 December 1780

Dear Sir

 Your two favours of the 16th. Instant came to hand yesterday and that of the 13th. (by some Accident at the Post Office) I did not receive till this morning otherwise the memorandums inclosed Should have been in forwardness by this time—two Bbls Spirits, the Muscovada Sugar Loaf Sugar Certificates and Pipe of Wine were forwarded a week since & the other Articles shall follow as soon as possible—

 I wrote you the 12th. since which I have received the Amt. of the two Warrants on Mr. Smith—that Sum has enabled me to pay off Talbot Kersley Faw Hollingsworth &c. and to advance Mr. Elliott Seventy Odd thousand Pounds to compleat his Contract for Cattle to be delivered at Fort Pitt—

 I have not had time Since the receipt of your Letters to collect the Situation of the Beef—the Cattle are all Slaughtered and the Salters and packers have been constantly at Work—The post hour is near at hand must therefore conclude with Assurance that every Information I can obtain respectg Supplies shall be transmitted you in the course of the week of Capt Craig or sooner is Oppy Serves—

   I am Sir Yours &c G. M.

Mr. Hillegas got Orders from Congress to pay a Warrant in favr. of Col. Pickering in preference to yours— Col. Blaine

Peter Force Collection, Mss. 17,137, Series 8D, Ephraim Blaine Papers, Library of Congress.

Blaine to Jabez Hatch

New Windsor 27th Decr. 1780

Sir

The new arrangement of the Quarter Master and Commissary generals departments, throw that part of duty and receiveing and forwarding all State Supplies upon the Quarter Master General his deputies & Assistants—have therefore to request your close attention to the undermentiond Instructions in Order to detect all attempts of imposition and do justice to the United States—In the first place live Cattle which is an Article of so much Consequence to the public, are generally deliver'd in droves by the State Agents, to the person who is appointed to receive them, for which he give a receipt for the number of Cattle & the Estimated weight of beef; great Errors are daily committed in this business, though every Method I have been capable of has been used to prevent it by haveing person [sic] appointed upon Oath to apprize, but from a General Disposition of rather doing justice to individuals than the public, and in some cases want of knowledge all estimates fall amazeingly short. to prevent which as much as possible, you must fix upon persons of Probity who are competant Judges, who you will pay by the day while Employed they ought to live near where the Cattle are to be delivered, whose duty shall be carefully to Inspect all Cattle so delivered rejecting such are not fit for use, and with a person appointed by the State Agent to Estimate the neat weight of beef upon Oath shou'd they disagree in Opinion a Third person to be chozen as an Umphire, who shall determin the weight—those Cattle to be forwarded to the place of consumption under the directions of a carefull drover, who is to bring duplicate invoices with him one to be deliver'd the receiver of Cattle with the army or the person at the post where delivered, and the other returned with his receipt for the number and Estimate weight as your Voucher for delivery, no Cattle to be receiv'd or forwarded, without being properly branded—I have reason for doubting some of the drovers for selling and Exchanging Cattle upon the road—in order to prevent it, none ought to be intrusted but honest carefull men, and all their returns of Lost Cattle made upon Oath—precaution must be taken to Establish necessary Magazines of forage upon the Communication to this place for the support of such Cattle as you may forward.

All other stores ought to be receipted for Expressly specifying the Quality & Quantity, and forwarded as above directed, mentioning the deficiency if any that the person who had care of transporting may be charged with the damage and the same stop'd out of his pay Or Certificate—great punctuallity must be observed in forwarding the supplies without which the army will undoubtedly starve.

Be particular in makeing me Monthly returns of all supplies receiv'd from each State, specifying the quantity forwarded, to what post, and what remains on hand—The pay of drovers and each person as you are Obliged to employ in my department, must be in the new money, and you will engage them upon the lowest and most reasonable terms you possibly can.

The places pointed out by his Excellency General Washington for depositing the provisions in your district you have inclosed. the live Cattle demanded from the State of New Hampshire woud wish delivered at the most convenient place upon the Verge of the state to be forwarded here, and all live Cattle in the State of Massachusetts bay at Springfield, or Great Barrington, as may best suit the public—

The State of Rhode Island will have Little more than will equal their own Consumption, all their State supplies to be delivered at Providence—

I shall be happy in Corosponding with you, and beg every information you possibly can give respecting my Department I remain with great respect Sir—
  Your Most Odbt Huble. Servt.
    Eph Blaine C G P—
(Copy)
Colo Hatch

> Hatch was Deputy Quartermaster General at Boston. Mss 9004, Shepley, v. 8, p. 150, Rhode Island Historical Society.

Morton to Jacob Morgan

        Philada: 27 December 1780
Sir
 I am informed by Letter from Col. Blaine at Head Quarters that the Army have been several Days upon half Allowance of Bread and that his chief dependence for that necessary Article was upon the resources of this State and the Exertions of the Commissioners in forwarding an Ample Supply of Flour before we are deprived of the Advantage of Water Transportation—
 There should be at least a Supply for two months at Camp and in the Magazine at Trenton before the frost impedes the Navigation of the Delaware and I make no doubt but you will take the most speedy measures in your power for that purpose—* If you will be kind enough to inform me respectg. your prospects I will take the Earliest Opportunity to transmit them to Col Blaine,
   for whom I am Your Obt Servt
    Geo: Morton

P-S- Is there any Flour at or on the way to Easton—
 *There is also wanting two Hhds of good Spirits for Head Quarters—I shall be sending a number of small Articles

for the use of His Excellencies Family on Saturday and would wish to have the Spirits go by the same Conveyance—

Col. Jacob Morgan—Supt. Purchasers—

> Peter Force Collection, Mss. 17,137, Series 8D, Ephraim Blaine Papers, Library of Congress.

Blaine to Samuel Huntington

New Windsor 31st. Decr. 1780

Sir,

I find there will be great difficulty in supplying the troops at West Point and the Other Cantoonments of the army in this neighbourhood through the winter—our Magazines of beef do not exceed seven days supply exclusive of six hundred head of cattle which I have salted down in bulk one half in the Garison and the residue at different posts convenient to the troops—we have no flour, the army have been several days upon half allowance, I have Just been informd six or seven hundred Barrels are at Ringwood but there is not teams to bring it all forward—the Quantity of cattle I expected from the Eastward will fall considerable short—I have wrote the Executive of New Hampshire, Massachusetts Bay, and Conecticutt, to adopt every possible means of procuring the weekly supplies which I have Required, and assured them a neglect of which will be a dissolution of the army—as this Country do not appear to have any Resources or means of relief shou'd we be necessitated.—

The Pennsylvania line at Morris Town must be supplied with meat from Jersey and Pennsylvania, and our princaple dependance of Flour through the winter must be from Pennsylvania. If our wants will admit, will admit, I coud wish that part of the State Quoto to be delivered at Philadelphia, with the Flour demanded from the State of Deleware and One third of the Maryland Quota, to be reserved as a Magazine for next Summer and all we want for winter support including the requisitions from this state to be drawn from Easton that being most Convenient—I have wrote his Excellency Govr. Reed upon that subject and Requested him to press the Commissioners of the County of Northampton, Berks, Lancaster, and York to use every possible exertion in procuring their Quotas of Flour and Delivering it in the Magazine at Easton. and I hope there is not the least doubt but the [sic] will be able to equal our Cunsumption—I shall not return to Philadelphia untill I have the state Provisions in such a train as will afford a regular supply for the army—General Heath who now Commands at West Point is an exceeding frugal Officer and shows the greatest desire of adopting every measure which may save the issue of Provisions, there is no place of Entertainment in the neighbourhood of the Garison which subjects him to great expence—he has applied to me for some little necessaries for the use of his table—I inform'd him I could not procure those Articles he wanted without an order from Congress that I shou'd write them and hoped in a few days to have an answer, which I beg your Excellency to favour me with by the first Opportunity

Permit me through your Excellency to return Congress my sincear thanks for their favourable Opinion of my Past conduct and reapointing me to the office of Commissary General of purchases—and assure them I shall ever think myselfe happy if by my exertions I can render them and my Country any service—I have been in their Employ since June 1776 and have never been anxious about my saliry, but I find this mode of conduct will not do and that I cannot support my selfe and family without great injury to my private interest. I look upon my selfe an Oeconomist and have a regular Account of the sums which I have expended in the execution of my duty this year to lay before Congress, in adition to which I have to add three thousand five hundred pounds loss upon Horses which leaves very trifling of the years pay—the expence of every necessary of life in travelling is double in hard money what it was in the years 1776 and 77, and what it may be in the new Emissions, time will prove—in the arangement of my department I can git no persons agreable to serve in the principle Employments, <u>for the saliries allowed</u>. Major Forsyth has agreed to supperintend the southern District, but in expectation of having a Compensation for his service sufficient for his support—my Assistant at Camp has left me, and Mr. Geo. Morton the young man to whom I intrust my whole business when absent, and who has charge of receiving and Paying away all public money, which passes through my Office has given me notice to engage another—that he cannot support himselfe upon the monthly pay allowd him—I have found him very faithful and if I continue in the Service, wish not to part with him—I beg Congress to allow such pay in Specia or Other money equivalent as will enable me to engage those persons to Continue—

As to my duty and Office it is the most perplexed and disagreeable of any in your Service, I am envied by many who suppose from my appointment I am making a fortune—on the Other hand the delays daily commited by the State agents in forwarding supplies causes a scarcity of Provisions and altho I have taken every precation and given the most pointed instructions, I am condemn'd without enquiry by three fourths of the army as being the cause—These circumstances make the Business very disagreable to men of any spirit, indeed I have Often wished I had never engaged in it—

I am expos'd to a very great Expence in entertaining those people who come after me upon business and who cannot be supplied else where and indeed they are Justly entitled to it. being Often Obliged to return without a shilling in there pockets.

those expenditures when colected from the Commissaries Books and Otherwise yearly settled, will amount to a very great sum—have therefore to Inform your

Excellency, that unless Congress make good my saliry in Specia or Other money Equivalent (for the last year and this) and allow all reasonable traveling expenciss when on public duty, with a daily allowance of six rations and forage for four Horses (a number necessary to Execute the duty) I cannot continue in the Service without Injury to myself, I am confident my proposals are Reasonable and will appear so to any person who Knows the Expense of traveling at this day—if Congress approve I shall continue to render the public every service in my power. Otherwise request them to accept of this as my Resignation and appoint another—I will Continue here untill I have a Certainty of regular supplies coming in from the different states for the support of the army—and have the honor to be, very Respectfully
    Your Excellency's Most Obdt.
     and very Hble Servt.
      Eph. Blaine C.G.P

The Honble. Saml. Huntington

Addressed: Public Service, His Excellency Samuel Huntington Esquire, President of Congress
Noted: Letter from E Blaine
New Windsor Decr. 31. 1780
Referred to Mr. Montgomery, Mr. Clarke, Mr. Duane.
   Mr. Adams, Mr. Varnum

   Papers of the Continental Congress, r182, i165, p331-35, National Archives.

Morton to Benjamin Stoddert

         Philada. 4 January 1781
Sir
  Your favor of the present respecting the Garrison of Fort-Pitt I recd. and have to inform you that One hundred hd. of

Cattle (for which Col. Blaine has contracted are now in motion, and I hope will soon be deliver'd for the relief of that Post—

The necessary Application to the Superintendent of Purchasers of this State, for Salt has been made & some part of that Article is already forwarded—
<pre>   I am Sir Yours &c.
                    G: Morton</pre>

Capt. B. Stoddart Secy B War—

> Peter Force Collection, Mss. 17,137, Series 8D, Ephraim Blaine Papers, Library of Congress.

Blaine to Mr. Munell

Sir,

Please to deliver to my boy what grain you can spare I wll Obtain you a Rect. from the forage Master also the Butter and what ever else you have procured.

5th. Jany. 1781   Your Hble Servt.
<pre>   Eph Blaine C.G.P</pre>
Mr. Munell [S]: A

On the reverse: Delivered for the use within Mentioned Twelve Bushells of Buck wheat Januy. 5

> Morristown National Historical Park, Lloyd W. Smith Collection, Box 152, Box152.

Morton to Jacob Morgan

<pre>   Philada: 8 January 1781</pre>
Sir

There is a Hhd of Rum much wanted for the use of the Continental Schooners. I beg you will give Capt. Hazelwood Orders to Purchase & send to the Issg. Store one or two Hhds for that purpose as they cannot do without it at this Season of the Year—

                I am Sir Your Obt Servt.
                      Geo: Morton

Col. Jacob Morgan—

> Peter Force Collection, Mss. 17,137, Series 8D, Ephraim Blaine Papers, Library of Congress.

Blaine to George Clinton

                      New Windsor 10th January 1781.

Sir,

I presume your Excellency has rec'd the requisition of Congress some time ago for the supplies of our army this year, and that means is adopted by your legislature to procure them in due time. His Excellency General Washington has pointed out the places of deposit in each state. The quantity of Provisions required by your State is sixteen thousand barrels of Flour; two thousand eight hundred Barrels of beef; one thousand five hundred barrels of Pork; 441½ hundreds weight of stalled beef; and thirteen hundred and twenty hundred weight of Grass beef for next summer's use; all the salt provisions and four thousand Barrels of Flour to be delivered this month, the stalled beef subject to my order as well the grass beef which is to be delivered next summer; wou'd wish the stall'd beef delivered in the following proportions viz: one fourth part to be delivered the tenth of February; one other the 10th of March; one the 10th of April; and the residue the 10th of May.

      Congress have pointed out the periods in which the flour is to be delivered. I need not mention to your Excellency the great punctuallity there ought to be observed by the state agents in procuring and delivering the supplies required, and the uneasiness the want of one day's provisions occasions with the soldiery, to prevent which, I beg that your executive and

Legislature may give full and ample powers to your agent to obtain the supplies required, and that your Excellency will give very pressing and pointed Instructions for the execution thereof, without which it will not be in my power to keep up a regular supply for the Army. Sundry applications have been made to me by the Inhabitants of this state and persons from others to exchange flour, which if I adopted wou'd undoubtedly be an advantage to the public, but be attended with difficulty to your State, or at least prevent them from furnishing their Quoto of Flour, and not add a single Barrel to our magazine. I should think myself happy if consistant with my duty and the public interest I cou'd render your State any service, but wou'd beg leave to mention, that if persons are admited to exchange or barter flour before the state supply is furnished, it will not be in the power of your agent to comply with his orders; was I to encourage the exchange I could undoubtedly engross all the spare flour in the State in the course of three weeks. If the Quantity required was nearly furnished, I wou'd undertake to Exchange a Considerable Parcel at least a sufficiency for the magazine at West Point, but shall decline any encouragement whatever untill I have your opinion fully upon that subject. The new arrangement of the Quarter Master and Commissary Genl. Departments, orders the receival and forwarding of all Public Stores to and from the places of deposit to be performed by the deputy Quarter Master or his store keeper. I shall beg the favour of an answer by first Opportunity and have to honor to
be, very respectfully, your Excellency's
most Obed't and most H'ble Serv't
Eph. Blaine, C. G. P.

Gov'r Clinton.

Public Papers of George Clinton, First Governor of New York vol. 6. (Albany: State of New York, 1902; reprint, New York: AMS Press, 1973), 558-60.

Morton to the Treasury Board

        Philadelphia 11th. January 1781—
Gentlemen
  You will receive herewith an Estimate of Rum seized by Capt. Craig in September last for the use of the Army, and Mr. John Taggarts Account and Contract with Udney Hay Esqr. for rum delivered for the Garrison at West Point Amounting to Nine hundred five thousand One hundred and Sixty One and 46/90 of a Dollar.—Mr. Daniel Lyons A/c is now included with the Accounts of those Gentlemen in whose favor the Warrant was Issued on the—Supreme Executive Council of this State, as the Circumstances of the seizure of his Liquor were similar to theirs—you will also receive a letter from Capt. Mc.Connel and others to Colo. Blaine—a resolution of Congress of the 4th. Instant and the Warrant on the State of New-Jersey indorsed payable to John Taggart and Daniel Lyon which Mr. Taggart has refused to accept as inadequate to his just demands.—
  Agreeable to the resolution of Congress before mentioned the Accounts are new modelled the propriety of which and mode of payment I submit to the Judgment of your Honble Board and am—
       Gentlemen Your Most Obedt. Humble
         Geo: Morton
Honl. Board Treasury

Peter Force Collection, Mss. 17,137, Series 8D, Ephraim Blaine Papers, Library of Congress.

Morton to the Treasury Board

Gentn.
  Agreeable to an Order from Mr: Joseph Donnel I have given up Col. Hays Certificate for Rum purchased for the Garrison at West point—The Acct. which will be handed you

herewith Amounts to 700.035 Dollars out of which he is to receive from Col. Hay 406.800 Dollars as his part of two Warrts. dated the 9th: Ult. on the L Offices in the States of Massachussets Bay & New-York—for the purpose of paying him & Major Hale—
    I have the Honor to be Yours &c
    Geo: Morton for E: Blaine Esqr.

Honorable Treasury Board

> Peter Force Collection, Mss. 17,137, Series 8D, Ephraim Blaine Papers, Library of Congress.

Blaine to Thomas Sim Lee

    Head Quarters New Windsor January 18, 1781

I presume your Excellency has received the requisitions of Congress a considerable time ago for the supplies of our army this year—and that means have been adopted by your Legislature to procure them in due time. Congress have pointed out the proportions of delivery, and his Excellency General Washington the places of deposit and the Quantity of Provisions to be stored at each magazine, two thirds of the Quota of Flour and Salt provisions required from your State is to be reserved as a Magazine for the southern army—the fresh beef rum and salt is to be subject to my order—the salt and rum will not be wanting before the Spring and Summer at which time I shall order the disposal of it—the salted beef to be delivered in the following proportions Viz. (and for which I beg your Excellency's pointed instructions to the State agent for a faithful complyance therewith) one sixth part to be delivered the 20th Feb[y] one the 20th March, one the 26th Apr[l] one the first of May, one the first of June, and the residue the fifteenth of July.

  I need not mention to your Excellency the great punctuality there ought to be observed by the States in procuring and delivering the supplies required, and the uneasiness the want of One days provisions ocasions with the soldiery—to prevent which, I beg such powers may be given your agents as will enable them to execute, without which it will be impossible for me to keep up a regular supply for the Army.

The requisitions of Congress were barely calculated to support the troops they have reason to expect in the field next Campaign—and from the present prospects of State supplies I dread the most fatal consequences will ensue, the troops at West point and the other cantoonments of the army in this neighbourhood have been several days upon half allowance of bread, and but a very temperary supply of meat, if our situation is such in the most plentiful season of the year, and when the army is much reduced. I leave you to Judge what it must be next summer with twenty or thirty thousand men in the field operating against the enemy the consequence must undoubtedly be their desolution for want of subsistance, without the States use ten fold exertions in procuring the supplies.

Congress have ordered me to make monthly returns of all state supplies and for that purpose to call upon the executive of each State—have therefore to request your Excellency to give express orders to your State agent to furnish me with an accurate return of all supplies obtained from your State in the year Eighty and to whom delivered—and to make proper monthly returns in future to my Office at Philadelphia, when I settle the accounts of the agents who acted for me in your State the last year, shall furnish you with a return of all provisions purchased on Continental Acc^t let no cause whatever prevent you from furnishing the supplies required by Congress

The new arangement of the Quarter Master and Commissary Generals departments points out the delivery of all State supplies to the deputy Quarter Master or his Store

Keeper at the Magazines or place of deposit who is to receive and forward the same.

Eph: Blaine C.G.P.

J. Pleasants Hall, ed. *Journal and Correspondence of the State Council, January 1, 1781 - December 31, 1781* (Baltimore: Maryland Historical Society), 47:26-27.

Blaine to Caesar Rodney

Head Quarters New Windsor 18th Jany 1781.

I presume your Excellency has received the requisitions of Congress a considerable time ago for the Supplies of our Army this year—and that means have been adopted by your Legislature to procure them in due time—Congress have pointed out the proportions of delivery, and his Excellency General Washington the places of deposit.—The quantity of Provisions required from your State is very small and may be easily furnish'd if power is given to your Agent to execute—

I need not mention to your Excellency the great punctuality there ought to be observed by these States in procuring and delivering the supplies required, and the uneasiness the want of one days provisions occasions with the soldiery, *to prevent which* I beg your Executive & Legislature to adopt such means as will fully afford the Supplies required—without which it will be impossible for me to attempt to feed the Army—the requisitions of Congress were barely calculated to support the Troops they have reason to expect in the field next campaign, from the present prospects of State supplies I dread the most fatal Consequences—the Garrison at West Point, and the Troops cantoon'd in this Neighborhood have been several days upon half allowance of Bread and have but a very temporary supply of Beef, if our Situation is such in the most plentifull season of the year and when the Army is much reduc'd—I leave you to judge what it must be next summer with twenty or thirty thousand men in the field operating against the Enemy—the consequences must undoubtedly be then disolution for want of Subsistance, without the States use tenfold exertions in procuring the Supplies.

Congress have ordered me to make monthly returns of all State supplies and for that purpose to call upon the executive of each State, have therefore to request your Excellency to give express orders to your Agent to furnish me with an accurate Return of all Supplies obtain'd from your State in the year Eighty and to whom delivered—and to make proper Monthly returns in future to my Office in Philadelphia—

When I settle the Acc<u>ts</u> of the Agent who acted for me in your State last year, I shall afford you a return of all provisions purchased on Continental Account—let no cause whatever prevent you from furnishing the Supplies demanded by Congress—

George Herbert Ryden, ed., *Letters To & From Caesar Rodney, 1756-1784* (Philadelphia: Historical Society of Delaware, 1933), 394-95.

Blaine to Samuel Huntington

Head Quarters New Windsor 19th. Jany. 1781

Sir

I think it my duty to inform Congress of every Circumstance which concerns the supplies of our army—and my uneasiness respecting them, I fear none of the states will come up to their expectations and that many fall exceedingly short—Inclosed I send you a coppy of a letter which I received from Colonel Champion, it will inform you the expectations I have from that state, and from many others similar information—those failures of supplies will one day or Other will be attended with the most fatal consequences—to prevent which I beg Congress to write the most pressing letters to each of the states to use every possible exertion in procuring the provisions required with punctuality—I expect shortly to have returns of all the state supplies furnished last year and shall transmit them to Congress the moment I have it in my power—

The troops at West Point and those Canton'd in this neighbourhood, have been some time on Scant allowance of bread—and the present appearances give me little hope of a reasonable supply of beef Cattle, we have no fresh meat upon hand and the troops are now fed upon what little corned and salted meat I had laid up for Spring use—which is not more than twenty days support—If our situation is such in the most Plentiful season of the year, when our Magazines ought to be filled with salt provisions—I leave your Excellency to Judge what it must be next Campaign when three times the number of men are in the field—the consequence must undoubtedly be their disolution for want of subsistence—without the states use fourfold Exertions in facilitating their respective purchases in due time—I find a very great loss will arise upon all the cattle which are received with the army— and altho I have taken every precation and adopted every Judicious measure to have proper Estimates they are all laid much to high—those which I have had slaughtered under the directions of careful people have lost One fifth upon the estimated weight—the drovers had it not in their power to make proper provision of forage for the cattle upon the communication will add some to the loss of beef upon the cattle which have been drove late in the season, the troops have been destitute of rum ever since they came into winter Quarters. there is about seventy Hhds at Springfield. but I have not the least hopes of geting it brought forward before the Spring—

    I have the honor to be with the
        greatest respect—your Excellency's
           most Obdt. and most Hble Servant
              Eph. Blaine C.G.P.

Saml. Huntington, Esqr.

On Reverse: "Read Jan 27
 Copies of the within sent to the States Eastward"

>Papers of the Continental Congress, r 182, i 165, p. 389-90, National Archives. A copy appears in *Public Papers of George Clinton*, 6:599-600, a copy sent by Huntington to Clinton on January 27, 1781, pleading for provisions and other supplies. It was also sent to "the several States from Pennsylvania to the Eastward."

Blaine to William Livingston

Head Quarters New Windsor 19th. Jany. 1781

Sir

I presume your Excellency had received the Requisitions of Congress a considerable time ago for the supplies of our army this year, and that means have been adopted by your Legislature to procure them in due time.—Congress have pointed out the periods of delivery, and his Excellency General Washington the places of deposit.

I need not mention to your Excellency the great punctuality there ought to be observed by the States in procuring and delivering the supplies required—and the uneasiness the want of one days provisions Ocasions with the soldiery—<u>to prevent which</u>, I beg your Executive and Legislature to adopt such means as will fully afford the supplies required.—without which it will be impossible for me to attempt to feed the army—the requisitions of Congress were barely calculated to support the troops they expect to have in the feild next Campaign—from the present Prospects of state supplies I dread the most fatal consequences will insue—the Garison at West Point and the troops cantooned in this neighbourhood have been several days upon half allowance of bread and have but a temporary supply of meat, and the troops in Jersey have been several days upon scant allowance of meat, and have been princapally supplied with the little salt beef which I wanted to have Kept for spring use—if our situation is such in the most Plentiful season of the year and at a time when our Magazines, ought to be fill'd with salt Provisions, and the army much reduced, I leave you to Judge what it must be next summer with twenty or thirty thousand men in the field waiting to Operate against the enemy, the consequences must undoubtedly be their disolution for want of subsistance—without the states use tenfold exertions in procuring supplies—

Congress have ordered me to make monthly returns of all state supplies and for that purpose to call upon the executive—have therefore to request your Excellency to give express orders to your agents to furnish me with an Accurate return of all supplies Obtaind from your state the last year, and to whom delivered—and to make regular monthly returns in future to my Office in Philadelphia, let no cause whatever prevent you from furnishing the supplies required by congress—I have the honor to be very respectfully, your Excellency's
     Most Obdt Hble Servt.
     Eph. Blaine C. G. P.
Govr. Livingston
Public service
Addressed: His Excellency William Livingston Esquire
    Trenton pr Express

William Livingston Papers, Roll 14, New York Public Library.

Morton to Jacob Morgan

Philada: 19th. Jany 1781

Sir

  The Issuing Commissary at Carlisle writes Col. Blaine that he is almost destitute of Meat for the Supply of the

Artificers at that post—he has been furnished with that Article for some time past by Major James Smith late an Assistant under Col. Blaine, but the Public are so much indebted to him for former Contracts he will not render any further Supplies, neither is it proper he should as Col. Blaine is not Authorised to make any purchases whatsoever without a Special Order from the Board of War or Commander in Chief—

Mr: Lyon refuses to purchase Beef without an Order from you or Council, with which if you'll furnish him he can purchase a number of good Cattle from Major Smith upon easy terms, paying part of the Money on delivery of the Cattle and giving Assurance of the remainder in a limitted time

The Gentleman who brot: the Letter will return tomorrow morning—must therefore beg an Answer this Afternoon that I may be enabled to write Mr. Alexander Blaine the Issuing Commy. upon the Subject—

    I am Sir Your most Obt Servt
      Geo: Morton for E. Blaine Esqr.
Col. Jacob Morgan

> Peter Force Collection, Mss. 17,137, Series 8D, Ephraim Blaine Papers, Library of Congress.

Morton to the Treasury Board

    Commissary Generals Office 26th. Jany. 1781
Gentlemen

I have examined an Account for Provisions furnish'd by Messrs: Peter Mallet & Co. for the use of the Troops in North Carolina Amounting to One Million One hundred and Eighty four thousand Nine hundred and Twenty Two and a half Dollars, on which I beg leave to make the following remarks.—

First. The Chief part of the supplies were purchased with Carolina State money, the depreciation of which was considerably greater than the Continental Currency into which

the A/c is reduced at 8/ pr Dollar, this information I have from Mr. Porterfield who presented the A/c.—
Secondly. The prices of every Article purchased excepting the Meat is enormons, when compared with the prices here at that, (or even the present) time.—
Thirdly. No. 17 is an A/c. of Provisions furnished, their own property Amountg to Eight hundred Seventeen thousand Seven hundred and Thirty Six Dollars for which there is no rect.
Fourthly. It appears that no purchases were made before the month of June, notwithstanding considerable quantitys were delivered in Feby., April & May—This may be the Provisions contained in the charge No. 17 which is dated in December last—perhaps to enhance the price.—
Fifthly, Some of the charges against Colo: Armands Legion are not properly supported, as there are no receipts on his orders to shew the quantity of Provisions delivered thereon—
Sixthly. The quantity of Provisions purchased and delivered agree in every particular except to 14/ of Sugar which is deficient, provided the charges against Colo. Armonds Legion are admitted—
    I have the Honor to be Gent.
     Your Most Obedt. Servt.
      Geo: Morton
Treasury Board—

Peter Force Collection, Mss. 17,137, Series 8D, Ephraim Blaine Papers, Library of Congress.

Blaine to Ebenezer Foote

          New Burgh 6th. Feby. 1781
Sir
  The Bearer Mr Crouse is going over the river to stay with you and assist in Receiving and delivering the beef Cattle, you will try to fix him at some convenient place, inclos'd you have an order upon Mr. Keese for Long forage, you must Keep

a very regular acct. of all the Cattle you Receive, and deliver them to the issuing Commissaries taking rects. from them agreable to the estimates which you Receive,
        I am Sir Your Hble Servt.
        Eph. Blaine C.G.P.

> Foote served as a Receiver of Cattle for the Commissary Department. Hays Family Papers, Dickinson College Library.

Morton to the Treasury Board, Estimate of Sundries Delivered in October 1780

Estimate of Sundries delivered by Colo. Thomas Hart in the month of October last for the use of the Southern Army pr Certificates of William Pendergast D: C: G of Ps. and Major Genl. Gates.—

1780
Octr. 31   15463 lbs of Beef including
                  5th. Quarter @ 4 1/3 pr Ct £318..1..10 ½

                1560 lbs of Mutton   do.   32..3..6
                1000 Bushells of Corn 5   250..
                Specie   £601..2..4 ½

                Exchange @ 75   £45,083..18..17
Commissary Genls. Office
    Philadelphia 9th. Feby 1781

                for E: Blaine Esqr. C: G: P
                Geo: Morton

Honorable Board Treasury Prest—

> Peter Force Collection, Mss. 17,137, Series 8D, Ephraim Blaine Papers, Library of Congress.

Morton to James Duane

Philada: 12th. Feby, 1781

Sir
    I recd: your favor to Col. Blaine requiring an Account of the Debts due in his department in answer to which I beg leave to inform you that it is not in my power to furnish you herewith, as none of the Accounts from the Eastern States are yet come to hand—Col. Blaine writes me from Head Quarters that he is collecting a number of Accounts from those parts—many of his Assistants in the Middle Department have not settled their Accounts tho' the most pressing Letters have been sent them for that purpose—notwithstanding those difficulties I hope on Col. Blaines arrival in Town he will be able to furnish an Estimate for the information of Congress—
    I have the Honor to be Sir
        Your Most Obt Servt
        Geo: Morton for E: Blaine Esqr. C.G of Ps.
P. S. Col. Blaine is expected in ten Days—

Honorable Mr. Duane.

    Duane was a Delegate to Congress from New York. Papers of the Continental Congress, M247, R41, i34, p213, National Archives.

Blaine to Alexander Hamilton

New Burgh 19th. Feby. 1781

Dear Sir
    youl please to inform his Excellency Genl. Washington, that I have Just returnd from Fish Kill that the whole of the provisions necessary for the detachment will move this Evenning—I have sent fifty head of good Cattle and five Hhs. rum. Mr Stevens D C I has ordered a person to attend at Peeks Kill, to take charge of the stores,
    I remain with much Esteem and reguard Dr. Sr

Your Most Obdt. Hble Servt.
Ephr. Blaine C.G.P.

Colo Hamilton

Hamilton was an Aide-de-Camp to Washington. George Washington Papers, Library of Congress.

Blaine to Samuel Huntington

New Burgh 25th. Feby. 1781.

Sir

I Expected being at Philadelphia long ear this in order to have my Accts. aranged and laid before the treasury board for settlement by the tenth of March—but the scarcity of provisions and great difficulty there is in keeping up a regular supply has induced his Excellency to detain me here untill the magazines is in such a state as to remove any doubt of want— the langour which prevails with all the state agents in executing their respective purchases are such that present Appearances are not favourable, indeed I have not the least expectation of any state complying with the requisitions of congress—and the advantages many of the people take who are disposed to comply with the Laws for delivering in their quotas and assessments of supplies is such that the most ordenary of the different Specie of Provisions which their farms Produce or they are called upon to furnish is delivered in and they use every possible means to have it estimated as high as in their power—and we shall never be better while the states are called upon to furnish supplies and they [sic] people are paid with Certificates—or untill you can adopt measures to procure your supplies by contract—

Cattle have gone from every part of this and the Eastren states to Rhode Island, the market has been so gluted with flour and beef that hard money wou'd have purchased it as cheap as it has ever been Known in that place, <u>indeed</u> all the good cattle go there we get only the refuse—

I dread the opening of next Campaign, supposeing the army in the field you have reason to expect, I know the Difficiency's of the states with cause a scarcity of Provisions with the soldiery which will undoubtedly end in a dicession from their duty or a general mutiny which may not be in the power of their Officers to Quell, I wish to god the states had those objects in view, and wou'd use ten fold the exertions they have done to comply with your demands and prevent those evils which will one day or Other, be our misfortune.

all my public transactions in the year 1776, with Mr Buchanan in 1777, and Wadsworth in 1778, 9, and under my own direction are unsettled, I wish not to let them remain longer and as I shall have the princaple part of my Accts. ready by the 20th. of March or first of apl.—and as those gentlemen do not appear to be ready for a final settlement and my Account are daily increasing—I must beg and request a Special order of Congress to give them a preference with the auditors or Claims Accts. to have them properly adjusted as If I continue in the service I shall spend as little of my time as possible in this business—I hope in a few days to be enabled to make you a return of all state supplies furnished up to the first of last January—the salaries allowed the people employ'd in my department are such that I am distitute of a single person to assist me, indeed they are declare it is not sufficient for their support nor can the [sic] live upon it, I shall say nothing more upon that subject untill I come to Philadelphia,

And remain with all Due Respect,
Your Excellency's Most Obdt:
and most Hble. Servant
Ephraim Blaine

Sl. Huntington Esqr.

Papers of the Continental Congress, M247, r182, i165, p341-44, National Archives.

Blaine to Samuel Huntington

New Burgh 8th. March 1781,

Sir,

The depreciation of Continental money has been so rapid that Justice ought to be done those persons who have demands against the public and have received no acknowledgments for the same.—the resolutions of the Honorable the Congress of the 26th. of last August ample provision indeed it opens a field for fraud without their Officers are Exceedingly attentive and faithful in settling all their public transactions—I have been ever averse to granting my people a power of issuing Certificates for the paymt. of debts and very few have passed Except in this state, I have been very pressing to obtain the returns and Accounts of my Deputies and assists. in order to have them finally Adjusted, and assuring them that ample justice shou'd be done all those who had legal demands, your agents was generally from One to twelve months in arrears for purchases and very seldom enabled to pay Cash down for their purchases and Contracts, by which means the Community at large have suffered by the depreciation,

I have had sundry applications to make restitution for depreciation between the time Contracts have been made and the Accounts finally settled and paid—I have Reason to believe that from Representations made to the Honorable Congress that they have been induced to give some sanction to those claims, which if introduced except in very particular cases will be attended with the utmost confusion and Embarrassment against all settled Accts. cost the united States a very large sum of money—as every person will be disposed to take unreasonable and unjust advantages of the public—therefore it is my humble Opinion that no allowance ought to be made (but in extraordinary cases) only to those who are still unpaid—

The public sustains a very great loss upon the live cattle delivered by the respective states, they fall short from twenty to thirty PrCent upon each hundred weight as estimated. I can adopt no method under the present plan of procuring supplies to remove this evil—I wish Congress had it in their power to advance money for the purchase of live cattle, for people could execute that business the public wou'd have their beef upon more reasonable terms and of a better quality—the present mode is by no means proper as I am never Certain of a Regular supply for they [sic] army—the small supply of live Cattle which I have received through the winter and am now receiving has Obliged me to make use of the little salt Provision which was on hand indeed I do not expect a single Barrel will remain at the opening of next Campaign—these circumstances and how they [sic] army will be feed makes me dread the Consequences which may follow—I have now on hand about thirty five days supply of Flour and twenty of salt Provisions (no Cattle). I hope to have my Accts. prepared to lay before the board of treasury by the first of April—I have the honor to be with all due Respect,
        your Excellency's
          Most Obedt. Hble Servt.
            Eph. Blaine C.G.P.
Sal. Huntington Esqr.

Papers of the Continental Congress, Roll 92, i78, v4, p127-133, National Archives.

To George Washington

New Burgh 9th March 1781,

Sir,
    I know it is your Excellency's wish and the desire of Congress that no more posts shou'd be established but such as might be necessary for the deposits of state supplies upon a line of communication from the Eastren to the southern states as pointed out by your Excellency—any aditional posts are

attended with a very considerable expence, and consume large quantities of our best Provisions—when they are appointed by the authority of any particular state and under the condition of pay and rations from, Congress. I could wish such states wou'd make provision without breaking up the supplies required by Congress—except in Cases where any state is invaded by the enemy and the militia are called out into Actual service to operate in conjunction with the Continental army or a detachment thereof under such circumstances and no Other the supplies out to be furnished from the public Magazines—there are three or four posts contained in the state of connecticut, which have drawn very considerable quantities of Provision from our public Magazines and are now applying for part of the little salt provisions put up in that state for Continental use—I wish your Excellency wou'd speak to Governor Trumbull upon that subject, and shou'd these posts be continued, that he wou'd adopt measures to furnish them without Encroaching upon the continental supplies,

    I have to honor to be very Respectfully,
    your Excellency's most Obdt.
    and very Hble Servt,
    Ephr Blaine, C.G.P.

Genl. Washington

George Washington Papers, Library of Congress.

Blaine to George Morton

10th. March 1781,

Sir,

Procuring provisions for the garison at West point and the troops cantooned in that neighbourhood has induced his Excellency General Washington to retain me here, he has been some days absent upon a Journey to Rhode Island upon his Return I expect to set out for Philada. which will be about the

20th. pray what progress are you making in the settlement of my Accts. has the delinquents all come in, such as are still difficeint write them in the most pressing terms, and assure them a further neglect will attended with disagreeable consequences—I have obtain'd all the Eastren returns but Mr Cuylers and his I expect every hour, if Mr Mc.Clay has not been down from sunberry write him to attend the first of apl. at which time he will find me at home—I hope you have recd. returns of the supplies furnished by the state of Delaware and Maryland and that their purchases are very Considerable, write me all news by the next post,
    I am with much regard, sir
    Your Most Hble Servt.
    Eph. Blaine, C.G.P.

Peter Force Collection, Ms 17,137, Ephraim Blaine Papers, Series 8D, Reel 74, Library of Congress.

Blaine to Charles Stewart

    NewBurgh 21st. March 1781,
Dear Sir,

Your favour by Mr Kitts came safe to hand—which is the only letter I have Recd. from you since you left this, I wrote you four three of which I have reason to suppose you recd. and your not answering them is the only cause why you have not heard from me this two months—I am never at head Quarters but the Genl. asks for you, when you were coming up, and when I had heard from you, I have as Often told him weekly by which means I have made a lye for each of the thirteen states—

we have now upon hand about ten days supply of mean and twenty of Flour, <u>when thats done</u>, the resources of this state will be totally consumed and our Dependance for flour must be in Jersey and Pennsylvania—I hope the southern

Magazines afford a considerable quantity, if the states mean to feed the army now is the time to procure it, Mr Morton's information to me that all supplies will be stop'd in Pennsylvania to feed the Convention troops, it is very extrodinary if the Convention troops and the pennsylvanians, which recruting shou'd consume all the flour required from that state, we have had very little for the currant year, if those troops interfer with the supplies of our army for god sake apply to Congress to have their throats cut—Mr Stevens your deputy, is an attentive man he has given me great satisfaction, and is very deserving of his appointment—

I thank you for your Kind information and shall ever esteem the many marks of your friendship which I have experienced since our first acquaintance in the highest view,

as to Congress and the board of War making new Arangements and Mr Pickering their little god Almighty I have not the least Objection, but I do not think it Generous in the board of War to adopt the measure without giving me information—I made Mr. Pickering acquainted with the defects of my department and told him I had mentioned the mater to Congress and inform'd them that without sundry Alterations I wou'd not continue, but wou'd certainly resign, I wish after six years service Mr. Pickering may give the public the same satisfaction I have done, I am sure his abilities and attention to public duty and Oeconomy in disposing of public money, will never be greater than myne, however new brooms sweep clean and Congress seem fond of them,

the settlement of my Accounts and means of Obtaining money to pay my Deputies and assistants their respective Ballances is my Greatest concearn—

you Know my sentiments about continuing in service since since the present uncertain mode of supplies has been adopted—my only wish this months was to quite with reputation which I hope will be in my power, I have kept the contents of your letter secret but in confidence to Colo.

Tilghman, the Genl. return'd from his Journey to Rhode Island yesterday, I have asked leave of Absence this morning which is the third time, and believe I shall obtain it sunday or monday, immediately after shall proceed to Philadelphia, I am sorry for the disapointments you have met with in not being able to defray the expenciss of your department—the poor finances of Congress induced them to make trifling Excuses of payment (and that is my great concearn) all your friends here are well but angry at your not writing them, my Compliments to all acquaintances, and

     believe me with the greatest reguard,

      Dr. Sir, Your Most Obdt. Servt.

       Eph. Blaine
Colo. Stewart

Addressed: Charles Stewart Esquire

    Comy. Genl. of Issues Philada.

Charles Stewart Papers, 1752-1818, Collection 262, New York State Historical Association.

To George Washington

         New Burgh 21st March 1781,
Sir,
  All my public transactions in the year 1776, with Mr Buchanan in 1777, Mr Wadsworth in 1778-9 and since under my own direction remain unsettled, those Gentlemen quiting public service and engaging in private business has caused great delay in the settlement of their Accts.—indeed the necessary exertions have not been used to bring their deputies to an immediate settlement—I have long since made application to Congress for their special order to the treasury board to admit of my Accts. whenever ready—this has been done and the time fixed was this month—I wish not to delay this necessary business—and beg to have your Excellency's

permission to attend thereto—shou'd I continue in the Service which I believe will not be the case without many alterations in the department, and Power given me to purchase and means of payment, whenever the states failed in furnishing the necessary supplies for the support of the army, there is no time I can be better spared than before the Campaign Opens, shou'd your Excellency order any General movement of the army, I shall be ready to attend at a moments warning, my assistant and Colo. Stewarts deputy will give constant attendance and make the Necessary reports to your Excellency the State of the magazines and their information of supplies—shou'd Circumstances Occasion my quitting the service nothing would give me greater pleasure than an assurance of your Excellency's approbation for my past conduct—and shou'd my future aid or assistance render my Country and your Excellency any service you have only to command,
     I have the honor to be with great respect
       Your Excellency's Most Obdt.
        and Most Hble Servant
         Eph. Blaine
Genl. Washington

<small>George Washington Papers, Library of Congress.</small>

Blaine to George Washington

         New Burgh 23rd. March 1781,
Sir,
  The information I have received from Philadelphia is very alarming and gives me great concearn, Mr. Hazelwood state agent for the City has informed my assistant that he has directions from Concil to send no more Provisions to the grand armey untill further Orders—the Convention troops being on their March from Virginia to Quarter in some part of that state

I have not received Colo. Hays return to know the quantity of Flour I can expect from this state before harvest, but from report I doubt very inconsiderable—Jersey is doing little and I believe the Governor and Council of that state are using very Indifferent measures to procure the Supplies required—

In this situation what is to be done—my applications are so frequent I believe many of the Executives look upon them Impertinent—the assembly of Pennsylvania is now siting will your Excellency please to write them—the whole supplies of flour received from their agents the last and present year do not exceed ten thousand Barrels—a few weeks neglected at this season may loose [sic] all the surplush flour in the States of Maryland, Deleware, and Pennsylvania—Mr. Phelps agent for Massachusetts assures me sixty stall'd cattle weekly untill the middle of may—

the Magazine at West Point fish Kill &c. equal One thousand barrels of flour, five hundred barrels of beef, twenty five Hhds. of rum, and One hundred and twenty cattle, part of which was delivered yesterday, five hundred barrels of Flour at Ringwood, and, About an equal quantity at Morris and Trenton—very few stores at Philadelphia except five hundred barrels of beef, put up by my directions last December,

with your Excellencys Permission I wou'd wish to set out next Monday or tuesday immediately upon my arrival at Philadelphia, Colonel Stewart will return—

I have the honor to be very respectfully your
  Excellency's, Most Obdt. and very Hble Servant
    Eph. Blaine C.G.P.

Genl. Washington

George Washington Papers, Library of Congress.

Blaine to Hugh Hughes

NewBurgh 29th March 1781

Sir,

As the states are call'd upon to furnish salt Provisions, the Continent will have no Occasion to engage more Coopers than may be necessarily employd at the Magazines and posts—underneath you have my Opinion the number which ought to be engag'd in my department; the Garrison at west point will Require two Coopers to repair and Keep in Order all the old Casks which may be emptd. at that Post Kings Ferry, Peeks Kill, Or at Albany, One at Fort Schuyler, one at Great Barrinton, and One at Clavarac, I wou'd wish Good stuff prepared at NewBurgh to number One thousand or fifteen hundred tight Barrels, the Necessary number of Coopers to prepare that Quantity of stuff and Repair what old casks may be emptyed at New Windsor and Fish kill Landing to be employ'd—the above mentioned number will be very sufficient to answer the Demands in the Commissary's department within your district—you will therefore Please to engage them upon the same or proportionable terms with Other—Artificers in public service, I remain with Esteem Sir,
    Your Most Obdt Hble Servt.
    Eph. Blaine CG.P

Col Hughes

> Hughes was a Deputy Quartmaster General for the State of New York. Sold by Swann Galleries, 104 East 25th Street, New York, New York, 10010, Lot 2367, on November 20, 2014.

Blaine to Nehemiah Dunham

Sir   Philada. 6th. Apl. 1781.

I have Just returnd from the Army and am preparing my Acots. for a final settlement, have therefore to request you to use every possible Exertion in closing yours by the first of may and attending at my Office for the above purpose be very particular in your Returns of delivery and see that they corespond with your Acots purchases—I have some

expectation of money in the month of may, and beg your attendance at that time I remain Sir
          Your Very Hble Servt.
          Eph Blaine

Nehl. Dunham Esqr.

> Peter Force Collection, Roll 75, Ephraim Blaine Letterbook, Library of Congress.

Blaine to Samuel Huntington

          Philad: April 6th 1781

Sir

    A number of People who have claims against the Public for Rum seized in the vicinity of West Point by Order of Major Genl. Howe and Warrants have been granted for part payment—As those Gentlemens claims differ from the Resolutions of last August or any mode pointed for my Government in Settling public Accts. I would wish to have an Invervicw with the Comittee who settled those Accounts and reported the Warrants, in Order to know what depreciation is to be allowed—

    I have the Honor to be very respectfully—
        Your Excellencys Most Obedt.
        & Most Humble Servant—
          Eph: Blaine C.G.P.

His Excellency the President of Congress

> Papers of the Continental Congress, M247, r182, i165, p405, National Archives.

Blaine to Nathaniel Appleton

          Philadelphia 6th. April 1781

Sir

Mr. Kelsey a Merchant of this City will present you with two warrants for the payment of sundry parcels of rum seized in the Vicinity of West Point for which there was former Warrants granted, if those drafts have been paid, you will please to observe the following disposal of the money, the amount of Mr. Fetchums money was 100,235 Dollars which in the new money make two thousand five hundred and Five Dollars seventy nine, Ninetieths which you will please to pay Mr. Kean or Order as he has a large demand against the public and taken this as Cash; the other two Warrants indorsed to Colo. Udney Hay is settled, you will please to stop payment of the present Orders, Mr Keans money excepted, and the residue I will see properly settled in the Treasury Office, and send you an Order to pay the Ballance to Mr. Miller my Agent at Boston who is largely in Advance for the public and very much distressed

    I am with much esteem
      Sir your Most Obedt. Humble Servt.
        E. Blaine

Nathl. Appleton Esqr.
C: of the C Loan Officer Boston—

> Appleton was Director of the Continental Loan Office at Boston. Peter Force Collection, Roll 75, Ephraim Blaine Letterbook, Library of Congress.

Blaine to Samuel Huntington

            Philada. 9th April 1781

Sir

  Inclosed you have an Account of State Supplies so far as in my power to procure them, I wrote the Executives and beged them to order their Agents to make me Monthly returns of all Provisions furnished. I have frequently wrote their superintending Agents but to no purpose. Jersey has not furnished me with a single return since the appointment of their

Commissioners in February 80.—The present mode of procuring supplies will never answer the Expectations of the Honble Congress & Commander in Chief, and the uncertain methods of furnishing has never put it in my power to have one Months compleat supply; at any one period since the States undertook to furnish, and I have often been days without a Single ration to issue—

Now is the time to procure and lay up Six months supplies of Flour, if delayed this and next month it will be impossible to procure it,—Our Public Magazines empty, the prospects of an Active Campaign, be Assured without ten fold Exertions of the States your Army will undoubtedly Starve.—

The Estimates herewith delivered you are for part of the debts due in my Department, and for which numbers are in the greatest distress, have in the most pressing terms to beg and intreat Congress to adopt some mode of payment to enable me to discharge those demands.— What method am I to pursue in the settlement of my Accounts, and payment of debts, shall I confine myself to the resolution of Congress of the 26th. of last August, this is a matter of great consequence therefore beg to be inform'd—

When I accepted of the appointment of Commissary General in January 1780, I acquainted Congress if I could not engage people to act under the new system, I would employ them upon the most Oeconomical terms in my power, this I was Obliged to do or let the service suffer, and upon my return from the Eastern states and Part the Southern, I represented to Congress the terms on which my deputies were engaged, have therefore to request your Excellency to apply to Congress to pass a resolve to make good all my engagements upon Commission or Salary.—

The delay which Mr. Buchanan and Mr. Wadsworth Commisary's General will meet with in the settlement of their Accounts owing to the Death of some of their deputies and neglect of others, gives me much uneasiness and as I wish to

be discharged from those incumberances beg directions may be given the Treasury Board to Order the settlement of my Accounts as deputy to those Gentlemen.—
I have the Honor to be with
Due respect—Your Excellencys
Most Obedient Humble Servt.
Eph. Blaine C.G.P.

Samuel Huntington Esqr. President of Congress

> Papers of the Continental Congress, M247, r182, i165, p397-98, National Archives.

Blaine to Isaac Carty

Philada. 10 April 1781.
Dear Sir
Congress having receiv'd information of the intention of the Enemys coming into Delaware Bay with a design of plundering Provisions and Forage, it herefore behooves you to use every possible exertion to forward to this place or Trenton all the Flour and meat Kind in your possession the property of the State—at the same time please to observe that no State Supplies become the property of the United States untill deliver'd into the Public Magazine—the bearer Mr. Morton will give you every assistance in forwarding the Provisions—
Information has been made Congress of ten or twelve thousand Barrels of flour being in the neighbourhood of Wilmington I wish to God your Governor and Council would impower you to seize it for the United States—
Your Return of State Supplies for the last and present year are much wanted, pray be very particular in making them monthly to my Office and give me every information respect'g Supplies—
I remain Dear Sir Your Most Obt. Servt.
Eph Blaine C.G.P

Major Isaac Carty

> *Delaware Archives: Revolutionary War* (Wilmington: Public Archives Commission of Delaware, 1919), 3:1356.

Blaine to Donaldson Yeates

Philada. 10th Apl. 1781.

Sir

Congress and the Board of War receiving Information of the Enemy's intention of Coming into the deleware Bay with a Design of Plundering and taking Provisions and forage, its therefore Necessary to use every possible Exertion in forwarding all public stores to Trenton—the bearer hereof Mr. Morton my assistant, goes down on purpose to Expedite the removal of all public Stores—those delivered into the Public Magazines are the property of the united States, those in the hands of the state agents the property of the states to whome the [*sic*] belong, however it is the duty of every public Officer to give every assistance for the removal and preservation of Public property, and on that princaple make no doubt you will do every thing in your power, shou'd the enemy come up the delewarr and Prevent your Craft from bringing up the stores by water—your only remidy will be to remove those you cannot forward to this place or trenton, up in the County toward the Cross roads or Brick Meeting House, however your own Judgement must determine from the information you receive, I remain with Esteem and reguard Sir

Your Most Obdt Hble Servt—
Eph Blaine C.G.P.

Donaldson Yeats Esqr
DQMG States of Maryland & Delewarr

> Peter Force Collection, Roll 75, Ephraim Blaine Letterbook, Library of Congress.

Blaine to the Board of War

Philada. 10th. Apl. 1781,

Gentlemen

Inclosed you have a Return of State supplies so far as in my power to Procure them, I wrote the Executives and urged them to order their agents to make monthly returns of all provisions furnished—I have frequently wrote those who have been appointed supperintending Agents but to little purpose—Jersey has not furnished me with a single return since the appointment of their Agents in February 80, I expect returns from my deputy in the southern Department by every post—

Genl. Wayne has called upon me for supplys for a Detachment of One thousand rank file who are ordered southerly, this detachment with their followers will equal fifteen hundred Daily Rations, the place where the rendezvous at York Town and the Country through which the march to Fredericksburgh will afford them ample supplies of Flour, but how they are to be furnished with meat lay with the state agents or your Honble. board to determine, I know of no supplies upon that Communication Except some little at Alexandria, and two hundred and eight Barrels of beef which I have receiv'd in this City, if no other mode can be adopted, Country Waggons which are returning to the Susquehanah ought to be engaged to carry part of this beef to York Town, but cou'd live cattle be procured to wou'd be a great saving of transportation,

I have the honor to be with due Respect Gentlemen
    your Most Obdt. & Most Hble Servt
      E Blaine

Honble. Board of War

    Peter Force Collection, Roll 75, Ephraim Blaine Letterbook, Library of Congress.

Blaine to Joseph Reed

Philadelphia, 12th Apl, 1781.

Sir

I have had the perusal of a letter from your Excellency in Council to the Honorable Board of War, and must confess I was astonished at the expressions made use of against me—they are ungenerous and I do not deserve them from the Executive Council of Pennsylvania. You may look upon the information of assistant Commissaries of Purchases in what light you think proper, but those of my acquaintance and appointment are Gentlemen of probity, Character and reputation, and I presume if your Excellency compare them with the different characters of men in general you will find them such as I represent. My Information to the Commander in chief has ever been Impartial and founded upon Just representations, and I shall make it appear from you superintendants returns and the report of Mr. Hazelwood, your agent, that I have facts to support every information given had they been three fold.

When the Magazines are nearly exhausted, and it is evident no state have comply'd with the order of Congress, and the state of Pennsylvania which was our princaple dependance for bread notoriously deficient, thousand [*sic*] depending upon me for their daily support; my representations to the General became necessary and an Incumbent duty, and your Knowledge of Military Operations if impartial must undoubtedly determine in my favour—however I have made them and am Conscious of the Justice of my assertions, and those and every other which I have made shall support.

I remain with all due respect,
your Excellency's most Obedt Hbble. Servt,
Eph. Blaine, C. G. P.

Directed,
    Public.
    To His Excellency Joseph Reed, Esqr,
        President of the State of Pennsylva, Present.

Samuel Hazard, ed., *Pennsylvania Archives: Selected and Arranged from Original Documents in the Office of the Secretary of the Commonwealth....* 1st. series, volume 9, (Philadelphia: Joseph Severns & Co., 1854), 72-73.

Blaine to George Washington

Philada. 13th. April 1781—

Sir

    I am order'd by Congress to proceed immediately as far as Dover in the Delaware State, and Accomack upon the Eastern Shore of Virginia, in order to secure and remove all Public Stores upon the Peninsula between the two Bays— indeed Congress would have done right to Order a siezure of all Salt Provisions Flour and Forage in that Country, as two thirds of it will go to the Enemy—they have a compleat Command of the Bay up to Rock Run—

    I have it from good information that the Delaware State and the Counties upon the Eastern Shore have now manufactor'd twenty Thousand Barrels of Flour, a considerable part of which is in the Brandywine Mills, I offer'd to secure the whole provided I was invested with power—The matter is refer'd to Governor Rodney and the Council of safety upon the Eastern Shore, it will rest with the Governor, but I am in hopes the Council of Safety will Act with precaution & Spirit & if I am not disappointed your Excellency may expect a pretty little Magazine of Supplies—The Frigates are order'd down to Lewis Town to cover the Landings in the Delaware State, to which all the Supplies are to be collected and Trenton is fixed on the placed of Deposit—

Your Excellency may be assured of my utmost Exertions, and that every power I am invested with upon this Occasion shall be extended as far as possible—

The sixth of this month there was 520 Bbls of Flour at Ringwood 750 at Sussex Court House with other small Stores 200 at Morris Town 250 at Trenton and 450 at Easton—One thousand Barrels of Flour public property will be forwarded in a few Days which lays in the Delaware State (also a very considerable quantity of Forage)—no Provisions in this City except a little Flour, when the Collection is made on the Eastern Shore shall inform you.

I have the Honor to be with every Sentiment
of Esteem & regard Your Excellencies
Most Obdt. & Most Hble Servt.
Eph: Blaine C. G. P.

George Washington Papers, Library of Congress.

Morton to Jacob Morgan

Philada: 17th. April 1781

Sir

The Garrison at this Post have been several Days destitute of Meat & Mr. Bradford Commissary of Prisoners has made Application to Col. Blaine for a regular Supply of that Article for Six hundred Prisoners—I know of no way of accomplishg. the matter but by Application to you—if Fish can be procured two or three Days in the Week it will answer the purpose as well as Meat and come upon more reasonable Terms—

I am Sir Your most Obt Servt
Geo: Morton for E. Blaine C. G. P.

Col. Jacob Morgan
Superindendt. of Purchases—L. Pennsylvania

Peter Force Collection, Roll 75, Ephraim Blaine Letterbook, Library of Congress.

Blaine to Thomas Sim Lee

Annapolis 20th. April 1781

Sir

I am ordered by the board of War to remove to places of safety all public provisions and Stores which come within my department, in the State of Delaware, and Eastern shore in Maryland.

Keeping in Idea that Trenton is to be the grand Deposit in all cases practicable.—Your Excellency and Council will please to give orders for the removal of all stores under the above discription upon the Eastern shore to the most convenient Landing upon the Delaware, prefering those above Dover, where I shall have persons appointed to receive and forward the same.

those of the Western shore wou'd wish deposited to or near George Town upon Potomack, except a small temporary Magazine at Baltimore and Frederick Town, for passing Troops those places being upon the line of communication to the southern Army.

the danger which the Eastern shore and Delaware are exposed to will require every Possible exertion for the removal of Public Property—

I have the Honor to be very respectfully
Your Excellency's Most Obedient Humble Serv[t].
Eph Blaine C.G.P.

His Excellency Govr. Lee—

Archives of Maryland, ed. J. Hall Pleasants, vol. 47, *Journal and Correspondence of the State Council of Maryland, 1781* (Baltimore: Maryland Historical Society, 1930), 199.

Blaine to Caesar Rodney

Wye River 23d April 1781

Sir

I set out this morning for Chaptank Bridge from whence I shall proceed by way of Joney cake Landing to Dover, and hope to be with you by One OClock on tuesday the Honble board of War inform me by Letter, that they ordered down two Continental armed Schooners, to protect the small craft and shallops which may load with public provisions and other Stores in your state; your Excellency will please to give the necessary Orders of expediting the Loading of such craft as may be at the difft. landings where public property may be collected, and that taken in preference to any other, the Board inform me some shalops were to come down with the Armed Vessels in order to Load; all possible supplies upon the Eastern shore will be collected to the Head of Chester

I have the Honor to be very respectfully
Your Excellency's Most Obedt. Humble Servt.
E. Blaine

His Excy Govr. Rodney

Peter Force Collection, Roll 75, Ephraim Blaine Letterbook, Library of Congress.

Blaine to the Board of War

Dover 25th. April 1781

Gentlemen

I have been around the Western shore at Hartford, Jopha Baltimore, Malbro: and Annapolis, delivered your letter to the Govr. and Council, from whence I proceeded to the Eastern shore, Talbot Court-House and delivered your Other letter to the Special Council; previous to my coming, they had resolved to keep all supplies in the hands of their Agents, and gave

Orders accordingly, but upon my representation of the wants of bread in the Northern Army and presenting your Orders, they agreed to have all the supplies collected to the Head of Chester a place the Govr. had fixed previous to their Orders, I have seen a Number of their Agents and in fact, the case is they have done nothing; the Council has not as yet recd. One [sic] their supperintending Commissary's has little information, & their County contractors have done nothing, the whole Eastern Shore cannot produce One thousand Bbls. public Flour, believe I might say five hundred, the western shore have produced about 1500 barrels, a good deal of which the Marquis used for his Troops.—Upon the whole their is large quantities of Flour but very little belonging to the States or Public.—the Agents of this State will be able to furnish perhaps Six hundred Bbls. and about seven or Eight thousand Bushells of Forage; I shall stay here a day or two untill the Boats are nearly loaded, and then proceed to Philadelphia; and if some more certain Method is not adopted, give up pretentions of supplying your Army for be assured you cannot do it—I have been convinced long since that the present plan will never answer the demands of the army,

   I have the honor the be very respectfully
    Gentlemen your most Obdt Hble Servt
     Eph Blaine C.G.P

The Honble the Board of War

> Peter Force Collection, Roll 75, Ephraim Blaine Letterbook, Library of Congress.

Blaine to Captain Montgomary and the Officer Commanding the Armed Schooners

       Dover 27th. of April 1781

Gentlemen

Mr. Carter waited upon the Govr. and me at this place for orders where to direct the shallops under your convoy where to load with Flour and forage, belonging to the public; agreeable to the Govr. directions you will dispose of the Shalops in the Manner I have within directed, those being the places pointed out by him to load at, I have made out the arangement agreeable to your Memorandum, supposing the Vessels to be at the sundry landings therein mentioned but should it be necessary to make some Alterations for the conveniency of landing and Water, your are [sic] the Judges and therefore conduct yourselves accordingly.—you will proceed to Lewis Town Creek when Mr. Fury a Gentleman from this Town and the Contractor for Sussex County will wait upon you, and give every Assistance in their power to expedite the loading of those four Shallops,—And should they have more public property than the four can carry, they have Orders to impress Craft for the removal of all public propery—Col: Carty Agent for this County, will give attention to the loading the Vessels you have left in this County, shou'd your men want provisions I have given directions to Mr. Fury to provide for them below, the danger of the bay will require every possible exertion in the execution of this business, and proceeding up to Phia.

I remain Gentleman Your Most Obedt. Humble Servt.
E: Blaine

Capt. Montgomary and the Officer Commanding the Armed Schooners—

> Peter Force Collection, Roll 75, Ephraim Blaine Letterbook, Library of Congress.

Blaine to Henry Hollingsworth

Christia Bridge 28th. April 1781

Dear Sir

A number of Shalops are now loading with Flour and forage in this State. there are more at Duck Creek than can Obtain freight, if any quantity of stores is collected at the Head of Chester wou'd request you to have them sent over immediately, as armed Vessels are down the Delaware bay to Guard them,—Would wish to have all the Flour in Hartford County brought to the Head of Elk, provided the navigation between those places are safe, and beg you to forward all the flour in your possession without a moments delay, favour me with a return of Stores the very first Opportunity and believe me—

Dr. Sir Your Humble Servt.
Eph: Blaine C:GP

Col: Hollingsworth

> Peter Force Collection, Roll 75, Ephraim Blaine Letterbook, Library of Congress.

Nathaniel Stevens to Morrell and Wynkoop

Fishkill—28th. April—1781—

Sir,

His Excellency General Washington being desirous of having a quantity of Shad fish procured for the Army, by Exchanging Salt for the Same, I have to request that you will immediately proceed to all the several Fishing places up the North River and procure to the amount of 300 Barrels or more if they can be had for three pecks of Salt for 220 pounds of Cleaned fish, you will apply three pecks of Salt for the cure of every Barrel of the Fish, or to every 220 pounds.—

You will call on Mc.Cullen for Barrels, & the Commissary at Clavarack for Salt—

His Excellency is very anxious to have carefull and trusty persons employed to See to the putting of them in the Casks and the application of the Salt, which I wish you to look well to—

I am Sir your most Obt. Servant
for Colo. Blain C. Genl. of Purchases
N. Stevens D. C. G. Issues

(Copy)
James Morrell Esqr. A.S. Agent

Stevens was the Deputy Commissary General of Issues at Fish Kill, New York. Charles Stewart Papers, 1752-1818, Collection 262, New York State Historical Association.

Blaine to Samuel Huntington

Philada. 1st. May 1781

Sir

My Letter to your Excellency, of the 26th. last month covering an estimate of the Sums due in my Department have not been considered by the Honorable Congress, at least I have had no information thereon.—

The Settlement of my Accounts is absolutely necessary and the mode is a matter of the greatest Consequence, and I shall not attempt to give Certificates until properly instructed by Congress—

Many of my People are in the greatest distress, some of whom have been in this City ten Weeks and dare not to return to their homes without Money to Satisfy their Creditors—have therefore in the most pressing terms to Solocit Congress to adopt some mode to enable me to Settle with those who have just Demands against my Office for Supplies furnished when the Army was in the greatest distress.—

The deficiency of State Supplies will convince your Excellency and Congress of the necessity of taking Provisions in the Vicinity of Camp & occasionally making Contracts with people, where part Credit could be obtain'd, without which the Army must have disbanded—

A reference to my former Letter and some remedy recommended by Congress to Satisfy these People who have demands against me, will be acknowledged a favor by
Sir Your Excellencies
Most Obedient & Most Hble Servant
Eph. Blaine, C.G. P.

His Excellency S. Huntington Esqr.

On the reverse: May 8, 1781
Referred to Mr. T. Smith
Mr. Clark
Mr. Motte

Papers of the Continental Congress, r182, i165, p. 401-402, National Archives.

Blaine to the Board of War

Philadelphia May 1st. 1781

Gentlemen

I have been through the Western and Eastern shore Maryland, and State of Delaware and find the Magazines are empty, and afford very trifling supplies, indeed many of the County Contractors have done little or nothing.—The Govr. and Council of Maryland are disposed to do every thing in their power, have wrote in the most pressing terms to their supperintendants and have Ordered the County Contractors to use Exertions in procuring supplies required, but the Winter being far advanced before the Law passed and the County Agents received their instructions, little has been done; those of the Western shore have procured about two thousand Barrels of Flour some little salt provisions and rum; the Eastern Shore have not five hundred Barrels of Flour and I believe very little other provisions, but cannot be particular as no returns have been made the Govr. and Council or their superintendants.—I have recommended the forwarding all the supplies on the Western Shore near to George-Town upon the Potomack except a temporary Magazine at Baltimore and Frederick, those places being upon the line of Communication to the Southern Army; those of the Eastern shore to be collected to the Head of Chester from whence they are to be transported to Duck Creek Landing—the State of Delaware have about five hundred Barrels of Flour no salt meat, and from information, eight thousand Bushels Corn, I have disposed of the shallops agreeable to my return made you, for the conveniency of taking in all the flour and grain, and expect every particular belonging to the Public will come up under the Convoy of the Armed Schooners.—

There is a very considerable quantity of Flour and an imensity of India Corn in the Country, all store Houses filled except the Public Magazines which are Empty and afford little relief—the want of money and the slow and uncertain manner in which state Agents execute will ever keep the Army from being regularly supplied, Indeed my disapointments have been so repeated and distresses of the Army so great that I have determined to quit the service, I expect Col: Hollingsworth returns by the next post at which time shall inform you more particularly the provision which may be expected from the Eastern shore but believe it will very little exceed what I have mentioned—I have the honor to be with due respect,

Gentlemen Your Most Obedt. Humble Servt.
Eph: Blaine C: G: P

The Honble Board of War—

> Peter Force Collection, Roll 75, Ephraim Blaine Letterbook, Library of Congress.

Blaine to the Board of War

Philada. 4th. May 1781

Estimate of Money wanted to procure the following Articles for the use of the Commander in Chief's Table &c Viz—
150 lb Coffee
120 Loaf Sugar
6 Bohea Tea
10 Green ditto
200 Cheese
400 Gammons—
2Ct..2..0 Musa: Sugar
12 Bottles Mustard
12lb Pepper
3 [W] Brushes—

The above Articles will Amount to One thousand Dollars of the New Emissions—

Eph Blaine C.G.P.

Honorable Board War—

Papers of the Continental Congress, M247, Roll 160, i147, v5, p91, National Archives.

Blaine to the Board of War

Philada. 9th May 1781.

Gentlemen

Your favour of the 2nd. Instant covering a Letter from Colonel Hay agent for the state of New York, wherein he proposes terms for the barter or exchange of flour I have received and carefully perused the same—if any of the states had comply'd with the requisitions of Congress and enabled me to lay up Magazines of Flour I shou'd be disposed with the Approbation of your Honorable board to adopt any plann which might be an advantage or saving to the public, but when the States are all notoriously difficient in furnishing their quotas and no Magazine Laid up in any state a proposal of

Barter in my Opinion is unnecessary and will answer very little purpose—

I agree with Colonel Hay that a Barter will be attended with very great advantages to the public provided it can be carried into execution but the same advantage will undoubtedly attend Individuals who make the exchange in bringing their produce to Market, but if the price of Flour upon Hudsons River shou'd exceed what it brings in this City—in that case the difference must be allowed the Possesor, indeed you will be Obliged to give it or want the flour as every person in that business will study the advantage of his market, (and that rule must Govern your agent) in making the exchange—Inclosed you have Coppies of Letters which I wrote Govr. Clinton and Colo. Hay last winter upon that Subject, to which I never recd. an answer,

I have the honor to be very Respectfully,
Gentlemen, Your most obdt Hble Sert
Eph. Blaine

Honble Board of War

> Peter Force Collection, Roll 75, Ephraim Blaine Letterbook, Library of Congress.

Blaine to Joseph Reed

Philada. 9th. May 1781.

Sir

Your favour of the 7th Instant inclosing a Resolution of the assembly I acknowledge to have received. and am to inform your Excellency and Council that I Know not of a single certificate issuing from the Officers of my department for the payment of any debts Contracted within this State—shou'd there be any the [*sic*] have been given without my Knowledge and contrary to my express Orders—I forsaw evils attending the giving my deputies and assistants a power to issue those certificates in payment of debts and concluded it wou'd be a hindrance to the settlement of Accts. altho very large sums is due from my department to the inhabitants of this state—shou'd any have been issued I shall endeavour to discover them and inform your Excellency previous to the 24th. of the month,

> I have the honor to be very Respectfully
> Sir your Most Obdt. Hble Servt.
> Eph. Blaine

His Excellency Govr. Reed

> Peter Force Collection, Roll 75, Ephraim Blaine Letterbook, Library of Congress.

Blaine to the Committee on the Commissary Department

Dr The United States to Sundry Persons Vizt 1780

May 8	Samuel Roy	36 head Cattle	£288..0
June 10	Adam Cook	9 do.	£7 63..0
	20 John Randles	4 do. @	7..1030..0
July 10	John Purveyance	26 do @ 7..10	195..0
	19 Michael Coiner	4 do @ 7..10	30..0
	do. do.	1 do	3..0
Aug 9	James Irwin	3 do @ do 10	30..0
	12 John Moor	1 do d	9..10
	16 John McAlheny	1 do. do.	7.10
	do William Holmes	2 do do 7..10	15.0
	18 William Chambers	2 do @ 12	24..0.0
	20 Brewer Reeves	5405 lb Mutten 4½	
			101..6..10½
	Henry Norris	2 Cattle	24..6.0
	John Moor	400 Galls Whisky 5/	100..0.0
			£920..12..10 ½

Gentlemen,

The Vouchers for the above Acct. have not been Rendered to my Office, but I know Mr. Smith deliver'd the above Mentioned beef for the supply of the troops at Carlisle agreable to my advice to him, and which was the only method Cou'd be adopted for furnishing that post with Provisions Philada. 10th. May 1781.
Eph: Blaine C.G.P.

The Hble. the Committee on the Comy. Departmt.

On the reverse: James Smith Acct of Purchases—

> Papers of the Continental Congress M247r182, i165, p409, National Archives.

Blaine to Nathaniel Stevens

Philadelphia 12th. May 1781

Dear Sir

Your favour of the 11 Ulto. came safe to hand with your return and sundry other inclosures for which I thank you, shou'd have wrote you long ere this, but upon my coming home from the Army I was six days in Town when I was ordered down to Potomack and the Eastern shore Maryland; and since my return have been exceedingly unwell with a bad Cold and pain in my Breast.—Col: Stewarts return to Camp will inform you of the state of your Departmt. and that no attention has yet taken place, he has been exceedingly disapointed in geting money, indeed that is the case with all of us; the Public have none to give.—I have by repeated applications to Congress obtained a Committee to adopt some mode for the settlement of All my Accounts and fixing some General plan for the discharging the same, this Committee will take under their Consideration all public demands and I presume will adopt the same System to every other Department, they have been two days met, I am to attend them

on Monday, and hope in the course of a week to know their determination, which I will communicate to you and Col: Stewart—pray give me every information you possible can respecting supplies and the present state of your Magazines be assured nothing will give me greatly pleasure than to hear you are properly supplied.—I have no News worth your Notice to communicate; remember me kindly to all Friends and believe me with much regard—
    Dear Sir Your Most Obedt. Humble Servt.
    Eph: Blaine C:G of Ps.

Nathl. Stevens Esqr. D:C:GI—

N:B shou'd Mr. Abraham Lott near Morris-Town, and Mr. Fash of Mount hope, offer to deposit any flour at the Magazine, West-Point, New-Windsor, or Fishkill, you will please to Order the receival; and give a Certificate to entitle them to an equal quantity at Morris-Town or Ringwood which will Oblige
  Sir Yours &ca. &ca. E: Blaine

> Peter Force Collection, Roll 75, Ephraim Blaine Letterbook, Library of Congress.

Blaine to John Lawrence

          Philada. 12th May 1781,
Sir
  the Inclosed is an Order of Congress of the 20th. of March last with the Order of the Continental Treasurer of the ninth Instant for the One Million of dollars which I suppose My Deputies have Recd. from you on the warrent in my favour on you Dated the 24th. of January 1780 which warrent ageable to the within Order you will please to return that it may be Canceled and charge the monies therein paid to the warrent of the 29th. of June last in favour of the Continental Treasurer,

shou'd any further papers be necessary only mention it, and I shall take Care to have them forwarded, I remain sir,
Your Most Obdt. Hble Servt. Eph Blaine C.G.P

John Lawrence Esqr
Treasurer for the State Conecticutt. Hartford

> Peter Force Collection, Roll 75, Ephraim Blaine Letterbook, Library of Congress.

Blaine to the Committee

Philadelphia 14th May 1781

Gentlemen

Having Acted as Deputy Comy. General of Purchases for the middle department under Mr Buchanan and Mr. Wadsworth who were Commissary Genls. of Purchases, and haveg. all those Accts. principally settled have reason to believe it will be a Considerable time before those Gentlemen are prepared for settlement—I beg that an Order of Congress may pass in my favour directing the Treasury Board to give Instructions for the immediate settlement of those Accts.—and that the amount of each seperate Acct. may be carried to the Credit of those Gentlemens Accts. in the treasury Office—upon my producing Certificates for the sums of money received from each of them—this will be relieving me of a very great charge and if longer delay'd will be a greater injury to individuals and the public—the Immediate settlement of all public Accts. are Absolutely Necessary in order to remove the uneasiness of the people and give them some certain Assurance of payment—there is so little public confidence and Virtue in the people owing princapally to the depreciation of the money, that any plann you adopt will meet with Opposition yet the longer the delay the greater the Evil—shall therefore take the Liberty of giving you a few hints with my Opinon thereon which are as follows—all Accts. brought into the public

Offices in this place to be Liquedated by the Chamber of Accts here, fix a place in each state where one or two Auditors of your appointment with One appointed by the Executive of each state shall meet, who shall notify all persons of every Department within such state who have demands against the public to attend for the immediate adjustment of the same—the auditors to be catious [sic] to take notice of the amount of every month and quantity purchase, [sic] comparing all such sums with Specia agreable to the General Scale of Depriciation (or the depriciation of each Respective State) and when the Accts. of each department is so settled with the Auditors to transmit a Coppy to the treasury Board and One to the head of each department Specifying the Amt. in Continental money and Specie agreable to the Exchange—then if money cannot be procured to pay such Ballances—Specia Certificates bearing a Legal interest to issue for the above purpose—the interest of which with such a proportion of the princaple as you think proper, to be punctually paid annually, I presume a plann of this Kind with some money to enable the agents to pay small debts to the necessitous might answer and I am sure will be satisfactory to every true whig—I have the honor to be with every sentiment of Esteem, Gentlemen

Your Most Obdt. Hble Servt.
Eph: Blaine C.G.P

the Honble. Committee

> This was probably to the Congressional Committee on the Commissary Department. Peter Force Collection, Roll 75, Ephraim Blaine Letterbook, Library of Congress.

Blaine to Robert Forsyth

Philadelphia 14th. May 1781

Dear Sir

I did not return from the Army 'till the tenth of April, and great part of the time since have been down the Eastern

shore Maryland, trying to remove all public Provisions upon that Peninsula between the Delaware and Chesepeck Bay, but to my great mortification after going all through that Country found very little Public property.—our distress's will never be at an end respecting the supplies of the Army; nor never will the state Agents answer the end of their appointments in feeding them.—the present plan must be altered, and new means adopted if Congress mean to keep an Army in the Field without which they cannot—You can have no dependance on the State of Maryland for Beef, they have it not; nor have their Agents adopted any proper measure to procure salt meat of any kind, what will be done God knows.—I have made application to Congress to have some plan adopted for a final settlement of my A/cs., and to think of some means of payment, a Committee is now sitting upon that business, what measures they will recommend cannot inform you, but presume they will appoint or order Auditors to attend in each State for that purpose, who are to reduce all Debts to Specia value when they became due, and Certify the same to the Treasury Board who will adopt some mode of paymt. I have made application in your favour for a large sum of money and have mentioned the necessity of purchasing every kind of provisions your Country can furnish to reduce the necessity of long transportation— This the approve off [sic] but when money can be Obtained to Execute the purchase God knows—The moment the Committee report, and Congress approves I shall inform you of that and every other transaction respecting our Department,
    I am with much Esteem—and regard
      Dear Sir Your Most Obedt. Humble Servt.
       Eph: Blaine

Major Forsyth—

<small>Peter Force Collection, Roll 75, Ephraim Blaine Letterbook, Library of Congress.</small>

To George Washington

Philada 14 May 1781

Sir

I have return'd some days from Maryld: and the Delaware State and find the Supplies procured for Public use very triffling and that the State Contractors have done but little—I could not obtain permission to seize private property, indeed the Governor & Council had not the power of giving it, altho a very large quantity of Flour and an immensity of Indian Corn might have been procured—the Flour cheifly in the hands of Millers and Speculators—All the Provisions upon the Eastern shore I have Order'd to be collected at the Head of Chester from whence it's to be transported to Duck-Creek Landing where Craft are waiting to take it in—The whole Eastern shore Supplies now purchased will not exceed twelve hundred barrels of Flour and two hundred and fifty Barrels of Beef and Pork—those of the Western shore are more considerable and I have given Directions to have them collected as near to George Town as will Admit of safety.

The State of Delaware have done little in the purchase of Flour, and have procured no Meat altho great Things are in their power—had the Assembly laid the Millers under small Contribution they might have had all their Quot[o] of Flour procured and delivered into the Public Magazines some time ago—I have collected from the Agents in that State six hundred Barrels of Flour and eight thousand Bushels of Corn which will all be at Trenton in a few Days provided no accident happens in the Bay.

There are little or no Magazines in this State—the Governor and Council have furnish[ed] their Commissioners with large Sums of Money to expedite their purchases of Flour (which is very plenty) but the Villainy which prevails in this City amongst the Mercantile and speculating Interest, and the measures daily pursued by the disaffected People in the Barter of hard Money, Counteracts every Public Measure and has depreciated and ruined the Circulation of all paper Currency, indeed the Contractors can buy nothing, and no person can subsist in this place without hard Money to procure the Necessaries of Life—this has induced the Council to call a special Meeting of the Assembly on the 24th Instant to endeavour to adopt some certain plan to procure the Supplies acquired, and comply with other public Demands.

The Board of War have ordered me to proceed to York Town and see that proper Provision is made to supply General Waynes Detachment from that place to Fredericksburgh—I have procured a pipe of Wine and some necessaries for Your Excellency & Family which shall be forwarded in two Days from this place.

Upon my Return from York Town shall give your Excellency every further information in my power respecting Supplies.

I have the Honor to be with every sentimt of
Esteem & Regard Your Excellencies
Most Obedient & most Humble Servant
Eph. Blaine C.G.P.

George Washington Papers, Library of Congress.

Blaine to Charles Stewart

Philada. 15th. May 1781.

Sir I have nothing of Consequence to write you only the very extraordinary Change our money has taken since you left the City—the Council having information that the Exchange between hard money and Continental was two hundred and twenty five for One in their state, also being inform'd that Jersey had rais'd the exchange to One hundred and fifty, Mr. Rittenhouse made this discovery by the Large quantities which was brought to his Office, upon which the Council raisd the Exchange One hundred and seventy five for One, next day being market, Continental was Six & Seven hundred for One and State from four to six, indeed none seem disposed to take it—the Villiny Commited in this City from the Avariciousness of Whigs and disafection of torys is sufficient to Dam all paper Currency in Circulation—the agents of this state have had a Large supply of money and wou'd have purchased Considerable quantities of Provisions had not the depreciation of the new money been so rapid—this sudden change in the money has induced Council to call a special meeting of the assembly the 24th. of this month, to adopt means to procure supplies for our army and answer the public demand

  the Boats are not come up yet, you need not expect more than fifteen hundred barrels of flour from my sothern Journey—an embargo is laid upon all Vessels in this harbour, and I pray god the Merchants may be laid under Contribution which have purchased flour, Mr. Holker and them get every barrel which comes to this place and for twenty Shillings pr hundred hard money—a Committee of Congress are now meet [sic] to adopt some system for the payment of their debts what measures the [sic] will Establish I cannot inform you but suppose it will be comparing the Value of all sums with Specia when Contracts become due and giving Certificates in Specia for those sums bearing an Interest of five pr Cent, however this is only my Oppinion but I believe its all they have in their power, the Board of War have ordered me to york town to see that sufficient supply of Provisions is procured to Carry Genl. Waynes Detachment to Fredericksburgh—I have been exceeding unwell with a Cold and pain in my heart ever since my Return from Maryland—give my Compts. to all friend
    and believe me with much Esteem Dr. Sir Your
      Most obdt Servt. Eph Blaine
Colo. Chs. Stewart

  Peter Force Collection, Roll 75, Ephraim Blaine Letterbook, Library of Congress.

Blaine to Abraham Lott

Philadelphia 15th. May 1781.

Dear Sir

Your two favours came to hand, the former when I was absent in Maryland Else shou'd have been answered, the latter by Mr. Beverante—I have wrote Mr. Stevens Deputy Commissary Genl. of Issues who lives at Fish Kill Town, to Receive any flour offered in your name at Fish Kill or West point and give a Certificate to Entitle you to an equal Quantity from the Magazine at Morris Town, I have no Certainty of receiving any pork, therefore wished not to have yours without in my Power to repay at Morris—Inclosed you have a few lines to Mr. Blair who acts as Issuing Commissary at Morris and who will deliver you such Quantities of his best flour upon producing Mr. Stevens Rect: as you are entitled two, [sic] this Exchange is much in favour of the Public and I acknowledge it as such—and at any time when in my power to give you One upon equal terms you have only to Command—and wish it was in my power to serve you in any Other way,

I remain Dear Sir,
Your Most Obdt. Hbl Servt.
Eph Blaine

Mr Abram. Lott

Abraham Lott fled from New York City after the British occupation in 1776 and settled at Beverwyck near Morristown, New Jersey. Peter Force Collection, Roll 75, Ephraim Blaine Letterbook, Library of Congress.

Blaine to John Jacob Faesch

Philadelphia 15th. May 1781

Dear Sir

Your letter came to hand a considerable time ago, and should have been answered ear [sic] this, but my being absent in Maryland prevented; I am now to inform you that I have wrote to Mr. Stevens D:C:G:Is. at Fish Kill Town to give orders to receive such quantities of Flour as you may offer to deliver at Fish Kill land or West Point and to give you a Certificate to receive equal quantity and quality from the Magazine at Morris Town which I have not the least doubt he will comply with.—Inclosed you have a few lines to Mr. Blair keeper of the Magazine at Morris Town upon that subject, shall be happy at any time if within the line of my Duty to render you any service and remain

      Dr. Sir Your Most Obedt. Humble Servt.
      Eph: Blaine

Mr. Fash

> Faesch was the proprietor of the ironworks at Mount Hope, N.J. He supplied the Continental army with much-needed cannon, shot, and general ironwork during the war. Peter Force Collection, Roll 75, Ephraim Blaine Letterbook, Library of Congress.

Blaine to Unidentified

      Philada. 19th May 1781

Sir

Their is forty five Barrels of Mercht. flour at Mr. Helm's Mill in your County the property of Colonel Grayson which he has disposed of two me on public Acct. for which you have an Order Inclosed—have therefore to request you to receive it in public Acct. and give the bearer Mr. Moody a rect. in Colonel Graysons name, for the number of Barrels neat hundred of flour and price in hard money or the Exchange which will oblige sir

      Your Most Obdt. Hble Servt.
      Eph. Blaine C.G.P

> Peter Force Collection, M 13,778, Series 8D, Roll 74, Library of Congress.

Blaine to Henry Hollingsworth

Philadelphia 19th May 1781.

Sir

I expected have heard from you long ear this and to have been inform'd what Quantity of provisions the Contractors in your district had procured, in Order to make returns to the Commander in chief Board of War &c. but am sorry It has not been in my power—Inclosed is an Order of the Board of War for my Government by which you will see the great necessity of punctuallity in making monthly returns of your purchases Deliveries and the provisions remaining on hand—therefore request you to give such Orders to your Agents as will Oblige them to Comply and enable you to perform that Necessary part of your duty. favour me with a line by first safe Opportunity
and Believe me sir
your Most Obdt. Hble Servt.
Eph. Blaine

Colo. Hollingsworth, supperdt. of supplies
Eastern Shore Maryland

> Peter Force Collection, Roll 75, Ephraim Blaine Letterbook, Library of Congress.

Blaine to Udny Hay

Philadelphia 19th. May 1781—

Sir

When you return to North River you will please to examine the quantity of Provisions which may be deposited at Clavarac & Kenderhook and give directions for the disposal of them in such manner as will answer the wants of the Garrison at West point, the Troops in the neighbourhood and those of the Northern Department.—I have reason to expect a considerable quantity of salt provisions and rum will be deposited at Great Barrinton and that the Quarter Master will use every possible exertion to have it forwarded to Clavarac— You will also collect all the Accounts of such parcels of rum as was siezed in the vicinity of West Point and Fish Kill either by Order of Genl. How or any Officer commanding in your Department, and as soon as those Account [sic] are procured favour me with an Acct. of them, Inclosed is an Order of the board of War for my line of Conduct from which you will see the necessity of making monthly returns, and beg you give such Orders to your people as will enable you to make them without Disappointment—

    I am with much Esteem and regard Sir
     Your Most Obedt. Humble Servt.
      Eph. Blaine

Col: Hay—

Peter Force Collection, Roll 75, Ephraim Blaine Letterbook, Library of Congress.

Blaine to Donaldson Yeates

        Philadelphia 19th. May 1781

Sir

Your favr. of the 17th. Instant I recd. this morning and am happy to find such a quantity of Flour is deposited at Geo: Town provided that is a place of safety, but should rather wish it was five or Six Miles back in the Country, I made application to your Goveror [sic] and Council to have all the supplies of provisions upon the Western shore (Except those of Hartford County) colected near to George Town Potomack in Order to have it convenient to the Southern Army I have reason to believe that the most Active part of this Campaign will be in the state of Virginia and that provs. will be much wanted there, therefore would not wish a single Bbl of Flour, Beef or Pork brought this way except those of Hartford which

with all the supplies upon the Eastern shore wish you to forward to this place with all possible dispatch,—I have wrote to Col: Hollingsworth but can Obtain no returns of the provisions procured in his District—I approve of Major Forsyths plan of sending provisions up Potomack Creeck as every Advantage ought to be take of Navigation provided it reduces the Expences of land transportation and there is no risque in the attempt, however I shall leave this matter entirely to your Judgment.—I know there has been little regularity observed by the state Agents, and it is wrong in the state keeping up any posts but those pointed out by the Commander in Chief—however it is done but presume not [sic] part of the provisions Issued by the state Agents is to be accounted for as part of the Continental supplies nor will the Continent pay the Expences of keeping up any post, but those properly established,—
I remain with much regard & Esteem
Your Most Obedt. Humble Servt.
Eph: Blaine

Donaldson Yates Esqr.
D:Q:M— Maryland

Peter Force Collection, Roll 75, Ephraim Blaine Letterbook, Library of Congress.

Blaine to the Board of War

Philadelphia 23rd. May 1781—

Gentlemen

A resolution of Congress of the 26th. of August 1778 empowered the Commander in Chief or the Commanding Officer of a seperate Army to fix the rations issued to our Troops—The impossibility of procuring the small parts of rations allowed by resolve of Congress the 4th. of Novr. 1775 to supply the Army, induced the Commander in Chief to fix a ration to one pound of Flour, one pound of beef, or three quarters of a pound of pork and in lieu of Milk, Molasses, rice & a a jill of rum or other spirits—The articles of soap and Candles must be procured from the tallow of the Cattle used with the Army the proceeds of which will be sufficient for that purpose. The above mentioned ration in my opinion is sufficient for the Troops, and the rum is an equivalent for the small parts thereof rations. Fish is an article the Soldiery do not like, nor will they accept of it only chance Days when there is a scarcity of beef.

The value of the above mentioned rations will depend on the places where you engage your contractors to deposit or and in my opinion the under mentioned allowance for reasonable places of deposit will be sufficient

        Viz   1 lb. Flour 2 ½
including 5th. Quarter   1 Beef or ¾ pork 6   } 11 d
                         1 Gill rum 2 ½

Agreeable to the above rations you will please calculate your supplies and when you fix upon your places of deposit and the method in which you mean to have the supplies delivered I make no doubt you will have many persons offering to engage.—

                      I have the Honor to be &
                      Eph. Blaine C.G.P.
The Honble Board of War
Copy of Colonel Blaines Letter to the Board of War

    This copy was sent with the Board's letter of June 7 to Washington. George Washington Papers, Library of Congress.

Blaine to the Board of War

                            Philadelphia 24th May 1781
Gentlemen

The request of the Honble Congress of the 25th. of Feby. 1780 calling upon the states for the supplies of our Army has not in any One Instance been fully comply'd with, nor is it in my power to give you any further information than what my return Contains, the States of Jersey, Delaware & Maryland have made me no returns, nor has it been in the power of Major Forsyth to Obtain a regular return of the provisions furnished in the Southern department, two or three of the Agents being captured.—however your Honor's may be assured that the State Agents never furnish'd supplies equal to the daily demands, and that is One reason why the Continental agents are so largely in debt—the requisitions of Congress of the 4th. of Novr. for supplies for the Year 1781 from Newhampshire to North Carolina do not furnish your Magazines with Eight Weeks supplies for your Army

I have the honor to be very respectfully.—
Gentlemen Your Most Obedient Humble Servt.—
E: Blaine

Honble Board of War

Peter Force Collection, Roll 75, Ephraim Blaine Letterbook, Library of Congress.

Blaine to Oliver Phelps

Philadelphia 25th May 1781,

Dear Sir

I Expected to had [sic] it in my power to have sent you money long ear this but have been disapointed. a Committee of Congress have been appointed to adopt some mode for the payment of the debts but have not yet determined, the momt. I am acquainted with the plann shall inform you, and be assured nothing will satisfy me but money or an Order upon your state for the Ballance of your Acct. and Mr. Millers of Boston The Convention troops are Ordered from Maryland to Rutland in your state there is about two thousand three hundred of them

Exclusive of the Guards which will be three or four hundred I have therefore to request you to adopt Measures to lay in two Months supply of Provisions at that place and give such directions to your assistants as will afford them a temporary supply from time to time while they remain at that post—their route is from Fish kill to Springfield from thence to Rutland—I am now seting out for York Town Onn the Susquehanah in Order to make provisions for their march and Immediately on my return shall write you

    I remain with much Esteem and Reguard
     Dear sir Your Most Obedt. Hble Servt.
      Eph Blaine

Oliver Phelps Esqr. Springfield

  Peter Force Collection, Roll 75, Ephraim Blaine Letterbook, Library of Congress.

Blaine to Samuel Huntington

        Philadelphia 26th. May 1781

Sir

  I take the liberty of troubling your Excellency upon a Subject which gives me great uneasiness and which I beg you to represent to the Honorable the Congress sundry persons under my directions from repeated and pressing applications for supplies and their desire to serve the Public, have involved themselves in ruin, without money or Orders is granted to cover their demands.—Many of which have borrowed Continental and hard money and others have taken public money which was put into their hand for other purposes, Mr. Philips of Springfield in particular Amount of their particular debts will not be large; have therefore in the most pressing terms to intreat Congress to adopt some means of payment and not let those demands come under the general system of the payment of Debts, by Certificates; in a few days I can state an

exact Account of the sums and persons so circumstanced, nothing could induce me to make a partial representation to Congress but a desire of doing justice to those people whom I have ever found attentive and faithfull in executing my Orders, and to relieve them from the distresses they now labour under for complying therewith—I therefore intreat your Excelly. to press upon Congress in Order that Justice may be done those who in this particular manner have served them, the Commander in Chief, the Army and
    Your Excellency's
      Most Obedt. Servt. Eph: Blaine
His Excellency the Presidt. of Congress—

> Mr. Philips is probably Oliver Phelps. Peter Force Collection, Roll 75, Ephraim Blaine Letterbook, Library of Congress.

Blaine to James Wood

      York Town 30th. May 1781
Dear Sir
 I am ordered by the board of War to make Provisions for the Convention troops and their guards amounting to near three thousand men, and have it laid in at convenient places upon the route in which the [*sic*] are Ordered to march—I have already given the necessary Orders and the places of deposit between Frederick Town and North river is this place, Reading, Easton, Sussex Court House, and Fish Kill Landing—Flour and Whisky will be procured but have reason to doubt a difficulty in Obtaining meat—I shall Employ some person who will meet you at this place, and give attention to the supply of those troops untill the [*sic*] reach Rutland in Massachusetts Bay—I am now upon my way to Carlisle where I shall remain a few days if you cou'd inform me the time you expect to reach this place will do my selfe the honor of waiting upon you—
 I remain with much Esteem and Reguard, Dr. Sir

Your Most Obdt. Hble Servt.
Eph. Blaine C.G.P

Colo. Wood

> Colonel Wood was Colonel of the Eighth Virginia regiment and had been superintending the Convention Prisoners from Burgoyne's army, who had been moved to Virginia in 1779. They were being moved to Pennsylvania, as Cornwallis was moving into Virginia. Papers of James G. Blaine and Family, Acc. 16,822, Container 3, Library of Congress.

Morton to William Colfax

Philada. 30 May 1781

Sir

You will receive by the bearer Philip Cole the following Articles for the use of His Excellency the Commander in Chief & Family—Viz—

2 Hhds Mada. Wine No. 2- 44 } 89 Galls.
         6- 45

1 Bbl Musa. Sugar	2 Ct..1..4 Nt
1 do. Loaf ditto	133 lb 4 oz
1 do Coffee	177 lb Nt.
9 lb Green Tea	
6 Bohea Tea	
5 Bottles Mustard	
6 lb. Pepper	
1 Jar Pickles &	
2 Brushes—	

The above Articles should have been forwarded long e'er this if Money had been furnished for that purpose—you may expect shortly some good Spirit two or three Barrels of Biscuit and if in Cash the Gammon & Cheese mention'd in your memorandum—at present if those Articles were procured I could not get a Waggon to take them—In one of the Boxes is a Sample of the Wine by which you can discover the

Adulteration, if any—Col. Blaine has been at York Town some days—for whom—
> I am Sir Your very Obt Servt
> Geo: Morton

Capt. Colfax—

> Captain Colfax from Connecticut, was serving in the Commander-in-Chief's Guard. Peter Force Collection, Roll 75, Ephraim Blaine Letterbook, Library of Congress.

Morton to Charles Stewart

Philada. 4th. June 1781—

Sir

Your favour by Col. Broderick came to hand last friday—Col. Blaine set out from here yesterday week for York Town & Carlisle in Order to make some Provision for the Convention Troops, who are order'd back to Rutland—I forwarded some Wine, Loaf & Muscado Sugar, Coffee, Tea, Pepper, Mustard, Pickles &c. by Col. Blaines own Waggon last Wednesday, which hope will be at Head Quarters before this reaches you—

The Brig Holker arrived here yesterday in twenty three days from Martinique, in her Timmy Mullins came passenger, he brings an Account of the arrival of 26 Ships of the Line with fifteen thousand Troops at that Place—that after the Fleet had seen the Transports safe in Port, they pushed out immediately and attacked the British Fleet of seventeen Sail of the Line (which had been riding triumphant off Fort Royal several Weeks) Mr. Mullins saw the Action which lasted an hour and three quarters Six of the British were disabled and towed out of the Line into St Lucia—the Languedoc in like manner returned to Martinique—after this Contest the French immediately sent over Troops to St Lucia & as the British Fleet did not appear when the Holker Sail'd it is expected that the place must be in possession of our good Allies before this time—paper Money retrieves its Credit, but very little but hard Cash in Circulation, Exchange about 4 @ 5 for one—

By Col. Hollingsworths Return for last month, there is on hand—in Kent County 200 Bbls Flour in Worcester, 65 Bbls Pork (forty of which order'd by the Governor to Baltimore & Annapolis) and in Dorchester County 750 Bushs. Wheat—those are the whole Supplies of the Eastern Shore of Maryland—what little was in the Delaware State is forwarded & the fluctuating State of the Money has prevented the State Purchasers from doing any thing considerable for some weeks past—

    I am Sir with Respect
     Your most Obt Servt
      Geo: Morton

Coll. Chas. Stewart—
  C. G of Issues

Addressed: Col. Charles Stewart
  Commy General of Issues Head Quarters

Charles Stewart Papers, 1752-1818, Collection 262, New York State Historical Association.

Blaine to James Wood

          Reading 17th. June 1781,

I expected to have had the pleasure of seeing you at this place but am disappointed. Captain Alexander the person whom I have appointed to attend the Convention Troops upon there March to the Eastward and use every endeavour in his power to procure supplies at the sundry posts upon the route, and attend to your Orders and Instructions, upon meeting the Hessians troops in Marsh Creek, and thinking you would be up Immediately did not proceed but return'd with them to this place, where he will remain untill he hears from you, he is a Gentleman on whom you may rely, and will closely attend to your Instructions and put every part of them into execution,

>   I remain with much Esteem and Reguard
>   Dear Sir, Your Hble Servt.
>   Eph: Blaine C.G

Colo. Wood
Commanding the Convention Prisoners

Addressed: Public Service
           Colonel James Wood
           Commanding the Convention troops, Lancaster

Papers of James G. Blaine and Family, Acc. 16,822, Container 3, Library of Congress.

Blaine to the Board of War

>   Philada. 20th June 1781.

Gentlemen

Inclosed you have an Estimate of three or four kinds of rations which in my Opinion are a sufficient Allowance for the army, you have also the supposed Cost but much will depend upon the places of deposit and mode of delivery. beef at six pence pr lb in sinking the fifth quarter which if properly managed will exceed One forth [sic] the Value of the beef to the public the small parts of Rations are of little Advantage to the soldiery and can never be furnished an Army. indeed it only tends to creat confusion and disorder in settling Accts.—the mode Established by the Brittish in issuing provisions in my Opinion is the best that can be adopted. what constitutes a ration is Bread Meat and rum always allowing the necessary quantity of soap and Candles—when rice pease or Vegetables are issued there is a Deduction of either bread or meat & the Generally the Article which is Scarcest—this method they have pursued and it undoubtedly answers well—the money which your agents will have to pay Regimental Quartr Masters for parts of rations due your Soldiery and from which they will have very little benefit will amount to more money than the Brittish troops receive for their pay—I wou'd therefore beg leave to mention to your honors that in my Opinion the ration N<u>o</u> 3 ought to be Establish'd with the Alteration that when troops are in Quarters and Vegetables can be procured, that the [*sic*] shall be issued, and the allowance of rum detained, or a deduction of Bread or Meat in proportion to the Vegetables issued stop'd from this ration.

    I have the honor to be very Respectfully Gentlemen
        Your Most Obdt. Hble Servt.
            Eph Blaine C.G.Ps.

the Honble. Board of War—

> Peter Force Collection, Roll 75, Ephraim Blaine Letterbook, Library of Congress.

Blaine to Frederick Augustus Conrad Muhlenberg

                      Philadelphia 22d. June 1781
Sir

    His Excellency Genl. Washington is now preparing to open the Campaign and intends being in the field the first of July how his Army is to subsist is a matter of great importance to every Friend of America and gives me the utmost concern, all the Magazines upon North River, Sussex Court House, Trenton Philadelphia; Easton, Reading, Lancaster, Christian [*sic*] and the Head of Elk, does not equal two thousand Bbls. the small magazine at Easton will soon be consumed by Convention Troops, the Flour in Jersey and New-York state nearly exhausted, little on none to be expected from Maryland; the supplies of that state being ordered southerly, and your Agent not able purchase a single Barrel in this situation the Magazines will soon be exhausted, the flour all bought up for private purposes and no relief in your power untill afforded by the new Crops; in this situation it will be impossible for the

Commander in Chief to act Decisively indeed I may say impossible to keep the Army from disbanding—

I have therefore in the most pressing terms to request you to urge your Honble House to adopt measures which may tend without delay to secure a supply of Bread, without which there can be no Campaign the state is far deficient in the quantity demanded by Congress, this State must furnish the present supplies of flour as little can be expected from our Neighbouring states before harvest, say the begining of November, from those circumstances you will see the necissity of fixing upon proper ways and means to facilitate the purchases of that Article while in your power, Easton and Philadelphia ought to be the places of purchase except such quantities as may be necessary for the Consumption of Established posts,

I have the honor to be very respectfully—
Sir Your Most Obedt. Humble Servt.
Eph: Blaine

His Excy. Frederick A Muhlenberg

Peter Force Collection, Roll 75, Ephraim Blaine Letterbook, Library of Congress.

Blaine to Robert Morris Jr.

Philadelphia 23d. June 1781

Sir

By a resolution of Congress I am authorized to Exchange with Mr. Nickelson agent for the State of Virginia now in this City, as much of the Flour within the State of Pennsylvania, Delaware or Maryland belonging to the United States as you shall think proper, I beg leave to inform you that all the flour which has come to my knowledge and now remains on hand, is contained in the inclosed return The Agents in Maryland & Delaware have had very pressing orders to purchase and

perhaps their exertions may have aded Considerably to the public Magazines—
  I remain Sir Your Most Obedt. Humble Servt.
      Eph: Blaine
Robt. Morris Esqr.

Return of Flour in the States of Pennsylvania, Maryland and Delaware supposed to be at the
 following Posts Vizt.

York Town	350
Carlisle	850
Head of Chester and Duck Creek X Roads	400
Head of Elk	150
Baltimore Co.	400
Geo: Town	<u>1200</u>
	Barrels 3350

  Morris was a prominent leader during the American Revolution, and was a signer the Declaration of Independence. He had been appointed Superintendent of Finance by the Continental Congress. Peter Force Collection, Roll 75, Ephraim Blaine Letterbook, Library of Congress.

Blaine to the Board of War

          Philadelphia 23d. June 1781
Gentlemen
  Inclosed you have a return of all the flour which remains on hand within the States of Pennsylvania Delaware and Maryland, since my last returns, the Exertions of the Agents may had aded Considerable quantities to the public Magazines—
  I have the honor to be very respectfully Gentlement
    Your Most Obedt. Humble Servt.
      Eph. Blaine

Honble Board of War

Return of Flour in the States of Pennsylvania Delaware and Maryland supposed to be at the following Posts Vizt.

York Town	350
Carlisle	850
Head of Chester & Duck Creek X Roads	400
Head of Elk	150
Baltimore Co.	400
Geo: Town	1200
Barrels	3350

Peter Force Collection, Roll 75, Ephraim Blaine Letterbook, Library of Congress.

Blaine to Donaldson Yeates

Philadelphia 24th. June 1781

Dear Sir

Congress have directed me to make an exact return of all stores in my department to Mr. Morris the Financier, who is now making arrangements for future supplies—have therefore to request you without delay to furnish me with a return of all stores at Christian, Elk, Head of Chester and Hartford County, the supplies of that District being ordered to the Magazine at Elk, the flour at and near George-Town to remain untill further Orders, except the Southern Army are in need of it and Navigation of Potomack Creek clear from the Enemy, in either cases and provided their [sic] is no danger of the Enemy at Fredericksburgh wou'd wish you to forward part.

I remain Dr Sir Your Most Obedt. Humble Servt.
Eph: Blaine

Donl. Yates Esqr.

Peter Force Collection, Roll 75, Ephraim Blaine Letterbook, Library of Congress.

Blaine to Robert Morris Jr.

Philadelphia 2d July 1781

Sir

Inclosed you have a return of the persons who are on Established pay in my department since the new arangement took place; previous to that I had Agents in each state who superintended the receival and forwarding of all provisions and supply'd the posts with what was necessary. I have had no late return from Major Forsyth, and as posts and places of deposite are Established by the Commanding Officer of the Southern Army, cannot inform you what number of Persons he may have employed to answer the calls of a moving Army. Drovers, Coopers &ca. are engaged Occasionally according to the demand we have for them, always taking care not to keep them a moment in Service when we can do without them. I have no returns from the Southward since the first of last January nor can I inform you when to expect them, and believe the principle reason is that One half the supplies of the Southern Army are taken by impress, and it is not in Major Forsyths power to Obtain a proper Account. I shall use every means in my power to procure Accurate returns from the other States and when accomplished shall waite upon you with them.

I have the Honor to be very respectfully Sir
Your Most Obedient and Most Humble Servant
E: Blaine

Robt. Morris Esqr.

Return of Persons employ'd in the Commissary Genl. of Purchases Department agreable to the Last Arrangement shewing their Duty, Station, pay &c. July 1st. 1781

Names	Residence	Duty and Station	Pay per month
Ephraim Blaine	Philada. Pennsylvania	Commissary General of Purchases	177

Names	Duty and Station		Pay per month
George Morton	ditto ditto	Cashier and Book keeper in the Commy. Generals Office	40
Alexdr. Williamson	ditto ditto	Assistant in ditto	40
George Kitts	Grand Army	Receiver of Live Stock	50
Nathl. Stevens	North River	Assistant Commissary General of Purchases to Estimate and deliver Cattle	
Nichs. Crouse	New York	Assistant Commissary General of Purchases to Estimate and deliver Cattle	
Robert Forsyth	Frederickbg. Virginia	Deputy Commissary General of Purchases Southern Department	
George Buckner		Clerk to ditto	
John Meals		Clerk to ditto	
Noah Emory	New Hampshire	Assitant Commissary of Purchases	
William Miller	Boston Massachusetts	to Receive and forward State Supplies and furnish the Establish'd Posts	
Oliver Phelps	Receiver of Supplies for Rhode Island and Connecticut	One Clerk allowed Mr. Phelps	
Henry Champion Sr.	Colchester Connecticut	to Receive and forward Live Stock from the Eastern States and see them provided with Forage	
Udny Hay	Poughkepsie New York	Receiver and forwarder of Live Stock	
Daniel Walters	West Point	Receiver of Cattle and Supt. of Slaughters	
Jona. Morgan	North River	Receiver of Cattle at	

Jona. Morgan	North River	Receiver of Cattle at the Barracks and Fish Kill Landing	
David Duncan	Pennsylvania	Superintendt. of the Western Department	
Saml. Dunham	New Jersey	Receiver of Cattle	

NB. Exclusive of the within there are two Butchers to each Brigade of the Army, one at every principal post. Drovers and Coopers are Occasionally employed.

Peter Force Collection, Roll 75, Ephraim Blaine Letterbook, Library of Congress.

Blaine to Samuel Miles

Sir,   Philada. 3rd July 1781,
Please to furnish me with three good Teams to carry stores to head Quarters—woud wish to have covered Waggons with locks and Keys in order to deprive the Carters from Embezeling any part of the stores—two teams may carry the whole provided I can have my team ready to go with them, which will not have more than half a load—wou'd wish to have them ready to Load to Morrow, I Remain Sir
Your Most Obdt. Servt.
Eph. Blaine C.G.P.
Colo. Miles

> Miles had been commander of the Pennsylvania Rifle Regiment, and had been captured at Long Island and later exchanged. At this time was serving in Philadelphia as a Deputy Quartermaster General.
> Peter Force Collection, Roll 74, Ephraim Papers, Library of Congress.

Blaine to Charles Stewart

Philadelphia 5th. July 1781.
Dear Sir,
I expected to have been with you long Ear [sic] this but the want of money and a power of ading to our supplies has been the cause of my delay, Mr. Morris is now at the head of

every department and will make Considerable alterations in the Quartermaster departmt. and myne; and all your assistants at posts and magazines will be reduced, as he means to have those places supply'd by special Contract the Contractor to issue the rations and be paid so much for each, he has now published requesting people to give in their proposals for the supply of this place and Lancaster and believe will get it under ten pence pr ration—the ration Established is One pound of bread a pound of Beef or ¾ of pork, and a Jill of rum with the former allowance of soap and Candles—he seems to be disposed to husband out the Contracts to different people that no person will have it in their power to make any thing worth their attention—Mr. Morris has got every power the Assembly of this State can give him, he has got compleat hold of their purse string and has assured them he will procure their Quota of Supplies—his old favourites are coming in play, your friend Mr. Lowry one of his principles—he intends Contracting for the supplies of the main and Southern Army's. I shall call upon him and Know his proposals before I set out to Camp which will be about this day week,—I shall resign to morrow but claim every advantage of pay and Rations untill I am discharged from my Accts. or have made a final settlement—I cannot Obtain One Shilling of money the time and payment of Old Debts is left to Mr. Morris and I presume he will have such heavy demands upon himselfe that nothing can be done for some Considerable time.

    I am preparing Stores sufficient for his Excellency's table during the Campaign and hope to have them forwarded by next tuesday—your friends are all well, remember me Kindly to our Circle of Friends at Camp, and Believe me with much Esteem and reguard Dr. Sir

Your Most Obdt. Hble Servt.
Eph. Blaine

Col Stewart

Excuse hast and the badness of my Scrawl, being celebrating the fifth Anniversary of our Independence

N. B The reports of Genl. Green taking 96, is not yet confirm'd—the Marquis's light [Troo]ps and Tarltons Cavelry have [had] a touch, and Mr. Tarlton has been severely handled, our Loss is 9 Kill'd 13 Missing and thirty wounded, the Enemy's loss is sixty Kill'd upon the spot One hundd. Wounded, Colo. Butler has now the Command, the Brittish are at Williamsburg—our troops twenty Miles Above—

> Charles Stewart Papers, 1752-1818, Collection 262, New York State Historical Association.

Blaine to Jacob Hiltzheimer

Sir,
  four teams will be wanting to load for Head Quarters, you will therefore please to give Orders for that number the loading will be all Ready next Monday Morning, two Chest will be wanting to pack China and Other Crockery, they must Long so as to pack 3 Qt. Bowls and dishes,
6th. July 1781   Your Hble Servt
           Eph Blaine C.G.P.
Mr Hiltzheimer

> Hiltzheimer, a long time resident of Philadelphia, ran a stable and provided transporation for the Americans.
> Peter Force Collection, Roll 74, Ephraim Blaine Papers, Library of Congress.

Blaine to the Board of War

Gentlemen   Phia. 11th. July 1781
  I have made enquiry and find it impossible to procure the articles wanting for the use of his Excelly General

Washingtons Table on credit, therefore have it not in my power to forward them; the Waggons are waiting—Shall I load the Wine, spirits and Neats tongues, and discharge the others—will waite your answer and am Gentlemen very respectfully—
Your Obedt. Servt.
Eph: Blaine

Honble Board of War—

> Peter Force Collection, Roll 74, Ephraim Blaine Papers, Library of Congress.

Blaine to George Washington

Sir   Philada. 14 July 1781—
Inclosed you have an Invoice of Sundry Articles for the use of your Excellency's Table Loaded in five Waggons and put under the particular Care of a Waggon Conductor, All the Stores are of the best quality, the Wine is properly cased and all the other Articles put up carefully—beg your Excellency to Order some person to examine and see that the Stores are properly deliver'd before the Waggon Master & his People are discharged—There is one Pipe of Wine and some other Articles which will be forwarded next Week—should have had the Table Linnen made up but not knowing the length of your Tables or Marqui, thought it best to forward it and the Diaper for Toweling whole in Order that it may be made proper sizes—
I wish the Stores safe and have the Honor to be with all due respect—
Your Excellencies Most Obedt. &
most Humble Servant—
Eph: Blaine C. G. P.

George Washington Papers, Library of Congress

Enclosed with above:
Invoice of Sundries sent to Head Quarters for the use of his Excellency General Washingtons Table—
Philadelphia 14th. July 1781

6 Quarter Casks Madaira Wine   Containg. 198 Gallons
1 Ditto   sweet Ditto   from Mr. Morris
2 Tierces Jamaica Spirit   82   }
2 Barrels Ditto Ditto   61   Total 143 Gallons
1 Ditto French Brandy   34 Do.
1 Ditto Shrub   30 ½ do.
6 Barrels Hares Bottled Porter contg. 24 Doz:
1 Hhd.
1 Tierce   } Morris's Do. Beer   24 Do.
2 Bbls
2 Bbls. Containing   350 lb of (English) Cheese
1 Tierce containing   231 lb 14 Oz. Loaf Sugar,
                                double refined
1 Box   do.   375 lb best Spanish Sugar
1 Bbl   do.   187 lb of Coffee
2 Casks Raisins
1 Small Box contg 10 lb. of Mustard
1 Box of China contg. 2 Doz: Coffee Cups with saucers, two
             Tea-Potts a Cream Jugg and Six Bowls
1 Barrel of Hams   170 lbWt.
2 Box containing 12 Bottles Oyl 12 Bottles Olives
           & 6 Bottles of Kitchup
6 Kegs Sturgeon
2 do. Pickled Oysters
6 Doz: Knives and Forks
½ lb Nutmegs ½ lb. Cloves ¼ lb Cinnamon ¼ Mace
1 ps. Diaper   35 Yards   Cost 40/pr Yd.
16 Yards Do.   Do.   8/
1 Table Cloth
6 Yards Sheeting

2 Bottles of Kitchup

[Margin Note with brackets for items from oysters down]
Note, these Articles together with the China are contd. in a large Chest, also Mustard

George Washington Papers, Library of Congress.

Blaine to the Board of War

Return of sundry Articles sent to Head Quarters for the Use of his Excellency General Washington—
Philada. 14th. July 1781—
Vizt.
- 6. Qr. Casks Madeira Wine cased Contg. 198 Gallons—
- 1. ditto   sweet ditto   from Mr. Morris
- 2. Tierces Jamaica Spirit 82   }
- 2. Bbl   ditto ditto   61   Total 143 Gallons
- 1. ditto French Brandy   34 ditto
- 1. ditto Shrub   30 ½ ditto—
- 6. Bbls. Hares bottled Porter Containing 24 dozen
- 1. Hhd.
- 1. Tierce } Morris's bottled Beer do.   24 ditto—
- 2. Bbls
- 2. Barrells containing   350 lb English Cheese
- 1. Tierce ditto   231 14 Oz. Loaf Sugar
- 1. Box   ditto   375 Spanish ditto
- 1. Barrell ditto   187 Coffee—
- 2. Casks Raisins
- 1. small Box containing 10 lb. Durham Mustard
- 1. box China—Contg. 2 dozen Coffee Cups with Saucers two Tea Potts a Cream Pot and 6 Punch Bowls
- 1. Barrel Hams   170 ¼ Wt—
- 2. Boxes Contg. 12 Bottles Oil 12 do. Olives and 6 do. Catchup

6. Kegs pickled Sturgeon
2. do. do. Oysters
6. dozen Knives and forks
½ lb. Cloves ½ Nutmegs ¼ Mace and ¼ Cinnamon
1. Piece Diaper   35 Yards
P. do.   ditto   16 ditto
1. Table Cloth
6 .Yards Sheeting

NB. Mr. Morris proposes giving a Draft upon some person in the State of Connecticut who will pay One thousand dollars for the Genls. Table—

Eph Blaine CGB

Honorable Board of War
Margin Note:
NB. 4. Bbls. Irish Beef and Pork
1. do.   do.   Tongues
20. Green Tea
2. Bags Almonds Wt. abt. 150
1. pipe Madeira Wine
400. Smoked Tongues
4 Bbls Biscuit

These Articles are procured and ready to send off as soon as Teams can be got for that purpose—

George Washington Papers, Library of Congress.

Blaine to the Board of War

Gentlemen   Philadelphia 18th. July 1781

The bearer hereof Capt. Alexander is the Person whom I appointed agreeable to your instructions to attend the Convention Troops upon their March to Rutland in Massachusetts Bay, as those Troops have been delay'd at

Reading, he has returned, thinking there was no farther service for him—he is entitled pr agreement to twelve Shillings and Six pence pr day, for himself and Horse, and reasonable Expences, have therefore to request your Honble Board to settle his Acct. which will greatly Oblige
    Gentlemen Your Most Obedt. Humble Servt.
      Eph: Blaine
Honble Board of War—

> Peter Force Collection, Ephraim Blaine Papers, Reel 74, Library of Congress.

Blaine to Samuel Miles

Sir   Philada. 27th. July 1781
 there is near four hundred blls. of Flour and seventy Blls. of pork at Duck Creek Landing which is much wanted. & I am in doubts if delay'd much longer the Pork will perish. have therefore to request you to Order down two of the Continental Arm'd Schooners and least there shoud be Danger please to Order them Double man'd,
    I Remain Sir Your &c.
     E Blaine
Col Miles

> Peter Force Collection, Ephraim Blaine Papers, Reel 74, Library of Congress.

Blaine to Thomas McKean

Sir   Philadelphia 30th. July 1781
 The new arrangement for the Supplies of the Army leaves me no Duty to execute, therefore take the liberty through your Excelly to inform Congress that I return them my most grateful thanks for the many Honors they have confered upon me in the appointment of Commy Genl. of Purchases and

to accept of this as my resination At the same time please to assure them, that when in my power to render my Country or them any service they have only to Command—I have always made it my study to Execute the Duties of my Department with the strictest integrity care and Economy and altho' often disappointed by the mercenary disposition of many of the Inhabitants of these States I hope my Conduct has met the approbation of Congress—

As all my Publik transactions in 1775 & 76 my Accounts with Mr. Buchanan and Mr. Wadsworth in 77 and 78 and those under my notice since my appointment of Commissary General remains unsettled, I shall pay close Attention to that Business and use every endeavour to expedite a final settlement, and while engaged on that duty shall expect my Pay and Emoluments—Part of my A/cs. are now ready to lay before Auditors or the Persons who may be appointed to settle the same.—

Inclosed you have a list of Specia Contracts and other Debts which ought to be settled, request your Excellency's influence with Congress that some mode may be adopted to discharge them—many of your Honble Members know the situation of my people and the necessity for the payment of those demands to keep them from total ruin—

I have the Honor to be very respectfully Sir
  Your Excellency's Most Obedient
    & Most Humble Servt.
     Eph: Blaine

His Excy. Thos. Mc.Kean Esqr.

> McKean, from Delaware, was a Signer of the Declartion of Independence and serving at this time as President of the Continental Congress.
> Peter Force Collection, Roll 75, Ephraim Blaine Letterbook, Library of Congress.

Estimate of Money Due

Estimate of Money due to Sundries for Special Contracts, Services &ca. &ca.

Isaac Sorrel for Beef purchased last fall	£1.356..7..6
John Little for Ditto	50.
Jacob Hiltzhimer Ditto	24..9..3
William McMullin Ditto	108..18..6
James Smith for Cattle &ca. supplied the Post of Carlisle last Summer	800.
Richard Robinson for Beef purchased last fall	31..4..2
Isarel Morris Junr. for Services &ca	150
George Kitts and Sons Ditto	200.
George Morton for services, sundry small Accts. for Office expences, Cooperage of Beef &ca. &ca.	500
Specia	£ 3,220.19..5

	Dollars
Azariah Dunham, for Liquors &ca. purchased for the Army in Jersey in April, May June & July 1780	121,148
Pay of Drovers, Butchers, & ca. with the Army at West Point &ca.	348,852
Charles Miller, Ballance of his Account of Purchases at Boston in the year 1780	250,000
Contl. Dollars	720,000

Oliver Phelps ballance of his A/c of Expences forwardg Cattle from the Eastern States	£3,002..12..5
James Munnel for necessaries supplied Head Quarters last Winter	350
New Emission	£3,352..12..5

N:B a Warrant for 470,00 Dollars was granted on Mr. Hilligas the 28th. of October last for the purpose of paying Azariah

Dunham, and the Butchers at Camp of which there remains unpaid 404,333 80/90 Dollars—
Also a Warrant on the Managers of the Lottery Office dated 22d. Novr. last for 100,000 Dollars in part Paymt. of Beef, no part of which has been received—

> Peter Force Collection, Roll 75, Ephraim Blaine Letterbook, Library of Congress.

Incomplete Letter

Sir,   Philada. 4rd Aug. 1781.
    Inclosed you have an Acct. of sundry Articles provided for the Commander in Chief, (by Order of the board of War) request the favour of you to grant me money to pay the same

> Peter Force Collection, Roll 75, Ephraim Blaine Letterbook, Library of Congress.

Blaine to Robert Morris, Jr.

Sir   Philadelphia 6th. August 1781
    My going to Camp is the cause of this early application to you for supplying the Garrison at Fort Pitt and its dependencies, propose the following terms Vizt.—To supply the Troops upon that station with the ration you have published from the first of September untill the 1st. of January,— I shall expect Nine pence half penny pr ration and if the time you mean to engage includes the Winter and Spring (or say for twelve Months), I shall expect Eleven pence half penny pr ration my reason for making so great a difference is, that Garrison ought never to have less than three months salt provision on hand—and no stall'd Cattle to be purchased in that Country and the salt to carry by land from this place those expences will make the ration come very high. I have the Honor to be very respectfully—

Sir Your Most Obedient Servt.
Eph: Blaine

Honl. Robert Morris Esqr. Supt. of Finance

>Peter Force Collection, Roll 75, Ephraim Blaine Letterbook, Library of Congress.

Blaine to Thomas McKean

Sir   Philadelphia 7th. August 1781
I am ready to proceed to Camp to settle my A/cs. there, and in the neighbourhood of West-Point—but can with no degree of Justice discharge the drovers and Butchers who have been employed there; without money to pay them their wages part of a warrant granted me the 11th. of last October was intended to have paid them for their last years Services. Mr. Hillegas was never enabled to pay the Amt. of said warrant, have therefore to request Congress to grant me a warrant for an Equivilent in the New Emission—to enable me to discharge those people, and pay some Special debts due with the Army—
I have the Honor to be very respectfully —
Your Excellency's
Most Obedt. Humble Servt.
Eph: Blaine

P. S. The sum due on the above mentioned Warrant was 404,333 1/3 Drs. equal to 10108 1/8 Drs. N: Emission Exca. @ 40—

The Honble Thos. McKean Esqr. President of Congress

>Peter Force Collection, Roll 75, Ephraim Blaine Letterbook, Library of Congress.

Blaine to the Board of Treasury

THE UNITED STATES

1780   To Jacob Thomas   Dr.
June 25th. To 3 Hhds. N. England Rum Contg 232 Galls.
         @ £48..15/ pr Gall £11,310
    2 Hhds. West India Rum Contg 208 Galls.
         @ £60 pr Galln £12,480
    Exchange @ 60 is Specia   396..10
    13 ½ Mot. Interest @ 6 pr Ct.   26..15..2 ½
    Commissary Genls. Office 8th. August £ 423....5..2 ½

Gentlemen

     The above rum was seized by order of Major Genl. Howe as will appear by Col: Udney Hays Certificate dated 10th July 1780 which will be handed you herewith by Mr. Reyer Schermerhorn the above Exchange was Current in this City at the time of seizure request your Honble Board to adopt some mode of payment and am—
     Gent. Your Most Obedt. Humble Servt.
              George Morton for Eph: Blaine Esqr. C:G:P:

Honble Board of Treasury—

> Peter Force Collection, Roll 75, Ephraim Blaine Letterbook, Library of Congress.

Morton to the Board of War, with a letter by Charles Miller to Blaine, July 11, 1781.

Copy of a letter from Charles Miller Esqr. Agent for the State of Massachusetts Bay dated— Boston July 11th. 1781
Sir
     I am requested to inform you that this State has four or five thousand Gallons of exceeding good Teneriffe Wine

which they would send on to the Army provided you would receive it in lieu of W. I. Rum Gallon for Gallon—I must desire your answer by the first Opportunity; if you agree to the proposal I shall send it on to Springfield as soon as possible—
    I fear this State will be very backward in procuring their Quoto of Rum as they are very destitute of Cash—
        I am Sir Your most Obt Sert
            Chas. Miller—
Ephraim Blaine Esqr.

Gentn.   Philada. 10 August 1781—
    The inclosed Letter from Charles Miller Esqr. Agent for the State of Massachusetts Bay came to hand this morning— As Col Blaine is not in Town I beg your Honors would instruct me in what manner I am to answer it—
    I have the Honor to be with due respect
        Gentn. Your most Obt Huml. Servt
            Geo: Morton

Peter Force Collection, Roll 75, Ephraim Blaine Letterbook, Library of Congress.

Blaine to Charles Stewart

    Tuesday [Morn]ing Morris Town 10 OClock Augt. 1781.
Dear Sir
    I unfortunately was delay'd in crossing Dob's ferry untill twelve OClock Yesterday, came to Mr. Odgen's last night—Mr. Chaloner has been with Mr. Dunham last night and engaged with him for the supply of the french troops through Jersey—I have not had an Oppertunity of seeing him, as he is set out to purchase flour & Cattle, I shall write You from my next Stage—I have call'd upon Mr. Dunham to furnish two hundred head of cattle and all the flour he can to supply our troops—upon their march, I am in haste Dr. Sir
            Your Obdt. Sert.

Eph. Blaine
Col Stewart
Addressed: Public Service
                Charles Stewart Esquire
                Commissary Genl. Issues with the Army
Docket: From Col Blaine 21 Augt 1781

> Charles Stewart Papers, 1752-1818, Collection 262, New York State Historical Association.

Blaine to Azariah Dunham

Dear Sir   Morris Town 21 Augt. 1781
   Am exceeding Sorry I had not the pleasure of seeing you at home on many Accts:—a large detachment of our Army are upon their march to this State, and will want a considerable quantity of Provisions—have therefore to request you to urge the Contracters to use every possible Exertion to procure both beef and flour, two hundred head of good Cattle will undoubtedly be wanting and that without delay—
                I am in haste Dr. Sir
                Your obdt. Hble Servt
                Eph Blaine

Colo. Dunham

> Peter Force Collection, Roll 75, Ephraim Blaine Letterbook, Library of Congress.

Blaine to Charles Stewart

                        Morris Town 21st. Augt. 1781
   you may perhaps think my demand upon Mr. Dunham for two hundred Cattle is large but shou'd the Army proceed southwardly it will be an advantage to have a small stock on

hand—do you press him all possible, I shall write you from Mr. Lowrey's, & remain Dear Sir.
> Your Obdt. Servt.
> Eph. Blaine

N.B I shall try to squeese friend Challoner at Philada. I have Reason to believe he has undertaken to furnish the french troops

Addressed: Public Service
                   Charles Stewart Esquire
                   Com. Genl. Issues
P Express   with the Army.

Charles Stewart Papers, 1752-1818, Collection 262, New York State Historical Association.

Blaine to George Morton

Sir   Philadelphia 25th. August 1781
You will proceed to the Head of Elk, and waite upon Colo. Hollingsworth state agent for the Eastern shore Maryland, and engage him to deposite in the magazine at that place three or four hundred Barrels of the Flour demanded from that state, also, three hundred Barrels of salt provisions; should he fall short of the quantity of flour and salt provisions, you will call upon Mr. Yates Q: M: and request him to order Teams to remove the flour and pork from Duck Creek X roads to Elk shou'd the supplies Obtained from Col: Hollingsworth and those at Duck Creek prove difficient; you will write James Calhoun Esqr. Agent for the Western shore to make up the difficiency without loss of time, inclosing him a Copy of Mr. Morris's letter, the Governors Letters you will inclose to Mr Colham—Use every possible endeavour to have this business completed, and return as soon as possible
> I remain Sir Your Odedt. Humble Servt.
> Eph: Blaine

Mr. Geo: Morton

> Peter Force Collection, Roll 75, Ephraim Blaine Letterbook, Library of Congress.

Blaine to Thomas Sim Lee

Sir   Philadelphia 25th. August 1781

Inclosed is a Letter from Mr. Morris respecting the Supplies of your State, there is an immediate demand for three hundred Barrels of Salt Provisions and four hundred Bbls. Your Excelly will please to urge a special Compliance and give farther directions for the purchases of your Specific Supplies the receival of which I will attend to in a very few days.

I have the Honor to be very respectfully
Your Excys. Most Obedt. Humble Servt.
Eph: Blaine

Govr. Lee

> *Archives of Maryland*, ed. J. Hall Pleasants, vol. 47, *Journal and Correspondence of the State Council of Maryland, 1781* (Baltimore: Maryland Historical Society, 1930), 446.

Blaine to James Calhoun

Dear Sir   Philadelphia 25th. August 1781

I have received special orders from Mr. Morris the Financier Genl. to deposit at the Head of Elk four hundred Bbls. of flour and three hundred Bbls of Salt provisions, I have wrote Colo. Hollingsworth to furnish the above quantity without delay, and have sent down Mr. Morton my Assistant to see the Order comply'd with; should Colo. Hollingsworth not have it in his power to compleat the Order, have directed Mr. Morton to call upon you, for whatever quantity may be difficient, and beg your immediate compliance therewith. A very considerable demand of Specific supplies will shortly be

required from your State; the inclosed Letters from [*sic*] His Excy. the Govr. relates thereto which please to forward by Express—perhaps I shall have the pleasure of seeing you in a few days and remain
>Dear Sir Your Most Obedt. Humble Servt.
>Eph: Blaine

James Calhoun Esqr. Baltimore

>Calhoun was Deputy Quartermaster General for the Western Shore of Maryland. Peter Force Collection, Roll 75, Ephraim Blaine Letterbook, Library of Congress.

Morton to Blaine

Sir   Head of Elk 27 Augt. 1781—

I arrived here yesterday afternoon & immediately waited on Col Hollingsworth—he informs me he can fully Supply the quantity of Flour demanded, but there is not one pound of Salt Provisions in this part of the Country—I have just now sent off the Letters for the Governor of Maryland and Mr. Calhoon to whom I have wrote pressingly respecting a Supply of Salt Provisions, and in Case that Article can not be procured, I have requested that a number of good Cattle might be sent to this post immediately, where they can be pastured and used fresh as exigency may require 'till the Weather will admit of Salting them down—I shall now proceed to Duck Creek Cross Roads and examine into the State of the Pork at that place—if good shall Order it here directly, but if care has not been taken to repack & pickle it I fear it will not be fit for use—I can't say whether I shall return this way again or go immediately from Dover to Philada:—but in this particular shall Act as I think the Service may require—the Flour that is here is not merchantable as very little more than the Bran & Shorts are taken out, but will make good Bread if used soon—should any part Sour it

can be replaced, as there is Wheat in the Mills for that purpose—
I am Sir Your most Obedt Hble Servt
Geo: Morton

Col. Ephraim Blaine Commy General of Purchases Philadelphia

Peter Force Collection, Roll 75, Ephraim Blaine Letterbook, Library of Congress.

Morton to James Calhoun

Sir   Head of Elk 27th. August 1781

Annexed you have Mr. Morris's Orders to Col Blaine respecting the forming of a small Magaze. of Provisions at this Post—Col Hollingsworth inform[s] me he will be fully able to furnish the quantity of Flour demanded, but there is not one pound of Salt Provisions to be procured here—to you therefore we must look for a Supply of that necessary Article, and as it is impossible to say how soon it may be wanted, no time should be lost in procuring it—if Salt Provisions can not be had some Cattle should be sent here immediately & put in good pasture, part of which might be used fresh as exigency requir'd, and the remainder could be Salted as soon as the Weather would Admit—I shall proceed immediately from here to Duck Creek Cross Roads where I am informed there is a small quantity of Pork, but if particular Care has not been taken to have it repacked and pickled I fear it will not be fit for use—

You will receive herewith a Letter from Col. Blaine inclosing two others for His Excellency the Governor of your State who I hope in Conjunction with Council will enable you to execute this necessary Business to your own Satisfaction & the Advantage of the Public—
I am Sir with respect &c. &c.—
G Morton

James Calhoon Esqr.   Copy—

Peter Force Collection, Ephraim Blaine Papers, Roll 74, Library of Congress.

Blaine to Tench Tilghman

Dr. Sir,   Philada. 5th. Septr. 1781

  The bearer hereof Mr. George Morton is my deputy and will attend to the supplies of the army untill I come up—you will find him attentive careful and dilijent in the Execution of his duty—have therefore request the favour of your attention to him and beg you to give him the Earliest information the movements of the Army—[sic]
      I am with much respect Dear Sir
       Your Most Obdt. Hble Servt.
        Eph Blaine

Col Tilghman

Peter Force Collection, Roll 75, Ephraim Blaine Letterbook, Library of Congress.

Blaine To Unidentified

Sir   Philada. 6th. Septr. 1781

  I am under the necessity of troubling you upon a request which gives me pain knowing the many applications you have from the heads of every department upon the same Business and the small support you have had from the states to enable you to execute—the fine people under my direction have been a very considerable time without money and are in great distress particularly those who are exposed to traveling, the receivers and drovers of cattle are all going to leave me. One of the principles was Obliged to sell his Horse upon his way from North river to defray Expenciss the formerly [sic] sold cattle for the above purpose but that gave such an Opening for fraud I utterly refused and wou'd not admit of it under any pretence whatever—to enable them those persons and Others in my employ to execute their respective duties money Sufficient to Support them is Absolutely Necessary and beg and intreat you to advance me a sum sufficient for the above purpose, two of those people with return to North River and attend to the receiving all public cattle and forwarding to this place weekly such parcels as can be spared from supplying the Eastren Army—I wish you to write Gov. Livingston to grant a press warrent to procure pasture for such cattle as may be forwarded from King's ferry to Trenton, or to adopt some Other mode by which they may be well fed,

  I am very respectfully Sir
    Your Most Obdt. & Most Hble Servt.

  Peter Force Collection, Roll 75, Ephraim Blaine Letterbook, Library of Congress.

Blaine to George Morton

Sir   Philadelphia 6th. Sepr. 1781

  You will proceed after the army to the Head of Elk, and whenever necessary call upon the state Agent for a plentifull supply of Provisions—Should the Army proceed from the Head of Elk before I overtake you, you will Apply to Head Quarters for the Line of March keep in front and see that proper supplies are laid in at the different Magazines upon the line of Communication sufficient for their Support—Leave nothing undone to facilitate this business; and urge thos people into an immediate compliance who are appointed by Law to execute.— Should a seizure of supplies be necessary you will apply to the Commander in Chief, or to the Officer Commanding the Detat. for a Guard and proper Order to execute the same. The person who has taken charge of the Cattle to Elk (Mr. Mórgan) has my word of Honor to be permitted to return, your will try to engage a good Man who is capable of keeping A/cs. taking and giving rects. and a Judge of Cattle none else will do.—When you come up with the Drovers you will give the Master Drover money, and

enable him to come to this place—A few Days will enable me to follow you however miss no Opportunity in giving me every information, and get all the supplies you can from the Delaware State.—No part of the Salt provisions must be Issued at the Head of Elk Fresh is very plenty in that part of the Country and the state must furnish it, I wish you a good Journey and remain
     Sir Your Obed Humble Servt.
       Eph: Blaine

Mr. Geo: Morton A: C of P—

> Peter Force Collection, Roll 75, Ephraim Blaine Letterbook, Library of Congress.

Blaine, Memorandum of Money Wanted

Memorandum of money wanted for the Commissary Genls. Department.—
To Ephraim Blaine to enable him to pay the Expences of his Departmt. from this to Virginia.
£250..

Ebenezar Foot and Joseph Morgan receivers of
Cattle to return to North River
12..10

To Geo: Morton & Alexander Williamson
Assistants in my Office.
37..10

to send by Mr. Ford to enable him to forward
Cattle to this place.
75..   £375

> Peter Force Collection, Roll 75, Ephraim Blaine Letterbook, Library of Congress.

Blaine to Nathaniel Stevens

Dear Sir   Phila. 7th Septr. 1781
    I have Ordered Mr. Foote to return to North river and attend to the recieval and Delivery of all public cattle which may be forwarded from the Eastren State, [sic] and have given him particular Orders to have great care taken of said cattle and pay close and proper attention to his duty, I have also Ordered him to forward to this place weekly such cattle as can possibly be spared from the supply of your army—and those cattle ought to be the best or such as will bear Driving—four hundred & fifty Miles—I have also ordered him not to sell any cattle under any pretence whatever let his necessity for Money be ever so great, I have also assured him that reasonable Sums of money will be furnished him to advance the drovers which may come in with the Cattle—that and every Other part of his Duty I beg you may see him perform, and such directions and Advice as he may stand in need of I beg you to afford it him upon every Occasion—I wou'd wish One careful drover with a Corporals guard to come on to this place with each drove of cattle, let their route be Morris & Trenton at which place the soldiers can draw provisions—those men shall return from this city, and a new Guard and drovers shall be employ'd here to proceed with the Cattle—I fear our Army now going southerly cannot be supplied with beef, therefore shall expect One Hundred head Weekly—will you pay attention to Management of the tallow and receive what Mr. Forbes can procure into some convenient Magazine, let Mr. Welch have no more than may be Necessary to supply your Army with soap and a Reasonable allowance of Candles—you will be so kind as to furnish me with an Acct. of all Contracts or Expenditures of money in my Department for what trouble you may have in executing such business as belongs to the Commissary General of Purchases be assured of a proper Reward, let me here [sic] from you by every Oppertunity and believe me Dr. Sir

Your Most Obedt Servt.
Eph Blaine CGP

Nathl Stevens Esqr D C G of issues

Peter Force Collection, Roll 75, Ephraim Blaine Letterbook, Library of Congress.

Blaine to Ebenezer Foote

Sir   Philada. 7th Septr. 1781

You will proceed immediately to North River and take charge of the Public Cattle which may be forwarded from the Eastren states—all that can Possibly be spared from the supply of Genl. Heaths army must be forwarded to this place weekly, and every Week for supplying the Southern Army, you will make Regular returns to Mr. Stephens and take his advice upon Every Occasion, he will assist you in Obtaining the necessary guards from General Heath—a careful drover will come on with each parcel of Cattle with whom there ought to be a Guard of One Corporal and five men, those men to draw fituage rations while employ'd in that business—be very exact and particular in Delivering every Drove of cattle you forward and give Orders to the drovers to give Certificates describing the quality of such pastures as the [sic] may procure for the Accommodation of the cattle upon the road to this place—you will order your drovers to Deliver their cattle to Capt Little Who will give a proper rect. to you for them, herewith you will receive Seven pounds ten Shillings towards the defraying of your expenciss from North River to this place and Returning for which you will render a particular Acct. the hundred Dollars now advanced you is to furnish the drovers with money to defray their own Expenciss upon the Journey and give them a very particular charge to use every possible Economy in their Expenditures, when that sum is expended render me an Acct. and I will furnish you with more money, Mr. Stevens will

assist you in Obtaining a tent and such Other Necessaries as the Quarter Masters Stores can furnish.
I remain Sir Your Obdt Servt.
E Blaine

Peter Force Collection, Roll 75, Ephraim Blaine Letterbook, Library of Congress.

Blaine to George Morton

Sir, Philada. 9th. 1781

I have Just time to Acknowledge the Receipt of your letter by Express and am glad to find the troops have a regular supply of bread & beef. I forwarded from this place yesterday twenty four Hhd. common and five Hhd. of West India Rum some soap and Candles and this day have Started under the care of Crouse Sixty head of Cattle, inform me by very first Oppertunity what number of the troops have march'd what rout they have taken and which road has the Genl gone. give me every Information respecting Supplies,
I remain Sir Your Obed. Hble Sert
Eph Blaine

Mr Morton

Blaine to Udny Hay

Sir Philadelphia 9th. Septr. 1781

Having the most sincere desire to settle all my Public Accounts, must request you to call upon all those persons within the state of New-York who have furnished any Articles, or performed any services for my Department since your Appointment as Agent.—(Purchases made by Mr. Cyler or his deputies excepted) and settle with them Agreeable to the resolution of Congress and the Vouchers the [sic] produce— And make a return to me as soon as in your power—You will also settle with Major Hale for the money he received at

Boston; I hope he will refund all the money which he received except what was allow [sic] him by Congress, and come in for the depreciation with others—The persons who had those particular warrants granted them are very Importunate for their money, and exclaim much against me for not paying them, this Matter lays with you; and I make not the least doubt you will settle it properly—I remain with Esteem and Regard,

      Sir Your Most Obedt. Humble Servt.
        Eph: Blaine
Udney Hay Esqr.

  Peter Force Collection, Roll 75, Ephraim Blaine Letterbook, Library of Congress.

Blaine, Necessarys for General Greene's Table

An Estimate of Necessary's wanted for the Use of Genl Greens table Philada. 11th Sepr 1781

Two Quarter Casks Maderia wine	£ 50
1 Quarter Cask red port	12..10
250 lb. best Havanah Sugar	9..7..6
100 lb. of Cheese	11..5
100 lb. Coffee	5
6 lb. Green Tea	10..10
4 lb. Pepper	2..10
6 lb. Mustard	3..10
32 Gallon Best Spirits	20
	124..12..6
Wanted for the use of Genl. Heath	112..10
	£237..2..6

    Eph Blaine C.G.P.

[Verso]
Inform Majr. Burnett that Robt. Morris Esqr. will furnish the within mentioned Articles—
    Eph Blaine

Mr. Williamson

> Andrew Williamson was an assistant in Blaine's Philadelphia office. Major General Nathanael Greene was at this time in South Carolina, commanding the Southern Army. Major General William Heath was commanding in the Highlands of New York.
> Peter Force Collection, Roll 75, Ephraim Blaine Letterbook, Library of Congress.

Blaine to Henry Hollingsworth

September 15, 1781

All the Cattle which are comeing in from the Eastward with those furnishd by your district are to be delivered to Mr Yeates D. Q. M. Gl for the State of Maryland who has received Instructions how to dispose of them, you will deliver him all the Cattle you possibly can, and press the County Contractors to procure the supplys required without delay—the necessity of Provisions Southardly and the great demand, will require your utmost exertion and punctual compliance with every demand—the season for salting provisions is near at hand and if our Army remains to the southard very large requisitions will be made for Salt provisions have therefore to request you to make preparation in salt and Barrels for the above, purpose I shall wait upon your Governor and Council upon my way down, and represent to them the necessity of prepareing the above mentioned Articles and make no doubt but they will make proper provision.

> *Archives of Maryland*, ed. J. Hall Pleasants, vol. 47, *Journal and Correspondence of the State Council of Maryland, 1781* (Baltimore: Maryland Historical Society, 1930), 495.

Blaine to Henry Hollingsworth

Dear Sir Williamsburgh 23rd. Septr. 1781

You must use every possible Exertion in colecting flour & beef Else our army will undoubtedly Perish. what cattle you have now on hand in Cecil & Kent Counties you will deliver Colo. Yeates as fast as he can have them slaughtered—the Others Colected upon the Eastren shore shall inform you by next post at what places I shall receive them, for god sake forward large supplies of Flour—am in hast Dr. Sir

Your Obdt. Hble Servt.
Eph Blaine CGP

Col. Hollingsworth

> Photocopy, Gilpin Collection, Box 8, Cecil County Historical Society.

Blaine and Charles Stewart to Thomas Nelson

Sir, Williamsburgh, 25th. Septr. 1781

In order that no time might be lost in getting forward the Supplies for the Army, Application was made yesterday by Charles Stewart Esqr. Commissary General of Issues to General Lincoln to send Boats to the following places—Vizt.

```
to George Town for 1185 Bbls. Flour
   Baltimore         400 do. do. & 100 Bs. Bread
   Head of Elk       300 do. do.
                    1885 & in a week

To George Town for 1500 Bs. Flour
   Richmond          400 do. do.
   Petersburgh       300
   Annapolis         150
   Fredericksburgh   250 & 1000 Bus: Corn
   Dumfries          150
   Elk (collecting)  500
                    3250
```

5130 In the whole exclusive of considerable quantities of Indian Corn supposed to be collected by this time—As soon as Returns of any Additional quantities come to hand the places of deposit shall be set forth to Governor Nelson or the Quarter Master General that the further necessary Instructions may be given to the Commanders of the Vessels—as it is expected that great part of the Cattle collected in Maryland must be Slaughter'd at the landings on the East side of the Bay and Salted there where Casks may be difficult to procure three or four good light Boats fit to carry Meat Salted in Bulk will be wanted in a few Days for this Special purpose to proceed to Vienna in Dorchester County & Snow Hill in Worcester County to transport the Beef to the Army—at these places proper person will be Station'd to Superintend the Business of Slaughtering & forwarding the Meat to the Army—Your Excellency will please to give the necessary Orders to the Persons appointed to Superintend the transportation of the Stores to use the utmost dilligence to bringing to the Army the before mention'd Supplies, as the wants of the Army require great & immediate Exertions—With much Respect we are—

        Your Excellency's Most Obedt. &
        most Humble Servants—
        Chas. Stewart
        Commy. Genl. of Issues
        Eph. Blaine C.G.P

His Excellency Governor Nelson

Thomas Nelson was Governor of Virginia and commanded that state's militia at the Siege of Yorktown. Sold by Swann Galleries, 104 East 25th Street, New York, New York, 10010, Lot 2367, on November 20, 2014.

Blaine and Charles Stewart to George Washington

Sir   Williamsburgh 26th. September 1781
    Governor Nelsons plan for swimming the Cattle across the River has failed, but he adopted another and sent Col Wills with a party of Militia with Orders to Slaughter the Cattle and bring the Beef over in Boats—this will answer, some of the

Beef is already at the landing, and we hope will continue to come as fast as wanting until the Drove on the west side are exhausted—Governor Nelson has also given Directions to arrange the Craft under proper Superintendents and send them to the places where Flour & Corn are deposited in this State & Maryland, of which places we have given him the most accurate Returns in our power, by them it appears that near five thousand Barrels is and will be ready in a few Days—and from the Zeal shewn by Governor Nelson we hope it will arrive in time to keep the Troops supplied—On examining the Map of the Eastern Shore, we think Cherry Stone a proper Landing for the Supplies to be furnished by the two Counties in Virginia, and that Snow Hill & Vienna are also proper for the Maryland Shore—Should Your Excellency think a third place needful we apprehend Chop tank will answer & shall on knowing Your Excellency's Sentiments, write to Governor Lee to Order the State Agents to deliver their Supplies at those places.

In order to have the Supplies as Certain as possible E. Blaine proposes to Cross the Bay and instantly set on foot the Business of Slaughtering and conveying to Camp the Collections in Maryland and those two Counties in Virginia— We observe with concern that the Department of Commissary of Hides is much neglected, and the Tallow so much wanted to make Soap & Candles is in a great measure lost and destroyed—We wish not to interfere with the Duties of other Men, but in order to have the Soap and Candles furnished we will if agreeable to Your Excellency Appoint one or more persons to Superintend this Business and make Contracts on the best terms we can for Soap & Candles to Supply Your Army—

We have the Honor to be with the greatest respect—
Your Excellency's
Most Obedt. & most Hble Servts.
Chas Stewart Commy Genl Issues
Eph. Blaine C.G.P.

His Excellency General Washington

George Washington Papers, Library of Congress.

Blaine to Thomas Sim Lee

Williamsburgh September 27, 1781

His Excellency the Commander in Chief approves of three places of Deposit upon the Eastern Shore of your State for the collection of Beef Cattle. Viz. Oxford landing upon Choptank River for the Supplies of Queen Ann, Talbot & Caroline Counties—Vienna upon Nanticoke River for Dorchester, and Snow Hill for the County of Worcester. I will Order Agents to attend at those places to receive and forward the Stores. Your Excellency will please to Order the Contractors to bring in their Cattle to those places agreeable to the Orders they receive from my Agents, and to be punctual in a compliance therewith—they must also provide good pasture convenient to the places of slaughter, and I beg Sir you will give them Orders to afford every necessary Assistance in this Business. I shall order what Public salt remains in your State to be collected to those places but am doubtful it will by no means equal our demand. Packing down Meat at this early Season requires large quantities of Salt. Your Excellency & Council will please to order the purchase of five or Six hundred Bushels, one half of which to be sent to Oxford & the residue to Vienna & Snow Hill.

I shall set out tomorrow for Northampton & Accomack and take those places in my way to Annapolis.

The large Consumption of Provisions in our Army will require the utmost Exertions of every Person who is the least concern'd in procuring Supplies. Your Excellency will please to repeat your Application to the State Commissioners and enjoyn them to be punctual in executing your Orders in the purchase of Provisions.

Number of our Soldiers are falling sick—the Season, Climate, & fatigue our Army will undergo for some time, will oblige the Commander in Chief to Order large quantities of Spirits to be Issued—we shall want a considerable quantity of Whiskey from you as speedily as it can be procured.

The whole Army moves down towards York to morrow morning at five oClock, and its said they will not halt until they are within one Mile of Cornwallis's Works. It is reported he is strongly fortified therefore in a few Days the Opperations of both Armys will become very serious.

Archives of Maryland, ed. J. Hall Pleasants, vol. 47, *Journal and Correspondence of the State Council of Maryland, 1781* (Baltimore: Maryland Historical Society, 1930), 507-508.

Blaine and Charles Stewart to George Washington

Sir Williamsburgh 27th. Septr. 1781

The Rum on hand and on the Way from Elk, with twenty five Hhds. to be sent by Mr. Morris, & fifty Hhds. to be received from the State of Maryland, will last twenty two days allowing ten pr. Ct. for wastage in Boating Carting &c—therefore suppose the whole to arrive, which is by no means certain, the Troops will want about the 18th. of October.—but it appears to us that during the Seige double allowance will be wanted for the Troops especially those in Trenches, and as many are daily falling sick, if Mr. Morris can send fifty Hhds. more, it may be of most singular service.

We have the honor to be with the greatest Respect
Your Excellency's Most Obedt.
& Most Humb. Servants
Ephm Blaine C.G.P.
Charls Stewart C.G. Issues

His Excellency Genl. Washington

George Washington Papers, Library of Congress.

Blaine to John Cropper

Sir Old Point Comfort 1 Octr. 1781
Not having a fair Wind to cross to Cherry Stone—I have concluded not to land upon the Eastern Shore until I arrive at Oxford Landing upon Choptank River—Our Army & the french are all Assembled before York Town & are in want of Provisions—you will adopt Measures to give in every in your Power—[sic] What Beef Cattle may be collected in your district you will please have Slaughtered, Salted in Barrels & sent off—it will be immediately issued—I remain Sir
Your most Obt. Hble Servt.
Eph. Blaine C.G.P
Col Cropper

> Cropper, of Accomack Virginia, had commanded the Eleventh Virginia and was now a colonel of Virginia militia.
> Library of Virginia, http://image.lva.virginia.gov/GLR/02350

Blaine to Caesar Rodney

Sir Choptank River Oxford Landing 4th October 1781—
I am upon this Shore ordering the Supplies of Provisions Forward to our Army in Virginia—the French Army & Navy with our Continental Troops and Militia consume Sixty thousand Rations per day—we have no Magazine established and are only feeding them from day to day—and I fear it will be impossible to keep up a regular Supply without the utmost exertion of this State and yours in forwarding to the most convenient Landings upon the Chesepeak the Supplies required by Congress—have therefore in the most pressing terms to request your Excellency to order the Exertions in your Agents and a punctual compliance in procuring those Supplies and delivering the same at the places of deposit to Donaldson

Yeates Esquire State Quarter Master who will adopt proper measures to have them forwarded to the Army with the utmost dispatch—choptank Bridge and the other Landings which lead to Chesepeack Bay would be very convenient places to receive your Supplies.

Our Army have invested Lord Cornwallis and his Army in the Town of York and last Sunday, which was the day I left our Army they had taken possession of all his out Works and redoubts on Monday all our heavy Artillery would be brought from Burwells ferry on James River, and our Engineers was to have run a line Circumlocution at more than five hundred yards from the Enemy's Works which inclose the town from which Line, our Army will advance by regular Approaches until they Subdue his Lordship with an Army of Seven thousand men which I have not the least doubt will be accomplished in the course of twenty Days—Men who are day & night upon fatigue and exposed to the greatest Danger ought to be regularly Supplied with Provisions and every refreshment they are entitled to—for God sake give me every Assistance and let no excuse prevent the Commissioners from doing their duty

I have the Honour to be very respectfully
Your Excellencys Obedt. Hble Servt.
Eph. Blaine C. G. of P.

Governor Rodney

Delaware Archives: Revolutionary War (Wilmington: Public Archives Commission of Delaware, 1919), 3:1357.

Blaine to Mathew Tilghman

Oxford, October 16, 1781.

Your favour by Mr Blake I have just received, and have only to observe that the requisitions of Congress in beef from the respective States is neat beef, and they afterwards add pay for the hide and tallow, this convinces me that the State ought to pay the expence of Slaughtering and that expence will not exceed the cost of procuring hands, paying pasturage while driving the Cattle to places where I would be Justifiable in receiving them.

In the first place it is impossible for me to attend to the slaughtering of the Cattle in the respective Counties, in the second I have not one shilling of money to defray the expence allowing it to be a Continental charge, however as I do not wish to through any difficulty upon your State, shall agree to the following proposals Viz. That if Mr Morris with a Committe of Congress say the expence of Slaughtering the Cattle shall be a charge against the United States, I will pledge my honour to you to see it paid. If that of the State why it is done—any additional expence which may attend the trying of the tallow and procuring barrels to put it in, and drying the hides I shall engage to pay, but be assured the slaughtering of the Cattle lays with the State. I have requested the Commissioners to sell the hides, but would rather wish them to dispose of them to good Tanners who would tan them on the shares—such of the people as will carefully slaughter their Cattle and are dispos'd to keep the fifth quarter I agree to keep the beef but this I leave to your direction, and if the hides and tallow can be saved they are much wanted for the Army.

I have been delay'd exceedingly by unfavourable winds and as there is a prospect of getting down the Bay this morning I am prevented of the honor of waiting on you. The Governor and Council have engaged to send a boat to Mr Blake to load with beef I shall take particular care to send boats to the sundry landing places to take in beef. I have enquired the price of hides at Baltimore and find they will bring four pence hard money p lb.

I would wish the Commissioners to obtain that sum for what they may sell, making a reasonable deduction for the expence of drying the hides and freight to Baltimore.

To The Honble Mathew Tilghman Esq.
President of the Special Council, Talbot Court House
(By Mr Blake)

>Tilghman had been in the Continental Congress and was a major leader in Maryland throughout the war.
>*Archives of Maryland*, ed. J. Hall Pleasants, vol. 47, *Journal and Correspondence of the State Council of Maryland, 1781* (Baltimore: Maryland Historical Society, 1930), 525.

Blaine to Robert Forsyth

Dear Sir,   York Town 25th. Octr. 1781.

I returnd from the Eastren shore the morning Lord Cornwallis Caputalated; [*sic*] the hurry of business and Viewing the troops as they march'd from this place has been the cause of my not writing you before. I shall be here some days, when I set out shall take your town upon my Return to Philadelphia when I shall have it in my power to inform you of every m[   ] Relative to the department and your pay—Inclos'd you have a Copy of an order from General Washington—and Request you to Apoint some careful prudent person to attend to the supplies of the British Prisoners untill they reach their destination & proper Measures are adopted for their support, the person you send will apply to the County Commissarys who have the Governors Orders to furnish him with the Necessary Provisions—for the Above purpose and shou'd their supplys prove insufficient the inclosed Order will Justify him in purchasing what Provisions may be necessary to Answer the Demand,—for which I will engage payment;—but by no means presume to purchase upon any Other princaple—

If you can by some means procure a little hard money good are much cheaper here than you can get them else where, and if you cannot come down favour me with your Demands
  I remain with much Esteem and Reguard
    Dr Sir Your Most Obdt Servt

Eph Blaine

Majr Forsyth

Forsyth had been an aide-de-camp for General Nathanael Greene. At this time he was Deputy Commissary of Purchases in Virginia, and was later Commissary of Purchases for the Southern Department. Charles Stewart Papers, 1752-1818, Collection 262, New York State Historical Association.

Blaine to Thomas Nelson Jr.

Sir,   York Town 25th. Octr. 1781.

The bearer Mr. Jackson is the Commissary of Issues who is to attend the Brittish prisoners—and has letters from me to Major Forsyth requesting him to send some person to attend and see that proper provisions are made upon the Communication to their place of distination—you will be so kind as to Inclose Major Forsyth an Order upon the County Commissary's to furnish him with the necessary provisons untill proper Measures are taken for their support—I shall do myself the honour of waiting upon you before I leave Camp, and adopt any measure which may be agreable to your Excellency for that purpose,

I have the honor to be very Respectfully
Sir your Excellency's Most Obdt.
and Most Hble Servt.
Eph. Blaine
C.G. of Purch.

Govr. Nelson
Addressed: Public Service
His Excellency Governor Nelson
Williamsburgh

Charles Stewart Papers, 1752-1818, Collection 262, New York State Historical Association.

Blaine to Henry Hollingsworth

York Town, October 26, 1781
The Army being detached from this place and few or no Troops remaining here, have to request you to forward no more provisions of any kind to this place—when further operations or the Canteen^{mts} of the Army take place shall give you information where to forward your supplys—what beef Cattle you have upon hand preparation must be made to salt them down and have them properly Barreld—great care must be taken in this Business in order that the beef may be well cured to keep untill next Summer—however this is the business of your State, and will require particular attention
Ephraim Blaine.

Archives of Maryland, ed. J. Hall Pleasants, vol. 47, *Journal and Correspondence of the State Council of Maryland, 1781* (Baltimore: Maryland Historical Society, 1930), 550.

Blaine and Charles Stewart, to Lord Cornwallis

Sir York Town 1 Novr. 1781.
We are informed by His Excellency General Washington that the Salted provisions found at this post and Gloucester at the surrender is to be appropriated to Victualing the Transports destined for New York On condition that a like Quantity of equal quality be delivered at Kings Ferry or West point, at North River. In order to know at which of those posts it will be most convenient for Your Lordship to have it replaced & at what time it may be done We now address You that We may make the necessary preparations to receive it.
We are you Lordships most Obedient Servants
unsigned

His Excy Lieut. Genl. Earl Cornwallis
York Town Virga,

Charles Stewart Papers, 1752-1818, Collection 262, New York State Historical Association.

Charles Stewart and Blaine to William Davies

Sir, York Town, Novem'r 8th, 1781

We are honor'd by the rec't of your favour of the 1st Instant, and are perfectly convinced of the very great Exertions of this Government to supply this our own Army, as well as that of our good Allies, and of the distress that always has, and must attend collections of this kind—the only consolation to the sufferers at present, is that the principal object for which such supplies were exacted, is compleatly accomplished & the peace of this State restored thereby.

The uncommon Exertions of the Executive of this State and Maryland during the seige, threw into Camp a surplus of Beef Cattle—there are quite a sufficiency now on hand to support our Army, and the Prisoners in this State for one month to come.

We have made the most proper Distribution of them in our power, but the scarcity of salt may frustrate our Intentions, unless the State can speedily procure, and order to Fredericksb'g 400 Bus: to Winchester 600, and to Williamsburg the like quantity. We must intreat you will urge these Deposits that the cattle may be killed before Winter sets it—We think that sending such Cattle as are collecting in the Counties near Winchester, directly to that place, would be of singular advantage and a great saving, for at that place we presume the Prisoners will continue for a considerable space.

We shall order a supply of Provisions to Fredericksburg and leave a present support at Willamsb'g & this place, for the use of the Prisoners & Sick of both Armies that remain in this quarter, and shall instruct Major Forsyth, Deputy Commissary General of Purchases, and Mr. Robinson, Superintend't Commissary of Issues for this State, to keep the Board of war and Executive Authority fully informed at all times of the state

of the magazines, that no future wants may arise, and of Conseq'e no Exactions by made, but what the public Interests require. We would also beg leave to mention to you that the season is now at hand in which the State ought to lay up their magazine of Salt Provisions required by Congress, therefore make not the least doubt, but your Executive will adopt measures to procure as much salt Beef & Pork as their situation will admit of.
              We are with much personal esteem—
                  your most Ob't H'ble Serv'ts.
                       Chas. Stewart, Com'y Gen: Issues
                       Eph: Blaine C. G. Provisions

> Davies was Colonel of the First Virginia Regiment and in March 1781, Thomas Jefferson appointed him as Commissioner of the Virginia Board of War.
> Wm. P. Palmer, ed., *Calendar of Virginia State Papers and Other Manuscripts....*, (Richmond: James E. Goode, 1881), 2:587-88.

Blaine to Thomas Nelson

Sir,   Nov'r 16th 1781, Frederic'sb'g
     I intended doing myself the honor of waiting upon you at Hanover, but upon coming there, found you were gone to Richmond. My hurry to the Northward prevented my going to that place, in order to have communicated many matters relative to the present and future specific supplies required from your State; and to have fixed upon some plann for the disposal of the Public cattle which are now upon hand at Williamsburgh. the assessments of the cattle which were collected in this State, was for the use of the Allied Army.— there remains now upon hand, two thousand three hundred head, half of which are not fit for use—I made application to the Commander in cheif, who told me he wou'd make application to Count Rochambeau, to order the receival of their

proportion of such as were fit to Kill—Since his departure from York Town I made application to the french agents and requested them to appoint some person to receive their proportion, but this they have refused, as you will see by the inclosed, which was their Answer to Col: Stewart and myself—as those Cattle were collected for the Special use of both armies, I think it exceeding hard they shou'd remain a charge to the State and Continent, which they now are, as we have no Troops there to make use of them, and numbers are dying with the distemper. I have adopted every possible plann for the disposal of such as are fit for use, and have directed Major Forsyth to wait upon your Excellency and Council and take such directions as you are pleased to give for the disposal of those which are too poor to Kill—Seven hundred and fifty of the best are now upon their way to this place and Winchester, and if not immediately slaughtered, will be unfit for use. there is salt to answer the purpose here, but not a bushel at Winchester—you will please to give directions upon this head, and Order an immediate deposite at that place, where in my opinion, all the cattle yet upon hand and fit for slaughter, ought to be sent and salted up in bulk for the use of the Prisoners.

the Season is now at hand, in which magazines of Salt Provisions ought to be laid up for the use of the Continent. the requisitions of Congress upon your State is very large—have therefore to request your Excellency and Council to press this business with your Executive, that measures may be taken, in due time to procure the Salt Provisions required, particularly the Pork. the want of proper magazines of this necessary article, has ever been an injury to the summer supplies of our army, and being fed entirely upon fresh beef, and often of a very ordinary quality, has been the causes of fluxes, and many other diseases, which are very injurious to the soldiery. Colonel Stewart and me have wrote your board of war, upon the same subject, and hope it will meet with your approbation and theirs.

  I have the honor to be, with the greatest
    Respect Your Excellency's Most Obedt.
    and most Hble Servant.

  Wm. P. Palmer, ed., *Calendar of Virginia State Papers and Other Manuscripts....*, (Richmond: James E. Goode, 1881), 2:606.

Blaine to Henry Hollingsworth

          Philadelphia, November 30, 1781

  Your favour of the 28th Instant came safe to hand and am sorry its not in my power to furnish you with salt for the purpose of salting what Beef Cattle there remains upon hand. Governments are still In debt a large quantity and you must make application to them for what may be necessary for the above purpose

  Archives of Maryland, ed. J. Hall Pleasants, vol. 47, *Journal and Correspondence of the State Council of Maryland, 1781* (Baltimore: Maryland Historical Society, 1930), 563.

Blaine to Robert Morris Jr.

Sir   Philadelphia 27th. Novr. 1781
  Inclosed you have a return of the Stores borrowed from the French Army, and Amount of Provisions repayed and lent them in Virginia; also a return of the provisions furnished the Cartel Ships going to New York. Which provisions by Order of His Excellency Genl. Washington and Agreement of Lord Cornwallis is to be replaced at Kings-Ferry or West-Point the provisions furnished the French Cartel Ships going for Europe, is carried out by itself and is to be replaced or paid for. The States of Virginia and Maryland afforded us a plentifull supply of Provisions during the Seige. I made special Contracts, [*sic*]

except one with Col: Hendricks as I went down to the Army for Five hundred Bbls. of Flour, and one as I came up with Mr. Shaw for fifty Five head of Cattle sent the British Prisoners to Frederick-Town, who were in want of Beef many days those Contracts with Sundry expences for driving and Slaughtering Cattle and Cost of Barrels purchased for salting of Beef are all to pay.—The Acct. of Expences have not yet received, therefore have only aded small sums for which I request you to furnish me money to send those people whose Names are annexed in order to relieve them in some measure from their Duns who are very importunate to Obtain their money and for which there was special promises; as soon as in my power to Obtain the particulars shall them before you.—

The collection of Cattle in Virginia were for the use of the Allied Army but from some cause or Misunderstanding between Govr. Nelson and the French Agents, they refused receiving any of those delivered by Government. When our Troops were detached from York-Town, and little or no Continental demand for Beef there was two thousand Five hundred head of Cattle upon hand Numbers of which were dying daily with the distemper I made application to the Commander in Chief, who spoke to Count De Rochambeaux, and sent one of his Aids to Messrs. Wadsworth and Carter, about takg. their proportion of those Cattle; I afterwards wrote them pressingly, and requested their immediate answer in writing; a Coppy of which you have inclosed.—Upon receiving their answer I adopted the following disposal of the best of those Cattle, five hundred forwarded with Genl. St. Clairs detachment, Seven hundred sent to Fredericks burgh and Winchester for the use of the British Prisoners—three hundred to be slaughtered at Williamsburgh for the use of our Hospital and Guards—the remaining number are unfit for slaughter, and I have given Orders to Major Forsyth my deputy to wait upon the Govr. and Council and take their directions about the method of Sale, and recommend a credit of Nine Months, then to be paid in Specia or good Merchantable beef, this wou'd induce the Farmers which have Fodder to purchase and give a good price.—Mr. Stevens my Asst. at North River and Mr. Foot receiver of live Stock are in great want of money. Foot is sued and execution Issued against him. I have added three hundred Dollars for their use; which request you to furnish with the other sums.—Mr. Stevens is killing what Cattle are upon North River, and salting them in Bbls. and bulk; there is abought Eight hundred Old Bbls. upon hand which he is using for that purpose—There will remain upon the Eastern Shore Maryland One thousand Bbls. of beef, I will have particular returns in the Course of two Weeks, those provisions will answer for the consumption of the posts in that State, and the Prisoners at Frederick-Town untill contracts are made to supply them—I shall now mention my own situation, and must request your Assistance; all my property and connections in private business is at Carlisle except two or three small adventures in Trade which have as yet been of no Advantage and I assure you I am without money, have therefore to request your Aid in furnishing me with One hundred and fifty or two hundred pounds on Account of my Salary which will do me a particular favour—

            I remain with sentiments of regard Sir
                Your Most Obedt. Humble Servt.
                Eph: Blaine

Honble R: Morris Esqr. Superintendent of Finance

> Peter Force Collection, Roll 75, Ephraim Blaine Letterbook, Library of Congress.

Blaine to Nathaniel Stevens

Dear Sir   Philadelphia 5th. Decr. 1781
      Your sundry favours I have recd. but the hurry of business since my return from the Southard prevents my

answering any of yours except the last.—The Southern Army during the Seige, was plentifully supplied; and I am happy in telling you there has been no want of any One Article, except rum I am also pleased to find you have made a demand of the ballances of Beef due from the Eastern States agreable to the resolve of the Convention at Providence which I hope will be sufficient to supply the post of West-point and its dependencies; untill the Contractors Issue which will be the first of January—

I am sorry for your scarcity of Flour, was it not in the power of your State Agent to give relief—the Salt Provisions which are Ordered from the state of Connecticut with what you are puting up, will give the Contractors a pretty supply to begin with, they must pay dear for it.

I was informed yesterday that some Gentlemen of your state, their names are Sands, have contracted with Mr. Morris for West Point, I cannot inform you at what price, but they are Gentlemen I have not the pleasure of an Acquaintance with; nor do I know of their ever being in public service, therefore suppose we Old hands will be dismissed from service as poor as Job, and new Ones which have never borne any part of our difficulties get into business, when it's in their power to make money, my present situation and being loaded with public Accounts and Debts far beyond, indeed Millions above any prospect I have of payment has discouraged me from making any Application for new employment untill I get discharged from the Old, which I will endeavour accomplish [*sic*] this Winter, I have sent you by Hunt Sixty Dollars on A/c and remain in haste

      Dr. Sir Your Obedt. Humble Servt.
       Eph: Blaine
Mr. Nathl. Stevens

    Peter Force Collection, Roll 75, Ephraim Blaine Letterbook, Library of Congress.

Estimate of a Month's Pay for the Commissary General of Issues Department

Estimate of one Month's Pay for the Commissary General of Issues Department agreeable to the last Return received from the Deputies, from which several Returns a general one is made and presented to the Honorable Robert Morris Superintendant of Finance on the 6th December 1781.—

Districts	Number of Distracts	Number of A. C. of Issues	Number of Clerks	Number of Scale Men
Main Army	1	16	16	16
Eastern Department	1	4	4	4
Northern Ditto	1	11	7	11
State of Rhode Island	1	2	3	3
West Point and it's Dependencies		10	10	10
Fort Pitt and it's Ditto	1	4	4	4
Middle Department	1	42	27	36
	6	89	71	84

The Southern Department no exact Return of their Number has come to Hand yet.

6 Deputies at 100 Dollars per Month   600 Dollars
89 Assistants at 60 Ditto per do   5,340
71 Clerks at 35 Ditto pr ditto   2,485

84 Scale Men at 25 Ditto pr ditto	2,100
	10,525 Dollars.

Peter Force Collection, Roll 75, Ephraim Blaine Letterbook, Library of Congress.

Blaine to Solomon Maxwell

Sir, Philada. 7th. Decr. 1781

If any public flour remains at your post you will take the very earliest Opportunity of sending it to this place by the first craft which Offers—I expect a large quantity from the head of Elke. therefore wish you to adopt Measures that it may not remain any time with you—favour me with a line and a return what quantity I have reason to expect—and am Sir

Your Obdt Hble Servt.
Eph Blaine CG.P

Mr Maxwell or The Quarter Master Christian Bridge

> Maxwell was a wealthy merchant of Christiana Bridge, Delaware. He was acting as a Receiver of Supplies for New Castle County in 1781. Peter Force Collection, Roll 75, Ephraim Blaine Letterbook, Library of Congress.

Blaine to Isaac Carty

Dear Sir Philada. 7th. Decr 1781,

From the inclosed coppy of a letter from Mr Morris you will see the necessity of an immediate complyance in forwarding all the flour and salt Provisions in your state—have therefore to request you upon Rect. of this to forward all the flour and salt Provisions if any to this place without a Moments delay and intreat and beg you not to loose a moments time in the execution of this business as two Vessels are waiting to receive the provisions and a danger of the frost shuting up the

Navigation in the Delaware—there was a large Quantity of flour since last Summer at Duck Creek Cross Roads—what has been done with it if in remains have it forwarded immediately—should you have it in your power to send two hundd. bushl. of indian Corn have it done pray inform me by the Express what quantity of flour you can send up and what time I may Expect it.

      I remain Sir
        Your Most Obdt Hble Servt.
         Eph Blaine CGP
Majr. Carty

> Peter Force Collection, Roll 75, Ephraim Blaine Letterbook, Library of Congress.

Blaine to Henry Hollingsworth

Sir   Philada. 7th. Decr. 1781.

  The enclosed letter from Mr: Morris to me will show you his desire of having all the Specific supply's of flour and salt provisions in your district forwarded to this place, have therefore to request you upon Rect. of this to give special orders to your assistants to forward all your flour and Salt provision without a moments delay—the quarter Mastr. has been wrote upon that subject and will adopt the proper means of transportation, you will Keep a small reserve of provisions for the use of the post at Elk—as the season is far advanced and a danger of Shuting up the navigation in deleware also two Vessels waiting to receive the supplies—beg that no time may be lost in the execution thereof—please to favour me with a line by the return of the Express and inform me what quantity of flour and salted provisions may be expected from you

      I remain Sir—
        Your Most Obdt. Hble Servt.
         Eph Blaine C.G.P
Colo. Hollingsworth

Peter Force Collection, Roll 75, Ephraim Blaine Letterbook, Library of Congress.

Blaine to James Calhoun

Dear Sir   Philada. December 7, 1781

The inclosed letter from Mr Morris to me will shew you his desire of having all the Specific supplies of Flour and Salted Provisions in your State forwarded to this place, have therefore to request you upon rec^t of this to give orders to your Assistants to forward all your flour and Salt Provisions without a moments delay to the Head of Elk (except such as may be necessary for supplying the Prisoners at Frederick Town and such Troops as may be passing your Post at Baltimore as the season is far advanc'd and two Vessels waiting in the Delaware to receive those supplies beg that no time may be lost in the execution thereof — please to favour me with a line by the return of the Express and inform what may be expected to Elk,
I remain with Compts to Mrs. Calhoun Dear Sir
Your obedt. Hble Servant
Eph Blaine C.G.P

James Calhoun Esquire

Peter Force Collection, Roll 75, Ephraim Blaine Letterbook, Library of Congress.

Blaine to John Hanson

Sir   Philada. 10th. Decr. 1781

I do not wish to give your Excelley and Congress any trouble respecting my department—but the distresses of many of my deputies and assistants call loudly for Justice—and it is my duty to represent to you the difficulties which the [*sic*] labour under—mearly from my repeated application and their desire of serving the public and relieving the distresses and wants of our Army—

In my letter the 30th, of last July I represented to Congress the Situation of sundry of my deputies who, had Warrants upon the states of Conecticutt New York, Jersey, Deleware, and Virginia with two Warrents in my hand One upon the Continental treasurer the Other upon the Managers of the Lottery—great part of which warrents have never been paid—those warrents gave many of my people a Credit upon which they made large purchases—

Others whose public Credit had failed plidged their private Obligations for supplies at specia value a list of which was also inclosed—I need not enlarge by telling your Excellency that many of those persons are under the greatest distress and their property liable to seizure—this being a Matter Known by Members of your Honorable body—have therefore to request and entreat your Excellency and Congress to adopt some method to enable me to discharge their demands—and also to order a final settlement of all my Accts.—the delay of those settlements I am confident has been a much greater Injury to the public than any advantage and has formed a thousand excuses in the payment of public demands to person [sic] in my Opinion who have little or no claim against the united states—having a large number of my Accts. ready for settlement and the time being at hand in which my appointment as Commissary General of purchases will be of little real advantage to the public—and as I shall claim every Emolument there from untill the [sic] are finally settled—have therefore to intreat your Excellency & Congress to give orders or adopt some plann to facilitate that necessary business, and relieve me from a charge which gives me much concearn and real uneasiness having had the Disposal of such large sums of public money unaccounted for—

I have the honor to be with the greatest respect— your Excellency's Most Obdt.

and Most Hble Servant
Eph: Blaine

John Hanson Esqr. President of Congress

> Hanson, from Maryland, was elected President of the Continental Congress on November 5, 1781. Peter Force Collection, Roll 75, Ephraim Blaine Letterbook, Library of Congress.

Blaine, Circular to Maryland Counties

Circular
Sir   Philadelphia 14th Jany. 1781 [sic]
Immediately upon rect. of this you will please to forward to Col: Yates Deputy Quar. Master Genl. at the Head of Elk—all the neat proceeds of tallow arising from the public Cattle which were slaughtered under your direction in the County Queen Ann, also the Hides if you have not sold them—The Numbers of Cattle slaughtered and the Accounts thereof, with such rects. and Vouchers as you may have from any of my deputies or Assistants send to Col: Hollingsworth state Agent with whom I settle and pay of [sic] such ballances as may be justly due against the United States, and give him proper Certificates or receipts for such provisions as have been delivd. for the Use of Our Army during the last year
                I remain Sir Your Obedt. Humble Servt.
                Eph: Blaine

Mr. Charles Blake
Also sent To the Counties Talbot Dorset Summer sett Caroline & Worchester

> In 1780 Blake was appointed by the state as Commissary of Purchases for Queen Anne's County, Maryland.
> Peter Force Collection, Roll 75, Ephraim Blaine Letterbook, Library of Congress.

Blaine to Donaldson Yeates

Dear Sir   Philadelphia 15 Jany 1781 [sic]
    I have sent the bearer Mr. Morton to call upon you and Col: Hollingsworth for a special return of specific supplies within your district, and to adopt some means of geting the flour and salt provisions brought forward without delay—have to request that every measure in your poser or Col: Hollingsworth, may be executed to answer that purpose, Mr. Morris is exceedingly pressing favour me with a return of all supplies, recd. and during [sic] the last year and from what persons or post recd.
                I remain with much regard
                Your Obedt: Humble Servt.
                Eph. Blaine
Mr. Yates
N: B I have ordered all the public Tallow upon the Eastern shore, and such hides as has not been sold by the County Agents sent forward to you, if you can sell the hides at Phia. price do it and the Tallow with what is in your care forward to this place as soon as possible   E B

> Peter Force Collection, Roll 75, Ephraim Blaine Letterbook, Library of Congress.

Blaine to James Calhoun

Dear Sir   Philadelphia 15th. Jany. 1781—[sic]
    The Honble Mr. Morris has called upon me for a return of all specific supplies furnished by the respective states in the year Eighty One and has requested me to Order all the provisions in your state which is not wanted for the Troops, now stationed there to this place have therefore to request you to give me the necessary information as spedily [sic] as possible, and order the specific supplies collected to the public Magazines without delay you will please to send your returns

by Mr. Morton or the first safe opportunity and give him every information you can, shall be glad to hear from you and believe me with much regard—
                Dear Sir Your Most Odedt. Humble Servt.
                              Eph: Blaine
James Calhoon Esqr.

> Peter Force Collection, Roll 75, Ephraim Blaine Letterbook, Library of Congress.

Blaine to Henry Hollingsworth

Sir   Philadelphia 15th. Jany. 15, 1782

I have sent the Bearer Mr. Morton on purpose to call on you for a special return of all the supplies of provs. furnished for the last year, and to press you and Col: Yates to use every possible measure to forward what provisions may be on hand to this place—The information I had from the Honble special Council when at Talbot Court House, gave me assurances of a large quantity of wheat and flour that was colected and colecting upon your shore, the Army recd. very little from your district while in Virginia, therefore a considerable quantity must be on hand,—I gave this information to Mr. Morris when I came from the Southard, and he is very pressing to have the specific supplies colected; and returns of what each state has furnished the last year, made to his Office, <u>and has called upon me for that purpose</u> have therefore to request and intreat you to give me the necessary information as spedily as possible, and order an immediate collection of the specific supplies to the public Magazines I shall expect your returns by Mr. Morton and with respect—
                      Sir Your Most Obedt. Humble Servt.
                      Eph Blaine

Col. Hollingsworth

Peter Force Collection, Roll 75, Ephraim Blaine Letterbook, Library of Congress.

Morton to Blaine

Sir   Philada. 16th. February 1782

    The necessity I am in for Money, as well as my uneasiness at sacraficing my time without a certainly of a Compensation for my Services, while some People who have made fortunes in your Department will not attend a single Hour, even to the Settlement of their own Accts. obliges me to trouble you on this Occasion—

    The Balance of Salary &c. due me Per Acct: inclosed is £153 for which I have given you the necessary Voucher to lay before the Auditors of Accompts—What Money I have drawn prior to the first of May last, charging it in Specie agreeable to the depreciation at the time I recd: it, which is doing strict Justice to the public, will fall considerably short of my Salary for 23 months commencing the 1st. June 1779 at £15 pr month—without any Commissions or other Emolument—

    I am now indebted for my Board, and Tradesmen and others near £100—which I hope and expect the Public will enable you to advance me—The remaining Sum of £53 together with my Salary from the 1st. January and what may hereafter become due, I expect you will take it upon yourself to pay and charge the Public in such manner as you may think proper—On those Conditions I will spend a few Months to Assist you in explaining and Settling such Transactions as I have had an Opportunity of being acquainted with, and other matters as far as lays in my power—Should you think me Extravagant or ungenerous in what I have proposed I must take such part of the Salary due me as Mr: Morris is pleased to grant and seek a living in some other Employ—I can have a Salary equal to what I expect from you <u>regularly paid</u> any time I please to Accept it, and when last in Baltimore I had an Offer of entring into a Partnership which I am well assured would turn to good Advantage—I beg to be favour'd with your Answer in writing I remain with much respect—

     Sir Your most Obt. Hble Servant
      Geo: Morton

Col. E. Blaine

Addressed: Col. E. Blaine Privt.

Peter Force Collection, Ephraim Blaine Papers, Reel 74, Library of Congress.

Blaine to Robert Morris Jr.

Sir   Philadelphia Feby 19th. 1782

 I do not wish to add to the many difficulties you have to encounter with in the great undertaking of your public Office—but it is my duty to represent the situation of myself and many of those Persons who have been employed in the Department over which I have presided. And I have not the least doubt but you will afford every redress in your Power, final Settlements of all public Accts. are Necessary. A delay of which favours every delinquent and ill desposed person who has any intention of fraud—Previous to July 1777 what business I transacted for the United States was by order of Congress. The beginning of August following I was the first deputy which Acted for Mr. Buchanan Commisary Genl. of Purchases, and Continued under his direction untill the 15th. of May 1778—at which time Colo. Wadsworth began to Act, I continued under him untill the 4 of November 1779 at which time Congress was pleased to appoint me Commisary General of Purchases. The sundry Systems of the Commisariate and the Manner in which the Business was transacted Obliged me to Employ a Considerable number of People, some of which have not been so faithfull in the trust reposed in them. Others who have been Attentive, done their duty and rendered satisfactory Acots. and have considerable Ballances due, for a final Settlement of which They are very importunate. I wish some

measure may be immediately Adopted to give them assurances of this, and future Payment—I assure you Sir my situation is very disagreable, I am liable to insults every Day from Numbers who have Claims against the department, and are continually making Application for Money—I have recd. and Expended large Sums under the direction of Mr. Buchanan—Millions under Collo. Wadsworth and a considerable sum since my appointment of Commissary General, and the delay of Settlement has prevented my obtaining credit for one Dolr. I wish to know if my Cash Acot. and receipts for the payment of Money will not be a sufficient Discharge, if this business is long delayed—those I can have ready in a short Time and I hope to the satisfaction of every Public Officer and Gentlemen—There are sundry demands against me for debts contracted last Campaign and for which the People have my special Promise, what is still due will amount to about Nine Hundred Pounds, I request and intreat the favour of you to enable me to discharge those demands—Orders for part of which are now against me in Town—I have the Honour to be with the greatest respect—
    Your Most Obdt. And Most Hble Servt

The Honble Robert Morris Suppr. of finance

> Peter Force Collection, Roll 75, Ephraim Blaine Letterbook, Library of Congress.

Blaine to Donaldson Yeates

Sir   Philada. 24th. Feby. 1782
 your favour of the Seventeenth by Mr. Wright came to hand this morning and I am happy in finding you are able to forward the Specific supplies, what Success is Colo. Hollingsworth making in the Colection of flour. I shall expect a Considerable Quantity from him. the flour and beef which Remains at George town you will please to order forwarded to

Elk. Mr. Morris is Exceedingly pressing for those supplies therefore beg you to adopt every measure to have them sent on—have your Accts. for the Expenditure of monies in my department made out and be very particular in your Vouchers, and rects. every triffle is made an Objection in the Auditors Office, you are Justifiable in delivering the hides to Colo. Hollingsworth he is appointed by the proper Officer—you will decline the sale of any and all which may be forwarded to you deliver him forward all the public tallow by the first Opportunity it is now much wanted, shall be glad to hear from you by every Opportunity—and believe me with much Esteem and regard, Sir

Your Most Obdt. Hble Servt.
Eph Blaine C.G.P.

Colo. Yeates DQMG Elk
N.B I am of Opinion you ought to continue some person to receive the public stores while they are forwarding to and from Christian

> Peter Force Collection, Roll 75, Ephraim Blaine Letterbook, Library of Congress.

Blaine to Ebenezer Coffin

Dear Sir,   Philada. 6th. March 1782

Inclosed you have an order upon Colo. Thompson which I beg You to present this morning and get his Acceptance, shou'd have waited upon you myself but being now engaged in business am prevented—will call upon you in the Afternoon, and am,

Dear Sir Yours Sincerely
Eph. Blaine

Mr Coffin

> By the ninth of the Articles of Capitulation at Yorktown, the merchant-capitulants were promised an amount of tobacco equal in

value to the total sales price of the property these merchants had been permitted to sell following the surrender of Cornwallis. Coffin served as the representative of all of them.

Blaine and Charles Stewart to James Thompson

Sir,   Philada. 6th. March 1782

Please to pay Messrs. Ebr. Coffin & Company or order, the sum of six hundred and ninty One pounds fifteen Shillings and Eleven pence in gold or Silver, reckoning a Spanish Milled Dollar at seven Shillings and six pence, with Interest from the 15th. day of January last, and charge the same to Acct. of, Sir,
                         Your most Obdt. Servts.
                         Stewart & Blaine
Colo. James Thompson
     Prest.

Addressed: Mr. Coffin at Mrs. Dunlaps
Docketed E Blaine to Eb. Coffin and Blaine & Stewart order on Col. Thompson returned 6th. March 1782

Charles Stewart Family Papers, MS Am 1243 (10). Houghton Library, Harvard University.

Blaine to Robert Forsyth

Dear Sir   Philada. 18th. March 1782

Your favours of the 17th: Feby and 3rd. March inclosing Copies of Letters Returns and Estimates came only to hand the other morning and were immediately laid before Mr. Morris—also the Amount of Drafts drawn upon me in favour of Mr. Tate—He tells me that the Board of War had ordered such Prisoners as was left behind to be forwarded to Winchester, & Fredericktown in Maryd: where Contracts have been made to Supply them and that any Expence which may arrise on the Communication for Supplies either of Provision or

Transportation furnished those Troops must be a State Charge—however have reason to hope that part of those Drafts will be paid when presented and be assured my utmost Exertion shall be used for that Purpose—

I made Application to Mr. Morris to be informed whether you should proceed to join General Greene—His answer was that he believed General Greene would return to the Northward as he was of Oppinion that Enemy would Evacuate the Southern States, but desired me to inform you to be in readiness should that Event not take place—

New Methods are taken by Congress for a final Settlement of all Public Accts.—A Commissioner is to be recommended by Mr. Morris for each State and approved of by the Legislative Authorities, whose Business will be to adjust the Accts. between State & State respecting Specific Supplies & Services performed since the Commencement of the War until the first of January last—Five other Commissioners are to be appointed One for the Quarter Master Generals Department, one for the Commissaries, one for the Clothiers one for the Hospital & one for the Marine Department—who are to Settle and finally adjust all Public Transactions in those Departments—previous to the first of last January, God send this mode may take place immediately for I am heartily tired of Public Service—I thank you for the Return of Specific Supplies furnished by Virga.—Where are those of the Southern States—Is it in your power to Obtain them—I am much pleased to find your Accts. are nearly ready for Settlement—when the mode is finally Adopted & the Person Appointed I shall inform you—until then any attempt is unnecessary—Pray obtain a particular Acct. of those Cattle Sold at Williamsbuy [*sic*] I remain Dear Sir
    Your most Obt Hble Servant
     E: Blaine
      CGP

Major Forsyth

Peter Force Collection, Roll 75, Ephraim Blaine Letterbook, Library of Congress.

Blaine to Robert Morris Jr.

Sir   Philada. 20th. March 1782

Enclosed you have an estimate of Monies due for provisions furnish'd the guards and British prisoners in Virginia & Maryland and services perform'd in my department—for which orders are drawn and well Authenticated Vouchers deposited in my Office—Necessity Oblig'd Major Forsyth to adopt this plann Otherwise the guards and prisoners must have suffered for want of subsistance, he is an attentive good Officer and had my orders to procure provisions upon the best terms he could—provided that states shou'd fail in affording A Necessary supply—have therefore to entreat you Sir to enable me to Discharge those demands a disapointment will break my special promise and ruin the credit of those persons who have transacted the business—when Specific supplies have been demanded by Congress from the respective States I have ever avoided making Special Contracts but where there was the utmost Necessity or orders from the Commander in chief for that purpose—

you have also Enclosed a return of the specific supplies furnished by the state of Virginia from June 1780 untill December 1781, Major Forsyth has had great trouble in colecting the Returns from the state agents and store Keepers, negligence, want of method and Ability in many of the state Commissioners and the manner in which they delivered over their Supplies will make it impossible to be Exact but the return is as Compleat an Aggregate as in his power to Obtain

the flour at Duck creek Cross roads is in a perishable state and never was more than meal, shou'd an Opportunity Offer to send it up it will bring very little in this market, woud therefore take the Liberty of advising to Bargain will to Miller to have it unpack'd and such as will Answer have it rebolted with fresh Meal to make it Merchantable—Otherwise have it sold for what it will fetch—

you will pardon me for taking the Liberty of repeating to you my Anxiety of haveing the Enclos'd list of debts paid your Complyance with which will Keep Major Forsyth from a total ruin of Credit and greatly Oblige Sir

Your Most Obedt. and Most Hble Servt.
Eph Blaine C.G.P

the Honble. Robt. Morris Financier

> Peter Force Collection, Roll 75, Ephraim Blaine Letterbook, Library of Congress.

Blaine to Robert Morris Jr.

Sir   Philada. 30th. March 1782

I am exceedingly perplexed with those Persons who have special Demands against the Department of Supplies furnished and Services performed agreeable to the Estimate left in your Office the other Day and particularly so with those People who furnished Supplies at Fredericktown and Winchester—The People are waiting in Town for Money & are very importunate—I must take the Liberty of beging and entreating you to enable me to pay those demands—the Supplies have been furnished and proper Receipts taken from the Issuing Commissary for the Delivery of the Same which are deposited in my Office—The Deputy Commissary of Issues for the State of Virginia lives at Richmond and my Application to him for his Accts. and Vouchers of Issues will be improper and I presume he will pay no regard to it without a Regular Order from Col Stewart who is at the Head of the Department—Those Provisions were procured upon my special Promise and the Credit of Colonels Wood Snigars & Holmes who are bound for a principal part of the Money—Holmes and another Gentlemen are in Town and from their Representations are in distress—You will particularly

Oblige me by an Answer that I may have it in my Power to inform those Gentlemen what they are to expect—
I have the Honor to be with great respect—
Sir Your most Obt Hble Servant
E. Blaine
The Honorable Robert Morris Esqr.

Peter Force Collection, Roll 75, Ephraim Blaine Letterbook, Library of Congress.

Blaine to Robert Morris Jr.

Sir			Philada: 8th April 1782

Inclosed you have an abstract of the Provisions purchased by Mr. Tate for the Guards and Prisoners at Winchester and the Deputy Commissary of Issues Rect. for the Receival, as also a Receipt of Mr. Johns for Cattle purchased of Mr: Shaw and delivered at Fredericktown to Col Price—Those Cattle were deliver'd by Special agreement with me and the time long expired in which he shd: have had his pay—Those two Demands are the principal part of the Estimate left in your Office which with the other triffg. Accounts ought to be paid—Mr. Holmes has returned but has left Orders for part of the Money in Town, it will be serving the Public and confering a great Obligation upon me to discharge those Debts—my Word Honor and Reputation are forfeited by the Delay & indeed most innocently, as I had the Order of the Commander in Chief and never adopted the Plan but when the Troops were in the greatest distress for want of Provisions—Have therefore to entreat your Approbation and complyance with my Request and enable me to discharge those Demands particularly Shaws Debt—Indeed my People have done their Duty in the purchase of the Provisions and the Delivery thereof, and the Acct. of the Expenditure of the Provisions is the business of the Commissary General of Issues, his Deputies and Assistants—The Person who went with the British Prisoners had a Special Appointment from Col Stewart

for that particular Duty and will undoubtedly Account for such Provisions as he may have receiv'd on the March or at the Post of Winchester—
   I remain with much Esteem and Regard
    Hond. Sir Your most Obedt. Hble Servt—
     E. Blaine
Hon: Robert Morris Esqr.
 S. Finance—

> Peter Force Collection, Roll 75, Ephraim Blaine Letterbook, Library of Congress.

Blaine to Donaldson Yeates

Sir   Philada: 10 April 1782
 Your favour of the 8th. pr Giles came to hand this day and am sorry at the Information you give respecting the Flour which is forwarding from George Town and Baltimore—there is no hard Bread wanting for any Public use whatever therefore baking is out of the Question—I have considered and the only method which can be adopted to make the Flour Merchantable will be to have it [partial letter ends]

> Peter Force Collection, Roll 75, Ephraim Blaine Letterbook, Library of Congress.

Blaine, Subscription for the Purchase of a Ship

          Philada: 17 April 1782
£100.10
 In thirty days from the date hereof I promise to pay Thomas Fitzsimons Esqr. or Order One hundred Pounds ten Shillings for my Subscription for the purchase of a Ship to protect the Trade—
    Eph. Blaine

Peter Force Collection, Roll 75, Ephraim Blaine Letterbook, Library of Congress.

Blaine to John Hanson

Sir,   Philadelphia July 20th. 82.

I am under the Necessity of adressing Congress through your Excellency upon a very disagreable subject a subject of great Consequence to many worthy Citizens of the United States and particularly so, to some of those who have been Active in the present revolution—

A great number of my assistants as Depy. Commisary Generals, and Deputies as Commissarys Genl. [sic] are now sued and under Execution for public Debts, an Action has been lately Brought against me in this City by Garret & Sorrel Graziers—and many more Persons are only waiting the Issue of that Tryal to commence sundry other Suits—In this situation what are your Officers to do, if the Public Finances will not admit of Congress paying their Debts, it is undoubtedly the duty of those States who are Deficient and have not complyed with their requisitions to adopt means of payment, or to make Laws to indemnify your Officers untill their Public Accounts are settled, This is only Common Justice and I demand It of Congress. Many Things have been said about the Staff Officers being the cause of Depreciating Contl. Money by a Lavish Destruction thereof—and a Neglect of their Duty, this has very seldom taken place in my Department and I defy the Envy and malice of Man to charge me with a known neflect of duty in any one Instance, there is a large sum of Money due me between the first of December 1776 and the 14th. of September 1777 for supplies furnish'd the post of Carlisle for which I have never receiv'd one Dollar, I am exceedingly Distressed for Money and must entreat your Excellence to furnish me with Six Hundred Pounds in Money bills of Exchange or any thing which will command Money to enable me to pay Debts to that amount for the Discharge of which I have no other fund but the

Public, having Discharged all my Clerks last fall but one and begun the final settlement of my Public Accts. with Jonathan Burrall. I find I shall be under the Necessity of employing two or three Persons while engag'd in that necessary business for which I request the approbation of Congress—Your Excellency and Congress Complying with the forgoing request and adopting some measure to prevent many of your Servants from total ruin, will infinitely oblidge your Excelly
      Most obdient & Very Hble Sert.

His Excellency John Hanson Esqr.
President of Congress

> Peter Force Collection, Roll 75, Ephraim Blaine Letterbook, Library of Congress.

Blaine to Thomas Huggins

Sir   Philada. 31st July 1782
  I am now attending the auditors who is making a final settlement of my public Accts., under Mr. Buchanan and Mr Wadsworth—I have been looking over yours and find I can do nothing with them untill you come up, the whole Vouchers and Acct. of purchases are wanting for the month of February, if Mr. Ma[rv]el is not engaged and will come up with you I shall want him to stay two months but he must give up every Other business for that time—I shall expect you hear [sic] by the 6th. August, without fail, I remain Sir,
        Your Obdt. Hble Servt
        Eph. Blaine
Mr. Huggins
Elke

> Huggins had served as an Assistant Commissary of Purchases at the Head of Elk (now Elkton) in 1777 and 1778.

Peter Force Collection, Roll 75, Ephraim Blaine Letterbook, Library of Congress.

Blaine to Henry Miller

Dr. Sir   Philada. 1st August 1782.

I have daily difficulties from the Commissioner for settling the Expenditures of the Commissary Generals Department, for the Accts. of my deputies and Assistants indeed what makes him more importunate is the short time he has to remain in this State, he is Obliged to Attend in Hartford Connecticutt the fifteenth of October for the purpose of settling the Expenditures of my department in that State—let me Request you my dear Sir to come down prepared for a final close as well yours as the Accts. of George Eichelberger Decd, in the course of this month and be particular Respecting your Deliveries,

pray endeavour to settle the Amount of Majr. Smiths Warrant with Mr Hays your treasurer and bring down the means of payment with you, I have been laid upon my back ever since my Return to this City and perhaps as bad in the gout 12 days of the time as ever man was, why the Devil shou'd I have it, give my Love to Colo. Hartley, and tell him this ought to be a hint to him and you, not to attend the cold Spring to Often,

I am in hast Dr. Sir.
Your Obdt. Hble Servt.

Col Miller

Peter Force Collection, Roll 75, Ephraim Blaine Letterbook, Library of Congress.

To Robert Buchannan

Dear Sir,   Philada. 2nd. August, 1782.

Your favour I recd. and my Absence was the cause you did not hear from me long ear this, you must know that Mr. Burrell the Commissnr. for the Commissary department begins to get impatient at the delay of several of my deputies and Assistants, in not bringing in the residue of their Accts. for a final settlement, and suspect that large sums of public Money are detaind in their hands, you are Amongst the delinquents but I have used every Arguement in your favour such as your Absence for want of health &c. I have now my dear Sir, to request your Immediate attendance for the above purpose, if in your power to bear the fituage of the Journey, if not pray arange your Accts and send them by first safe Opportunity and I shall do every thing in my power to have them properly settled, your compliance with One or other of the Afforesaid proposals is Absolutely necessary else I shall have to waite on you at Baltimore.

Those contracts which you made with sundry persons where money was advanced and not comply'd with you will settle with such for the difficency of Money Agreable to the Scale of Depreciation ading Interest from the time they Recd. the money untill you settle, if good men take their own Bonds with interest payable in three or four Months if Suspicious demand Security, and those Bonds shall be admitted by me in the settlement with you, let me hear from you by the first Stage and believe me to be dear Sir
      Your Obdt. Hble Servt.

  Peter Force Collection, Roll 75, Ephraim Blaine Letterbook, Library of Congress.

Blaine to Robert Dodd

Sir,   Philadelphia Augt. 2d. 1782
 I am now attending the auditor who is appointed to a final Settlement of all Accts. in the Departments of the Commissary Generals of Purchases. Your accounts have not

been regularly Settled, and there appears a ballance due against you, and least you May have some further demands I have postponed giving in your Accts. untill you come down and have them finally Closed, this I request you may do next week, I shall delay you a very short time I remain Sir
       Your most Hble Servt.
Mr. Robert Dodd.

> Dodd was a purchaser at Flemington, New Jersey. Peter Force Collection, Roll 75, Ephraim Blaine Letterbook, Library of Congress.

Blaine to Ezekiel Forman

Sir,   Philada. August 28th 1782

 Your favour by Lieut. Shepard came Safe to hand and Observe the contents—I expect my Accts under the Direction of Col Wadsworth will be ready for settlement the first of next Octr. I wou'd not wish you to be at the expence of coming down your selfe, but by that time Endeavour to send your papers by some safe person who may be coming on Other business money there is none to pay you all you can Expect will be a Certificate which will bear Interest. I shall pay particular attention in laying your accts. before the auditor to have them examined
      and am sir Your Hble Servt.
Mr. Foreman

> Forman was a member of the Maryland Council of Safety. He was appointed by Congress as a commissioner of the Board of Treasury, from which he resigned in May 1781 after charges were brought against the Board business. Peter Force Collection, Roll 75, Ephraim Blaine Letterbook, Library of Congress.

Blaine to Robert Morris Jr.

Sir   Philada. 16th. Octr. 1782

Inclosed you have an Estimate of the quantity of provisions which is Absolutely necessary to deposit in the Garrison of Fort Pitt and its dependancies before Christmass—and the sum of money those provisions will cost—my credit and the person concearned with me will help a little, but money and as large a sum as you can spare will be wanted immediately—my princaple supplies must go from this side the mountains—as the people in that Country except a small settlement upon the Mononghala have been drove from their Habitations by the savages—

your furnishing me with the means will enable me to lay in a proper supply, keep the troops from complaining, this I am sure will give you satisfaction, and I shall give you no further trouble untill next Summer—

I have the honor to be with much Respect Sir
your Most Obdt. & Most Hble Servt,
Eph. Blaine

The Honble. Mr. Morris

Endorsed: a Copy of a Letter/wrote Mr. Morris/16th. 1782 Blaine had agreed to assume the expired contract to supply Fort Pitt for the remainder of 1782.

> Peter Force Collection, Roll 75, Ephraim Blaine Letterbook, Library of Congress.

Blaine to Moses Chaille

Sir   Philadelphia the 5 Novr.
Your favour by Mr. Stevenson Came safe to hand and Observe the Contents, when Mr. Morton Return'd from the Estren shore he informed me of you having a Quantity of Beef upon hand, and as I wrote to the Special Council very perticular upon that subject, Also to Colo. Hollingsworth state ajent for your shore and to you before I left Yorktown and all the other Commissaries I look upon the provisions in your

hand the property of the state, you are Certainly blameable in Keeping it upon hand all the winter & spring, it ought to been sent up the bay or disposed of in such a manner that the publick might suffer no loss by it—take Colo. Hollingsworth advice in the disposal of it and as Spedily as you possibly can, I remain Sir

      Your Obdt. Hubl Servt
Mr. Chaille
  Worster County Maryland

> Chaille of Snow Hill, had served in the Maryland Militia.
> Peter Force Collection, Roll 75, Ephraim Blaine Letterbook, Library of Congress.

Blaine to Elias Boudinot

Sir   Philada, 25th. Feby. 1783.

In November 1779 Congress was pleased to appoint me Commissary Genl. of Purchases for the United States of America, and upon the first day of Jany. following adopted regulations for the Government of the department, at this time the [sic] had hopes of stoping a farther depreciation of Continental money, and fixed the pay of the Deputy Commissary's two Pr Cent for all Merchantable Provisions on twenty fold the prices they were sold at in the Year 1774, untill the further Order of Congress &ca—On the 12th. day of January I accepted the appointment the appointment and proceeded the 18th on my Journey to the Eastren States[.] I could engage no person of probity and character upon those terms, therefore agreed to give two Pr Cent Commissions upon all their purchases, indeed necessity Required my adopting this measure in order to Keep up a supply for the army—upon my return the 29th March I wrote Congress and informed them of this and Every Other transaction Respecting my department to which a Committee agreed, but no Resolve passed to Justify my engagements—a Commissioner is now setling the Accts. of the Commissariate and Cannot make that allowance without an Act of Congress—have therefore to intreat your Excellency to request them to pass a Resolve to answer the afforesaid purpose and enable the Commissioner to proceed in the settlement—

    I beg leave to mention my Own Situation, I was exposed to a very great expence that Winter and Spring and including a Horse which cost me sixty eight pounds Specia which died upon my returning for [sic] the Eastward, and going from this City to Fredericks burgh Virginia and Returning to Head Quarters in Jersey, I expended the saliry which was allowed me for that years service. I therefore think myself Justifiable in requesting Congress to allow my traveling expences, or make such Other provisions as may appear to them Just and Reasonable, I have constantly studied the pubic Interest in the expenditures of their money, and One Circumstance was the sales of the Sugar and Rum at Boston for which I had an Order but finding the prices there exceedingly low I pospon'd the sales, gave orders to forward the rum to the army, and ship'd the three hundred some odd Hhds. of Sugar for Philadelphia, by which the public Cleared One hundred and twenty thousand pounds, paying all expence, those Sugars I might have ta[ken for] my own Debit, which with the Rum wou'd have neated a profit of two hundred and fifty thousand Pounds—in the management of this business both at Boston and in this City I was subjected to very considerable expence, and had no advantage what ever, I flatter myself Congress will not think unreasonably my demand that they will be disposed to make an Acknowledgement for my Services,

    I have the honour
        to be with the greatest Respect
            Your Excellency's Most Obdt. and
            Most Hble Servt.
                  Eph. Blaine C.G.P.

Elias Boudinot Esqr.

President of Congress

> Boudinot, of New Jersey, had served Commissary of Prisoners, and in the Continental Congress several times. He was elected President of Congress in November 1781. Papers of the Continental Congress, Roll 48, i41, v1, p447, National Archives.

Blaine, Property Advertised

FOR SALE,
SUNDRY TRACTS of LAND in the county of Cumberland and state of Pennsylvania, viz Two Tracts of Land in Middleton township, one mile from the two of Carlisle, both sides of Canodoquenit creek, known by the name of the Cain Lands; upon which there is a compleate merchant mill with two water wheels; the mill house of stone compleatly built, two stories high, 52 by 42 feet in the clear; the water wheels are both within the house to prevent the frost from injuring them in cold weather; adjoining the mill is a large stone building erected for a distillery; on those tracts there is two hundred and fifty acres of clear land, fifty acres of meadow in excellent order, and fifty more can be made at a trifling expence; there is buildings and out-houses to accommodate three families on different parts of the land.

Two other Tracts two miles from Carlisle, in the township aforesaid, containing seven hundred acres; on those tracts there is but one tenement, a young orchard of gafted [*sic*] fruit. This tract is situated so as to afford three divisions.

One other Tract adjoining the town of Carlisle; containing four hundred and fifty acres, with sixty acres of clear land; this will suit dividing into lots, to accommodate such of the inhabitants of the town as may chuse to purchase.

One other Tract four miles from Carlisle.

One other Tract situated upon the Provincial road, leading from Carlisle to Virginia and Pittsburgh, fourteen miles from the former, containing five hundred acres, with two small improvements, known by the name of Butler's Tract, or the Rich Lands.

Sundry Lots in and adjoining the town of Carlisle, and Tracts of Land in the townships of Rye, Greenwood, Fermanaugh, Derry, and Armaugh.

Any persons who are possessed of lands near this city, and disposed to enlarge their property by exchange, may be advantageously accommodated. The subscriber will attend at Carlisle from the 15th of April until the 15th of May, to shew the premises and make known the terms. If not Sold by the 15th of May will be Rented for a term of years.

March 26.   EPH. BLAINE.

The Pennsylvania Packet or the General Advertiser, April 5, 1783; April 24, 1783.

Statement of Property Purchase

June 6, 1783.

I do hereby certify, that in the month of *May*, 1781, I sold Colonel *John Davis* seven hundred acres of land, situate in *Middletown* township, *Cumberland* county, two miles from the town of *Carlisle*, and that a survey made by *Samuel Lyon*, deputy surveyor, containing two hundred and nineteen acres, seventy-six perches, and the allowance of six *per cent.* is part of the aforesaid tract, for which the said *Davis* paid me four pounds five shillings, per acre, *specie*; and I do hereby engage to make the said *Davis*, or his assigns, a deed of conveyance for the aforesaid two hundred and nineteen acres and seventy-six perches, clear of every incumbrance to the first of *March*, 1775. Given under my hand and seal," &c.

(Signed)   "Ephraim Blaine."

Reports of Cases Adjudged in the Supreme Court of Pennsylvania 2nd. ed. (Philadelphia: Thomas Davis, 1846), 12:132.

Blaine to Unidentified, Partial Letter

Sir, Philadelphia 31st July 1783
   My being in the Country is the cause why you have not heard from me since the first of Aprl. last, the Commissioner of Accts. for the Commissary Department is very uneasy at your delay

> Peter Force Collection, Roll 75, Ephraim Blaine Letterbook, Library of Congress.

Blaine to Patrick Ewing and Thomas Huggins

Sir, Philadelphia 31st July 1783
   My being back in the Country is the Cause why you have not heard from me this Several Months past, I am distress'd at your delay in not coming up to put a final settlement to your public Accts, had you no interest in the issue, my being bound for your conduct and expenditures of Money, and deprived on that Acct. from closing my Accts. with the public is a sufficient Reason, your Returns and papers which were lodged in my Office have been long since Left with Mr Barrell and he has examined them and made his Remarks thereon—pray delay not a moment in attending here for the afforesaid purpose and bring every other paper and Voucher which Remains in your hands—Mr. Barrell is Ordered to attend in Harford Connecticut upon the first day of Octr. next and will have very little time to loose, your Compliance with Much Oblige Sir,
   Your Most Obdt. Hble Servt.

Mr. Patrick Ewing Mr. Thomas Huggins.

> Peter Force Collection, Roll 75, Ephraim Blaine Letterbook, Library of Congress.

Blaine to John Dickinson

a Certificate of Gideons Richey Agent for the County of Bedford, dated the 11th day of July 1782. Your Memoralist therefore prays your Excellency and the Honorable Council to grant said Wood a pattent agreeable to the Law in that case made and Provided, and your Memoralist as in duty Bound shall pray—

      EPH BLAINE
      Philada. 28th August 1783
His Excellency
 John Dickinson Esqr.
  President of the Commonwealth of Pennsylvania

   Samuel Hazard, ed., *Pennsylvania Archives*, 1st ser. (Philadelphia: Joseph Severns, 1854), 9:244.

Whereas James Woods of the County of Cumberland in the Commonwealth of Pennsylvania hath lately purchased a certain Tract of Land situate in the County of Cumberland in Pennsylvania aforesaid Containing One thousand four hundred and ninety seven Acres, and allowance for highways &ca. late the Property of Harry Gordon, and Confiscated to the State agreeably to An Act of the General Assembly of the same State, in that Case made and provided, as by the Survey thereof will more fully appear.

 Know all Men by these Presents that I the said James Woods have made ordained constituted and appointed And by these Presents do make ordain constitute and appoint Colonel Ephraim Blaine of the City of Philadelphia my true and lawful Attorney for me in my name and to my Use, to transact and Manage the Premises, and for me and in my name to procure from the Executive Council of the State of Pennsylvania Patents and every Instrument of writing .relative to the Premises, And all Fees Perquisites and Charges for the same in my name to pay and discharge And finally to do execute and

perform all and every matter and thing respecting the premises as fully Amply and to all Intents and purposes as I myself might or could do were I personally present hereby ratifying allowing and confirming as good and Valid, all and whatsoever my said Attorney shall do in and about the Premises. In Witness whereof I have hereunto set my hand and Seal this Twentieth day of September in the Year of our Lord one thousand seven hundred and Eighty two-
     JAMES WOODS [Seal]
       Sealed and delivered in the presence of
     JAS. YOUNG JOHN WEST

 To His Excellency the President and the Honorable Supreme Executive Council of the Common Wealth of Pennsylvania—

 The Memorial of Ephraim Blaine Humbly sheweth— That your memoralists has a power of Attorney from James Wood of the County of Cumberld. to apply to His Excellency in Council for a Deed for the Lands of Harry Gordon which was sold as forfeited property—and the said Jas. Wood being the highest bidder purchased the same as will appear by a Certificate of Gideons Richey Agent for the County of Bedford, dated the 11th day of June 1782. Your Memoralist therefore prays your Excellency and the Honorable Council to grant said Wood a pattent agreeable to the Law in that case made and Provided, and your Memoralist as in duty Bound shall pray EPH BLAINE
      Philada. 28th August 1783
His Excellency John Dickinson Esqr.
President of the Commonwealth of Pennsylvania

  Thomas Lynch Montgomery, ed. *Pennsylvania Archives,* 6th series, (Harrisburg, 1907), 12: 243-44.

Blaine to Richard Peters

Sir,   Philada. 23rd. Octr. 1783

Being informed that you are One of a Committee of Congress who are fixed to determine the pay and Commissions of such of the Commissary Generals as have not been properly aranged—and take the liberty of writing you upon that Subject—when Congress was pleased to appoint me Commissary General there was no fixed Salary—I accepted of their appointment upon Conditions they wou'd pay my traveling Expenciss and make me a Reasonable Compensation for my services—you Sir are well acquainted with my Services and the trouble and fituage I had in procuring and Colecting supplies, in this business I was subjected to very Considerable expence—have therefore to Request Congress to allow my Reasonable treasonable traveling expenciss from the time of my appointment untill I quit the army, in adition to my pay as Regulated by the Board of War—and as my Request is so very Just and reasonable I hope it will meet with you approbation and that of the Committee.

    I have the honor to be with the greatest Respect
     sir your Most Obdt. and Most Hble Servt.
    Eph Blaine
the Honble. Richd. Peters Esqr.

addressed to The Honorable Richard Peters Esquire
     Princeton favd. by Captn. Little

> Philadelphia Peters had been Secretary to the Board of War and at this time was serving in the Continental Congress.
> Papers of the Continental Congress, Roll 182, i41, v1, p453, National Archives.

Blaine to Robert Morris Jr.

Sir,   Philadelphia 28th Octr. 1783
  I take the liberty of making you the under mentioned proposals for supplying the Garrison of Fort Pitt with

provisions, and shall ask for payment but Once every six Months, the Component part of a Ration as follows Viz.

1 lb of Bread or flour	3¼
1 lb Beef of ¾ Pork	5¼
1 Gill of Rum or Whiskey	¼
	10 d

if these terms are agreable please to write me a few lines by the first Opportunity which may Offer for Pittsburgh, that I may make the Necessary preparation for laying up a Winter supply.
I am with the greatest Respect Sir
Your Most Obedient Servant
E Blaine

Mr. Morris

> Peter Force Collection, Roll 75, Ephraim Blaine Letterbook, Library of Congress.

Blaine to William Bell

Dear Sir   Fort Pitt, 25th. Novr. 1783

I have this moment returned from being up the Monongahala River in pursuit of One of the Deputy Surveyors—and fortunately met with Colo. Marshall who has Fayette County which Extends from the Mouth of Sandy River to Kaintuck, and back to the Mountains. I have Obtained a deputation for Mr Lyon who goes with me as a Surveyor—Mr. Marshall has given me bad Encouragement Respecting Vacant lands—however I shall proceed on Friday Morning and adopt every possible measure to accomplish my business. I shall have excessive fituage and do not Expect it will be in my Power to return before the last of February—After I reach the Mouth of sandy River and Explore that Country and locate my lands I will have to ride One hundred & fifty Miles to Mr. Marshalls Office to Enter them. This will take considerable time, then after the surveys are made I must return them and have the drafts signed and Certified. Mr Elliot has been gone some days. When he has his business a little settled at the falls he will proceed to Green River and endeavour to lay up the warrants I have sent with him. You will be so kind as to hury up the goods which I wrote for by Mr Tate and Rather add to the list as many of the articles are much wanted. Speak to Mr Ludhom Mr A & Co and tell them to keep my note untill I return at which time they shall be punctually paid with Interest—You will much Oblige me in paying Mr. Gren the Waggoner who Brought up part of my goods the sum of fifty pounds, and I forgot to settle with Mr. Galaugher in record that for some delph ware which I bought from him. Pray will you pay him. pray endeavour to have our Indian cargo early in the Summer there will be a great demand. I shall have a very Considerable Remmittance to carry down with me upon my Return in money and piltry—

You will please to pay attention to my family, and should my son Return from France before I come home, I shall take it as a very particular favour if you will make it your business to See him often and give him your friendly advice. He is an unweildy boy and will stand in much need of it, please to present my Compliments to Mrs. Bell and believe me with much Reguard Dear Sir

Mr Bell.

To Mr. William Bell, Merchant, Philadelphia.

> Gail Hamilton, *Biography of James G. Blaine* (Norwich, Conn.: The Henry Bill Publishing Company, 1895), 34-35.

DOCUMENT CHRONLOGY

Ephraim Blaine to Samuel Huntington, January 5, 1780.
Blaine to Moore Furman, January 6, 1780.
Blaine to Jonathan Trumbull, January 9, 1780.
Blaine to Samuel Huntington, January 12, 1780.
Blaine to George Washington, January 16, 1780.
Blaine to Isaac Carty, Undated.
Blaine to Isaac Carty, January 25, 1780.
Blaine to George Morton, January 26, 1780.
Blaine to George Morgan, January 29, 1780.
Blaine to Moore Furman, January 29, 1780.
Blaine to Jacob Cuyler, February 1, 1780.
Blaine to Robert Hoops, February 1, 1780.
George Morton to William Evans, February 4, 1780.
Blaine to George Clinton, February 5, 1780.
Blaine to Morton, February 5, 1780.
Morton to John Mitchell, February 5, 1780.
Morton to Michael Kitts, February 5, 1780.
Morton to Mrs. John Naglie, February 6, 1780.
Blaine to the Board of War, February 6, 1780.
Blaine to Jacob Cuyler, February 6, 1780.
Blaine to Nehemiah Dunham, February 6, 1780.
Blaine to Azariah Dunham, February 6, 1780.
Blaine to Conrod Theodore Wederstrandt, February 7, 1780.
Morton to Matthias Slough, February 10, 1780.
Morton to Conrod Theodore Wederstrandt, February 12, 1780.
Blaine to Jonathan Trumbull, February 14, 1780, two letters.
Morton to John Chaloner and James White, February 22, 1780.
Morton to William Evans, February 24, 1780.
Blaine to Samuel Huntington, February 25, 1780.
Blaine to George Washington, February 25, 1780.
Morton to Benjamin Rogers, February 25, 1780.
Morton to John Chaloner and James White, February 25, 1780.
Morton to Jacob Arndt and Jacob Stroud, February 26, 1780.

Morton to Peter Aston, March 9, 1780.
Morton, Circular, to Robert Buchanan, Patrick Ewing, and Jacob Giles Jr., March 9, 1780.
Morton to Isaac Carty, March 9, 1780.
Morton to John Chaloner and James White, March 9, 1780.
Morton to the Committee of Congress, March 9, 1780.
Morton to Azariah Dunham, March 9, 1780.
Morton to William Evans, March 9, 1780.
Morton to Mathias Slough, March 9, 1780.
Morton to Conrod Theodore Wetherstrandt, March 9, 1780.
Morton to Conrod Theodore Wederstrandt, March 13, 1780.
Morton to John Chaloner and JamesWhite, March 14, 1780.
Morton to James McCallaster, March 14, 1780.
Morton to the Board of Treasury, March 17, 1780.
Morton to Benjamin Stoddert, March 17, 1780.
Morton, Circular to Assistant Purchasing Commissaries in the Middle Department, March 17, 1780.
Blaine to George Clinton, March 19, 1780.
Morton to John Chaloner and James White, March 20, 1780.
Morton to Benjamin Stoddert, March 21, 1780.
Morton to Ephraim Blaine, March 23, 1780.
Morton to Conrod Theodore Wederstrandt, March 25, 1780.
Morton to Henry Miller, March 25, 1780.
Blaine to George Clinton, March 26, 1780.
Blaine to Samuel Huntington, March 29, 1780.
Blaine to the Board of War, April 3, 1780.
Blaine to Nathanael Greene, April 3, 1780.
Blaine, Circular to John Chaloner and James White, Nicholas Patterson, William Evans, Jacob Arndt & Jacob Stroud, Peter Aston, Matthias Slough, Cornelius Cox, Henry Miller, James Smith, and William Maclay, April 5, 1780.
Blaine to Thomas Sim Lee, April 5, 1780.
Blaine, Estimate of Money Due to Commissary Staff, April 6, 1780.
Blaine to the Board of Treasury, April 10, 1780.

Blaine to George Washington, April 10, 1780.
Blaine to Moore Furman, April 11, 1780.
Blaine to Moore Furman, April 12, 1780.
Blaine to Thomas Sim Lee, April 15, 1780.
Blaine to Robert Buchanan, April 20, 1780.
Blaine to Johann de Kalb, April 21, 1780.
Blaine to Robert Forsyth, April 30, 1780.
Blaine, House Rental Agreement, May 1780.
Blaine to Robert Forsyth, May 6, 1780.
Blaine to Nehemiah Dunham, May 8, 1780.
Morton to William Stewart, May 9, 1780.
Blaine to Robert Hoops, May 9, 1780.
Blaine to Robert Lettis Hooper Jr., May 9, 1780.
Charles Stewart and Blaine to George Washington, May 9, 1780.
Charles Stewart and Blaine to Committee of Congress at Headquarters, May 9, 1780.
Blaine to Henry Champion, May 10, 1780.
Blaine to Isaac Carty, May 12, 1780.
Blaine to Robert Hoops, May 12, 1780.
Blaine to Conrod Theodore Wederstrandt, May 12, 1780.
Blaine to John Davis, May 14, 1780.
Blaine to George Washington, May 18, 1780.
Blaine to Isaac Carty, May 20, 1780.
Blaine to Joseph Reed, May 20, 1780.
Morton to Isaac Carty, May 20, 1780.
Blaine to George Washington, May 21, 1780.
Blaine to the Treasury Board, May 24, 1780.
Morton to Peter Aston, May 25, 1780.
Blaine to To the Board of War, May 25, 1780.
Blaine to the Honorable Committee of Congress, May 25, 1780.
Blaine to Charles Stewart, May 26, 1780.
Blaine to George Washington, May 27, 1780.

Blaine, Circular to Wederstrandt, Ewing, Buchanan, and Richardson, May 27, 1780.
Blaine to Thomas Sim Lee, May 27, 1780.
Blaine to Azariah Dunham, May 27, 1780.
Blaine to Christian Wirtz, June 5, 1780.
Blaine, Circular, June 8, 1780.
Blaine to William McCauley/McCauly, June 8, 1780.
Blaine to the Board of War, June 13, 1780, two letters.
Blaine to Robert Forsyth, June 13, 1780.
Morton to Robert Hoops, June 17, 1780.
Morton to James McCalester, June 17, 1780.
Blaine to the Committee of Congress, June 26, 1780.
Morton to William Evans, June 28, 1780.
Blaine to the Board of War, June 29, 1780.
Blaine to Samuel Lyon, July 2, 1780.
Blaine to Peter Aston, July 3, 1780.
Blaine to Robert Forsyth, July 3, 1780.
Blaine to Nicholas Lutz, July 3, 1780.
Blaine to Charles Stewart, July 3, 1780.
Blaine to Joseph Baker, July 4, 1780.
Blaine to Charles Miller, July 4, 1780.
Blaine, Advertisement for a Runaway, July 6, 1780.
Blaine to Joseph Hugg, John Patton, John Ladd Howell, and the Executors of George Echelberger, July 9, 1780.
Blaine to John Little, July 1, 1780.
Blaine to the Commercial Commitee of Congress, July 13, 1780.
Blaine to Samuel Lyon and Christopher Wirtz, July 13, 1780.
Blaine, Advertisement for a Runaway Slave, July 15, 1780.
Morton to the Board of War, July 17, 1780.
Blaine to George Washington, July 19, 1780,
Morton to Jacob Giles Jr., July 19, 1780.
Morton to Wederstrandt, Patrick Ewing, Isaac Carty, and Thomas Richardson, Undated.
Morton to Thomas Harwood, July 22, 1780.

Morton to Nicholas Lutz, July 24, 1780.
Blaine, Receipt, July 26, 1780.
Blaine to William Greene, July 30, 1780.
Morton to the Board of War, July 31, 1780.
Blaine to the Board of War and Ordnance, August 1, 1780.
Morton to John Chaloner and James White, August 1, 1780.
Blaine to Thomas Sim Lee, August 3, 1780.
Morton to James McCalester, August 3, 1780.
Blaine to Joseph Reed, August 3, 1780, two letters.
Blaine to Caesar Rodney, August 3, 1780.
Morton to William Maclay, August 4, 1780.
Blaine to the Committee of Congress at Headquarters, August 7, 1780.
Blaine to George Clinton, August 9, 1780.
Morton to Robert Hoops, August 10, 1780.
Blaine to George Clinton, August 14, 1780.
Blaine to William Greene, August 14, 1780.
Blaine to William Livingston, August 14, 1780.
Blaine to Thomas Sim Lee, August 14, 1780.
Blaine to the Committee of Congress, August 15, 1780.
Blaine to George Washington, August 15, 1780.
Morton to Ludowick Weltner, August 17, 1780.
Morton to John Weitzel, August 17, 1780.
Morton to Nicholas Lutz, August 17, 1780.
Morton to Samuel Lyon and Christian Wirtz, Undated.
Morton to John Weitzel, August 17, 1780.
Blaine to George Morton, August 18, 1780.
Blaine to Richard Kidder Meade, August 21, 1780.
Ephraim Blaine to Robert Hanson Harrison, August 22, 1780.
Morton to Nicholas Lutz, August 23, 1780.
Morton to Archibald Dick, August 23, 1780.
Morton to James McCalester, September 1, 1780.
Morton to Alexander Blaine, September 5, 1780.
Morton to James Smith, September 5, 1780.
Blaine to George Washington, September 12, 1780.

Blaine to Samuel Huntington, September 15, 1780.
Blaine to Caesar Rodney, September 17, 1780.
Blaine to Mr. Jones, September 18, 1780.
Blaine to Zebulon Butler, September 18, 1780.
Blaine to David Deshler, September 20, 1780.
Blaine to Nehemiah Dunham, September 20, 1780.
Blaine to Samuel Adams and the Committee for the Commissary Department, September 20, 1780.
Blaine to Joseph Reed, September 21, 1780.
Blaine to the Board of War, September 22, 1780.
Blaine to Daniel Brodhead, September 22, 1780.
Blaine to David Duncan, September 22, 1780.
Blaine to Charles Stewart, September 22, 1780.
Report of Pay Due, Undated.
Blaine to Samuel Adams, Committee Chairman, October 1, 1780.
Blaine to Jacob Morgan, October 3, 1780.
Blaine to Charles Stewart, October 3, 1780.
Blaine to Unidentified, October 4, 1780.
Queries for the Committee of Congress, October 5, 1780.
Blaine to Jacob Cuyler, October 6, 1780.
Blaine to Charles Miller, October 6, 1780.
Blaine to Unidentified, October 7, 1780.
Blaine to Tench Tilghman, October 7, 1780.
Blaine to Charles Stewart, October 8, 1780.
Blaine to Asa Waterman, October 10, 1780.
Blaine to Nehemiah Dunham, October 13, 1780.
Morton to David Deshler, October 16, 1780.
Blaine to Samuel Huntington, October 17, 1780.
Blaine to Henry Hollingsworth, October 20, 1780.
Blaine to Henry Champion, October 24, 1780.
Blaine to Henry Champion Jr. October 24, 1780.
Blaine to Nehemiah Dunham, October 24, 1780.
Blaine to Noah Emory, October 24, 1780.
Blaine to Charles Miller, October 24, 1780.

Blaine to Samuel Huntington, October 26, 1780.
Blaine to the Treasury Board, October 26, 1780.
Blaine to the Board of War, October 27, 1780.
Blaine to Joseph Carleton, October 28, 1780.
Blaine to Udny Hay, October 29, 1780.
Blaine to Samuel Osgood and the Committee of Purchases at Springfield, October 29, 1780.
Blaine to Oliver Phelps, October 29, 1780.
Blaine to Charles Miller, October 30, 1780.
Blaine to Major Henry Champion, October 30, 1780.
Blaine to Samuel Huntington, October 31, 1780.
Blaine to John Patton, Conrad Theodore Wederstrandt, James Smith, Joseph Hugg, Morris & Huff, John Ladd Howell, Patrick Ewing, Matthia Slough, Charloner & White, Azariah Dunham, Peter Aston, William Maclay, William Stuart, Henry Miller, Robert Lettis Hooper Jr., and Isaac Carty, November 1, 1780.
Blaine to Abijah Phillips, November 2, 1780.
Blaine to Governor Joseph Reed, November 9, 1780.
Blaine to George Washington, November 10, 1780.
Blaine to Samuel Huntington, November 12, 1780.
Blaine to Zebulon Butler, November 12, 1780.
Blaine to Samuel Huntington, November 12, 1780.
Blaine to Nehemiah Dunham, November 18, 1780
Blaine to Robert Elliot, November 20, 1780.
Blaine to Samuel Huntington, November 20, 1780.
Blaine to Caesar Rodney, November 20, 1780.
Blaine to Frederick Augustus Conrad Muhlenberg, November 20, 1780.
Blaine to Thomas Sim Lee, November 20, 1780.
Blaine to William Livingston, November 22, 1780.
Blaine to William Churchill Houston, November 23, 1780.
Blaine to the Board of War, November 24, 1780.
Blaine to Frederick Augustus Conrad Muhlenberg, November 28, 1780.

Blaine to the Board of War, November 29, 1780.
Blaine to Joseph Reed, December 1, 1780.
Blaine to Robert Forsyth, December 2, 1780.
Blaine to the Treasury Board, December 4, 1780.
Blaine to the Board of War, December 4, 1780.
Blaine to Thomas Sim Lee, December 8, 1780.
Morton to Donaldson Yeates, December 8, 1780.
Morton to the Board of War, December 1780.
Morton to Jacob Morgan, December 9, 1780, two letters.
Morton to Udny Hay, December 9, 1780.
Morton to Joseph Reed, December 11, 1780.
Morton to Ephraim Blaine, December 12, 1780.
Morton to the Treasury Board, December 13, 1780.
Morton to the Treasury Board, December 14, 1780.
Morton to Ezekiel Forman, December 22, 1780.
Blaine to Unidentified, December 25, 1780.
Morton to Ephraim Blaine, December 26, 1780.
Blaine to Jabez Hatch, December 27, 1780.
Morton to Jacob Morgan, December 27, 1780.
Blaine to Samuel Huntington, December 31, 1780.
Morton to Benjamin Stoddert, January 4, 1781.
Blaine to Mr. Munell, January 5, 1781.
Morton to Jacob Morgan, January 8, 1781.
Blaine to George Clinton, January 10, 1781.
Morton to the Treasury Board, January 11, 1781.
Morton to the Treasury Board, Undated.
Blaine to Thomas Sim Lee, January 18, 1781.
Blaine to Caesar Rodney, January 18, 1781.
Blaine to Samuel Huntington, January 19, 1781.
Blaine to William Livingston, January 19, 1781.
Morton to Jacob Morgan, January 19, 1781.
Morton to the Treasury Board, January 26, 1781.
Blaine to Ebenezer Foote, February 6, 1781.
Morton to the Treasury Board, Estimate of Sundries Delivered in October 1780, February 9, 1781.

Morton to James Duane, February 12, 1781.
Blaine to Alexander Hamilton, February 19, 1781.
Blaine to Samuel Huntington, February 25, 1781.
Blaine to Samuel Huntington, March 8, 1781.
Blaine to George Washington, March 9, 1781.
Blaine to George Morton, March 10, 1781.
Blaine to Charles Stewart, March 21, 1781.
Blaine to George Washington, March 21, 1781.
Blaine to George Washington, March 23, 1781.
Blaine to Hugh Hughes, March 29, 1781.
Blaine to Nehemiah Dunham, April 6, 1781.
Blaine to Samuel Huntington, April 6, 1781.
Blaine to Nathaniel Appleton, April 6, 1781.
Blaine to Samuel Huntington, April 9, 1781.
Blaine to Isaac Carty, April 10, 1781.
Blaine to Donaldson Yeates, April 10, 1781.
Blaine to the Board of War, April 10, 1781.
Blaine to Joseph Reed, April 12, 1781.
Blaine to George Washington, April 13, 1781.
Morton to Jacob Morgan, April 17, 1781.
Blaine to Thomas Sim Lee, April 20, 1781.
Blaine to Caesar Rodney, April 23, 1781.
Blaine to the Board of War, April 25, 1781.
Blaine to Captain Montgomary and the Officer Commanding the Armed Schooners, April 27, 1781.
Blaine to Henry Hollingsworth, April 28, 1781.
Nathaniel Stevens to Morrell/Monnell and Wynkoop, April 28, 1781.
Blaine to Samuel Huntington, May 1, 1781.
Blaine to the Board of War, May 1, 1781.
Blaine to the Board of War, May 4, 1781.
Blaine to the Board of War, May 9, 1781.
Blaine to Joseph Reed, May 9, 1781.
Blaine to the Committee on the Commissary Department, May 10 1781.

Blaine to Nathaniel Stevens, May 12, 1781.
Blaine to John Lawrence, May 12, 1781.
Blaine to the Committee, May 14, 1781.
Blaine to Robert Forsyth, May 14, 1781.
Blaine to George Washington, May 14, 1781.
Blaine to Charles Stewart, May 15, 1781.
Blaine to Abraham Lott, May 15, 1781.
Blaine to John Jacob Faesch, May 15, 1781.
Blaine to Henry Hollingsworth, May 19, 1781.
Blaine to Udny Hay, May 19, 1781.
Blaine to Donaldson Yeates, May 19, 1781.
Blaine to Unidentified, May 19, 1781,
Blaine to the Board of War, May 23 or 24, 1781.
Blaine to the Board of War, May 24, 1781.
Blaine to Oliver Phelps, May 25, 1781.
Blaine to Samuel Huntington, May 26, 1781.
Morton to William Colfax, May 30, 1781.
Blaine to James Wood, May 30, 1781.
Morton to Charles Stewart, June 4, 1781.
Blaine to James Wood, June 17, 1781.
Blaine to the Board of War, June 20, 1781.
Blaine to Frederick Augustus Conrad Muhlenberg,
    June 22, 1781.
Blaine to Robert Morris, June 23, 1781.
Blaine to the Board of War, June 23, 1781.
Blaine to Donaldson Yeates, June 24, 1781.
Blaine to Robert Morris, July 2, 1781.
Blaine to Samuel Miles, July 3, 1781.
Blaine to Charles Stewart, July 5, 1781.
Blaine to Jacob Hiltzheimer, July 6, 1781.
Blaine to the Board of War, July 11, 1781.
Blaine to George Washington, July 14, 1781.
Blaine to the Board of War, July 14, 1781.
Blaine to the Board of War, July 18, 1781.
Blaine to Samuel Miles, July 27, 1781.

Blaine to Thomas McKean, July 30, 1781.
Blaine, Estimate of Money Due, Undated.
Incomplete Letter, August 4, 1781.
Blaine to Robert Morris, August 6, 1781.
Blaine to Thomas McKean, August 7, 1781.
Blaine to the Board of Treasury, August 8, 1781.
Morton to the Board of War, August 10, 1781, with a letter by Charles Miller to Blaine, July 11, 1781.
Blaine to Azariah Dunham, August 21, 1781.
Blaine to Charles Stewart, August 1781.
Blaine to Charles Stewart, August 21, 1781.
Blaine to George Morton, August 23, 1781.
Blaine to Thomas Sim Lee, August 25, 1781.
Blaine to James Calhoun, August 25, 1781.
Morton to Blaine, August 27, 1781.
Morton to James Calhoun, August 27, 1781.
Blaine to Tench Tilghman, September 5, 1781.
Blaine to Unidentified, September 6, 1781.
Blaine to George Morton, September 6, 1781.
Blaine, Memorandum of Money Wanted, Undated.
Blaine to Nathaniel Stevens, September 7, 1781.
Blaine to Ebenezer Foote, September 7, 1781.
Blaine to George Morton, September 9, 1781.
Blaine to Udny Hay, September 9, 1781.
Blaine, Necessarys for General Greene's Table, September 11, 1781.
Blaine to Henry Hollingsworth, September 15, 1781.
Blaine to Henry Hollingsworth, September 23, 1781.
Blaine and Charles Stewart to Thomas Nelson, September 25, 1781.
Blaine and Charles Stewart to George Washington, September 26, 1781.
Blaine to Thomas Sim Lee, September 27, 1781.
Blaine and Charles Stewart to George Washington, September 27, 1781.

Blaine to John Cropper, October 1, 1781.
Blaine to Caesar Rodney, October 4, 1781.
Blaine to Mathew Tilghman, October 16, 1781.
Blaine to Robert Forsyth, October 25, 1781.
Blaine to Thomas Nelson, October 25, 1781.
Blaine to Henry Hollingsworth, October 26, 1781.
Blaine and Charles Stewart, to Lord Cornwallis,
    November 1, 1781.
Charles Stewart and Blaine to William Davies,
    November 8, 1781.
Blaine to Thomas Nelson, November 16, 1781.
Blaine to Robert Morris, November 27, 1781.
Blaine to Henry Hollingsworth, November 30, 1781.
Blaine to Nathaniel Stevens, December 5, 1781.
Estimate of a Month's Pay for the Commissary
    General of Issues Department, December 6, 1781.
Blaine to James Calhoun, December 7, 1781.
Blaine to Solomon Maxwell, December 7, 1781.
Blaine to Isaac Carty, December 7, 1781.
Blaine to Henry Hollingsworth, December 7, 1781.
Blaine to John Hanson, December 10, 1781.
Circular to Maryland Counties, January 14, 1782.
Blaine to Donaldson Yeates, January 15, 1782.
Blaine to James Calhoun, January 15, 1782.
Blaine to Henry Hollingsworth, January 15, 1782.
Morton to Blaine, February 16, 1782.
Blaine to Robert Morris, February 19, 1782.
Blaine to Donaldson Yeates, February 24, 1782.
Blaine to Ebenezer Coffin, March 6, 1782.
Blaine and Charles Stewart to James Thompson,
    March 6, 1782.
Blaine to Robert Forsyth, March 18, 1782.
Blaine to Robert Morris, March 20, 1782.
Blaine to Robert Morris, March 30, 1782.
Blaine to Robert Morris, April 8, 1782.

Blaine to Donaldson Yeates, Partial Letter, April 10, 1782.
Blaine, Subscription for the Purchase of a Ship, April 17, 1782.
Blaine to John Hanson, July 20, 1782.
Blaine to Thomas Huggins, July 31, 1782.
Blaine to Henry Miller, August 1, 1782.
Blaine to Robert Buchanan, August 2, 1782.
Blaine to Robert Dodd, August 2, 1782.
Blaine to Ezekiel Forman, August 28, 1782.
Blaine to Robert Morris, October 16, 1782.
Blaine to Moses Chaille, November 5, 1782.
Blaine to Elias Boudinot, February 25, 1783.
Blaine, Property Advertisement, March 26, 1783.
Blaine, Statement of Property Purchase, June 6, 1783.
Blaine to Unidentified, Partial Letter, July 31, 1783.
Blaine to Patrick Ewing and Thomas Huggins, August 1, 1783.
Blaine to Henry Miller, August 1, 1783.
Blaine to Robert Buchannan, August 2, 1783.
Blaine to John Dickinson, August 28, 1783. 2 letters
Blaine to Richard Peters, October 23, 1783.
Blaine to Robert Morris, October 28, 1783.
Blaine to William Bell, November 25, 1783.

INDEX

This index contains all names mentioned. It also lists most items of supply that appear. Exceptions are things contstant referenced such as cattle with 327 mentions, flour with 273 mentions, and salt/salt provisions with 229 mentions. As Ephraim Blaine and George Morton are the authors of most of these letters, they are not indexed as such.

Adams, Samuel, 137, 177, 232
Alexander, Captain, 298, 312
Almonds, 312
Appleton, Nathaniel, 219;
   letter to, 259
Arndt, Jacob, 13;
   letters to, 30, 50
Arnold, Bendict, 157
Aston, Peter, letters to, 31, 50, 75, 95, 190
Bacon, 89, 97, 114, 118, 161
Baker, Joseph, letter to, 99
Bell, Mr., 33, 72
Bell, William,
   letter to, 383
Berry, Sidney, 61
Beverante, Mr., 287
Blaine, Alexander, 244
   letter to, 136
Blaine, Ephraim, 14, 17, 22, 23, 25, 26, 29, 30, 31, 32, 33, 34, 35, 36, 37, 39, 40, 41, 42, 72, 75, 90, 91, 106, 108, 109, 110, 112, 119, 123, 130, 131, 132, 133, 136, 137, 167, 216, 217, 220, 221, 222, 223, 228, 233, 236, 243, 244, 247, 267, 297, 319, 324, 327, 368, 374;
   letters to, 43, 220, 225, 318, 323, 359

property purchase, 378
Blaine, Rebecca, Mrs., 79, 95
Blair, Mr., 287, 288
Blake, Charles, 339, 340, 341, 356
Bland, Theodorick, 137
Board of Treasury, 55, 59, 61, 77, 89, 91, 93, 96, 102, 112, 166, 172, 174, 248, 251, 255, 262, 281, 282, 283; letters to, 54, 74, 178, 214, 221, 222, 236, 244, 246, 318
Board of War, 2, 20, 25, 40, 41, 59, 89, 119, 149, 179, 205, 209, 216, 220, 223, 244, 254, 263, 265, 268, 269, 285, 286, 289, 290, 316, 344, 346, 363, 382; letters to, 17, 49, 75, 86, 87, 92, 105, 112, 113, 148, 178, 206, 208, 214, 217, 264, 269, 274, 275, 276, 291, 292, 295, 299, 302, 308, 311, 312, 318
Boeman, Mr., 157
Borden, Joseph, 166
Boudinot, Elias, letter to, 375
Bradford, Capt., 48
Bradford, Thomas, 267
Bread, 3, 7, 17, 35, 36, 41, 46, 64, 83, 93, 156, 162, 165, 180,

Bread, 299, 307, 323, 330, 333, 368, 383; shortages of, 7, 13, 18, 32, 33, 46, 69, 76, 87, 168, 215, 216, 228, 238, 239, 241, 242, 265, 270, 301
Broderick, Anthony, 53, 297
Brodhead, Daniel, 88, 150, 151, 221; letter to, 149
Brown, Capt., 106
Buchanan, Robert, 34, 52; letters to, 32, 58, 81, 371
Buchanan, William, 9, 249, 255, 261, 281, 314, 360, 361, 370
Buckner, George, 305
Burnett, Ichabod, 331
Burrall, Jonathan, 370, 372, 379
Butler, Richard, 308
Butler, Zebulon, 223; letters to, 143, 196
Calhoun, James, 52, 321, 322, 323; letters to, 322, 324, 354, 357
Candles, 180, 187, 292, 299, 307, 328, 330, 335
Carleton, Joseph, 179
Carpenter, Increase, 34
Carson, Joseph, 143
Carter, John, 348
Carter, Mr., 271
Carty, Isaac, 30, 34, 42, 43, 53, 271; letters to, 7, 8, 33, 66, 70, 72, 109, 190, 262, 352
Chaille, Moses, letter to, 374
Chaloner, John, 43, 53, 91, 103, 319, 321; letters to, 25, 30, 33, 38, 42, 50, 112, 190
Chambers, William, 278
Champion, Henry, 2, 4, 27, 47, 53, 54, 55, 65, 69, 79, 113, 134, 135, 139, 240, 305; letters to, 66, 171
Champion, Henry, Jr.,

letters to, 172, 187
Charles Armand Tuffin, Marquis de la Rouërie, 245
Cheese, 296, 310, 311
Clark, Abraham, 232, 274
Clingham, Capt., 119
Clinton, George, 277; letters to, 14, 41, 45, 121, 123, 234
Clinton, Henry, 80, 115, 116, 117
Coffee, 276, 296, 297, 310, 311, 331
Coffin, Ebenezer, 363; letter to 362
Coiner, Michael, 278
Cole, Philip, 296
Colfax, William, letter to, 296
Colham, Mr., 321
Congress, letters to, 34, 65, 78, 91, 103, 120, 127, 147, 154, 158, 281
Cook, Adam, 278
Coperthwaite, Christopher, 16
Cornell, Ezekiel, 137
Cornwallis, Charles, 337, 339, 347; letter to, 343; surrender of, 341
Cox, Cornelius, 3, 53; letter to, 50
Craig, Capt., 225, 236
Cropper, John, letter to, 338
Crosby, Mr., 33
Crouse, Michael, 245, 330
Crouse, Nichs, 305
Cuyler, Jacob, 14, 41, 45, 48, 49, 53, 180, 253, 330; letters to, 11, 18, 159
Dallam, Richard, 54, 216
Darah, John, 104
Davies, William, letter to, 344
Davis, John, 378; letter to, 68
Deshler, David, letters to, 144, 167

Dick, Archibald, letter to, 135
Dickinson, John, 380
Dodd, Robert, 372
Donaldson, Mr., 58
Donnel T., 219
Donnel, Joseph, 236
Duane, James, 177, 196, 199, 232; letter to, 247
Duncan, David, 150, 306; letter to, 150
Dunham, Azariah, 53, 315, 316, 319, 320; letters to, 19, 35, 83, 190, 320
Dunham, Mr., 21, 43, 64, 70, 134, 138
Dunham, Nehemiah, 3, 43, 53, 57; letters to, 19, 61, 145, 166, 174, 197, 258
Dunham, Samuel, 306
Echelberger/Eichelberger, George, 101, 371
Eliot/Elliot, Mr., 221, 384
Elliot, Robert, 221, 225; letter to, 198
Emory, Noah, 53, 305; letters to, 175, 224
Erskine, Jno., 123
Erskine, Mr., 43
Evans, William, letters to, 14, 25, 35, 50, 92
Ewing, Patrick, 7, 34, 39, 40, 43, 52, 53, 74, 77; letters to, 32, 81, 109, 190, 379
Fackness, Mr., 19
Faesch, John Jacob, 280; letter to, 287
Faw, Mr., 225
Fell, John, 177
Fetchum, Mr., 260
Fish, 62, 79, 81, 168, 267, 272, 292, 310, 312
Fitzsimons, Thomas, 368
Flahavan, Mr., 43

Flint, Royal, 7
Foote, Ebenezer, 327, 328, 349; letters to, 245, 329
Forbes, Mr., 328
Ford, Mr., 327
Forman, David, 138
Forman, Ezekiel, 30, 37, 112, 196; letters to, 223, 373
Forsyth, Robert, 44, 48, 49, 54, 59, 74, 77, 79, 81, 161, 168, 178, 189, 194, 196, 199, 214, 231, 291, 293, 304, 305, 342, 344, 346, 348, 365, 366; letters to, 59, 60, 89, 96, 212, 282, 341, 363
Fourth of July, 308
Fradis, Mr., 103
Furman, Moore; letters to, 3, 11, 56, 57
Fury, Mr., 271
Galaugher, Mr., 384
Garret, Mr., 369
Gates, Horatio, 88, 163, 165, 246
Giles, Jacob, Jr., 368; letters to, 32, 108
Gordon, Harry, 380
Greene, Nathanael, 190, 213, 308, 364; letter to, 49; necessarys for, 331
Greene, William, 166; letters to, 111, 124
Gren, Mr., 384
Hale, Major, 219, 237, 330
Hamilton, Alexander, 194; letter to, 247
Hanson, John, letters to, 354, 369
Hart, Thomas, 246
Hartley, Thomas, 371
Harwood, Thomas, 81, 109
Haslet, Mr., 53
Hatch, Jabez, letter to, 226
Hay, Udny, 53, 121, 183, 185, 193, 194, 236, 257, 260, 276,

Hay, Udny, 277, 305, 318; letters to, 179, 219, 289, 330
Hays, Mr., 371
Hazelwood, John, 164, 221, 233, 256, 265
Heath, William, 230, 329, 331
Hendricks, James, 348
Henry, John, 196, 199
Hides, 180, 198, 335, 339, 340, 356, 357, 362
Hillegas, Michael, 87, 221, 222, 225, 315, 317
Hiltzheimer, Jacob, 60, 220, 315; letter to, 308
Holker, John, 286
Hollingsworth, Henry, 7, 221, 225, 275, 291, 298, 321, 322, 323, 324, 356, 357, 361, 362, 374, 375; letters to, 170, 271, 289, 332, 343, 347, 353, 358
Hollingsworth, Livy, 103
Holmes, William, 278, 366, 367
Hooper, Robert Lettis, Jr., 13, 53, 220; letters to, 63, 190
Hoops, Robert, 15, 34, 43, 53; letters to, 13, 62, 67, 90, 122
Houston, William Churchill, letter to, 205
Howe, Robert, 259, 290, 318
Howell, John Ladd, 90; letters to, 101, 190
Hugg, Joseph, 38, 53; letters to, 101, 190
Hugg, S., 103
Huggins, Thomas, letters to, 370, 379
Hughes, Hugh, letter to, 257
Hunt, Mr., 350
Huntington, Samuel; letters to, 1, 5, 26, 46, 139, 167, 176, 188, 194, 198, 229, 240, 248, 250, 259, 260, 273, 294
Hynshaw, Mr., 122

Ingersoll, Jared, 196, 199
Irvine, William, 56
Irwin, James, 278
Irwin, Robert, 42
Jackson, Mr., 342
Jas. Young, 381
Johns, Mr., 367
Jones, Mr., 75, 103, 137; letter to, 143
Jones, Whitehead, 53
Kalb, Johann de, letter to, 59
Kean, Mr., 260
Keese, Mr., 245
Kelsey, Mr., 260
Kiersly/Kersley, Mr., 221, 222, 225
King, Mr., 19
Kitts, George, 102, 103, 191, 197, 305, 315
Kitts, Michael, 17, 79, 103; letter to, 16
Kitts, Mr., 217, 220, 253
Lafayette, Marie Jean Paul Joseph Roch Yves Gilbert du Motier, Marquis de, 116
Lawrence, John, letter to, 280
Lee, Henry, 59, 134, 143
Lee, Thomas Sim, 29, 335; letters to, 51, 57, 82, 114, 126, 202, 215, 237, 268, 322, 336
Lincoln, Benjamin, 80, 333
Litle, Mr., 21
Little, Capt., 329
Little, James, 123
Little, John, 115, 118, 315; letter to, 102
Livingston, Mary, 12
Livingston, Mr., 177
Livingston, William, 12, 15, 326; letters to, 125, 203, 242
Lott, Abraham, 280; letter to, 287
Lowrey/Lowry, Mr., 307, 321

Ludhom, Mr., 384
Lutz, Nicholas; letters to, 97, 110, 132, 133
Lyon, Daniel, 236
Lyon, Mr., 9
Lyon, Samuel, 130, 131, 133, 136, 244, 383; letters to, 94, 104, 132
Lyon, Samuel, survey by, 378
Maclay, William, 53, 253; letters to, 50, 119, 190
Mallet, Peter, 244
Marshall, Colo., 383
Mathews, Mrs., 220
Maxwell, Solomon, letter to, 352
McAlheny, John, 278
McCallaster/McAlister, James, 22, 39, 44, 88, 112; letters to, 91, 119, 136
McCaraher, Mr., 14
McCauley, William, 85; letter to, 85
McConnel, Capt., 222, 223, 236
McCullen, Mr., 272
McKean, Thomas, 33, 39, 43; letters to, 313, 317
McMullin, William, 315
Meade, Richard Kidder, letter to, 134
Meals, John, 305
Miles, Samuel, letters to, 306, 313
Miller, Charles, 47, 53, 181, 182, 183, 185, 260, 293, 315, 319; letter from, 176, 318; letters to, 160, 175, 186
Miller, Henry, letters to, 45, 50, 100, 190, 371
Miller, Mr., 155, 164
Miller, William, 305
Mitchell, John, letter to, 15
Montgomary, Captain, 270
Montgomery, Joseph, 232

Moor, John, 278
Morgan, George, letter to, 10
Morgan, Jacob, 221; letters to, 155, 218, 228, 233, 243, 267
Morgan, Jona., 306
Morgan, Joseph, 326, 327
Morris, Israel, Jr., 38, 163, 164, 165, 315
Morris, Jr., Robert, 303, 306, 307, 312, 321, 322, 324, 331, 337, 340, 350, 352, 353, 354, 357, 358, 359, 363, 364; letters to, 301, 304; 316, 347, 360, 365, 366, 367, 373, 382
Morton, George, 20, 53, 95, 214, 231, 254, 262, 263, 305, 315, 322, 325, 327, 357, 358, 374; letters to, 9, 15, 122, 252, 321, 326, 330
Motte, Isaac, 274
Muhlenberg. Frederick Augustus Conrad; letters to, 200, 207, 300
Muirhead, Andrew, 110
Mullins, Timmy, 297
Munell, Mr., letter to, 233
Murdoch, George, 52, 54
Mustard, 276, 296, 297, 310, 311, 331
Naglie, John, 17
Naglie, Mrs, John, 16; letter to, 17
Neilson, John, 166
Nelson, George, 60
Nelson, Thomas, Jr., 334, 335, 348; letters to, 333, 342, 345
Nicholson, George, 301
Nisbit, Mr., 165
Noble, Mr., 39, 88, 91
Norris, Henry, 278
Ogden, Mr., 319
Osgood, Samuel, letter to, 183
Paca, William, 23

Pape, John, 110
Patterson, Nicholas, 9; letter to, 50
Patton, John, letters to, 101, 190
Pendergast, William, 246
Pepper, 276, 296, 297, 331
Pery, Mr., 157
Peters, Richard, 381
Pettit, Charles, 11
Phelps, Oliver, 53, 257, 305, 315; letters to, 184, 293
Philips, Mr., 294
Phillips, Abijah, letter to, 191
Pickering, Thomas, Jr., 184, 225
Pickering, Timothy, Jr., 254
Pork, 9, 15, 16, 17, 20, 38, 57, 64, 65, 66, 68, 70, 73, 77, 78, 79, 80, 89, 97, 105, 109, 150, 151, 161, 168, 171, 173, 174, 176, 182, 185, 188, 200, 202, 203, 204, 212, 213, 234, 284, 287, 290, 292, 298, 307, 313, 321, 323, 324, 345, 346, 383; for George Washington, 312; processing of, 68
Price, Thomas, 367
Purveyance, John, 278
Ramsay, Mr., 221
Randles, John, 278
Rawlings, Moses, 52, 110
Reed, Joseph, letters to, 71, 115, 116, 147, 192, 210, 219, 265, 277
Reeves, Brewer, 278
Richardson, Thomas, 52, 54, 109; letters to, 81
Richey, Gideons, 380
Riddock, D., 62
Risburg, Mr., 62
Rittenhouse, David, 36, 285
Robinson, Mr., 344
Robinson, Richard, 315

Rochambeau, Comte de, Jean-Baptiste Donatien de Vimeur, 345, 348
Rodgers, Mr., 52
Rodney, Caesar, 266; letters to, 117, 142, 199, 239, 269, 338
Rogers, Benjamin, letter to, 29
Roy, Samuel, 278
Rum, 48, 58, 98, 100, 108, 115, 116, 117, 153, 154, 155, 156, 162, 163, 164, 187, 219, 233, 236, 237, 247, 257, 290, 292, 299, 300, 307, 318, 319, 330, 337, 350, 376, 383
Rum, ordered to be seized, 169, 222, 236, 259, 260, 290, 318
Rum, shortages of, 142, 154, 168, 169, 188, 241
Rum, taken by Washington's order, 158
Sands, Mr., 350
Schermerhorn, Reyer, 318
Schuyler, Philip, 45
Scott, John Morin, 137
Shaw, Mr., 348, 367
Shepard, Lieut., 373
Shoemaker, Jacob, 132
Slough, Matthias, 53; letters to, 22, 36, 50, 190
Smith, James, 53, 140, 244, 279, 315, 371; letters to, 50, 137, 190
Smith, Mr., 196, 216, 221, 222, 225
Smith, S., 104
Smith, Thomas, 188, 274
Snigars, Colonel, 366
Soap, 180, 187, 292, 299, 307, 328, 330, 335
Sorrel, Mr., 369
Spear, Mr., 52
St. Clair, Arthur, 348
Steen, John, 135

Stevens, Nathaniel, 180, 247, 254, 287, 288, 305, 329, 349; letters from, 272; letters to, 279, 328, 349

Stevenson, Mr., 374

Stewart, Charles, 19, 43, 63, 64, 70, 256, 257, 279, 280, 333, 346, 366, 367; letters from, 63, 65, 333, 334, 337, 343, 344, 363; letters to, 78, 98, 151, 155, 164, 253, 285, 297, 306, 319, 320

Stewart, William, 104, 144; letter to, 62

Stoddert, Benjamin, letters to, 40, 42, 232

Stroud, Jacob, 13; letters to, 30, 50

Stuart, William, 53; letter to, 190

Sugar, 48, 87, 103, 104, 225, 245, 276, 296, 297, 310, 311, 331, 376

Sullivan, John, 137

Swim, Mr., 136

Taggart, John, 236

Talbot, John, 122, 221, 225

Tallmadge, Benjamin, 29

Tallow, 180, 187, 198, 292, 328, 335, 339, 340, 356, 357, 362

Tarleton, Banastre, 308

Tate, Francis, 363, 367

Tate, Mr., 384

Tatnall, Mr., 72

Tea, 276, 296, 297, 312, 331

Thomas, Jacob, 318

Thomas, John, 15

Thompson, James, 362; letters to, 363

Tilghman, Mathew, letter to, 339

Tilghman, Tench, 255; letters to, 162, 325

Tongues, 146, 220, 309, 312

Trumbull, Jonathan, 6, 252; letters to, 4, 23, 24

Vandering, Mr., 162, 164

Varnum, James Mitchell, 232

Wadsworth, Jeremiah, 2, 9, 11, 12, 77, 89, 96, 113, 172, 174, 249, 255, 261, 281, 314, 348, 360, 361, 370, 373

Walters, Daniel, 305

Washington, George, 20, 46, 48, 61, 79, 83, 111, 123, 124, 126, 127, 128, 140, 144, 145, 147, 148, 157, 158, 163, 165, 168, 169, 181, 183, 185, 199, 202, 207, 227, 234, 237, 239, 242, 247, 252, 253, 272, 291, 300, 301, 341, 343, 345, 347, 367; distressed by local citizens, 139, 142; food for, 296, 307, 309, 310, 311, 312; letters to, 6, 28, 63, 69, 73, 80, 106, 129, 137, 193, 251, 255, 256, 266, 272, 284, 309, 334, 337; postpones attack on New York City, 115, 117; supplies for, 276, 309

Waterman, Asa, 47, 53; letter to, 165

Wayne, Anthony, 264, 285, 286

Wederstrandt, Conrod Theodore, 30, 34, 43, 54, 58, 74, 77, 112, 203; letters to, 21, 22, 37, 38, 44, 67, 81, 109, 190

Weitzel, John, 132; letters to, 131, 133

Welch, Mr., 328

Weltner, Ludowick, 132; letter to, 130

West, John, 381

Wheat, 12, 13, 14, 19, 20, 31, 32, 33, 37, 39, 44, 49, 50, 54, 61, 68, 72, 73, 76, 144, 215, 298, 324, 358

Whiskey, 62, 145, 196, 278, 295, 337, 383
White, James, 43, 91, 103; letters to, 25, 30, 33, 38, 42, 50, 53, 112, 190
Williamson, Alexander, 305, 327, 332
Wills, Col, 334
Willson, William, 170
Wine, 225, 296, 297, 309, 318
  for George Washington, 163; 285, 296, 309, 310, 311, 312
  for Nathanael Greene, 190, 331

Wirtz, Christian, 94, 130, 131, 133
  letters to, 84. 104, 132
Wood, James, 366, 380, 381; letters to, 295, 298
Wright, Henry, 361
Wynkoop, Mr., 272
Yeates, Abraham, 219
Yeates, Donaldson, 217, 220, 321, 332, 333, 356, 358; letters to, 216, 263, 290, 303, 357, 361, 368

Heritage Books by Joseph Lee Boyle

"*My Last Shift Betwixt Us & Death*": *The Ephraim Blaine Letterbook, 1777–1778*

"*The distresses of the Army*": *The Ephraim Blaine Letters, 1780–1783*

"*Their Distress is Almost Intolerable*": *The Elias Boudinot Letterbook, 1777–1778*

From Redcoat to Rebel: The Thomas Sullivan Journal

"*this grand supply*": *The Samuel Hodgdon Letterbooks, 1778–1784*
Volume 1: July 19, 1778–March 31, 1781
Volume 2: April 3, 1781–May 24, 1784

Writings from the Valley Forge Encampment of the Continental Army:
December 19, 1777–June 19, 1778
Volume 1

Writings from the Valley Forge Encampment of the Continental Army:
December 19, 1777–June 19, 1778
Volume 2, "*Winter in this starved Country*"

Writings from the Valley Forge Encampment of the Continental Army:
December 19, 1777–June 19, 1778
Volume 3, "*it is a general Calamity*"

Writings from the Valley Forge Encampment of the Continental Army:
December 19, 1777–June 19, 1778
Volume 4, "*The Hardships of the Camp*"

Writings from the Valley Forge Encampment of the Continental Army:
December 19, 1777–June 19, 1778
Volume 5, "*a very Different Spirit in the Army*"

Writings from the Valley Forge Encampment of the Continental Army:
December 19, 1777–June 19, 1778
Volume 6, "*my Constitution got quite shatter'd*"

Writings from the Valley Forge Encampment of the Continental Army:
December 19, 1777–June 19, 1778
Volume 7, "*I could not Refrain from tears*"

Writings from the Valley Forge Encampment of the Continental Army:
December 19, 1777–June 19, 1778
Volume 8, "*called to the unpleasing task of a Soldier*"

www.ingramcontent.com/pod-product-compliance
Lightning Source LLC
Chambersburg PA
CBHW050327230426
43663CB00010B/1772